Getting Graphic

Programming Fundamentals in C and C++

Mark Finlay

Software by John B. Petritis

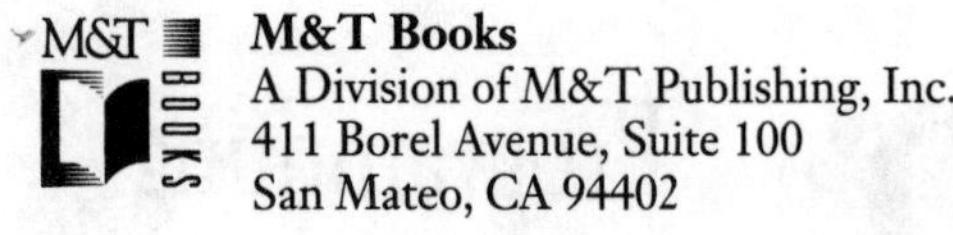

M&T Books
A Division of M&T Publishing, Inc.
411 Borel Avenue, Suite 100
San Mateo, CA 94402

Printed in the United States of America

Library of Congress Cataloging-in-Publication Data

Finlay, Mark
Getting Graphic : programming fundamentals in C and C++.
p. cm.
Includes index.
ISBN 1-55851-282-9
1. Computer graphics. 2. C (Computer program language) 3. C++ (Computer program language) I. Title.
T385.F55 1993 92-37961
006.6'6--dc20 CIP

96 95 94 93 4 3 2 1

Developmental Editor: Christine de Chutkowski
Copy Editor: Kristin Little and Laura Moorhead
Layout: Stacey L. Evans
Art Director: Margaret Horoszko
Cover Design: Lauren Smith Design

Getting Graphic

Programming Fundamentals in C and C++

To my wife Nikki for her patience and support, past, present, and future

Contents

Acknowledgments

There are quite a few people who have helped make this book possible. First and foremost, I would like to thank my part-time editor and full-time wife Nikki for all her help and understanding, especially when it seemed like this book would never be finished. In addition to her many other contributions, Nikki performed a considerable amount of editing and helped me rewrite major sections of the book.

Many, many thanks and kudos go to my fellow programmer and engineer, John Petritis. John is responsible for producing almost all the software in the book. Without John's dedication, thoroughness, and late-night stamina, the software would never have been completed, and it certainly wouldn't have worked as well as it does.

I am very grateful to Robin Maffett for helping me, the drawing impaired, produce many of the drawings and figures. Without her effort, there would be considerably fewer drawings and figures in the book.

I would also like to thank my technical editor Stephen B. Coy for his many sage comments and sound advice. Thanks also to my editor Christine de Chutkowski of M&T Books for her outstanding editing efforts and patience with an author who never seems to get the words out on time.

All the software in the book was written using the Borland C++ version 3.1. I used Microsoft Word for Windows 2.0 from Microsoft Corp. to write the text for this book.

I would also like to thank my family and friends for putting up with me while I wrote this book. Late nights are not always conducive to gracious behavior.

Finally, I would like to thank my sons Sean and Paul for making this project and everything else worthwhile. They were always there for inspiration and playtime.

Why This Book Is for You

This books is for anyone wanting to create computer graphics with a PC. You do not need previous experience with computer graphics, but you should be familiar with the C programming language.

This book is particularly helpful for beginners who will benefit from the extensive explanations for each drawing technique and the algorithms behind them. More experienced graphics programmers will find many interesting applications and tools not found in other graphics packages.

Some of the techniques you'll learn include:

- Drawing circles, ellipses, and polygons both in outline and solid-fill form
- Transforming objects by affine transformations to scale, rotate, and move objects anywhere on the screen in one easy step
- A complete plotting package for creating graphs of functions in several different styles
- Animating objects for fully-interactive drawings

You will need at least a 286-class system with a floating-point coprocessor and an EGA or VGA graphics card and monitor. The source code has been developed using the Borland C++ version 3.1 development environment for DOS. However, all the software conforms to the ANSI C standard and may be adapted to almost any development environment, such as Microsoft C or Zortech C++, with little or no modifications. The software can even be adapted to non-DOS environments, such as MS-Windows or X-Windows, by modifying a small set of device-specific routines.

Introduction

Suppose you've just been handed the latest financial data from the company's last quarter, and your boss wants you to produce a report summarizing the results. Or, perhaps, you've just received data from the lab's particle-beam experiment and you need to plot the data with log-log scales and then compare the results against the previous day's data. The best way to present data like that is through an illustration, such as a pie chart, bar chart, line graph, or some other graphic image. But hand drawing these images can take quite awhile.

Although you realize, this can be done on a computer, you've never done it before. So, how do you go about representing the data you have graphically?

Graphics pervade nearly all aspects of our lives. From advertising logos to every book, magazine, and newspaper, to information presented in charts and other illustrations, and every combination in between, graphics are the preferred means of presenting information and ideas.

People are visually oriented and can quickly grasp ideas presented in graphs or drawings that might be difficult, if not impossible, to understand when represented by any other means. Today, computer graphics are used in almost every discipline requiring visual representations. After reading this book, you'll learn how to create two-dimensional imagery on your computer.

The reasons to use a computer are the same as the reasons to use other drawing devices, such as paper and pencil: to present and illustrate concepts in an intuitive and meaningful way to others.

Moreover, the computer is the most powerful tool developed so far to create graphic representations of everything from complex scientific data to day-to-day business bar charts directly and easily. Flexibility and ease-of-use make the computer a valuable tool in the world of graphics. Additionally, low cost modern PC equipment makes computer graphics affordable for even the most tight-budgeted business or artist.

This book gives you the tools needed to create meaningful graphics and to help you avoid the pitfalls associated with using commercial graphic packages.

With this book, you'll first learn the basics of defining how graphics are physically displayed on your computer screen and how a drawing is structurally defined within the computer's memory. Then, you'll gain an understanding of a full range of topics for drawing, plotting, showing text, creating filled objects, and other related areas. Important design issues and limitations that you may have to consider for your specific application are pointed out.

The software in this book has been developed using the C programming language. It is assumed that you are already somewhat experienced with C programming, and you're able to compile and execute C code on your PC. The source code for all the software presented in this book is provided on the accompanying diskette. The code is in generic modules so you can adapt the software to your specific programming environment.

All code development was performed using Borland C++, version 3.1 for MS-DOS. Every effort has been made to adhere to an ANSI C implementation. The device-specific routines are stored in separate code modules that are easily adapted to your specific environment.

For best results, use of an EGA (enhanced graphics adapter) or VGA (video graphics array) graphics card is recommended. The disk that accompanies this book has several demonstrations taken from material in the chapters. These programs were created both to graphically depict particular ideas, and to provide a basis for you to create your own programs. Copy the sample programs and experiment with them to create new effects or enhanced demonstrations.

The software requires an 80286-class PC and, as previously mentioned, at least an EGA-level (or better) graphics card. Although not required, a floating-point coprocessor greatly improves the performance of many interactive demonstration programs.

Part I: The Basics

In Chapter 1, you'll have a brief history lesson that explains how for thousands of years, graphics were used to show geometrical relationships and ideas. But in modern times, the intimate relationship between algebra and geometry via coordinates has allowed people to explore more aspects of geometry than was previously practical.

You'll then review high school geometry and trigonometry by studying the equations of lines, circles, and ellipses (fortunately, no proofs!). This chapter presents useful computer graphics types, including polygons for representing filled areas and polylines for drawing arbitrary curves and plotting functions. Finally, you'll learn useful mathematical functions like *sine()* and *cosine()* and their uses.

Briefly reviewing C

Chapter 2 reviews the C language and syntax used throughout this book. Since you probably already have a working knowledge of C, this section acts as both a reminder and a reference for the conventions found in this book. A number of structures for vectors, matrices, points, and other graphical entities that take advantage of C's compact means of manipulating objects are defined.

Part II: An Introduction to Raster Graphics

Although Chapter 2 and the rest of the book concentrates on software, Chapter 3 presents some of the hardware you'll be using and how it will affect your work.

Through this chapter, you'll learn the differences between the raster graphics display of your PC and analog-display devices, such as a pen plotter or vector scope. These differences are important in understanding how various things, such as screen resolution, affect the display of your data.

A C graphics library

Having reviewed the mathematical, software, and hardware basics, you'll begin the real work by defining basic graphics libraries functions in Chapter 4. These routines include the display-dependent functions (for example, if you have an EGA, VGA, or SVGA display), along with the functions and methods needed to create display-independent code.

You'll also learn the basic point-drawing functions and line-drawing algorithms for drawing a line segment between two points on the screen. The use of color on VGA displays, particularly how colors may be selected and manipulated, will also be covered.

Chapter 4 also shows you how to make the most of your graphics card's limited range of colors and how to structure your program so that it produces the same drawing on a variety of different display cards, without requiring changes to the program.

Using the same approach as for the line-drawing algorithms, Chapter 5 presents the functions for drawing rectangles, circles, and ellipses. You'll then see how these techniques can be generalized to draw arbitrary curves and shapes.

Part III: Building on the Basics

In the following chapters, you'll build upon basic functions and develop methods to deal with the kinds of issues and problems you'll encounter when using and creating computer graphics.

Transforming objects

You often need to transform objects on the screen by operations, such as *translation* (moving an object to a new location), *scaling* (changing its size), and *rotation*. In Chapter 6, you'll develop the necessary mathematical tools to perform these operations on the various geometric entities defined in Chapters 4 and 5.

After exploring some linear algebra methods, you'll see how each of the individual transformations can be combined into a single operation using the 3 x 3 matrix from linear algebra. The matrix operations are then integrated into the modules to provide a concise and efficient means of transforming objects. Chapter 6 shows how various objects are related to one another by transformations, such as scaling a circle in one dimension to create an ellipse.

Clipping

As you produce more drawings and plot more functions, you will undoubtedly encounter a particular plot that requires a portion to be drawn partially off the screen, or at least off the scale of your plot's axes. Chapter 7 introduces the idea of *clipping* as a means of ensuring that your graphic objects are only drawn to the part of the screen where you want them to appear.

Among other things, clipping keeps your plot from overwriting the labels of your axes and making your plot unreadable. There are two basic methods presented. The first involves taking a graphical object, such as a polygon, along with a *clipping region* (for example, a rectangular area like your screen) and producing a new polygon that is guaranteed to lie completely within the desired region. This technique is then generalized to include clipping one polygon against another polygon. The second technique uses explicit checks inside the drawing functions to ensure that you don't draw to a point on the screen outside the desired area. Both methods have their respective benefits and drawbacks, which will be discussed along with when each technique should be used and when to use simpler methods.

One of the primary uses of clipping is in support of *windowing*, defining a rectangular region of the screen as the area for the program to operate. All of the window-based systems, including Microsoft Windows, must use both the *transformation operation* (moving all the objects on the screen around) and the *clipping operation* (preventing data from being written into other windows) to accomplish their task. Chapter 7 shows how this is achieved and why this requirement, among other things, slows window-based environments.

Solid objects

Until this point, the previous chapters dealt strictly with drawing the boundary or outline of geometric objects. In Chapter 8, you'll extend your drawing methods to include filling objects with a solid color and with a pattern. Chapter 9 then describes how to create bitmaps to represent patterns or images. You'll then see how the bitmaps may be used to represent icons that provide a much faster means for drawing fixed-pattern entities, such as cursors and simple text. Bitmaps are also used to store patterns for line drawings, including drawing dashed and dotted lines or more complex brush shapes that you see in most computer paint programs.

Chapter 10 presents various methods for drawing more complex text. In particular, you'll learn how to draw both bitmap-based text and vector-based text. The bitmap text can generally be drawn more quickly; however, it is more difficult to transform, especially with arbitrary scaling and rotation operations.

You'll also see some of the display artifacts (in this context, *artifact* means that the drawings have a peculiar or incorrect appearance) associated with both bitmap-based and vector-based text. You'll learn how to deal with this in more advanced graphics packages.

The Main Plot

Chapter 11 discusses the issues involved with plotting mathematical functions. Functions may be either mathematically expressed, as in a polynomial, or derived from a data file that specifies an independent variable (usually associated with the x coordinate) and a dependent variable (usually plotted as the y coordinate).

There is virtually an infinite variety of plot types, and by no means are all the methods presented in this chapter. (In fact, there are quite a number of books devoted to this topic alone). However, Chapter 11 points out many of the issues involved and how you might address them for your particular needs. Several methods are presented for making creative uses of color and how multiple plots can be presented in an uncluttered and meaningful way. You'll learn how to "lie" about data and create misleading or incomplete plots. While *you* would never do this on purpose, often others do so both intentionally (to overemphasize a particular aspect of the data) and unintentionally (by blindly taking the defaults of their particular plotting package). By becoming aware of such potential pitfalls, you can ensure that your presentations are always top-notch.

Part IV: Advanced Methods

Chapter 12 presents the most common methods of animating objects. You will have already seen some of these animation techniques used in the demonstration programs from previous chapters. This chapter covers the various operations that may be performed on a raster image and how the logical function, particularly *XOR*, acts as a nearly magic technique for animation. Through the use of the matrix representation of transformations, you'll learn how to move objects by any means—from simple translation for walking an object across the screen, to performing complex scaling and rotation operations that look far more involved than they really are.

Anti-aliasing

As the final topic, Chapter 13 covers the issues of cleaning the artifacts that are inherent in a raster image. The term *anti-aliasing* refers to a whole range of techniques for removing undesirable features, most notably jagged lines that are especially common in lines drawn at an angle.

Anti-aliasing is a complex issue with a great deal written about its development over the past 20 years. Chapter 13 focuses on some of the latest techniques for efficiently removing jagged edges from lines and circles, and it shows how to efficiently integrate them with the rest of the graphics modules.

Some fun examples

Armed with the tools from the previous chapters, you'll learn how to combine these tools to produce interesting and interactive programs by studying Chapter 14's sample programs. The first example is a simple clock face with moving hour, minute, and second hands. The next example simulates moving particles in a closed chamber using Newton's laws of motion with some interesting twists. The third example is an advanced version in which fish and sharks compete for survival on your screen.

Part V: Where to Next

The appendices of this book cover additional computer graphics topics as well as providing useful reference material. Appendix A deals with some of the issues and features that C++ provides to a graphics program. Appendix B includes a directory of the software found on the enclosed diskette as well as directions for using the *make* and Borland *project* files to build the software on your machine. And finally, the bibliography provides references for those intrepid programmers who want to explore computer graphics further.

Summing It All Up

This book only begins your exploration of computer graphics. There are so many different packages and standards that it is beyond the scope of this book to address them all. From Microsoft Windows to the X-Windows system for workstations, to the Macintosh and the plotting packages inside many business software packages, it is often difficult to know where to start. But all of these packages have common features similar to the ones found in this book.

Graphics packages provide calls to select colors and draw lines on the screen and provide many more sophisticated calls for drawing other graphic entities, such as circles and polygons. Chapter 15 further explores the various graphics standards and the future of computer graphics.

All the programs in this book are designed to provide an interactive and informative means of understanding how to create graphic representations and how your computer produces the wide variety of displays you see everyday. Using the source code provided, you can produce an array of interesting plots and drawings of your own. As you delve further, you can expand the modules to fit your particular needs.

One of the main benefits of working with computer graphics is that you can produce remarkable displays that are both interactive and fun to watch. Just consider the huge variety of computer games that abound. A principal feature of the best games is the quality of graphics they provide. My goal is to give you a start both in understanding how these types of images are produced and in actually producing such images for yourself. Have fun with the software and keep exploring the computer graphics medium— it only gets better!

CHAPTER 1

A Review of Basic Geometry and Algebra

Graphics are derived from the study of geometry. There is a compelling need for people to visualize problems and solutions via a drawn picture. This is evident throughout history, though the method for creating such pictures has changed greatly over time.

Early drawings were created using the simplest tools, paper and pen. Straightedges were used to draw lines and simple versions of compasses were used to draw circles. Many of the classic theorems of geometry can be derived using just these two tools.

Technically, you don't need drawings to develop many of the theories of geometry and algebra. But because of the elaborate visual processing functions of the human brain, a drawing can convey much more information about a concept than can symbolic statements. In other words, a picture truly is worth a thousand words. People are masters of visual interpretation and expression, and graphics provide a means for visually communicating complex ideas and concepts.

Three principle disciplines that motivated the need for accurate drawing methods are astronomy, architecture, and map making. Since precise astronomical measurements requires a thorough understanding of geometrical theorems, the ability to construct accurate instruments via detailed drawings, along with the ability to visualize the positions of astronomical bodies relative to one another, became more important.

Throughout history, many ingenious mechanical devices were developed to help draw and measure the complex motions of planets and stars. For example, telescopes required an intricate set of clocks and gears to track an object throughout the night as the earth turned. Through careful measurement and observation, these systems were refined so that they could accurately hold an object in a fixed position in a telescope's lens to allow for more detailed viewing at higher magnifications. This is just one example of using a mechan-

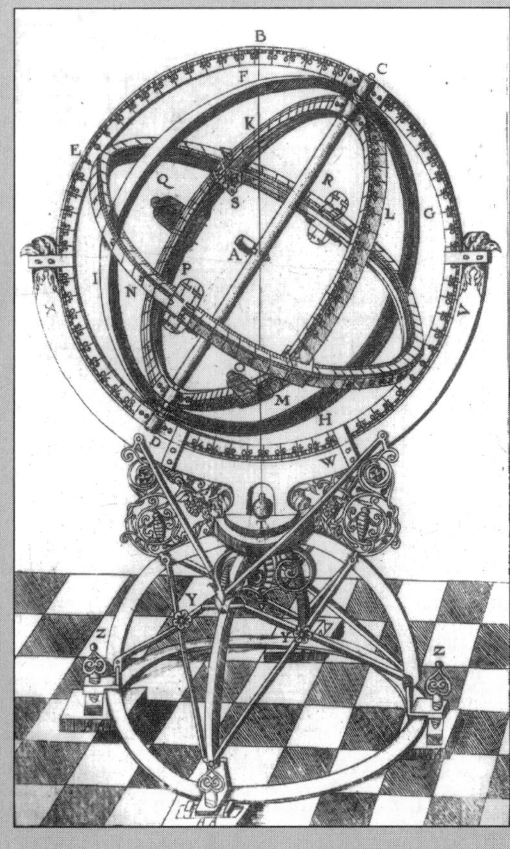

PHOTO COURTESY OF SNARK/ART RESOURCE, N.Y.

The astrolabe is an antique measuring instrument of great beauty and precision. Based on simple geometric prinici-ples, the astrolabe provides a means for finding your location using knowledge gained from previous astronomical observations of how the stars move through the heavens. The measurements taken by this instrument are simple functions of geometric relationships between lines, circles, and spheres.

Creating an instrument such as the astrolabe requires a solid foundation in both geometry and algebra. Once you understand these basic disciplines, you can begin creating your own models of whatever phenomena you are studying. The models can be mechanical, such as the astrolabe, or purely conceptual. In either case, graphic drawings are the principal means of communicating ideas to others, and computer graphics is a wonderful means for creating graphic images.

So, what better place to start than at the beginning by reviewing what you once learned and then forgot about geometry and algebra. Once armed with several concepts, you can construct drawings of two-dimensional objects, such as lines, circles, and ellipses.

ical analog of a mathematically described process, in this case, the motion of the planets.

Consider the spirograph. Here is an amazing toy that tracks the motions of fixed points on circles while one circle rotates within another circle. The variety of figures you can create with this simple device is quite astonishing. If you add additional features, such as ellipses instead of circles, the possibilities are endless.

The spirograph is similar to the kinds of devices used by ancient astronomers to model the motions of the heavens about the earth. In their model, everything moved in a circle with the earth at the center. As more "peculiar" motions, such as *retrograde motion* (the apparent reversal of a planet's trajectory across the sky), were observed, these astronomers created more elaborate models of the planets moving in smaller circles about some invisible center that moved in a circle around the earth. This is actually a reasonable approximation of a moon's motion around a planet. For ancient astronomers to visualize such a motion required great insight, excellent mathematics, and good drawing and mechanical skills.

As most architects would tell you, accurate drawings are crucial to the proper design of any building or structure. The utility of such drawings was recognized very early on as an essential means of planning. Accurate mechanical drawings helped planners visualize how final structures would look and provided a means of measuring how much material would be needed to build the structures. These drawings were also used as an aid in performing structural analyses to see if the structures would remain standing through typical wear and tear. We have come a long way, however, from the development of early mechanical drawing to the modern science of materials and mechanical engineering.

To produce drawings efficiently, architects adapted many techniques from the arts and geometry to develop what is now considered drafting. In earlier times, such drawings were essentially artists' renditions. While useful for visualizing the final results, they were often too inaccurate to use for actual measurements. Proper measurements were extensively labeled on drawings. This required that all critical measurements have separate labels since you could not assume that all elements were drawn in correct proportion. You can imagine how difficult it was to achieve a "clean" drawing.

Today, most people take for granted the ability to create renderings drawn to proper scale, that is, drawn so all the dimensions are proportionally correct and can be related to the final scale of the building or structure. Even more fundamental is our present ability to quickly and easily make copies of a drawing.

Using a computer, it is now incredibly easy to make changes and produce a clean final drawing. Just as the availability of low-cost word processing has completely changed how documents are produced, the advent of computer graphics is completely changing how drawings and images are created. The ability to easily add color, depth, and even work in three-dimensions provides unprecedented flexibility to artists, architects, and scientists alike.

Another drawing-intensive occupation is map making, which is also a very ancient art. There were probably few greater needs in early civilization than that of accurate maps. However, this was difficult without a proper understanding of the earth's shape or its movement through the heavens. Even with such knowledge, producing accurate maps that were useful at sea required great skill and patience.

Today, however, people are attempting to automate the process as much as possible. The use of sophisticated satellite imagery, digitized aerial photography, range-finding radar, and other such techniques have vastly improved our ability to produce extraordinarily detailed maps accurately and quickly.

You can derive a great deal of useful information from a map entered into a computer since the computer can further process the data. The power to perform complex analyses on digitized data is another great strength of computer-generated drawings. The computer provides the ability to look at a map in different or more effective ways. This is generating a revolution in the earth sciences for the monitoring and management of the planet's resources.

Geometry Requires Coordination

Euclidean plane geometry is a mathematical system that attempts to formalize our intuitive notion of space. Nothing in the real world is a perfect line or circle; these geometrical concepts are theoretical abstracts of observed physical entities.

Recall from your high school geometry how you proved various geometric relationships based upon a small set of postulates that define geometry. One of the basic proofs is by construction using straightedges and compasses. You never resort to direct measurement using a ruler since it can never be precise enough to prove an assertion. You can measure, for example, the three angles of a triangle to show that they always sum 180 degrees, but you are always limited by the precision of the measurement. From this point of view, algebraic manipulation of numbers is not really suitable for proving (or disproving) geometric relationships.

Because of this, many mathematicians of antiquity viewed algebraic analysis of geometric objects as inappropriate. Since they were able to construct so many different types of objects using these basic geometric techniques, it simply did not occur to many of the mathematicians to pursue other methods of analysis. Just studying and classifying the variety of constructible shapes was quite challenging. Exploring other means of geometrical analysis would have to wait for development of the now intuitive association of real-value coordinates with geometric objects.

For a long time, people have had the knowledge to measure a length along a given direction. The simplest measuring devices include knotted ropes, in which knots are evenly spaced along the length of a rope. Using such a rope, you can measure—however crudely—the distance between any two points that the rope can reach. The knots along the rope correspond to what is now thought of as *coordinates*, or the distance along a line from some fixed starting point. The spacing between the knots is defined as a length of one. So, a measurement of an object can be specified by how many knots long it is.

Today, of course, there are standardized units of length, such as feet and meters, so everyone can compare measurements. With the rope, however, the precision of any measurement is limited by the spacing between the knots. By introducing real-value coordinates, you can identify any point on the line by its distance from the starting point and, conversely, every coordinate value corresponds to a unique point along the line.

Similarly, you can extend this idea to measuring the area occupied by an object lying in a plane, such as a triangle. As with the knotted rope, an area can be measured by finding the number of *unit squares* (squares with sides measuring one) needed to cover the area. Again, you must use real-value measurements to precisely measure the area of an object. Also, once you know how to calculate the areas of simple shapes, such as triangles or trapezoids, you can study more difficult objects like circles by partitioning these objects into pieces made up of known shapes.

In fact, some of the Greek scholars actually came close to developing the idea of computing an area by integration. They computed the area of simple geometric objects by considering finer and finer partitions of the circle as thin trapezoidal-shaped pieces. The techniques of integration let you find the lengths and enclosed areas of complex curves that cannot be computed by simple geometric means. A development of this sort would have significantly advanced the development of geometry. However, without an algebraic basis, these types of studies were limited to a small set of easily constructed geometric objects, and still only provided approximations to the lengths and areas of most curves.

A *coordinate system* is the association of a set of real-numbers (one for a line, two for objects in a plane, three for solid objects, and so on) with the points of a geometric object. Several early scholars developed coordinate systems associated with certain types of objects, primarily the *conic sections* (objects created by slicing a cone with a plane). Attaching a coordinate system to an object simplified the process of computing areas and volumes. These early attempts, however, were not unified nor extendable to general studies of geometric objects.

In 1637, however, the French philosopher and mathematician René Descartes published his work *Discourse de la Methode*, which includes his discovery of the mathematics of analytic geometry. He shows that the geometric description (for example, a line is the shortest distance between two points) and the algebraic one ($Ax + By + C = 0$ for a line) were, in fact, equivalent if you set up an appropriate coordinate system in the plane.

Any theorem derived algebraically from equations that describe a curve is also true geometrically and vice versa. Every point in the plane can be associated with a coordinate set, with one coordinate for each dimension of space you are using. For the plane, there are two dimensions and a coordinate pair is represented as (x, y), where x is the distance of the point from the x-axis line and y is the distance from the y-axis line. These axes are two lines at right angles (or *orthogonal*) to one another. This relationship is illustrated in Figure 1-1.

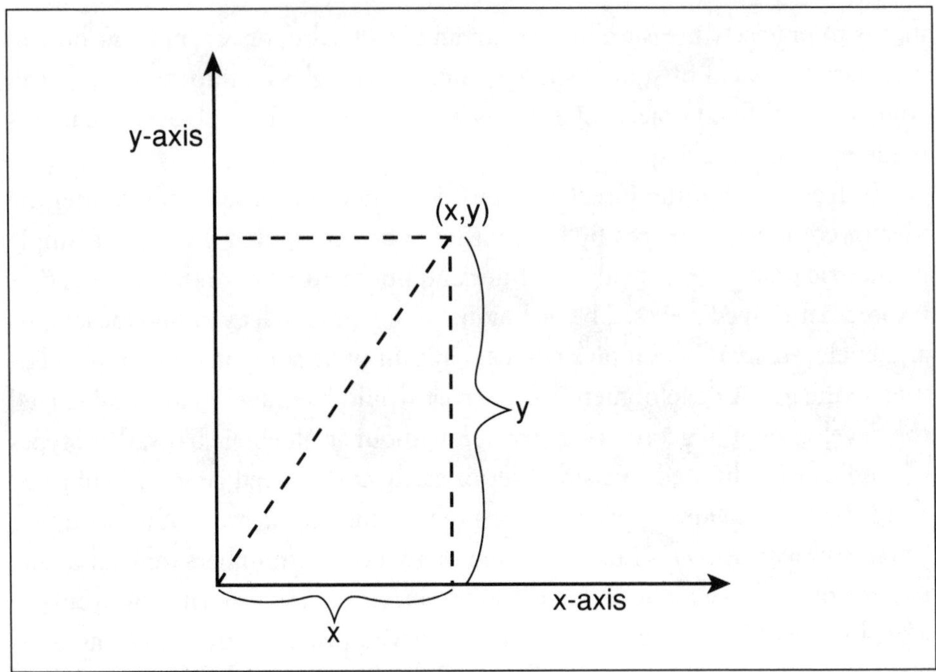

Figure 1-1. Cartesian coordinate system

Note that this definition can be treated geometrically if you consider the point (*x*,*y*) to be at one corner of a right triangle, as shown in the figure. *X* and *y* are then the width and height, respectively, of the triangle.

The notion that algebra and geometry could be combined and treated as equivalent is a powerful idea. This opened the possibilities of examination and analysis of more types of curves than previously considered. Using this idea, any equation could be represented as a curve in the plane. Before Descartes, most scholars only considered curves that could be constructed using a ruler and compass.

For a while, the merging of algebra and geometry brought an end to the study of geometry in the classical sense. The increased flexibility and ease of proving theorems algebraically was quite an improvement on pursuing geometric proofs in the traditional way. However, geometric analysis would reemerge with the discovery of spherical geometry (which is what mapping the earth is all about) and with the study of non-Euclidean geometries.

The Equation of a Line

A curve is a continuous set of points that define a path in a plane. For instance, a line is a type of curve while a circle is another type. A good way to think of a curve is as any figure you can draw without lifting your pen or pencil from the paper while drawing it.

By using the Cartesian coordinate system, you can represent any curve in the plane by specifying one or more equations that the points on the curve must satisfy. For a line, the general equation is:

$$Ax + By + C = 0 \qquad \text{(Equation 1-1)}$$

A line is fully specified by the coefficients A, B, and C. (In fact, it is over-specified since all three coefficients are not required. You can use a *normalized* equation in which $C = 0$ if the line goes through the origin, and $C = 1$ otherwise.) This form of an equation is referred to as an *implicit* equation. In the previous equation, there is no explicit relationship between x and y (for example, y is not a direct function of x in the equation). An *explicit* equation is one in which a variable is written as a function of the other variables. The line equation can be recast in the more familiar, explicit form of:

$$y = mx + b \qquad \text{(Equation 1-2)}$$

where $m = B/A$ and $b = -C/A$. Note that this equation does not work in the case of a vertical line, $A = 0$. There are several other cases in this book where you use the implicit form $f(x,y) = 0$ to specify other types of curves and surfaces.

Line segments

Equation 1-1 describes all the points along a line. For drawing purposes, you only draw line segments between two points, which you designate as (x_1, y_1) and (x_2, y_2). This is illustrated in Figure 1-2. You will, however, need the equation of the line containing these two points, which is:

Define: $dx = (x_2 - x_1)$, $dy = (y_2 - y_1)$
Then: $A = -(dy)$, $B = (dx)$, $C = dy * x_1 - dx * y_1$

You can verify this definition by substituting for both pairs of points with the result being zero. The form of Equation 1-2 is the most intuitive form of the line equation, even though it cannot be used for vertical lines. The constant *m*, referred to as the slope is simply *dy/dx*. Note that you can, however, choose another form of the equation that does work for vertical lines:

$$x = y/m + d \qquad \text{(Equation 1-3)}$$

For the line drawing algorithms, you will choose the most suitable representation based on the quantities *dx* and *dy*. For the moment, just note that quantity *m* represents the rate of change of *y* with respect to *x*. So a change of one in *x*, corresponds to a change in *m* in *y*. Similarly, a change of one in *y* corresponds to a change of *1/m* in *x*.

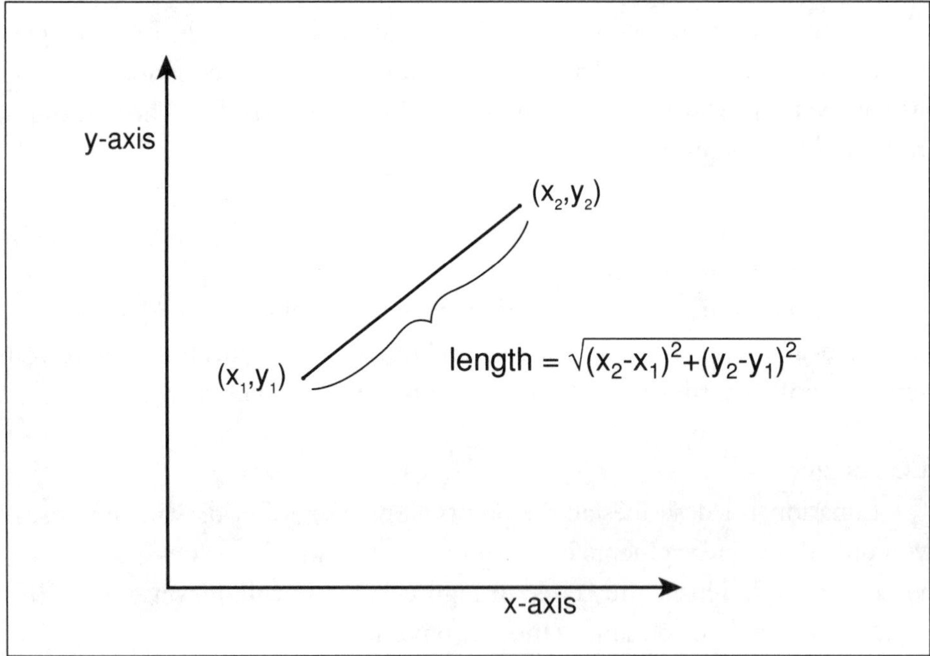

Figure 1-2. Line segment from (x1, y1) to (x2, y2)

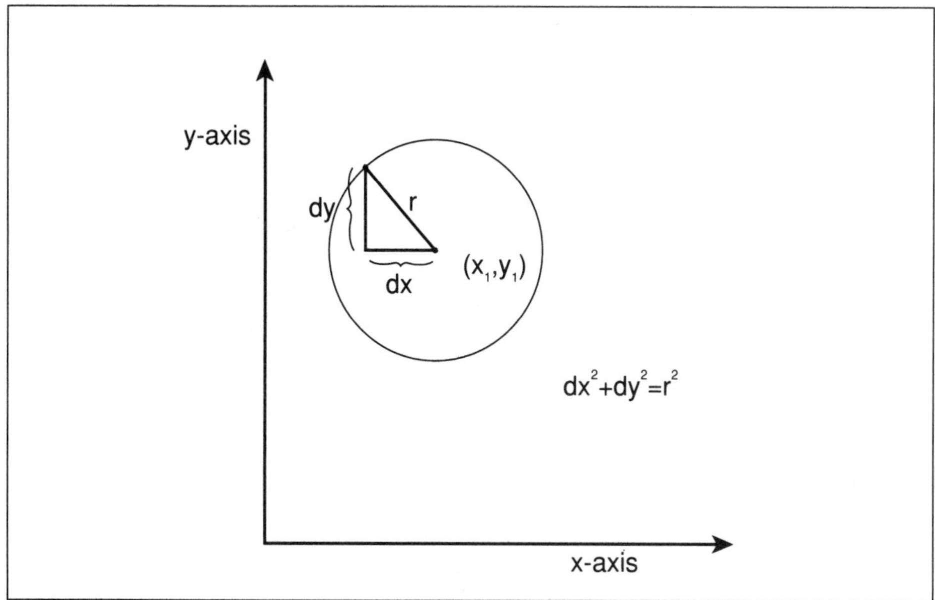

Figure 1-3. A circle centered at (x1, y1) of radius r

Circles and ellipses

The next most useful geometric figure is the circle. Recall that a circle is defined as the set of points equidistant from a selected center point. Using the Pythagorean theorem, the distance between two points is:

$$d = sqrt((x_2 - x_1)^2 + (y_2 - y_1)^2) \qquad \text{(Equation 1-4)}$$

where *sqrt()* returns the square root of its argument. This relationship along with a representative circle are shown in Figure 1-3. Note that the circle is centered at point *(x1,y1)* and has a radius of *d*. The equation for a circle can now be easily written as:

$$(x - x_1)^2 + (y - y_1)^2 - r^2 = 0 \qquad \text{(Equation 1-5)}$$

This specifies all points of distance r from the center point at (x_1, y_1). Unlike the line equation, you cannot solve this equation explicitly for y because it represents a *multivalued* function in y.

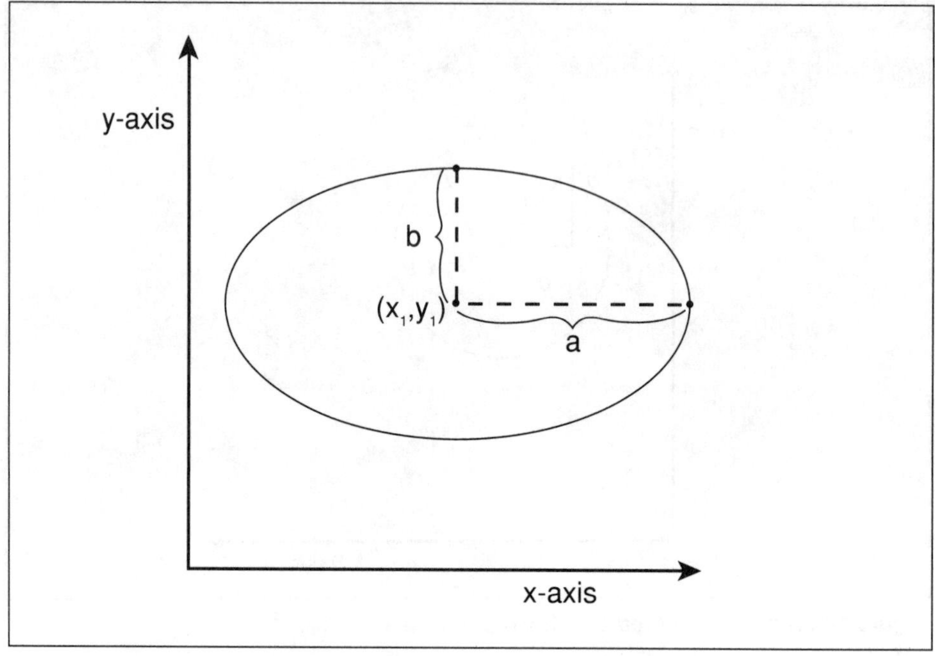

Figure 1-4. An ellipse centered at (x_1, y_1) with major axis of length a along the x-axis, and minor axis of length b along the y-axis

That is, for every *x*, there are two values of *y* on the circle, positive and negative. You can, however, plot the upper and lower semicircles separately. Later, you'll learn to exploit this property with the circle-drawing algorithm presented in Chapter 5.

Ellipses are circles that are stretched in either the *x*- or *y*-axis. The equation for an ellipse is very similar to that of a circle, except now I'll introduce some additional scale factors for both *x* and *y*. Equation 1-5 then becomes:

$$((x - x_1)/a)^2 + ((y - y_1)/b)^2 - r^2 = 0 \qquad \text{(Equation 1-6)}$$

A representative ellipse is shown in Figure 1-4. Equation 1-6 only allows for ellipses that are aligned with the axes. In Chapter 8, you will learn how to take this equation (and virtually any other) and generalize it to allow for rotated figures as well.

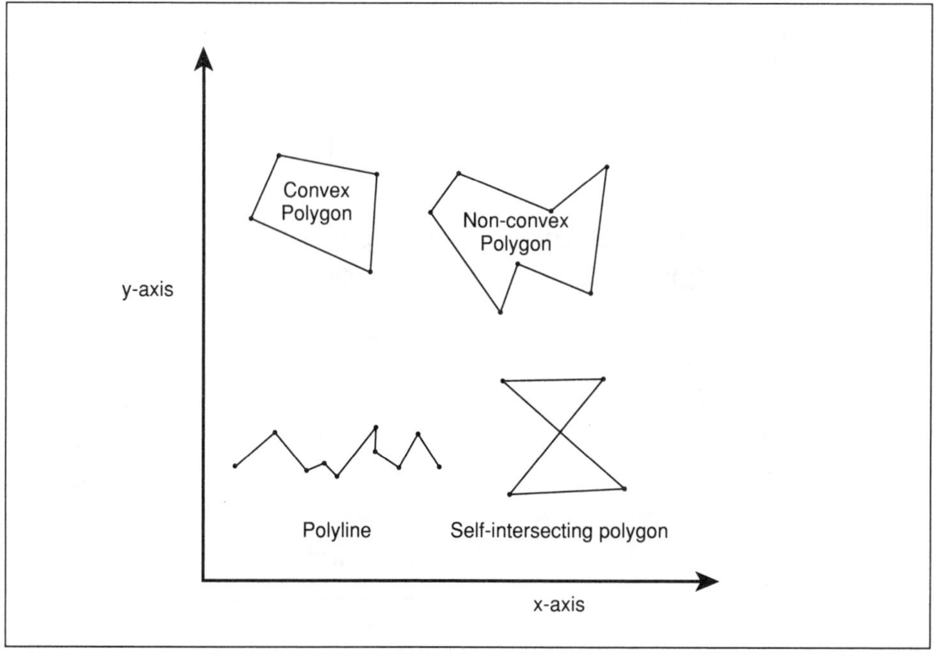

Figure 1-5. Different types of polygons

Polygons and polylines

You may recall that a *polygon* is any closed multi-sided figure. For instance, a triangle is a three-sided polygon, a rectangle a four-sided polygon, and so forth. Any series of points connected by straight-line segments is referred to as a *polyline*. A polyline may or may not be closed. The distinction between the two is that a polyline describes a path in the plane from a starting point to the last point in the polyline. A polygon is intended to describe an enclosed area. Therefore, one usual restriction for a polygon is that none of the edges cross other edges of the polygon. Examples of polylines, polygons, and invalid polygons are shown in Figure 1-5.

Since all display devices have finite resolution, you will usually end up approximating complex curves and shapes as polylines and polygons respectively. For instance, you can approximate the upper half of a circle by stepping along the x-axis and computing the corresponding y-value using the following equation:

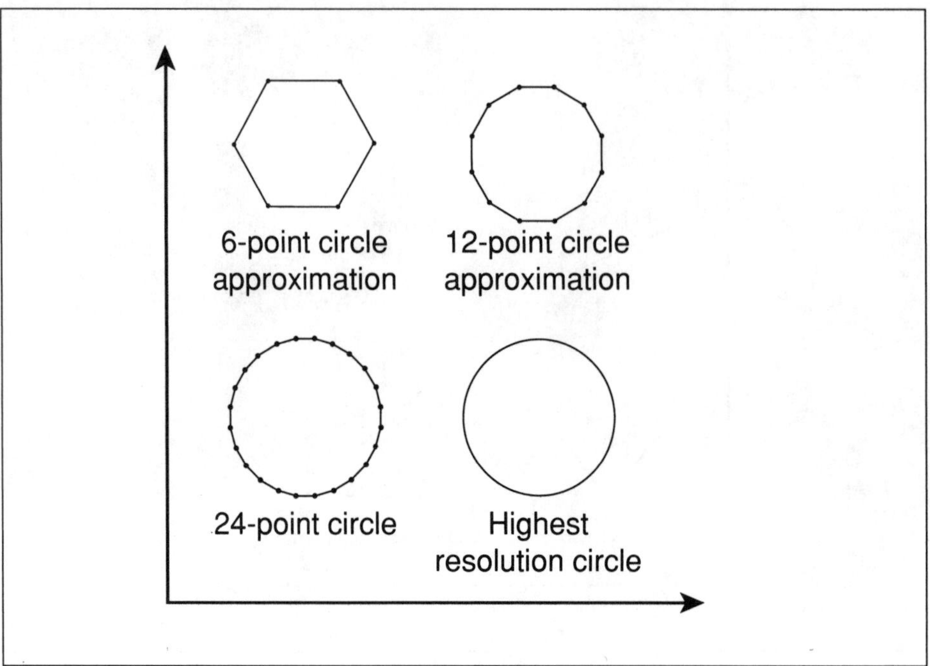

Figure 1-6. Approximating a circle using polygons. As more sides are used, the approximation becomes more accurate.

$$y = sqrt(r^2 - (x - x_1)^2) \qquad \text{(Equation 1-7)}$$

You then connect each *(x,y)* point with a straight-line segment, which forms an approximation to the circle. This process is shown in Figure 1-6. As you step in finer increments of *x*, you can produce a more accurate plot of the circle. If your step size is equal to the resolution of the display device, you can produce the most accurate plot available on that device. In Chapter 11, you will learn that most function plotting consists of evaluating points along the curve at regular intervals and connecting the points with straight-line segments.

Your main interest in polygons should be the ability to fill the area described by the polygon. For instance, to draw a filled circle, you need to know what part of the plot is inside the circle and what is outside. This is easy to determine for a circle; however, a more complex polygonal figure requires a little more effort.

One property that distinguishes a complex polygon from a simpler one is *convexity*. If you pick any two points inside of a convex shape and connect them with a line segment, the entire line segment is contained within the shape. A circle is a convex shape. A rectangle is a convex shape. Any *regular* polygon (all sides are the same length and all angles between adjacent edges are the same), such as a square, is convex. However, the last example in Figure 1-6 is not convex. Knowing that a shape is convex greatly simplifies the process of filling that shape.

Useful Functions

Once you have a mathematical description of a geometric shape, proceed with drawing that shape on the screen. An algebraic description is an ideal way to represent an object to a computer. A computer cannot "see" a drawing the way you can, but it can manipulate numbers and equations far more quickly than a human can.

You must, however, come up with the means for a computer to simulate what you can do with a pencil and paper, namely, to turn the algebraic equations into a suitable drawing. Just as you would use various tools to create a drawing, such as a ruler, compass, and protractor, you will need to develop a set of drawing tools that let a program do the same thing on the screen. The computer, however, will be able to draw much more quickly!

Before you dive directly into developing graphics programming tools, you must establish some conventions for how to treat angles, and you must introduce some useful mathematical functions that are necessary to implement many of the drawing algorithms.

The Proper Angle

In this book, you'll find angles represented in *radians*, the standard mathematical angular unit. While this seems a bit awkward from a practical standpoint, every math library expects angular arguments to be in radians. As you will recall, 360 degrees corresponds to *2 * PI* radians. You, therefore, have defined the following as constants in the graphics header file *ggraph.h*:

```
#define PI           3.14159
#define DEG_TO_RAD   (PI / 180.0)
#define RAD_TO_DEG   (180.0 / PI)
```

The two scale factors let you convert between the two units easily. Whenever dealing with angles, you'll often want to specify angles in units of degrees, instead of radians. Specifying the angle for a line as 45 degrees is more natural than specifying an angle as *PI/4* radians.

An angle is almost always used as an argument to one of the basic trigonometric functions *sine()*, *cosine()*, and occasionally *tangent()*. These functions let you convert angles into Cartesian coordinates. By universal convention, the C functions are called respectively, *sin()*, *cos()*, and *tan()*. These functions require that their argument be an angle in radians. In this book, I define versions of these functions that accept angles in degrees in order to simplify your programs. To maximize their efficiency, use the C macro capability and define the new functions *cosD()*, *sinD()*, and *tanD()* as follows:

```
#define    cosD(x)    cos( (x) * DEG_TO_RAD )
#define    sinD(x)    sin( (x) * DEG_TO_RAD )
#define    tanD(x)    tan( (x) * DEG_TO_RAD )
```

With the functions *sin()* and *cos()*, you can compute the (x,y) coordinates of a point given the distance, r, of the point from the origin and its angle, *theta*, with respect to the positive x-axis using the following equations:

$$x = r * cos(theta) \qquad \text{(Equation 1-8)}$$
$$y = r * sin(theta)$$

In fact, you can locate a point using r and *theta* just as easily as you can using x and y. The coordinates (r, *theta*) are referred to as *polar* coordinates. Whenever an object has a circular characteristic, such as a circle, an ellipse, or a spiral, polar coordinates are often more convenient for defining and manipulating the object. For example, in polar coordinates, the equation for the circle simply becomes:

$$r = r_1 \qquad \text{(Equation 1-9)}$$

(r is equal to the constant radius of the circle)

This is a much simpler equation than the corresponding Cartesian expression of Equation 1-5.

Don't Be Square

You've already seen the need to square a number and to take the square root in the equation of a circle and ellipse. You can improve the efficiency of squaring a number by again using the C macro facility to define the following macro:

```
#define square(x)       ((x) * (x))
```

By using this macro, the multiplication is performed in-line by the compiler, which is often more efficient than calling a separate function to compute the square.

The square root function, *sqrt()*, is the standard C built-in function to compute the square root of a floating-point number. This function is usually computationally expensive to use, and you'll want to avoid using it whenever possible. This function is necessary, however, when you need to compute the distance between two points in the plane. Fortunately, you won't need to do this very often!

Onto C!

Now that you have seen some of the basic graphic elements, you're ready to move on to creating drawing programs that display these objects on *your* computer screen. The next chapter begins with a look into the C language and shows how to apply it to the graphics programming task. After reading about the graphics display device on your computer, you'll learn how to make it actually do something useful. So, forward to Chapter 2 and learning how C makes graphics programming easy.

C Programming Techniques

Having a machine produce images is not a new idea. Since the nineteenth century, there have been mechanical devices for creating drawings from "live" input or for recreating mathematically defined shapes. These devices have provided the ability to create, and often more importantly recreate, accurate plots of many different types of functions.

However, only the computer provides complete control over the drawing process. The ability to program a computer and have it respond both to user input and to input data from a variety of sources gives it unparalleled flexibility to describe a drawing or image. Virtually any algorithm used for representing a drawing mathematically may be programmed into a computer. Furthermore, the computer provides an interactive means of viewing and manipulating a data or model. This is all accomplished through programming, and so the choice of how you express algorithms is quite important.

The source code presented in this book is based on C programming language. You'll need access to a PC on which you can run the example code found throughout the rest of this book. There were several reasons for selecting C:

- C is an extremely popular programming language. There is a seemingly endless number of compilers, developer's toolkits, and books available to help you in developing programs.

- All of the major graphics packages are based on C. This includes the MS-Windows developer's toolkits, DOS-based graphics packages, X Windows workstation-based platforms, and just about every other graphics-related package. Even those packages that were not developed in C almost always provide a C interface library.

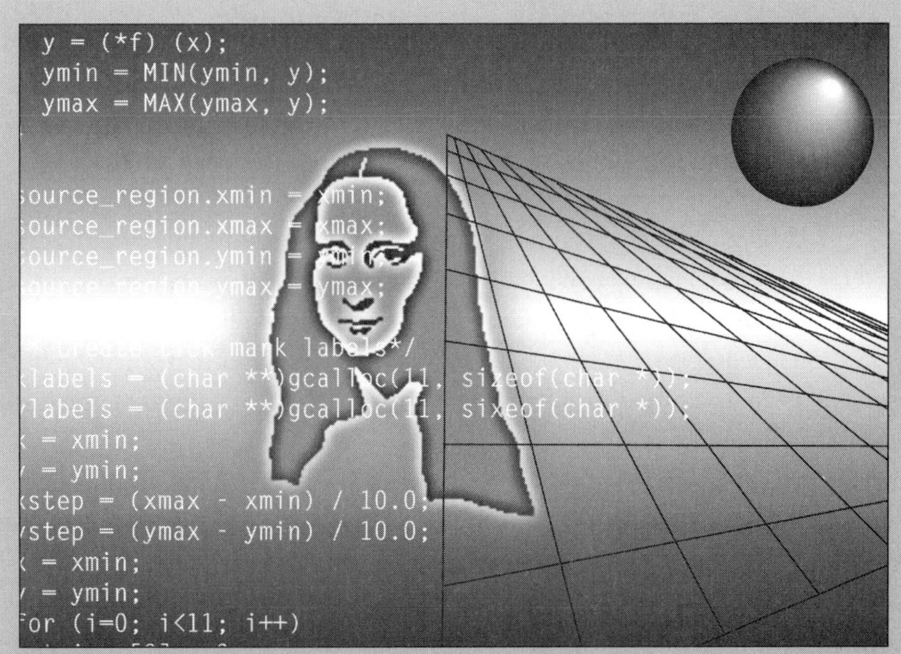
y = (*f) (x);
ymin = MIN(ymin, y);
ymax = MAX(ymax, y);

In order to create anything using a computer, you must learn how to speak its language. Think of programming languages as the raw material, the paint if you will, for creating a drawing. Any computer drawing or graphic is ultimately just a combination of ones and zeros created by someone's program. As with any artistic medium, you must learn how to efficiently use the tools of the trade, which for a computer includes the programming language.

In this chapter, you'll learn some guidelines for creating efficient, readable, and reusable code. These techniques will aid you in creating elegant graphics programs that you can build upon. Once you have coded an algorithm, you can easily reuse it as part of a more complex drawing program. By using the programming methods of this chapter, you will save yourself both time and effort as you create more elaborate drawing programs.

- You can create very efficient code and still maintain the elegance and stability provided by a high level language. As you will learn, you can manipulate objects in an efficient manner through the use of C structures and pointers.

- There are many example software packages and applications available to you once you have mastered the basics presented in this book. Since graphic programming is so pervasive, you'll probably find others who have developed code that you'll find useful in solving whatever application problems you might have. And chances are, the code will be in C.

As mentioned in the Introduction, I assume that you are already familiar with basic C language syntax and with the language's fundamental elements, such as the use of variables, operators (like + and -), and functions. The code in this book conforms to ANSI C and, for the most part, to K&R C, the standard in Brian W. Kernighan and Dennis M. Ritchie's *The C Programming Language* (Prentice Hall, 1978).

But just understanding how these various elements work does not always mean that you know the most appropriate way to use them in a given application. As with any complex language, there are always a dozen or more ways to accomplish the same task or express the same algorithm. You saw one small example of this in the previous chapter. You needed to compute the square of *x*, which could be implemented as either an explicit function or as a C macro. The function call is more computationally expensive; so you choose the macro method instead. However, for more complex functions, it is not obvious which method is the best approach. The rest of this chapter describes the file structure and programming style adopted for C graphics programming. Trust me when this book states that there are many other implementation choices that could be made, and none of them are ideal for *all* applications.

ANSI vs. Non-ANSI

To help ensure the greatest compatibility and ease of implementation, the code provided in this book is ANSI (American National Standards Institute) compliant. Several years ago, achieving compatibility and ease of implementation was a problem since many C compilers on the PC and other platforms were not necessarily standardized. This has changed in recent years to the point that all new compilers are created compliant to ANSI C. If you are using a noncompliant compiler, you shouldn't have much difficulty following the examples and material in this book, excluding the declarations of function prototypes described in the following section.

I strongly encourage you to program in an ANSI-compliant method by simply turning on the appropriate compile options for your compiler. This aids in moving your application to other platforms, and it also encourages you to write cleaner code. A lot of the nasty tricks that older C compilers let you get away with, and that ultimately cause trouble, can be detected by the compiler and subsequently avoided.

Headers and Modules

C source files are divided into two basic types, header files with an h-file extension and modules with a c-file extension. The modules represent the source code of your program. While no general rules really exist for how to organize these files, you should maintain each source module at a reasonable size. Avoid putting each function in a separate module or putting all your functions in the same file, unless it is a very simple program. A useful rule of thumb is to keep the length of all your function definitions to no more than a single page. This makes them easy to catalog when they are output, and it forces you to break complex functions into more manageable pieces.

Static Variables

Generally, it does not matter which file a given function is in as long as that function is global, or accessible to all modules. The most important feature of a source module is that any functions or variables declared as static within the module are known only to the functions of that module. This gives you the ability to add new functions to a module that cannot be accessed by functions outside the module. This means that the functions are local to your module; that is, other programs cannot use (or more importantly *misuse*) the modules. This is particularly important in large applications with many function names.

If you use a function name like *addcolor()*, it is likely that this name will be used by someone else unless you agree ahead of time on a naming convention. By using the static keyword, you have a local *addcolor()* known only by the functions of your module. So, you may use this function freely without fear of conflict with another programmer's use of the same name.

The same idea applies to the use of static variables. If the static declaration is made inside a function definition, then the variable will be retained after the function returns, just like a global variable. The variable may, however, only be used by that particular function. If a static variable is declared at the beginning of a module, outside of any function definition, then the variable is available to every function in the module. A static variable still refers to only one memory location. If function *foo1* changes it and then calls function *foo2*, *foo2* will see the changed value. Using a global variable can be quite tricky if the variable is set in multiple places in the program.

A good use for static variables within a function is to initialize pointers. For instance, the following code segment defines a temporary variable:

```
void process_circle(Circle *c)
Circle *c;
{
 static Circle *temp_circle = NULL;

 if(temp_circle == NULL)
  temp_circle = circleCreate(0,0, 1.0);

<rest of function>
}
```

When *process_circle()* is called the first time, the static variable *temp_circle* points to NULL (usually defined as *(void *) 0* or just zero). This then forces it to create the temporary circle by calling the *circleCreate()* function. The variable *temp_circle* may then be used as temporary storage or for whatever purpose you wish. Whenever *process_circle()* is called again, *temp_circle* will not be NULL, and so it will not bother creating it again. This saves execution time since you don't need to create and destroy the temporary circle each time *process_circle()* is called. This can be quite important for time-critical applications, such as image animation.

In general, you should avoid the use of global variables. They have their uses, such as keeping track of global state information to avoid having to pass extraneous arguments to all your application functions. But you can avoid most of this by putting all of the global information in a single global structure and using either functions or macros to access the data within the structure. Global variables should be treated as variables that are only modified during program initialization or when a major change of program state has occurred that affects most of the modules. Otherwise, create an appropriate structure to contain your state information and pass it only to the functions that need to use the information. You'll be glad you did!

Header files

The general structure of a standard header file is shown in Figure 2-1. Macros and structure definitions should be familiar to you. A .h-header file normally provides definitions for the following:

- Macro definitions
- Structure definitions
- Function prototypes

The function prototyping may be new, but it is conceptually simple. Instead of just declaring the return data type of a function, the function prototype also declares what the argument type should be. This lets the compiler check all the function uses throughout your program and report any argument mismatch errors (wrong number of arguments or wrong data type) at compile time. Such errors can be difficult to locate without this feature.

Function prototypes are not required by the C compiler. You may declare functions without them, but then you lose the benefit of the compiler automatically checking calls to that function. Additionally, the C++ environment does require function prototypes, so you might as well get used to using them now.

Place the declarations for all your global (or *extern*) functions in at least one header file. By doing this, you assure argument checking across several modules.

```
#if !defined(__HEADER_H)      /* You can also use the
                                 equivalent #ifndef statement */
#define __HEADER_H   1

/**************************************************************/
/*
     header.h

     Programmer(s):      Who gets blame if program doesn't work?

     Purpose:            Why did you spend time on this?

     Revision History:      Who changed it right before the
                            demonstration?
*/
/*************************************************************

     MACRO Definitions

*************************************************************/

#define      MAX(x,y)      ((x) > (y) ? (x) : (y))
#define      MIN(x,y)      ((x) <= (y) ? (x) : (y))

/*************************************************************

     Typedef declarations

*************************************************************/

typedef      float      angle;

/* Using this method, an angle variable could easily be changed
from using floats to doubles throughout the code */

/*************************************************************

     Structure Definitions
```

```
*************************************************************/

typedef struct circle_struct {
     int x,y;
     float radius;
} Circle;                /* It is generally good practice to have
                            typedefs for all of your structures */


/*************************************************************

     Function Declarations & Prototypes

*************************************************************/

Circle     *scaleCircle(Circle *circle, float scale);
void        circleCreate(void);
void        circleDelete(Circle *circle);
```

Listing 2-1. Structure of a C header file

The Zen of Macros

The C-macro capability provides a powerful (sometimes too powerful) means of defining symbolic constants and creating in-line expressions. A macro is processed by simple substitution. As the compiler scans a source file, any macro name that is encountered is replaced with the definition of the macro. The expression is then compiled normally. There are two basic flavors of macros:

```
#define   PI             3.14159    /* Defining parameters */
                                    /* In-line function */
#define   max(x,y)       ((x) > (y) ? (x) : (y))
```

The first type is the basic means for defining any particular constants you might want to use. For instance, you should define any program limits, such as maximum array sizes and time limits, using a macro. By doing this, you can change the macro at a later date and, more importantly, the symbolic name gives you a better indication of what the constant was meant to signify. For example,

```
#define MAX_ARRAY_SIZE   1000

double array[MAX_ARRAY_SIZE];
```

is much better than:

```
double array[1000];
```

It is even more useful when a limit or constant is a more complex expression, for example:

```
#define PI             3.14159
#define DEG_TO_RADS    180. / PI
```

Another common use of *#define* is in providing optional compilation control by employing the *#ifdef/#endif* directives. This gives you the flexibility to compile modules differently, depending on which environment you are using, such as between MS-DOS and MS-Windows or between different compiler manufacturer's implementations of C. So, you can retain some environment specific features without having to alter code when compiling under different environments.

Useful directives

You can use the *#ifdef* directive to solve the annoying problem of including header files multiple times. For instance, suppose header file *foo1.h* includes header file *foo2.h*. In your main module, *foo.c*, you include *foo1.h* and *foo2.h*. Without the proper precaution, you would receive lots of multiply-defined structure definitions, macro definitions, and so on when you tried to compile *foo.c*. The problem is that *foo2.h* is included twice. To avoid this, you can use the following in all your header files:

```
#ifdef __<HEADERNAME>_H
#define __<HEADERNAME>_H       1
.
<rest of header file>
.
#endif
```

where *<HEADERNAME>* is usually the name of header file, such as *FOO1* and *FOO2* in the previous examples. Notice that the convention used capitalizes the entire header file name in the *#define* and *#ifdef* statements. While not required, this helps avoid possible conflicts with the header filename elsewhere. With this technique, the header file definitions will only be included once, regardless of how many times it is included. You can also have all your header files cross reference one another without causing massive conflicts. This technique is used by all the system header files, such as *stdio.h* and *sys.h*, to avoid the multiple-definition problem.

The second main macro form is used to define simple functions. It is very similar to defining a function, except that there are no data-type declarations. The compiler processes the macro by taking whatever argument(s) you pass it and simply substituting it into the expression. As a matter of style, a macro is the *only* place you should use an operator like ?, which is considered unreadable otherwise. Although ? is a very efficient operator, all but the most savvy C wizards find it difficult to tell (or remember) what this operator does.

Note that in the macro definition you put *()* around each of the arguments. This is absolutely an essential step. Because a macro is processed by simple substitution, you can pass an expression as an argument. The compiler makes the substitution and then evaluates the resulting total expression based on the normal rules of operator precedence. This can result in wrong answers. For example:

```
#define     MUL(a,b)     a*b

int c;
c = MUL(1+2, 3+4);
```

The previous definition for *MUL()* does not put *()* around its arguments. So, when macro substitution is performed, the expression for *c* becomes:

$c = 1 + 2 * 3 + 4$

When the expression is evaluated, *c* will be equal to 1 + 6 + 4 = 11, instead of 3 * 7 = 21 as was intended. With more complicated macros, the errors can be more subtle. So always put the arguments in *()* in any macro expression.

Another interesting note about the use of function macros is that they let you define a function, such as max, that works on different data types. You don't need to define a separate max function for *ints*, *floats*, *doubles*, or any of the other defined types, because the macro substitution uses the > operator, which works on all these types. This was recognized as an early deficiency of C++, later rectified by providing the template feature.

A Few Pointers

Nothing seems to give more programmers trouble than the definition and use of structures and the corresponding structure pointers. C structures provide an elegant means of defining an object consisting of several unrelated elements, each of which may be a structure. Consider the following definition for a circle structure:

```
struct Circle_struct {
  int x, y;
 float radius;
};
```

This definition lets you manipulate the circle as a single entity. Now, you could make arrays of circles, or use a circle as an element of a more complex structure. You can make this definition more useful through using the *typedef* statement as:

```
typedef struct Circle_struct {
 int x,y;
 float radius;
} Circle;
```

In this definition, the symbol *circle_struct* is simply a reference for the definition of the structure. The *typedef* statement tells the compiler to treat the name *Circle* as another data type; in this case, it refers to the structure defined by *circle_struct*. You can now use the name *Circle* wherever you would use any other data type, such as *int* or *float*. For instance, you can now have functions with the following declarations:

```
Circle *scale_circle(c, scale)
Circle *c;
float scale;
{
 c->radius *= scale;
 return c;
}
```

The use of *typedef* increases the readability of the code, as you do not have to use unnecessary *struct* declarations now.

C provides dynamic memory allocation, primarily through the use of the functions *malloc()* (memory allocate) and *free()* (free memory allocated by *malloc*). *Pointers* are references to locations in memory. You traditionally think of pointers as addresses of memory; that is, the value of a pointer determines where the actual data is located in main memory. They provide a very convenient means of referencing structures and arrays, especially when these need to be passed as arguments to functions. C is a pass-by-value language; so, if a structure is passed as an argument to a function, the entire structure is copied and passed to the called function. This can be very inefficient and is never necessary. You should always pass structure arguments by a pointer, as in the previous example for *scale_circle*.

Pointers are also quite useful for indexing through arrays. Suppose you wanted an array of circles. You could process all of them as follows:

```
Circle circles[10];    /* An array of 10 circle structures */
Circle *c;             /* A pointer to a circle */
int i;

c = &(circles[0]);     /* Circles[0] is the first circle, the
                          & operator gives us the pointer to the
                          first circle */

for(i=0; i<10; i++) {
 process_circle(c);
 c++;
}
```

By using the ++ operator, you can easily step through the array of circles in a very efficient manner.

Naming conventions

In order to avoid conflicts with other graphics packages and with your own routines, a standard naming convention is used for most of the structures and functions throughout this book. As you use more software libraries, you will inevitably find that someone else has created a structure called *Circle* or *Point* or a function called *DrawCircle()*. Any standardized naming convention always makes the names longer and sometimes less intuitive. But this is much better than having to change your source code later to avoid conflicts with the new library you just purchased.

The conventions used in this book are reasonably straightforward. All of the graphics functions and structures begin with a lowercase *g*. Each word in the name is fully spelled out and each separate word begins with a capital letter. For example, the circle structure is named *gCircle*. The circle-drawing function is called *gCircleDraw()*. Structures are always typed with the following syntax:

```
typedef struct g<Type>_struct {
/* Definition of structure */
} g<Type>;
```

where *<Type>* is something like *Circle*. Most function names have the form:

```
g<Type><Action>();
```

where *<Type>* is the object type, like *Circle*, and *<Action>* describes the function, such as *MoveAbsolute*. By adopting a similar convention for your own routines, such as prefixing your function names and structure with your initials, you can save yourself a lot of potential grief.

Graphics programs, objects, and C++

C++ is the object-oriented extension to C that provides some very useful additions as well as increased utility. It is defined in such a way that it is a superset of ANSI C, for example, all ANSI-compliant C programs should compile under C++. This makes the transition to C++ less painful and faster since you don't necessarily have to rewrite all your code to use it (though in many cases, you would like to!).

For now, C still reigns supreme as the graphics language of choice. This will certainly change over the next several years as the object-oriented paradigm becomes more popular. In fact, graphics programs provide ideal candidates for object-oriented programming techniques. In this book, I have taken the middle ground by adopting some C++ techniques and implementing them in their closest C counterpart. While certainly not a complete object-oriented approach, it at least gets you thinking about how to structure programs to take advantage of what C++ offers.

An object is defined by two principle features: the data it contains and the *methods*, or functions, for manipulating that object. Methods provide the interface to the outside world—or other programmers—for modifying an object. A C structure solves half the problem in that you can define how data is stored for the structure. You can attach methods to a structure using pointers to functions. In fact, this is how C++ compilers implement methods, although in a more transparent fashion to the programmer. This approach is not used in this book since it obscures the basic graphics algorithms and produces less readable C code. Instead, this book supplies functions for each "object" that takes the object pointer as the first argument. This typically makes for more readable code at the loss of the flexibility that a truly object-oriented approach would provide.

As previously mentioned, all structures have a *typedef* definition so that they may be used in declarations just like standard data types. For each structure, you define three standard functions:

- Constructor
- Destructor
- Copy constructor

The constructor creates an appropriately initialized structure and returns a pointer to it. The destructor frees the structure, and more importantly, frees any data inside the structure that was allocated by the constructor. The copy constructor provides a means to create a copy of an existing structure. This constructor takes the following two arguments:

1. A pointer to the *destination* structure you want to copy to
2. A pointer to the *source* object to copy from

If the destination pointer is NULL, then the copy constructor creates a new object to hold the copy. If the destination pointer is not NULL, then the source object will overwrite the destination object. The copy constructor returns a pointer to the copied structure. A copy constructor of this form lets you overwrite existing objects instead of constantly creating new ones.

Our naming convention for these functions is:

```
structure *<structure>Create(<args>); /* Constructor */
void     <structure>Delete(<args>);    /* Destructor */
structure *<structure>Copy(structure *, structure *);
                                        /* Copy Constructor */
```

For example, the circle data type functions are *gCircleCreate()*, *gCircleDelete()*, and *gCircleCopy()*. Note that in this book, I have also adopted the naming convention that function names always begin with a lowercase letter, but variable types, such as *Circle*, begin with an uppercase letter. This helps to avoid confusion later. Similarly, the action verbs in a function name begins with an uppercase letter.

While C does not provide the C++ facility of virtual functions, you can at least adopt the convention that the same function (such as a drawing function) for different types of objects use a common naming convention. Thus, there is *circleDraw*, *lineDraw*, and *pointDraw* as functions to draw their respective objects. Note that all of the object functions pass a pointer called *this* as their first argument. In an analogy to C++, *this* is a pointer to the object acted on by the function. In C++, of course, *this* does not need to be passed explicitly. In most other respects, many of the C functions you have provided are coded in a very similar manner to how they would appear in C++. (Appendix A contains a more detailed description of how to recast software into a more object-oriented approach.)

For More Information

Although the definitive language reference is Kernighan and Ritchie's *The C Programming Language* (Prentice Hall, 1978), other valuable sources include *Applying C++*, Scott Ladd (M&T Publishing, 1992); *C++ Components and Algorithms*, Scott Ladd (M&T Publishing, 1992); and *C Elements of Style*, Steve Oualline (M&T Publishing, 1992).

Graphics Programming

While this chapter has extoled the virtues of C as a suitable programming language for computer graphics, up to now you have not had the opportunity to do any actual graphics programming. In the next chapter, you will learn about the various types of graphic devices that have been used in the past as well as those currently in use. Chapter 3 then describes the raster graphics hardware available on your system and how it operates to produce images you can create and manipulate yourself.

From there, you'll begin developing a programming library of graphic routines that provide the digital equivalent of the straightedge and compass. You'll then continue the exploration of the graphics frontier with a discussion of graphics display devices, past, present, and future.

CHAPTER 3

Graphic Display Devices

All types of graphics require a medium on which to draw images, whether it is paper, stone, marble, canvas, or a computer display monitor. Any medium, even a piece of paper, can be a graphics display if you think of it as a means of presenting a picture.

All you need to do is devise a means of drawing a shape, such as a circle, onto the medium. Although you normally think of a computer graphics display device as something like your PC monitor, in reality it's any medium to which you can transfer a specified shape, either by hand or by computer. For example, computer graphics applications are now being developed to control milling machines so that a computer can create three-dimensional sculptures.

The extent of available mediums for computer graphics is becoming virtually unlimited. In this chapter, you'll briefly look at the historical evolution of various graphics mediums. Then, you'll study the graphic output devices that are most commonly available for computer graphics. In particular, you will examine how your computer, graphics card, and display monitor combine to let you create and store images in a very flexible and powerful way.

Ideally, a graphics medium should meet the following three criteria:

1. It's easy to draw on.
2. It allows editing.
3. You can relate the drawing back to the objects being represented. For instance, you can take accurate measurements directly from a drawing of a house and relate these measurements to the actual house being drawn.

If you have an architectural drawing of a house, chances are you'd like to try various building options, and when finished, get appropriate measurements to use when actually building the house. Similarly, a road map is useful only if you

The principal means of viewing a drawing on a computer is with a CRT (cathode-ray tube). The CRT is the canvas on which all your drawing programs will paint. Unlike a real canvas, a CRT has many useful properties that make it an excellent graphics medium. A CRT display is easy to erase and redraw, and it can support animated drawings that cannot be performed with real paint and canvas without using expensive movie animation equipment. CRT's are very low cost and provide high resolution color displays.

By using the colors provided on most VGA and SVGA graphics cards, you can create images that appear to be almost photographic. In this chapter along with the rest of the book, you will learn how to use computer graphics to create images that cannot be easily made by any other means, and certainly that cannot be changed as quickly and easily as they can be changed on a CRT.

can determine where you are and how to get to another place from the information on the map.

Until the advent of computer graphics displays, graphic drawings satisfied the first and third criteria but had no real way to be edited, except with an eraser. This, however, has changed greatly in the last 10 years. To understand how this has come about, let's look briefly at the evolution of graphics displays and their drawing tools and instruments.

From the Beginning

In the past, people probably used sticks to draw the first pictures in sand. Of course, this isn't a very satisfactory method if you wish to preserve the picture for others to see. But sand drawing evolved into drawing on various other, more permanent, surfaces like stone and wood. The prevalence of stone drawings, for instance, is demonstrated by the large numbers of cave paintings discovered throughout the world.

The ability to create a permanent record encouraged the development of different forms of writing that let people record ideas for others to see, evaluate, and learn from. With a permanent record, a concept could grow and expand as others viewed it and made their own contributions.

Egyptian hieroglyphics are a good example of this. Hieroglyphics are a complex combination of elaborate drawings that required much refinement before the drawings became a viable form of writing. Today we are grateful that these were preserved in a medium as permanent as stone, otherwise much of what is currently known about the Egyptians would have been lost. Similarly, a great deal of what the world knows about Aztec culture is derived from the records left behind in Aztec tombs and pyramids. For example, the Aztec calendar is a graphical representation that shows the extent of the Aztecs' astronomical knowledge. Being able to make an accurate drawing was essential in creating this marvelous instrument for tracking the time of year. Carving it in a stone tablet is even more impressive, considering the time and care it takes to make any elaborate sculpture. Interestingly enough, our culture will probably have a more difficult time preserving its legacy as paper documents tend to deteriorate quicker than stone tablets.

Stone, however permanent, is much more difficult to work with than paper, and it is not nearly as portable. The development of various types of paper and pens provided a much easier medium to use for drawing and writing than any type of carving. Furthermore, paper can be easily sent to another person, whereas lugging stone tablets around is not very practical.

Today, paper remains the principle medium for transmitting our ideas to others. The difficulty with creating graphics is how to draw desirable images of objects on a medium, whether it is paper, canvas, or something else. To solve this problem, a number of graphics instruments have been developed that either simplify drawing objects, increase accuracy and precision, or both. Computer graphics addresses both of these issues and is a vast improvement over traditional drawing techniques.

Drawing by Hand

There are three basic drawing instruments used to create a two-dimensional drawing:

- Straightedges
- Graduated rulers
- Compasses

The straightedge makes it simple to draw a straight line between any two points. The graduated ruler provides the ability to draw a line of a specific distance as well as to measure the distance from another drawing. The compass lets you easily draw circles of different radii. Several variations of these instruments simplify drawing objects even further. The protractor lets you create angles with a specific number of degrees or draw arcs of a circle. Dividers are a variation of the compass that let you transfer an equal length from one part of the drawing to another, or transfer a length from the actual object being drawn. The T square lets you easily draw lines that are perpendicular to one another. The french curve lets you connect a small set of points with a smooth curve.

These types of drawing instruments, however, require that a person perform all the work and create the actual drawings. While this is necessary for many types of drawings, it is not efficient for other types, including plotting

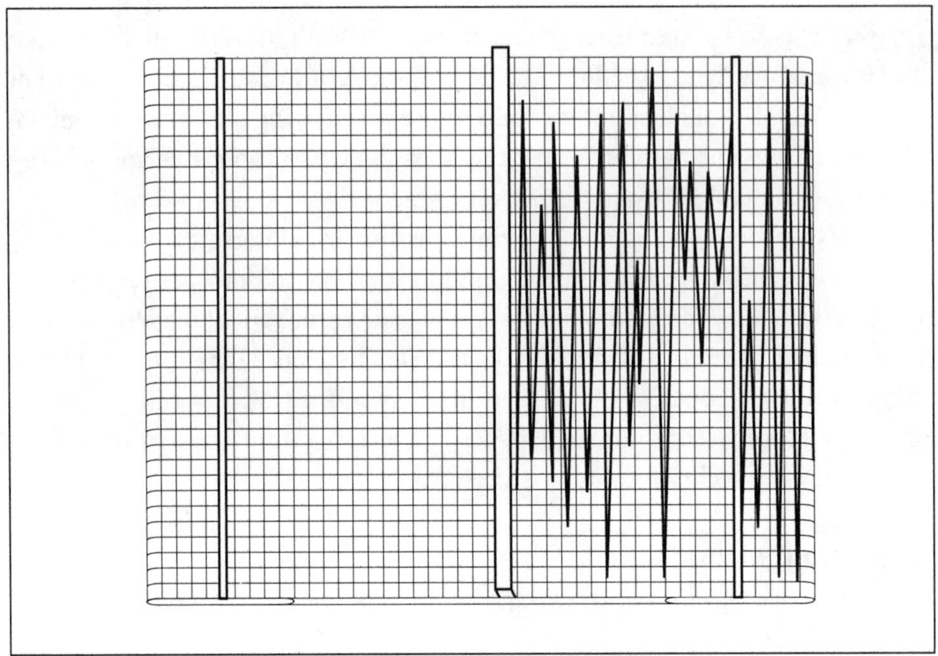

Figure 3-1. A seismograph for plotting earth movement data

equations, drawing graphs, drawing at different scales, and so on. The time to create precise architectural drawings and maps used to be measured in months or years, depending on the detail required. If the drawing (or any portion of it) can be described by some mathematical procedure or by data from another source, a machine can probably do the work more efficiently and repeatedly than any person could. People, therefore, have invented quite a number of electromechanical devices to create various types of drawings, most notably graphs of functions, in as automated a fashion as possible.

Plotting Devices

A good example of a device for creating a plot of some externally measured function is shown in Figure 3-1. The *seismograph* (a device that measures earthquakes), the *polygraph* (a device that measures pulsations), and the *electroencephalograph* (a device that measures brain wave patterns) are all based on a similar design for recording a plot. The principle is straightforward. A set of fine-inked needles are attached to an external voltage that fluctuates depend-

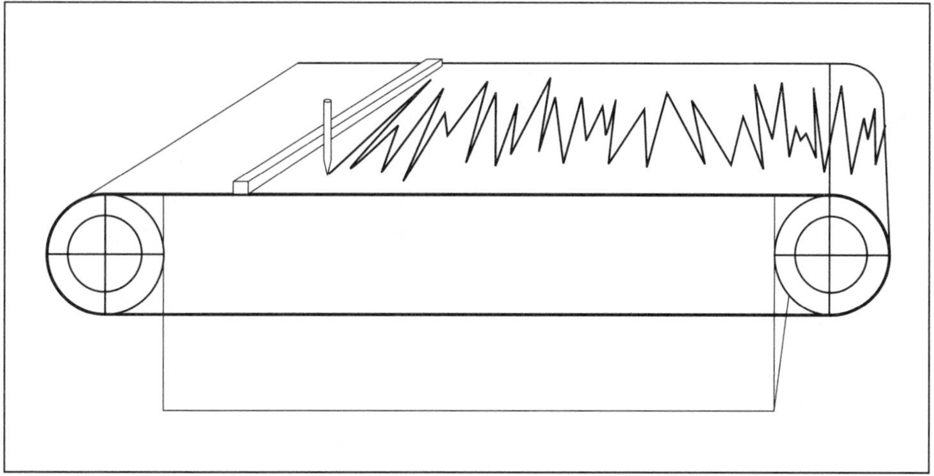

Figure 3-2. A typical pen plotter

ing on the incoming electrical signal. Each needle is attached to a small coil that causes it to move an amount from the center that is proportional to an applied electrical voltage. At 0 volts, the needle stays centered. If the voltage is negative, the needle moves in one direction, if positive it moves in the other direction. The roll of graph paper moves at a constant speed underneath the needles. This produces a graph of the input voltages as a function of time. This device can be used to produce a plot of any function if the function can be generated as a time-varying voltage. An electroencephalograph amplifies the electrical activity of the brain to supply the input voltages to the needles.

Adding another dimension to the plot

You create a more general plotting device if you can control both the horizontal motion (the moving paper) and the vertical motion (the needles). One solution for this is illustrated by the *pen plotter*. This device consists of a pen mounted in a special housing on the crossbar, so it can be positioned anywhere on the crossbar, as shown in Figure 3-2. The bar is then mounted so it can move perpendicular to the motion of the pen; that is, it slides freely along a set of rails, positioned by another small motor.

The position along each axis is then set by the voltage applied to the *x* and *y* inputs. This now gives us the ability to position the pen at any point in the rectangular region underneath the bar. As shown in the figure, the *x*-axis corresponds to the motion of the bar; the *y*-axis corresponds to the motion of the pen along the bar. To simplify the interface to the plotter, the position is usually directly related to the applied voltage. The input voltages might range from -10V to +10V, where -10V places the pen at one extreme and +10V places it at the other.

Additionally, the plotter provides a means of controlling whether the pen is up (not in contact with the paper) or down (you don't necessarily have to draw whenever the pen is moved). Now you can create a drawing defined entirely by electrical signals passed to the two controls of the pen plotter, one controlling the *x*-axis, the other controlling the *y*-axis. The pen is moved along a given line (or more often, along a given curve) by varying both the horizontal (*x*) and vertical (*y*) signals simultaneously. For instance, to duplicate the function of the seismograph plot, you apply a linear ramp voltage to the *x*-axis input to smoothly move the plotter across the page at a constant velocity. At the same time, the data signal from your sensors (or whatever source) is applied to the *y*-axis input.

The pen plotter is a powerful graphics tool that is still used today. It provides a relatively low-cost means of producing quality graphics output and can be flexibly controlled by a computer. Many improvements have been made to the basic pen plotter previously described, including the addition of multiple pens to create colored line drawings and improved accuracy and positioning precision. But the real flexibility of the pen plotter is that it can be controlled by a computer and, therefore, can be programmed to draw a variety of objects.

There are, however, many applications for which a pen plotter is not suitable. This device basically creates line drawings. All objects are drawn in outline form since the plotter has difficulties creating any solid drawing, even something as simple as a filled circle. This is because filling a region requires drawing many lines back and forth, just as you would do by hand. Normally, a plotter represents any area filled by cross-hatching or approximations that indicate the area is filled. While this is suitable for many drafting applications, it is not as if you are trying to create an actual image of what an object will look like. Another serious limitation is the number of colors available on a plotter. Even on a color plotter, you are limited to the number of different colored pens that are available. Drawing any reasonable color rendition requires a different approach to casting the desired image onto paper.

Since a pen plotter is a mechanical device, it also takes time for it to draw an image. The pen can only move at the maximum speed of the motors. A drawing with thousands of lines can take a long time to draw even on the fastest devices because of the inherent delay in physically moving a pen across a piece of paper.

Additionally, the speed is affected by the size of the final drawing. A small drawing will finish more quickly than a larger one of the same image.

Perhaps most importantly, you cannot edit a drawing that was created with a plotter. To make a change, you must alter the input data that describes your plot and then replot it. If the plot takes an inordinate amount of time to complete, this can be very frustrating.

CRTs to the Rescue

A cathode-ray tube (CRT) is essentially an electronic equivalent of the pen plotter. A focused electron beam is passed between two sets of parallel plates, one vertical and the other horizontal. A magnetic field is generated between the plates that deflects the electron beam, both horizontally and vertically. The beam then strikes a screen coated with a phosphorescent material that glows upon beam impact. Just as with the pen plotter, the beam can trace an image by varying the the voltages applied between the vertical and horizontal plates. The screen glows for only a short time after the electron beam hits, so the drawing must be continually redrawn, or *refreshed,* to keep it visible on the screen. The number of times per second that the screen must be refreshed depends on the time it takes for the image to fade, and this can vary widely depending on the type of CRT used.

The oscilloscope is the most common example of a CRT that can be directly controlled by an external voltage source. In its normal mode of operation, an oscilloscope automatically varies the voltage across the vertical plates to sweep the beam across the screen at a fixed rate. With no input for the *y*-axis, this produces a single horizontal line. When the beam reaches the end of a single sweep, it is turned off and the voltage is reset to start the sweep over again.

The next sweep begins when the oscilloscope is *triggered,* or told to start the next sweep. The trigger can be generated either at a fixed rate by the oscilloscope's electronics, or by an external signal. When a signal is applied to the *y*-axis, you can produce a direct plot of the signal on the screen. Because the oscilloscope is continually refreshing the screen, you can easily see any changes in the input signal. Many oscilloscopes let you apply a signal to both the horizontal and vertical plates simultaneously, which provides the same plotting capability that the pen plotter provides. However, now you have a dynamic display device with parameters, such as plot scale, that can be changed easily. Additionally, you can control the apparent intensity of the line by controlling the intensity of the electron beam and how long it stays in one spot on the screen.

Laser shows and displays seen at parks and rock concerts are another common example of this display technique type. These shows and displays use the same principle to draw figures as the oscilloscope, except they control a laser beam instead of an electron beam, and there is no need for a screen. The laser show also exhibits the same types of inherent problems as an oscilloscope, including that the entire display must be redrawn periodically or the image disappears. In order to avoid noticeable flickering, this must be at least 30 times per second. The total time to draw the image is proportional to the length of all the lines and curves being drawn.

As the image becomes more complicated, the rate at which it can be refreshed drops until the flicker becomes quite distracting. Obviously, this approach to line drawing has the limitation that the image complexity is fixed by the desired refresh rate. Furthermore, this method currently does not address the problem of pen plotters drawing pictures with filled regions, smooth colors, and images with photographic quality.

What's on TV

As with the oscilloscope, a CRT electron beam can be modulated to change the intensity of an image at the point on the screen that the beam is currently hitting. With the oscilloscope and pen plotter, you make a plot by changing the *x*-axis in a uniform manner to scan the beam and then the pen across the screen. A curve is then drawn as *y* is varied. In most oscilloscopes, the beam intensity does not change as the beam is moved around the screen.

To plot something as complicated as a photographic image, you must devise a means to change the beam intensity as a function of the image portion that you are drawing. The simplest method is to perform a *raster scan*. Figure 3-3

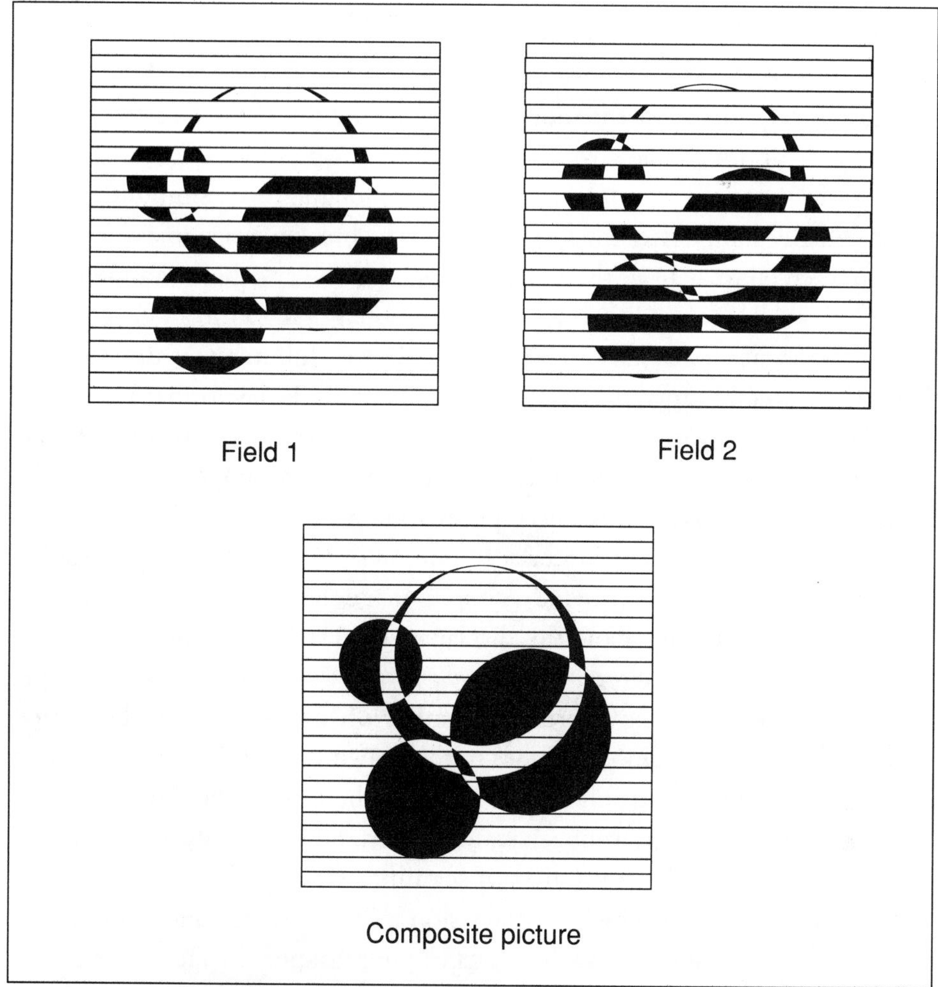

Figure 3-3 Raster scan of a CRT

shows this basic method. Starting at the top of the screen, the beam is smoothly scanned across the screen from left to right, maintaining a fixed-vertical location. As it is scanning, the beam intensity changes according to the image being reproduced. Once the beam reaches the end, it is turned off, reset to the image's left side; however, it is now lower in order to draw the next line.

Each line is referred to as a *scanline*. This process is continued until the bottom line is reached. The entire procedure is then started over again. In this instance, you do not need to know where the signal comes from to determine how to change the beam intensity. This signal is provided as part of the broadcast television signal. For the moment, you should only be interested in how the image is drawn on the screen.

This is essentially how television works, although greatly simplified. Television actually complicates the display process by breaking each image into two pieces, referred to as *fields.* Each field consists of every other scanline in the image. This is done to reduce the perceived amount of flicker in an image. Each field is drawn at 60 Hz (60 times per second), so a full image is drawn every 1/30th of a second on your television. This type of display format is referred to as *interlaced,* because each field represents only half the full picture. A *noninterlaced* display is one in which the full image (every line) is redrawn at the same time. Noninterlaced displays typically run at least twice as fast (or greater than a 60-Hz refresh rate) as interlaced ones in order to remove a perceptible flicker. However, they do provide a crisper image than interlaced displays do.

The important point about this display method is that the rate at which the image is drawn on the screen is *independent* of the complexity of the image. Unlike the oscilloscope, where the number of lines drawn on the screen depended on the the number of lines in the drawing, the CRT method uses a fixed number of scanlines. The image is created by varying the intensity of the beam as each scanline is swept across the screen. Since the rate at which each scanline is drawn and the number of scanlines is fixed, the entire image is redrawn at a fixed rate, which for television is 30 times a second. This allows for anything from simple line drawings to photographic images to be drawn on a television screen.

A color image can be produced by using three separate beams, one for red, green, and blue. The screen must be made using three separate phosphors, one which glows red, green, and blue for each beam. These phosphors are applied to the screen as colored dots, each color being slightly offset from one another. However, the spacing is close enough that the human eye cannot perceive any physical separation and so combines the intensity of each to produce the desired color. The three beams are scanned synchronously, but are offset from one another so that they only excite the appropriate color phosphor. So, a full color image can be produced using an appropriate CRT.

The new found flexibility of a raster-scanned CRT comes at a cost, though. Recall that you divided the screen into a number of scanlines, separated by a short distance on the screen. The number of scanlines covering the screen determines how detailed an image can be represented. The same is true horizontally; there is a "smallest-size element" that can be seen on the screen. This smallest viewable picture element is termed a *pixel*. An American television screen is divided into roughly 435 pixels horizontally by 350 pixels vertically. The phrase "roughly" is used because the television signal is analog in nature, and cannot be directly translated into a discrete number of discernable dots. To arrive at the number of pixels, you should consider the area of the screen over which the human eye can perceive a noticeable change in intensity. For television, this is limited by the way the signal is broadcast.

By using a raster CRT, you trade displayed resolution and fine detail for the ability to draw an image of arbitrary complexity. However, you still need to generate the signal for modulating the beam intensity that creates the picture. You, therefore, need a method for storing intensity values for the entire raster image that is to be displayed. Furthermore, you need a simple method of letting the computer generate and store the image to be displayed.

The Frame-Buffer Solution

All the display devices presented so far essentially use an analog means of representing an image. That is, something is drawn on a surface using a continuous drawing instrument, whether a pen or an electron beam. Such an instrument has the advantage of being able to draw a high-resolution image, limited only by the thickness of the pen or the width of the electron beam of the CRT. However, as has already been pointed out, it is not very suitable for representing solid images, such as photographs. The raster CRT offers a solution to this problem, but at the cost of decreased spatial resolution.

Breaking an image into a raster array of pixels is a natural means of representing an image for a computer. This type of representation is referred to as a *frame buffer*. It is a simple memory array in which each memory location contains the intensity to display at that location on the screen, as shown in Figure 3-4.

Every digital graphics board contains a frame buffer and the associated hardware to raster scan the values in memory and modulate the electron beam

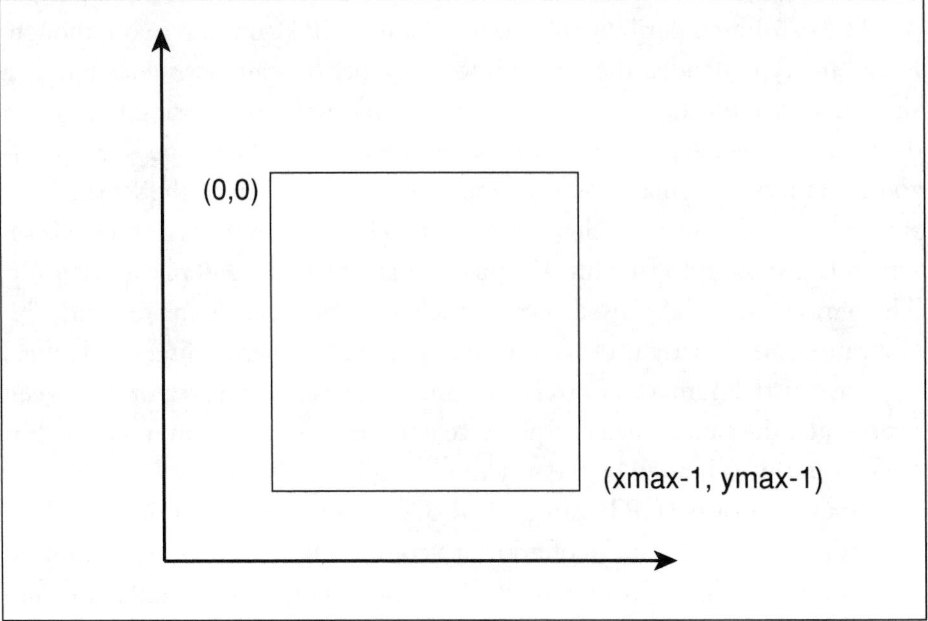

Figure 3-4. Memory layout for a raster frame buffer

according to the stored values. This process is entirely transparent to you as the programmer. You change the values by specifying the (x,y) coordinates of the pixel to be changed and the new value to store there. Changing the value stored for a pixel changes the image displayed on the screen. The rest of this book shows you how to set the intensity values in the frame buffer to generate images, such as lines, circles, and ellipses, in an intuitive and convenient way.

The resolution of the frame buffer determines the smallest area that can be represented. You cannot draw a region smaller than one pixel on the screen. This affects things such as how fine a line or circle can be drawn or how smooth a curve looks on screen. In general, the higher the resolution, the better the finished image appears. However, this requires more frame-buffer memory and more processing power because these additional pixels must be filled to draw the same object. If you double the vertical resolution then twice as many pixels must be drawn to create a vertical line. So, as with most things in life, there is no free lunch.

Low-cost frame buffer graphics hardware is a relatively new phenomenon. The price and availability are primarily driven by the following two factors:

1. Amazing improvement in memory speed, size, power consumption, and cost
2. Low-cost high-speed scanning hardware that converts the digital signal into analog voltages suitable for CRT display

Now that frame buffers are quite inexpensive and widely available, the power and flexibility of these cards can be fully exploited.

Today, frame-buffer resolutions on SVGA cards run up to about 1,280 x 1,024 pixels with noninterlaced displays. Almost all high-resolution displays use a noninterlaced format to produce crisp, clear images with well-defined colors.

Oddly enough, the primary limitation on higher-resolution displays is not because of the extra cost of the extra frame-buffer memory, but is due to the lack of availability of low-cost CRTs (under $1,000) that can operate at the speeds required for higher resolutions. As with most computer equipment, this too is improving, and you can expect to see higher resolution boards and monitors in the coming years.

Color frame buffers

Early frame buffers displayed images just as previously described, by directly scanning the frame buffer. But it didn't take long for computer graphics users to realize that there was a great deal more flexibility with the addition of an intermediate lookup table, also known as a *palette*, that converts pixel values to output display values. This is especially useful for the most common form of color display.

As mentioned earlier, a color display requires three separate intensity values, one for red, green, and blue. Instead of storing three intensity values at each pixel, and thus tripling the amount and cost of the frame-buffer memory required, only one value is stored in the pixel and it is used as the lookup table index into the palette. The palette then provides the red, green, and blue values that are actually displayed for the pixel. The intensity levels for each color are then sent to the output DAC (digital-to-analog-converter) that creates the output analog voltages that drive the CRT. By making the palette accessible to the program, you can assign any color to any index value and, more importantly, you can change this value dynamically, depending on your program needs. This is the method all EGA, VGA, and most SVGA cards use to display color images.

How many colors do you need?

In addition to the number of pixels stored vertically and horizontally for an image (referred to as the *spatial* resolution), you must also specify how many index values will be stored per pixel and how many discrete output intensity levels (usually referred to as *gray levels*) are to be displayed. The number of index values affects how much memory will be required in the frame buffer. For example, an EGA display allows 16 different index values, 0 through 15 for each pixel. This requires 4 bits per pixel of storage. A VGA display can operate at either 4 bits per pixel, or 8 bits per pixel, allowing index values ranging from 0 to 255. This requires twice as much frame-buffer memory to achieve the equivalent screen resolution of an EGA display.

The number of discrete output intensity values affects the amount of memory in the palette, but note that you only need as many palette entries as there are valid index values. For a VGA display, this is only 256 entries. Compared to the amount of memory used for the frame buffer, the palette uses a very small amount. The human eye cannot distinguish between more than about 64 intensity levels on most monitors, so providing one byte per color per pixel (256 possible gray levels, 3 bytes per palette entry total) in the palette is usually quite sufficient. However, this technique only allows a maximum of 256 different simultaneous output colors on the screen.

24-bit frame buffers

The one exception to the previous discussion is the newer SVGA cards that support storing separate red, green, and blue values at each pixel. In terms of memory, these cards require about three times the amount of frame-buffer memory as the equivalent VGA card. Instead of using a single color palette, a 24-bit SVGA card operates in one of two ways:

1. The red, green, and blue values are directly used as output intensity levels or
2. There are three separate lookup tables (one for each red, green, and blue) that the values are passed through on their way to the output DAC.

The first option is the most common. In the second option, the red intensity stored in a pixel is used as an index through the red palette table, the green is indexed through the green table, and the blue through the blue table. This allows for such things as color correcting an image without having to recompute it, but having these extra lookup tables does increase the cost of the card. Either type of 24-bit card can show all possible colors simultaneously as opposed to the 256 simultaneous colors of an 8-bit card. However, it does require more frame-buffer memory, which is becoming less and less of a concern as the price of memory continues to plummet. The main drawback is that to set a particular pixel requires writing at least 24 bits of data (3 bytes) instead of only 8 bits (1 byte). (Some cards actually provide 32 bits of data per pixel to support more sophisticated operations.) The 8-bit card will therefore be generally faster, albeit more limited in the types of images that can be drawn. The color limit is not very severe for the types of drawings you will probably be concerned with; however, it can be quite limiting for more complicated imagery, such as three-dimensional drawings, multimedia applications, or digitized photographs. Over the next several years, you will see these types of graphics cards become more common as the price of memory continues to drop and CPU performance continues to increase.

The frame-buffer advantage

Frame buffers provide a number of advantages over other display technologies, including the following:

- Graphics operations are fast. As you will see, graphics operations can be performed on a frame buffer at much higher speeds than those of just about any other display technology. The only physical action occurring (besides writing to frame-buffer memory) is the sweeping of the electron beam of the CRT, which is at a fixed rate and so does not affect the performance of the display.

- Frame buffers are now relatively low cost. The graphics display is no longer the driving cost of a computer system. On a PC, you can now purchase a frame-buffer graphics card and color monitor for about one twentieth of what it would have cost only 10 years ago. Although the price will probably not change greatly in the near future, the performance will continue to increase rapidly.

- A frame buffer can be both written and read back. The frame-buffer data is simply stored in a bank of memory, easily accessible to the computer. It can be read, rewritten, and manipulated in virtually any way desired. Special effects that are just not possible with any other display technology are quite simple and fast using a frame buffer.

- Multiple drawings can be drawn on top of one another, or *overlaid*, to add as many levels as desired. A good example of this is the ability to overlay a road map on top of a digitized photograph of an area, or to overlay multiple schematics for a complex wiring diagram. Being able to look at layers independently and together and color code them provides a very flexible analysis tool.

- Computer animation can be created. By changing the image in the frame buffer, the image displayed on the screen can be changed dynamically, just as is done for television. You can create an *interactive* display that shows not just a static sequence of images, but one that can generate simulations that are not possible without a computer and a fast graphics display. The computer makes it possible to visualize dynamic processes that would be impossible to view by any other means.

By connecting a frame buffer to a computer, all the other computing tools and peripherals like mass storage devices are available for use. Drawings can be easily edited through user interaction with a mouse or keyboard. They can be saved, copied, and changed without requiring someone to redraw the entire picture. It is no wonder that computer graphics applications have caught on so quickly when you consider the cost of making even simple changes to a hand-drawn drafting picture, map, or elaborate schematic diagram.

Drawing The Line

In the next chapter, you'll move on to developing a set of C routines for drawing into the graphics frame buffer on your computer. Many of the same routines would be just as applicable to drawing to a pen plotter. However, you'll learn how the animation capabilities of the frame buffer, along with the computer's ability to quickly change and redraw an image, can provide a more useful and fun means of graphic presentation than is possible on a plotter. So, on to making some of your very own pictures!

Drawing the Straight and Narrow

The best way to learn how to draw is to start using your tools, whether they are paint brushes or computer programs. In this chapter, you'll learn basic computer graphics operations for drawing points and lines on your display. These are the most fundamental drawing operations and the ones on which other drawing programs are based. All other graphics programming packages that you are likely to use have almost exact equivalents to the functions presented.

Since the point and line-drawing functions are used so frequently, it is important that they be both easy to use and efficient. An inefficient line-drawing algorithm makes any reasonably complex drawing take an inordinate amount of time to draw. Fortunately, today most point and line-drawing functions are implemented directly in the graphics hardware, making them extremely fast. This also frees your CPU from having to draw numerous individual pixels on the screen. This is quite important since frame-buffer resolutions keep getting larger.

Even though the line-drawing operation is often handled in the hardware, it is very useful to examine the line-drawing algorithm in detail in order to understand its properties, limitations, and how the method can be adapted to drawing other types of curves. Let's begin by describing the standard Cartesian coordinate system that you will be using for addressing the frame buffer.

The Raster Coordinate System

The basic raster coordinate system is shown in Figure 4-1. The coordinates of each pixel are represented by a pair of integer coordinates, (x,y). The x-coordinate corresponds to the column of the screen; the y-coordinate corresponds to the row. Note that (0,0) is in the upper-left corner of the screen. The lower-right corner of the screen has coordinates ($xmax$-1, $ymax$-1), where $xmax$ is the number of columns across the entire screen, and $ymax$ is the number of rows. Thus, x increases from zero on the left to a maximum value of $xmax$-1 on the right, and y increases from zero at the top of the screen to $ymax$-1 on the bottom.

The most basic drawing tool for creating lines is the straightedge. In this chapter, you'll learn how to draw lines by exploiting the fundamental relationship between geometry and algebra, known as the Cartesian coordinate system. Basic line-drawing algorithms are developed and implemented in several ways, so you can see the advantages and disadvantages of these methods for yourself.

In addition to providing the computer equivalent of the straightedge, this chapter also introduces several other tools you need for drawing, including drawing points, clearing the screen, and setting the color palette. The color palette of your graphics cards is essentially the same as a paint palette. You can pick a palette of colors by drawing from a huge set of base colors. And just as with real paint, computer graphics drawings present a sometimes overwhelming set of colors from which to choose.

Note that the orientation of *y* (increasing from top to bottom) is opposite of what you might expect from a normal Cartesian plot. This convention was chosen to conform with the way the raster is scanned by television, where scanline zero corresponds to the top of the screen. This is an unfortunate choice from a mathematical perspective. So, don't be too surprised if your first program draws its figures upside down from what you intended! (In later chapters, you'll learn how this problem can be avoided with a more general approach to establishing a drawing coordinate system.)

In Figure 4-1, each pixel represents a rectangular region of the screen, and that the integer pixel coordinates correspond to the center of this region. Depending on the type of graphics hardware and monitor you have, an individual pixel region may appear on the display as a square, round, or elliptical dot . You'll refer to setting an individual pixel as *plotting a point.* It is not a mathematical point; it is simply the smallest area you can manipulate directly. But remember that a pixel actually represents a small, yet finite, area of the screen. You'll explore the implications of this later, when you look at various types of graphic artifacts that result from the discrete nature of the raster display.

In a strictly mathematical context, curves are infinitely thin; that is, they have no width. When you draw a curve on any surface, you are implicitly drawing a curve of some finite width so you can see it. For instance, a pen creates a thinner curve than a paint brush. On the computer canvas, the smallest width you can draw is one pixel. In the following sections, you'll learn how to draw one-pixel wide lines. In Chapter 9, you'll look at drawing lines and curves that are more than one-pixel wide. You'll then see how the algorithm can be changed to draw lines of variable width.

Drawing a Point

Once you know the basic coordinate system of the screen, drawing points is straightforward. The function *gPlotPixel()* performs this operation. It takes the following three arguments:

1. An integer x- coordinate specifying the point to draw
2. An integer y-coordinate specifying the point to draw
3. An integer specifying the color index value to write into the frame buffer

The actual color displayed on screen depends on the color palette in use; this is described in the next section. However, before your program can use *gPlotPixel()*, it must initialize the display, set the color palette, and clear the screen. Additionally, you should determine the size of the frame buffer, that is, the number of pixels both horizontally (*xmax*) and vertically (*ymax*). Although this is not required, it gives you the flexibility to make your drawing look the same, regardless of the actual frame-buffer size.

The center of the screen will always be at the coordinate ($xmax/2, ymax/2$), no matter what these values are. In general, your program should be as *device independent* as possible. This means that instead of hard coding particular constants about the device (such as screen resolution), you should instead query the system for such constants. Today, most graphics systems let you inquire about many aspects of the display hardware, so that your program will run on as many different hardware configurations as possible. This flexibility, however, leads to some trade-offs that must be considered.

Efficiency Versus Ease of Use

As with any program, there is often a serious conflict between the efficiency of a particular implementation and the ease of use by programmers using different hardware. Graphics programs are certainly no exception and are, in fact, some of the worst offenders. These programs are often specific to particular display devices, operating systems, and other graphics-display characteristics, such as the number of colors supported by the device. The huge variety of graphics hardware available can make ease of use by others quite a daunting challenge. However, graphics libraries and standards are improving, which makes portability easier to deal with than it was in the "dark ages" of computer graphics.

In this book, a raster display device is characterized by the following major two attributes:

1. The dimension of the display (number of columns [*x*] and rows [*y*])
2. The number of colors available, or if a 24-bit display is being used, the number of intensity levels available for red, green, and blue

Many PC graphics cards operate in a number of different modes, each of which provides different combinations of the previous two attributes. For instance, even the standard VGA allows for two basic modes: a 640 x 400 frame-buffer resolution with 16 colors per pixel or a 320 x 200 frame-buffer resolution with 256 colors per pixel. Many SVGA cards allow other combinations.

The display mode your program should use depends on the desired application. Generally, you'll want to run your program in the highest resolution frame buffer that supports the number of palette colors required by your application. So, if your program needs at least 100 separate palette entries, it would run in the lower resolution, or 320 x 200 mode, on standard VGA hardware. If a mode with at least 100 colors is not available (such as an EGA card), your program should at least gracefully terminate with a message that the user might consider investing a few dollars in better graphics hardware.

The *ggraph.c* Module

To increase the portability of the code in this book, I have put all the *device dependent* frame-buffer functions in one module, the *ggraph.c* module found on the disk that accompanies this book. The corresponding header file, *ggraph.h*, contains the definitions for several of the common utility macros, such as *MIN()*, *MAX()*, *ABS()*, and *ROUND()*, along with the function prototypes for all the functions of the graphics package. The header file *gtypes.h* contains definitions for all the structures used by the software as well as macros defining some of the fixed-palette colors used in 256- or 16-color EGA/VGA modes.

A complete description of the organization and content of each module and header file can be found in Appendix B. Every other module in the book uses the functions in *ggraph.c* to initialize, draw points, and return to the operating system. All the programs can work on virtually any display device by putting in the appropriate calls for these routines.

The implementation shown is for Borland C++, version 3.1. If you are using a different compiler or operating system, then you only need to change the functions in *ggraph.c* to make the rest of the software fully functional.

The following two sections describe the basic sets of functions in *ggraph.c*. First, you'll study the various frame-buffer manipulation functions for initializing, reading, and writing to the graphics card. Second, you'll learn the functions for manipulating the color palette. A table of all the functions can be found at the end of the chapter. So, let's begin with the frame-buffer functions.

Frame-Buffer Functions

Before learning the individual frame-buffer functions, you need to know how pixels are represented in a graphics program. A single pixel of a frame buffer is stored in a data type called *gColor*. In the current implementation, a *gColor* is equivalent to an *unsigned long*, using a *typedef* statement. You use the *long* data type (32-bit integer) to support 24-bit frame buffers. The valid range of *gColor* types depends on the graphics mode of the display. For a 256-color mode, the values may range from 0 to 255. Any value outside this range uses only the low-order 8 bits. So, a value of 257 represents the same frame-buffer value as one. Whenever a pixel is drawn to or read from the graphics card, you should use a *gColor* variable to hold the value. This helps ensure your program's compatibility with many different types of graphics cards.

The following frame-buffer functions let you initialize the display, read and write individual pixels, blank the display, and return the screen to the normal display mode (or typically the text mode for DOS).

void gInitDisplay(int mode)

The *gInitDisplay()* function takes a single integer argument to set the desired operating mode of the frame buffer for the rest of the program. It must precede any other graphics call in your program and should only be called once. This is highly operating-system and device dependent. In this book, I've adopted the convention that passing a zero means *gInitDisplay()* should set the mode to the highest frame-buffer resolution available with the current hardware configuration.

For PC systems, a nonzero argument sets the video mode of the display hardware to a specific setting, and is thus dependent on the particular hardware that you have. You should consult your graphics hardware manual for the supported display modes. If you are adapting the software to a non-PC environment, then you may ignore this code or use it to set display characteristics that are specific to your system.

int gGetMaxX(void) and *int gGetMaxY(void)*

These two functions take no arguments and each returns an integer representing the maximum *x*- and *y*-resolution of the frame buffer. The returned values depend on the particular graphics mode set by *gInitDisplay()*.

void gPlotPixel(int x, int y, Color color)

This function provides the basic operation on which the rest of the graphics package is based. It takes two integer arguments representing the *x*- and *y*-coordinates of the pixel and a third argument, or *Color*, which is defined as a *long* value. A long value is used in order to provide support for 24-bit frame buffers. For most VGA and SVGA cards, only the least significant 8 bits are used.

gColor gReadPixel(int x, int y)

This function performs the opposite operation from *gPlotPixel()*. It returns the frame-buffer entry at location (*x*,*y*). This is quite useful for interactive applications.

void gClearScreen(void)

This function simply clears the entire frame buffer. Clearing means that every pixel in the frame buffer is set to zero. Normally, this displays a black screen; however, it could be any color, depending on the palette entry for value zero.

Technically, this call does not need to be device dependent. You could loop through the pixels of the frame buffer and set them to zero with *gPlotPixel()*. But most graphics packages provide a much faster screen-clearing function in the hardware. So, the call becomes device dependent.

void gCloseDisplay(void)

This function takes no arguments and terminates all graphics operations, which returns the screen back to the mode it was in prior to calling *gInitDis-*

play(). For MS–DOS-based systems, this clears the screen and puts it back into text mode.

The previous set of calls handle the device-dependent aspects of the frame buffer. You must also provide calls to access the color palette of the display.

Color-Palette Access

The palette functions are only useful on a VGA or SVGA display that operates in one of the 256-color modes (set by default with *gInitDisplay()*). In an EGA/VGA 16-color mode, the hardware color palette is not accessible to your program. In a 16-color mode, any attempt to write the palette has no effect and, when using *gPaletteGet()*, any readback from the graphics card always returns the settings of the default palette.

For easy manipulation of the color palette, this book provides you with a *gPalette* structure containing an array of *gPaletteEntry* elements. Each *gPaletteEntry* element is a structure that corresponds to a single entry of the palette. So, each *gPaletteEntry* contains a red, green, and blue color intensity for one palette entry. A *gPaletteEntry* is defined as the following:

```
typedef struct gPaletteEntry_struct {
 unsigned int red;
 unsigned int green;
 unsigned int blue;
} gPaletteEntry;
```

Each red, green, and blue value must be within the range 0 to 255, where 0 is darkest and 255 is brightest. So to make an entry white, you should set all three values to 255. As with every other structure, there is a *gPaletteEntryCreate()*, *gPaletteEntryDelete()*, and *gPaletteEntryCopy()* function. The *gPalette* structure defines an array of sequential palette entries as:

```
typedef struct gPalette_struct {
 int nentries;
 gPaletteEntry *p;
} gPalette;
```

The functions *gPaletteCreate( )*, *gPaletteDelete( )*, and *gPaletteCopy( )* are available to create, destroy, and copy palette structures. These structures may be used to contain the entire palette for your graphics hardware or any sequential subset of the palette. You only need a *gPalette* structure large enough to hold the part of the palette your program needs to access. By using the appropriately sized *gPalette* structure, you circumvent the problem of having the system storing data that your program doesn't actually need. For instance, if your program only needs three separate colors, then a *gPalette* of three entries is all that is required, even if the hardware supports 256.

In addition to the standard functions, there are several other functions for manipulating a *gPalette* structure. The function *gSetPaletteEntry( )* provides a simple means of setting the color of any entry in the palette. *gSetPaletteEntry( )* has five arguments. The first is the pointer to the palette structure being set, the second is the element number (starting at zero) to be set, and the last three are the red, green, and blue colors to be stored in the entry. For example, the following code sets up a simple five-color palette:

```
gPalette *palette;

palette = gPaletteCreate(5);
 /* Create a palette of 5 elements */
/* Make entry 0 black */
gSetPaletteEntry(palette, 0, 0, 0, 0);
/* Make entry 1 red */
gSetPaletteEntry(palette, 1, 255, 0, 0);
/* Make entry 2 green */
gSetPaletteEntry(palette, 2, 0, 255, 0);
/* Make entry 3 blue */
gSetPaletteEntry(palette, 3, 0, 0, 255);
/* Make entry 4 white */
gSetPaletteEntry(palette, 4, 255,255, 255);
/* Write the palette out to the hardware */
gPalettePut(0, palette, 5);
```

gSetPaletteEntry() only sets the entries of the palette; it does not actually write the palette out to the graphics hardware. You must call *gPutPalette()* to actually make a change to the display.

Under most circumstances, there is a color palette available of at least 16 entries. You have, therefore, defined a standard palette of 16 colors that lets you draw objects using the primary (red, green, and blue) and secondary colors (all combinations of the primary colors) as well as some additional common colors. The color values are defined in the header file *gtypes.h* as macros. Listing 4-1 shows the definitions of each symbolic color name and the corresponding entry of the palette. Anywhere a *gColor* value is required, you may use one of the symbolic names. This works as long as your program does not change the palette entries for the first 16 entries.

```
#define gBLACK  0
#define gBLUE  1
#define gGREEN  2
#define gCYAN  3
#define gRED  4
#define gMAGENTA 5
#define gBROWN  6
#define gLIGHTGREY 7
#define gDARKGREY 8
#define gBRIGHTBLUE 9
#define gBRIGHTGREEN 10
#define gBRIGHTCYAN 11
#define gBRIGHTRED 12
#define gBRIGHTMAGENTA 13
#define gYELLOW  14
#define gWHITE  15
```

Listing 4-1. The 16-default colors of the color palette. Whenever the color palette is initialized, these colors will be set for each of the corresponding entries of the palette.

The following presents the calling syntax and description of each palette-manipulation function.

gPaletteInit(void)

This function initializes the palette to the default setting. Color zero will be black, and color *gPaletteGetSize() - 1* will be set to white. The first 16 entries will be set to the corresponding color as defined in *gtypes.h*. For a 256-color palette, entries 16 to 255 will be set to a color scale that is useful for graduated color schemes.

gPaletteGetSize(void)

This function returns the maximum number of entries available in the color palette for the current display mode. This in turn determines the range of possible values for the color argument in *gPlotPixel()*. This value is almost always either 16 (corresponding to valid color values from 0 to 15) or 256 (corresponding to valid color values from 0 to 255). As noted previously, a 16-color palette cannot be changed by your program.

*gPalettePut(int start_entry, Palette *palette)*

This function sets the palette colors starting at value *start entry*. The color values from the palette structure are copied to the hardware color palette, setting all the entries from *start entry* to *(start entry + palette->nentries - 1)*. This function lets you set a range of palette entries; you don't necessarily have to set the entire palette at any one time. Additionally, this function allows you to set palette entries one element at a time if desired. Once *gPalettePut()* is called, a pixel value equal to *start entry* is displayed in the color of the first entry of *palette*, pixel value *(start_entry + 1)* is displayed in the color of the second *palette* entry, and so on.

*Palette *gPaletteGet(int start_entry, gPalette *palette, int nentries)*

This function retrieves the current palette settings beginning at *start entry* and continuing up to *nentries* elements. You may pass a *NULL* pointer for the second argument, indicating that *GetPalette* should create a new palette structure with *nentries* elements. If a non-*NULL* pointer is passed, then *gPaletteGet()* sets the first *nentries* elements of the passed palette structure to the values of the display's current color palette. If *nentries* is greater than *palette->nentries*, then *gPaletteGet()* destroys the passed palette pointer and creates a new one that is *nentries* elements in length.

Although seemingly complicated, this function actually makes manipulation of the color palette very flexible by automatically adjusting the size of the passed palette structure to get the number of entries you request. If the palette structure is too small to hold all the entries, then it is resized to hold the requested number of entries. If you pass a *NULL* palette pointer, then a palette of the correct size is created automatically. A standard way to use these calls is as follows:

```
gPalette *mypalette;
int max_palette_entries;

gPaletteInit();
max_palette_entries = gPaletteGetSize();
mypalette = gPaletteGet(0, NULL, max_palette_entries);
```

The pointer *mypalette* points to a palette structure that contains the entire color palette for whatever display your program is using. You may set any individual entries using *gSetPaletteEntry()* and then rewrite the palette to affect the display using *gPalettePut()*.

Drawing The Line

Armed with the functions in *ggraph.c*, you can now proceed to something a little more useful, namely drawing a line segment between two given points. Refer to Figure 4-2, if you wish to draw the line segment from point $(x1, y1)$ to point $(x2, y2)$. Let's define the following variables for later use:

$$dx = x2 - x1$$
$$dy = y2 - y1$$

Except for when dx is equal to zero, the slope of a line is $m = dy/dx$. For the moment, let's assume that both points lie within the frame buffer. In Chapter 7, you'll learn what to do if one or both of the points lie outside the screen.

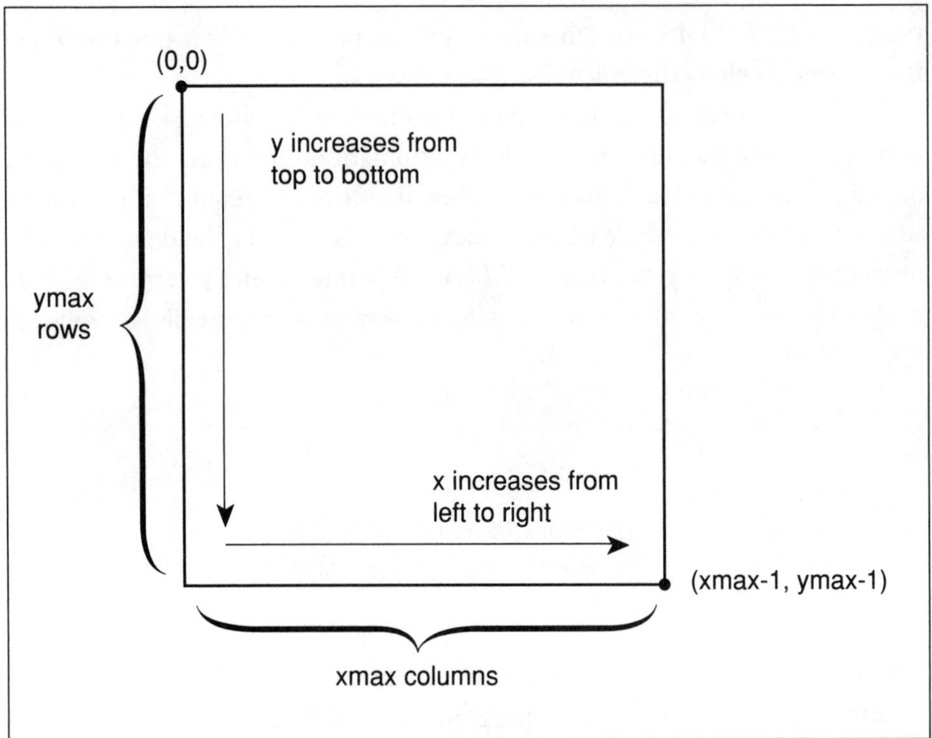

Figure 4-2. Drawing a line from (x1, y1) to (x2, y2)

Furthermore, you want the line segment to be drawn with the minimum width of one pixel. Drawing lines of varying thicknesses is discussed in Chapter 9.

As you can see from the figure, if the slope of the line lies between -1 and +1 *(ABS(dx) >= ABS(dy))*, then you want to set one pixel per column. For each column, you choose the pixel in the column that is nearest to the line. For the second case *(ABS(dy) > ABS(dx))*, you set one pixel in each row. Your task is to produce an efficient method of finding the nearest pixel in each column or row to the actual line.

To simplify the analysis process, you start with the simpler case of *ABS(dx) >= ABS(dy)*. Furthermore, you assume that *x2* is greater than *x1*. If this is not the case, you can simply swap the two endpoints. So, you can always proceed from left to right across the screen. This situation is shown in Figure 4-3. For

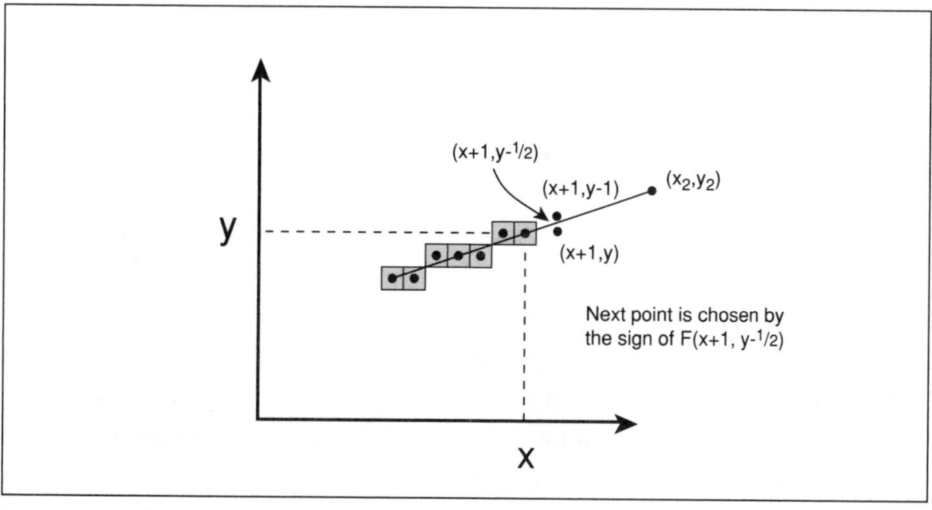

Figure 4-3. Finding the nearest pixels to a line segment from (x1, y1) to (x2, y2)

each column between *x1* and *x2*, you need to determine the closest pixel in the column to the actual line. Recall from Chapter 1 that you can write the equation of a nonvertical line as:

$$y = m * x + b \qquad \text{(Equation 4-1)}$$

where $m = dy/dx$
$b = y1 - m * x1$

For any given *x*-coordinate, you can determine the corresponding *y*-coordinate by evaluating the equation and *rounding* to the nearest integer with the *ROUND()* macro of *ggraph.h*. The line drawing algorithm is, therefore, quite simple:

```
float x, y, m, b;
int x, iy;

m = (float)(y2 - y1) / (float)(x2 - x1);
b = y1 - m*x1;
for(x=x1; x<=x2; x++) {
 y = m*x + b;
```

```
 iy = ROUND(y);
 gPlotPixel(x, iy, color);
}
```

This method, however, is not as efficient as it could be. First notice that you are using a lot of floating-point operations in order to maintain precision. In particular, you are performing an implicit floating-point promotion (converting the integer *x* to floating point), a floating-point multiply *(m * x)*, an add *(+ b)*, and a comparison operation (*ROUND(y)*). The second observation is that you can eliminate the multiply operation completely by converting to an *incremental* form. This is a method in which you use the *y* value of the previous column to compute the *y* value of the next column. This works because you always step a constant amount in *x*, namely, 1 pixel.

You first set the pixel at *(x1, y1)*. The next value of *y* is:

$$y_{new} = m * (x+1) + b = m * x + b = y_{old} + m \quad \text{(Equation 4-2)}$$

where y_{new} is the value of *y* for the current column and y_{old} is the *y*-value of the last column. The previous relationship holds for all instances of *x*. So, the next value of *y* is always equal to the previous value plus the slope *m*. This leads to the reformulated algorithm:

```
float m, y;
int x, iy;

m = (float)(y2-y1) / (float)(x2-x1);
y = y1;
for(x=x1; x<=x2; x++) {
 iy = ROUND(y);
 gPlotPixel(x, iy, color);
 y += m;
}
```

Notice that you have also eliminated any need for the evaluation of the *y* intercept value of *b*. Now there is one floating-point addition and a floating-point comparison for each value of *x*. In the next chapter, you'll learn how to recast many types of curve-drawing algorithms into an efficient incremental form. This method is sometimes referred to as DDA (*Digital Differential Analyzer*). A DDA is a device that numerically solves differential equations by incrementing (x,y) in small steps. The ratio of the increments is equal to the slope of the curve at the current point. For this example, the step size in x is +1, and for y is m. The DDA–line-drawing function is shown in Listing 4-2.

```
/* DDA algorithm */

void gLineDrawSimple( int x0, int y0, int x1, int y1,
        int color)
{
 int ix, iy;
 float x, y;
 float dx, dy;
 float m;
 float oneOverM;

 int temp;

 if ( x0 == x1) {
  /* Handle vertical case */
  ix = x0;

  /* Make y-coordinate increasing */
  if ( y0 > y1) {
   SWAP( y0, y1, temp);
  }

  for (iy = y0; iy <= y1; iy++) {
   gPlotPixel( ix, iy, color);
  }
  return;
 }

dy = y1 - y0;
dx = x1 - x0;
```

```
m = dy / dx;

if (ABS(m) <= 1.0) {

/* Make x increasing */
if ( x0 > x1) {
 SWAP( x0, x1, temp);
 SWAP( y0, y1, temp);
}

y = y0;
iy = ROUND(y);

for ( ix = x0; ix <= x1; ix++) {
 gPlotPixel( ix, iy, color);
 y += m;
 iy = ROUND(y);
}
} else {
 /* Make y increasing */
 if ( y0 > y1) {
  SWAP( x0, x1, temp);
  SWAP( y0, y1, temp);
 }

 x = x0;
 ix = ROUND(x);

 oneOverM = 1.0 / m;

 for ( iy = y0; iy <= y1; iy++) {
  gPlotPixel( ix, iy, color);
  x += oneOverM;
  ix = ROUND(x);
 }
}
}
```

Listing 4-2. DDA–line-drawing function

In the past, it was thought that floating-point operations were always significantly slower than integer operations on any CPU. This is no longer the case for many CPUs currently available, including i486-based systems. However, this performance difference is still true for many PC systems based on the 286 and 386 CPUs without a math coprocessor. Also, many hardware graphics cards do not support floating-point operations on the card itself. So, it is important to be able to perform the line-drawing algorithm without resorting to floating-point operations, even if it is not necessarily more efficient.

Midpoint Selection Algorithm

The original integer incremental line-drawing algorithm was developed by J. E. Bresenham and published in 1965. A modified form of this approach, called the *midpoint technique*, was developed by M. L. V. Pitteway in 1967. The midpoint selection method is easier to generalize to other types of curves, and has therefore become a standard technique for drawing many simple mathematical curves.

You want to perform solely integer operations in your drawing algorithm. So it seems desirable to stick with the incremental approach previously mentioned, where the next choice of the y value is based on the previous y. Also, as you can see from Figure 4-3, you really only have two choices for the next pixel. It must either be the one at (x_{new}, y_{new}) or the one at $(x_{new}, y_{new} - 1)$. For convenience, I refer to these two points as $p1$ and $p2$ respectively. You decide which one to choose by looking at the midpoint between these two points at $(x_{new}, y_{new} - 1/2)$. If the line is below the midpoint, choose point $p1$; if above, choose point $p2$. Now you need a function $F(x,y)$ that you can evaluate at the midpoint and determine whether the line is above or below the point (x,y).

You can create such a function by multiplying Equation 4-1 through by dy and then subtracting one side from the other:

$$F(x,y) = dy * x - dx * y + B * dx \qquad \text{(Equation 4-3)}$$

This function is zero for points on the line, simply from the way you constructed $F(x,y)$. It is negative for points below the line and positive for points above the line. You need to evaluate $F(x,y)$ at points $F(ix, iy + 1/2)$, where ix and iy are integer coordinates, or at the midpoints between pixels. You can force this expression to be all integer arithmetic at these points by multiplying F by two. Since you only care about the sign of F at the midpoint, you can multiply $F(x,y)$ by any positive constant and not affect the sign of the result.

The form of $F(x,y)$ makes it another candidate for an incremental evaluation. To do this, you introduce a new variable, D, called the *decision variable*. As you loop through x, D is equal to the value of $F(x + 1, y-1/2)$. You must then determine what to increment D by for the next midpoint evaluation at $x + 2$. This depends on whether you choose point $p1$ or $p2$. If point $p1$ is selected $(x + 1, y)$, then you need to evaluate $F(x + 2, y - 1/2)$:

$$
\begin{aligned}
F(x + 2, y - 1/2) &= 2 * dy * (x + 2) - 2 * dx * (y-1/2) + 2 * b * dx \\
&= 2 * dy * (x+1) + 2 * dy - 2 * dx * (y - 1/2) + 2 * b * dx \\
&= F(x + 1, y - 1/2) + 2 * dy \\
&= D + 2 * dy
\end{aligned}
$$

If $p2$ is chosen, then you need the value $F(x + 2, y - 3/2)$:

$$
\begin{aligned}
F(x + 2, y - 3/2) &= 2 * dy * (x + 2) - 2 * dx * (y - 3/2) + 2 * b * dx \\
&= 2 * dy * (x + 1) + 2 * dy - 2 * dx * (y -1/2) - 2 * dx + 2 * b * dx \\
&= F(x + 1, y - 1/2) + 2 * (dy - dx) \\
&= D + 2 * (dy - dx)
\end{aligned}
$$

As you can see, you increment D by either $2 * dy$ if $p1$ is chosen, or $2 * (dy - dx)$ if $p2$ is chosen. Your integer midpoint algorithm becomes:

```
int x, y, dx, dy, d1, d2;
gColor color;

y = y1;
dx = x2 - x1;
dy = y2 - y1;
d1 = 2*dy;
d2 = 2*(dy - dx);
```

```
d = 2*dy + dx;                  /* Initial value for d */
gPlotPixel(x1, y1, color);      /* Plot the first point */
for(x=x1+1; x<=x2; x++) {
 if(d <= 0) {                   /* Midpoint is below the line,
                                   choose p1 */
 d += d1;
 } else {
 d += d2;
 y—;
 }
 gPlotPixel(x, y, color);
}
```

Notice that within the inner loop, you compare a single integer, and then you make either one or two integer additions. This is quite an improvement over the floating-point algorithm previously described. However, if the CPU can perform floating-point operations as quickly as integer operations, then there is no significant performance difference between the two approaches.

A Complete Line Drawing

The previous algorithms only operated on the case that the slope was between -1 and +1. You can generalize the functions to include other cases by checking whether *ABS(dy)* is less than or greater than *ABS(dx)*. If *ABS(dy)* is greater than *ABS(dx)*, then you must loop through the rows rather than the columns. You can see that, by symmetry, you need only swap the *x*- and *y*-variables in the previous algorithms. The basic procedure is exactly the same. To avoid having to perform extra checks on the sign of *dx* and *dy* in the inner loop, the lines are divided into four cases based on *dx* and *dy*:

1. $dx > 0, dy > 0$
2. $dx < 0, dy > 0$
3. $dx > 0, dy < 0$
4. $dx < 0, dy < 0$

The complete midpoint–line-drawing function is shown in Listing 4-3 of the module *gline.c*.

```
/* Bresenham algorithm */

void gLineDraw( int x0, int y0, int x1, int y1,
                gColor color)
{
 int px, py;
 int dx, dy;

 int straight, angle, length;
 int *along, *normal;

 int i, D, temp, incAlong, incNormal;

 if ( x0 == x1) {
 /* Vertical line */

 /* Make y increasing */
 if ( y0 > y1) {
  SWAP( y0, y1, temp);
 }

 px = x0;
 for ( py = y0; py <= y1; py++)
  gPlotPixel( px, py, color);

 return;
 }

 /* Make line go from left to right */
 if (x1 < x0) {
 SWAP( x0, x1, temp);
 SWAP( y0, y1, temp);
 }

 px = x0;
 py = y0;

 gPlotPixel( px, py, color);
```

```
dx = x1 - x0;
dy = y1 - y0;

incAlong = 1;
incNormal = 1;

if (dy >= 0) {
if ( dx >= dy) {
 /* Octant 1, east-southeast */
 D = (2 * dy) - dx;
 straight = 2 * dy;
 angle = 2 * (dy - dx);
 length = x1 - px;
 along = &(px);
 normal = &(py);
} else {
 /* Octant 2, south-southeast */
 D = (2 * dx) - dy;
 straight = 2 * dx;
 angle = 2 * (dx - dy);
 length = y1 - py;
 along = &(py);
 normal = &(px);
}
} else {
if ( dx >= -dy) {
 /* Octant 8, east-northeast */
 D = (2 * -dy) - dx;
 straight = 2 * -dy;
 angle = 2 * (-dy - dx);
 length = x1 - px;
 along = &(px);
 normal = &(py);
 incNormal = -1;
} else {
 /* Octant 7, north-northeast */
 D = (2 * dx) - -dy;
 straight = 2 * dx;
```

```
    angle = 2 * (dx - -dy);
    length = py - y1;
    along = &(py);
    incAlong = -1;
    normal = &(px);
  }
  }
  for ( i = 0; i < length; i++) {
  *along += incAlong;
  if (D <= 0) {
   /* Move horizontally */
   D += straight;
  } else {
   /* Move at an angle */
   *normal += incNormal;
   D += angle;
  }
  gPlotPixel( px, py, color);
  }
}
```

Listing 4-3. Midpoint—line-drawing algorithm covering all line orientations. The number of different cases is to improve efficiency. Otherwise, you would have to test x and y inside the inner loops.

A Demonstration: gldemo.c

To demonstrate the how these various algorithms work, I have provided the *gldemo.c* program on the disk that accompanies this book. This program draws sets of vectors using exaggerated pixel sizes so you can see how the pixels are selected. In order to compare the efficiency of the two algorithms, the screen is divided into two halves, one using the DDA algorithm and the other using the midpoint algorithm. If you do not have a 486 system or one with a math coprocessor, there will be an appreciable performance difference between the two approaches. However, with a math coprocessor, the performance difference is much less.

Hardware Help

Most graphics hardware today, including many of the new SVGA cards, provide direct hardware support for drawing lines. This provides better performance than that achieved by having your program drawing every pixel along a line. These hardware implementations are all based on the midpoint algorithm (and some slight variations) previously shown. However, it is helpful to have the software-only versions of these routines to support older graphics cards that do not provide line drawing as a basic function.

More Interesting Objects

The ability to draw points and lines is fundamental to any type of computer graphics. Because of the raster frame buffer, you can draw virtually any type of curve on the computer if you specify the mathematical algorithm to do so. Drawing a line segment was the first, and most basic, operation.

In the next chapter, you will see how the midpoint algorithm can be easily adapted to drawing other types of curves and to drawing more general shapes that are often not provided in hardware. You do not need to know how the line-drawing algorithm works to make effective use of it. But just as painters must know that their paints and brushes apply different looks to canvases, computer graphic artists must know how the basic tools work so they may be combined and adapted to create richer, more interesting images.

Functions Found in This Chapter

Demonstration programs

`dpalet.exe`

Shows the default 256-color palette. This program only works using a 256-color mode, and thus requires a VGA or MCGA graphics adapter.

`dline.exe`

Demonstrates the various line-drawing algorithms. Each demonstration shows lines drawn using both normal pixels and magnified pixels. With the magnified pixels, you can clearly see how pixels are selected by the line-drawing algorithms. It also demonstrates why lines on the display screen appear more jagged as the frame-buffer resolution is decreased.

Frame-buffer functions

`int gInitDisplay(int mode);`

Places the computer in graphics mode. A mode value of zero lets the program autodetect to find the highest resolution graphics mode available. A nonzero-mode number forces a specific graphics to be set that is dependent on the particular graphics card you have.

`int gGetMaxX(void);`

Returns the width of the graphics-display screen in pixels.

`int gGetMaxY(void);`

Returns the height of the graphics-display screen in pixels.

```
void gPlotPixel( int x, int y, gColor color);
```

Draws a pixel on the screen. Note that color must be in the acceptable range for the display mode (for example, in a 16-color mode, a *color* value must be between 0 and 15).

```
gColor gReadPixel(int x, int y);
```

Returns the color of the pixel at the frame-buffer location (*x*, *y*).

```
void gClearScreen(void);
```

Blanks the graphics screen. In DOS, this happens automatically when a graphics mode is selected.

```
void gCloseDisplay(void);
```

Returns the system to its original display mode, which is typically text mode, before the call to *gInitDisplay()* is made.

Palette functions

```
gPaletteEntry *gPaletteEntryCreate(int red, int green,
                                   int blue);
```

Creates a single *gPaletteEntry* structure with the red, green, and blue elements set to the passed values. This function is generally not needed by most programs.

```
gPaletteEntry *gPaletteEntryCopy(gPaletteEntry *dest,
                                 gPaletteEntry *source);
```

Copies a *gPaletteEntry* structure.

```
void gPaletteEntryDelete(gPaletteEntry *pal);
```

Deletes a *gPaletteEntry* structure.

```
gPalette *gPaletteCreate(int nentries);
```

Creates a *gPalette* structure with *nentries* elements.

```
gPalette *gPaletteCopy(gPalette *dest, gPalette *source);
```

Copies a *gPalette* structure.

```
void gPaletteEntryDelete(gPalette *pal);
```

Deletes a *gPalette* structure.

```
void gSetPaletteEntry(gPalette *pal, int index,
                      int red, int green, int blue);
```

Sets the *index*th entry of a *gPalette* structure to the specified *red*, *green*, and *blue* values. Only the colors in the structure are changed. In order to see the change on the display, you must set the palette of the graphics hardware using *gPalettePut()*.

```
void gPaletteInit(void);
```

Initializes the 256-color palette of DOS graphics mode 19 (VGA 256-color mode) to the standard default set of colors, corresponding to the symbolic color names in the header file *gtypes.h*.

```
int gPaletteGetSize(void);
```

Returns the number of colors available in the current graphics mode.

```
void gPalettePut(int start_entry, gPalette *palette);
```

Writes the palette to the graphics display. This call only works in a 256-color mode. Remember that you can start writing to any location using *startentry*.

```
gPalette *gPaletteGet(int start_entry, gPalette *pal,
                      int nentries);
```

Reads *nentries* RGB elements from the palette of the graphics display and stores them in the *gPalette* pointed to by *pal*. This call only works in a 256-color mode. You can start reading from any location using *start_entry*.

Line-drawing functions

```
void gLineDraw( int x0, int y0,
                int x1, int y1, gColor color);
```

Draws a line from (*x*0,*y*0) to (*x*1,*y*1) using the specified color. The line is drawn using the midpoint--line-drawing algorithm.

```
void gLineDrawSimple(int x0, int y0, int x1, int y1,
                     gColor color);
```

Draws a line from *(x0,y0)* to *(x1,y1)* using the specified color. This line is drawn using the DDA–line-drawing algorithm.

CHAPTER 5

Circles, Ellipses, and Other Interesting Objects

So far, you've only seen how to draw points and lines. These are the simplest constructs of Euclidean geometry. By themselves, they do not make particularly interesting images. But in this chapter, you'll discover how to create far more elaborate drawings by connecting line segments to form *polylines* and *polygons*.

The drawing tools are then expanded by adding the equivalent of another basic tool for drawing circles, the compass. From there, you'll see how the circle-drawing algorithm can be adapted to draw ellipses, and with a little bit of work, to draw a variety of curves and elaborate shapes.

Drawing a Rectangle

The rectangle is perhaps the simplest figure you can draw using the line-drawing function *gLineDraw()*, described in the previous chapter. A rectangle is represented by two corner points, one corresponding to the upper-left corner and the other to the lower-right corner, as shown in Figure 5-1. The rectangle structure is therefore:

```
typedef struct gRectangle_Struct {
 float xmin, ymin;
 float xmax, ymax;
} gRectangle;
```

Drawing a rectangle is easy; you simply draw the following four vectors:

(xmin, ymin)	to	*(xmax, ymin)*
(xmax, ymin)	to	*(xmax, ymax)*
(xmax, ymax)	to	*(xmin, ymax)*
(xmin, ymax)	to	*(xmin, ymin)*

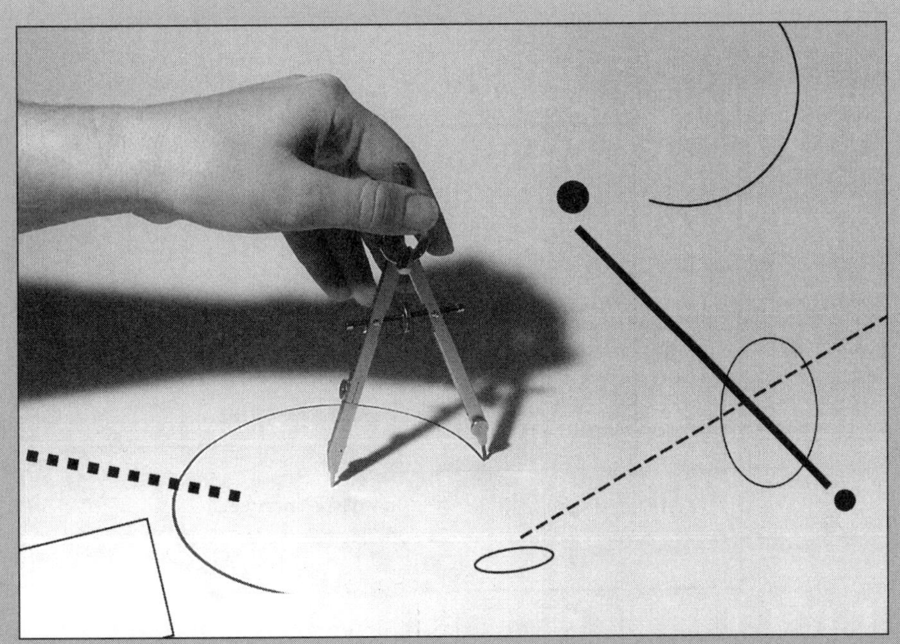

Having learned how to draw a line between two points, you can now move onto more complex objects. In this chapter, you'll learn how to draw more interesting figures, such as circles and ellipses. Just as there are several ways to draw a circle by hand, there are several ways to do it by computer as well.

As was done in the previous chapter, several different means of implementing the drawings are developed, each with its features and drawbacks. The chapter then proceeds with the development of more general types of drawing objects, the polygon and polyline, which are used to represent complex figures that may not have simple mathematical definitions. Any complex drawing, such as an architectural drawing or a map, uses many combinations of these simpler objects. It is important to draw these shapes accurately and efficiently, just as a draftsperson uses a compass to quickly and easily create such drawings by hand.

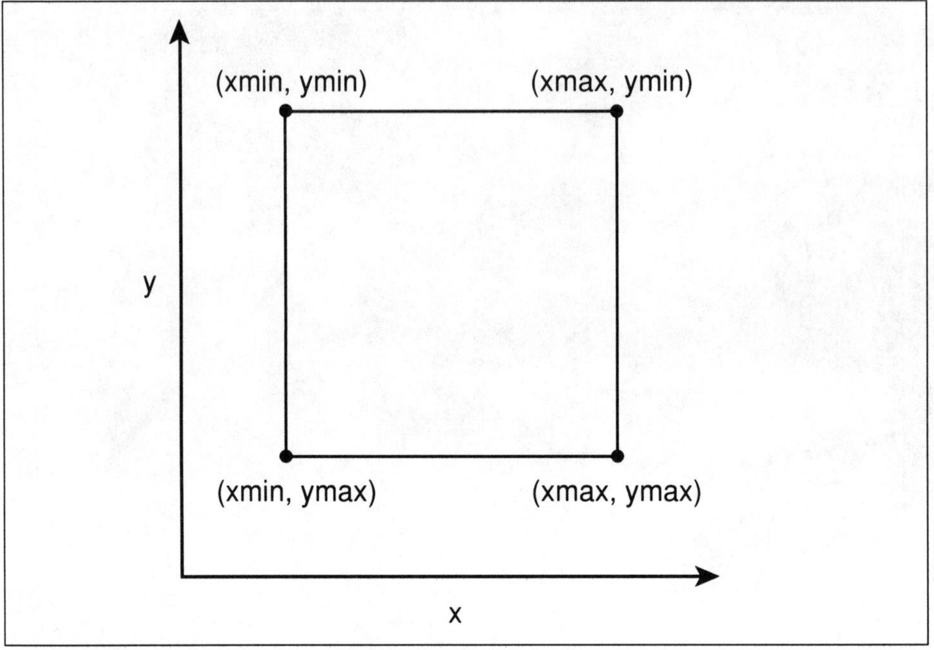

Figure 5-1. A rectangle is defined by its four corner points

You can simplify the rectangle-drawing algorithm somewhat because you do not need to use the general line-drawing function. Instead, you can directly fill in the pixels along the edges since they are vertical or horizontal. For instance, to draw the top and bottom edges, you can use a simple loop:

```
int x;
gColor color;
gRectangle rect;
for(x=ROUND(rect.xmin); x <= ROUND(rect.xmax); x++) {
 gPlotPixel(x, rect.ymin, color);
 gPlotPixel(y, rect.ymax, color);
}
```

You use a similar loop to draw the left and right edges. With this method, drawing the edges usually does not provide a significant performance improvement over direct line-drawing calls. In Chapter 8, however, you will see that it's a significantly faster approach if you need to fill the interior region of the rectangle with a color. Additionally, many graphics cards currently support rectangle operations (drawing, filling, and so on) directly in the hardware, just as with line-drawing operations.

The width of the rectangle is *(xmax - xmin + 1)*, and the height is *(ymax - ymin + 1)*. It is important to remember that the rectangle is inclusive; that is, all the pixels within the boundaries, including the edges, are part of the rectangle. Processing rectangles properly, which includes defining the elements correctly, is essential to any *windowing* system, such as MS-Windows.

Chapter 7 covers windowing and how to use the rectangle structure to specify the region of the screen that you wish to draw in. You don't want any portion of your drawing to appear outside of the window, because it might interfere with other windows. Fortunately, the clipping process takes care of this problem; however, it is important to know exactly how far the rectangle extends. By not carefully defining elements, you could easily be off by one pixel.

Drawing a Circle

After points and lines, the circle is the next geometric object you might consider drawing. It completes the set of standard Euclidean planar geometric objects. As you saw in Chapter 1, a circle is simply a set of points in the plane that are a fixed distance, r, from some center point $(x1, y1)$. You, therefore, define a circle as:

```
typedef struct gCircle_struct {
 float radius;
 float x, y;              /* Center coordinates */
} gCircle;
```

You can use the Pythagorean theorem to derive the algebraic relationship for the equation of a circle as:

$$(x-x1)^2 + (y-y1)^2 = r^2 \qquad \text{(Equation 5-1)}$$

This can be solved for y to yield:

$y = y1 +/- sqrt(r^2 - (x - x1)^2)$ (Equation 5-2)

Notice that you cannot simply plot *y* as a function of *x*. Each value of *x* has two values, one for the positive square root, the other for the negative square root. You have to plot two halves of the circle, the upper and lower semicircles. The most straightforward method for plotting the whole circle is:

```
float x, y, r2;
int ix, iy;
gCircle circle;
gColor color;

r2 = (circle.radius * circle.radius);
for(x= -circle.radius; x <= circle.radius; x = x+1.0) {
 y = sqrt(r2 - (x*x));
 ix = ROUND(x + circle.x);
 iy = ROUND(y + circle.y);
 gPlotPixel(ix, iy, color);     /* Positive y-value */
 iy = ROUND(circle.y - y);
 gPlotPixel(ix, iy, color);     /* Negative y-value */
}
```

Procedure 5-1. Plotting points on a circle

The problem with this plotting method is that it leaves gaps along the edges when *x* is close to the radius of the circle. As *x* approaches the radius, the change in successive *y*-values becomes greater than 1 pixel, resulting in gaps between adjacent columns.

A simple way to fix this problem is to use *gLineDraw()* instead of *gPlotPixel()*, and connect the points as they are generated along the circle. This results in the following modified procedure:

```
int lastx, lasty1, lasty2;

r2 = (circle.radius * circle.radius);
lastx = -ROUND(circle.radius);
```

```
lasty1 = 0;
lasty2 = 0;
for(x= -circle.radius; x <= circle.radius; x = x+1.0) {
 y = sqrt(r2 - (x*x));
 ix = ROUND(x + circle.x);
 iy = ROUND(y + circle.y);
 gLineDraw(lastx, lasty1, ix, iy, color);
 lastx = ix;
 lasty1 = iy;  /* Remember this value for y positive */
 iy = ROUND(circle.y - y);
 gLineDraw(lastx, lasty2, ix, iy, color);
 lasty2 = iy;  /* Remember this value for y negative */
}
```

Procedure 5-2. Plotting a circle with connecting lines

This method draws a complete circle with no gaps, but still produces erroneous results at the edges of the circle. In particular, the circle will now have a polygonal appearance alonge the edge, rather than looing like a smooth curve. Although these gaps are not very noticeable on smaller circles, they can be quite discernable on larger ones. Additionally, this algorithm has two other problems:

1. It uses extensive floating-point arithmetic, involving a square-root operation
2. Several of the pixels are drawn at least twice, especially near the top and bottom of the circle

Fortunately, there is a better way as shown in the next section.

Fast Circles

As with drawing the line segment, you want the most efficient drawing algorithm possible. To do this, you need to exploit the symmetry of the circle. You have already seen a partial result for this; namely, you can plot both the top and bottom halves of the circle simultaneously. There is no need to run through the equations twice. In order to simplify the rest of the analysis, you will assume that the circle is centered at (0, 0) and then offset the final com-

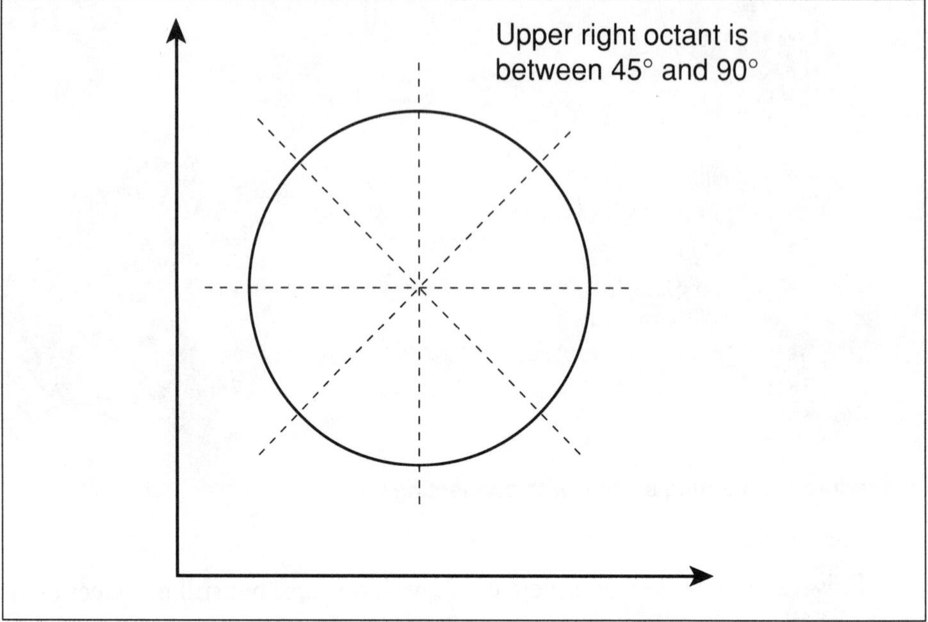

Figure 5-2. A circle can be divided into eight symmetrical octants. The circle-drawing algorithm draws the upper-right octant, and then fills in the other octants by symmetry.

puted pixel locations by the center coordinate *(x1, y1)*.

In the following discussion, you will use the standard mathematical coordinate system in which *y* increases from the bottom to the top. To get the *y*-coordinates for plotting on the screen, you take the computed *y*-coordinates, negate them, and then offset them by the circle center.

You can further exploit the symmetry of the circle by noting that if the point *(x,y)* is on the circle, then the following seven points are on the circle as well:

$$(-x,y),\ (x,-y),\ (-x,-y),\ (y,\ x),\ (-y,\ x),\ (y,\ -x),\ (-y,\ -x)$$

This is easily seen by substitution in Equation 5-1. The result means that you only need to find the points along a single octant (one-eighth of the circumference). Once a point along an octant is determined, all of the rest are found using symmetry. This reduces the computational complexity of the problem by a factor of four over the method previously shown. Although it doesn't mat-

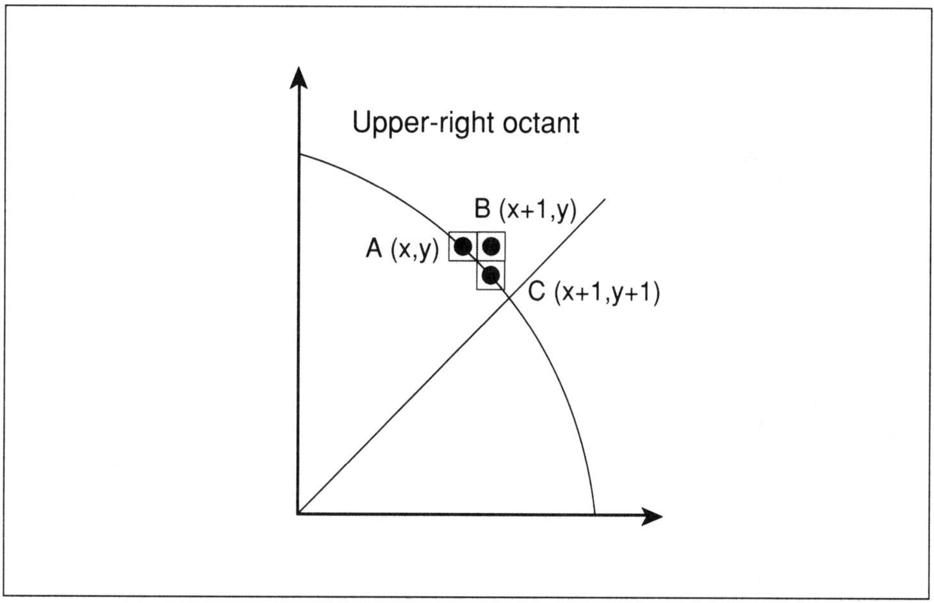

Figure 5-3. The upper-right octant of a circle is drawn via stepping by one in x. For each x, there are only two points to choose between, either the point directly to the right, or the point to the right and down 1 pixel. For pixel A, you must choose either B or C as the next pixel.

ter which octant you choose, pick the upper-right quadrant so you can follow Figure 5-2. For this octant, *x* runs from zero to radius/*sqrt* (2.0), which is at the 45-degree line. You must compute all the *y*-coordinates for each point within this range.

Recall that in the midpoint–line-drawing algorithm, you developed a method to choose the next pixel along the line by using a decision variable. You can adapt the same method to the circle. Along the upper-right octant, *y* cannot increase by more than one pixel for a one-pixel change in *x*. This means that, just as for the line, you need only test against one of two choices, as shown in Figure 5-3. Using the same notation as you did in Chapter 4, the circle-testing function is:

$$F(x,y) = x^2 + y^2 - r^2 \qquad \text{(Equation 5-3)}$$

The function $F(x,y)$ is greater than zero when the point (x,y) is outside the circle, zero when the point is on the circle, and less than zero when the point is inside the circle. As was done for the line, you will be evaluating $F(x,y)$ at points of the form $(ix, iy + 1/2)$, where ix and iy are integer coordinates. You can eliminate the fractional parts by multiplying F through by four. Since (1/2) ^{2} is 1/4; F(ix, iy + 1/2) would have terms divided by four in it and you want only integer results, which as previously stated, does not affect the sign of $F(x,y)$. The sign of $F(x,y)$, not the magnitude, is the basis for making decisions about which pixel to choose.

For the upper-right octant, the selected y-coordinate (row number) will always be less than or equal to the previous value. So, you'll need to evaluate $F(x,y)$ at $F(x + 2, y - 1/2)$ and $F(x + 2, y - 3/2)$. The decision variable D is equal to $F(x + 1, y - 1/2)$. This creates the following:

$$
\begin{aligned}
F(x + 2, y - 1/2) &= (x + 2)^2 + (y - 1/2)^2 - r^2 \\
&= x^2 + 4 * x + 4 + (y - 1/2)^2 - r^2 \\
&= 2 * x + 3 + (x + 1)^2 + (y - 1/2)^2 - r^2 \\
&= D + 2 * x + 3
\end{aligned}
$$

$$
\begin{aligned}
F(x + 2, y - 3/2) &= (x + 2)^2 + (y - 3/2)^2 - r^2 \\
&= x^2 + 4 * x + 4 + (y - 3/2)^2 - r^2 \\
&= 2 * x + 3 + (x + 1)^2 + 2 * y + 2 + (y - 1/2)^2 - r^2 \\
&= D + 2 * x + 3 + 2 * y + 2 \\
&= D + 2 * (x + y) + 5
\end{aligned}
$$

You can now perform the exact same type of procedure as you did for the line, except now the increments for D are functions of the current (x,y) point that is being processed. The algorithm may then be expressed as the following:

```
gCircle circle;
int x, y;
float d;

x = 0;
```

```
y = ROUND(circle.radius);
d = 5.0/4.0 - y;                    /* Initial value for d */
gCircleDrawEight(&circle, x, y, color);
                                    /* Plot the first point */
while(y > x) {                      /* Loop for upper octant */
 if(d <= 0) {                       /* We are outside the circle */
 d += 2*x + 3;
 } else {                           /* We are inside the circle */
 d += 2*(x+y) + 5;
 y--;
 }
 gCircleDrawEight(&circle, x, y, color);
 x++;
}
```

Procedure 5-3. Midpoint method for drawing a circle

The procedure *gCircleDrawEight()* plots the eight symmetric combinations of points, offset by the circle center. You used a real value of *d* since the initial value, according to our equations, involves a fraction. You eliminate the fraction simply by subtracting 1/4 from *d*'s initial value. The rest of the calculation then involves only integer arithmetic, so *d* cannot take on a fractional value. If you offset *d* by -1/4, the test for $d < 0$ becomes $d < -1/4$. However, since *d* is always an integer, it also must be less than zero. So, you can simply change the fraction 5/4 to 1 in the previous procedure and keep the entire computation strictly integer, assuming that the circle has an integer radius. Notice that you can easily adapt this procedure to work with circles of a noninteger radius and noninteger center points by simply changing the variable *d* back to floating point.

Circles With A Difference

You can, in fact, make one further improvement to the previous algorithm. The calculation of the decision variable, *d*, is a linear expression in *x* and *y*. The same method of using incremental differences can be applied to the computation of *d* itself. You introduce two new variables, *d1* and *d2*, that represent the increments of *d*, depending on whether you move to *p1* or *p2*. You compute the increments by observing:

$$d(x + 1, y) = 2*(x + 1) + 3 = 2 + 2 * x + 3 = d(x, y) + 2 \quad \text{/* Moving to p1 */}$$

$$d(x + 1, y + 1) = 2 * (x + 1 + y + 1) + 2 = 2*(x + y) + 2 + 4 = d(x,y) + 4 \quad \text{/* Moving to p2 */}$$

So, you increment *d1* by two for each pixel and *d2* by four for each iteration of the loop. These offsets are then added to *d* for each iteration. The completed circle-drawing procedure then becomes:

```
gCircle circle;
int x, y;
int d, d1, d2;

x = 0;
y = ROUND(circle.radius);
d = 1 - y;                        /* Initial value for d */
d1 = 3;                           /* Initial value for d1 */
d2 = -2*circle.radius + 5;        /* Initial value for d2 */
                                  /* Plot the first point */
gCircleDrawEight(&circle, x, y, color);
while(y > x) {                    /* Loop for upper octant */
 if(d <= 0) {                     /* We are outside the circle */
  d += d1;
 } else {                         /* We are inside the circle */
  d += d2;
  y++;
 }
 gCircleDrawEight(&circle, x, y, color);
```

```
        d1 += 2;
        d2 += 4;
        x++;
    }
```

Procedure 5-4. Midpoint method for drawing a circle using second differences

The increments *d1* and *d2* are referred to as *second differences* of the function $F(x,y)$, because they are the differences of *d*, the variable that represents differences for the function $F(x,y)$ (or differences of differences). This is an important technique that you will frequently encounter. Any incremental calculation can usually be made more efficient by introducing difference variables. For the circle, you needed to incrementally evaluate the second-order polynomial function $F(x,y)$. In general, a polynomial of order n (the largest exponent in the polynomial) can be incrementally evaluated using a set of n difference variables.

As you previously noted, the improved efficiency of using difference variables for the line is only valid when floating-point operations are slower than integer operations and when an integer multiply is slower than an integer add. These assumptions are not necessarily valid for many processors, and so there may be little performance difference between Procedure 5-3 and Procedure 5-2 on some machines. Procedure 5-1 will almost always be a little slower because of the overhead caused by the *sqrt*( ) operation.

Maintaining The Proper Aspect

Circles are very frequently used graphics shape, especially in drawing areas such as business graphics or architectural drawings. One common problem that often arises is that although you have used the previous circle-drawing algorithm to create a perfectly round circle into the frame buffer, the display on the screen shows a squashed circle instead. This is because the frame-buffer pixels are often not displayed with the same size in both the *x*- and *y*-axes. This difference in scale is referred to as the *aspect ratio* of the display. You compute the aspect ratio according to the following formula:

$$aspect = (screen\_width \,/\, screen\_height) \qquad \text{(Equation 5-4)}$$

where *screen_width* is the physical width of the screen, usually in inches, and *screen_height* is the height of the screen, usually in inches.. The pixels are square on the screen if the aspect ratio is the same as the ratio of the number of columns to the number of rows of the frame buffer. For example, a typical PC monitor has an aspect ratio of about 1.33, but standard VGA resolution of 320 x 200 has a ratio of 1.60. So, a circle will be displayed as elongated in the *y*-direction.

Your circle-drawing algorithm always draws a circle in the frame buffer under the assumption that pixels are equally spaced in both *x* and *y*. To draw a circle on the screen, you must scale one of the axes (usually the *y*-axis) to account for the aspect ratio of the screen. The scale factor for the *y*-coordinates can be obtained using the following scale factor:

$$yfactor = aspect * (ny / nx) \qquad \text{(Equation 5-5)}$$

where *ny* is the number of rows of the frame buffer and *nx* is the number of columns. Scaling the *y*-axis means that you are no longer drawing a circle, but instead that you must draw an ellipse into the frame buffer. This leads, coincidentally, to the next topic. You'll see how to handle the aspect-ratio problem for all of the drawings in Chapter 6.

Ellipses

The ellipse represents a "stretched" circle, as shown in Figure 5-4. The geometric interpretation of an ellipse is based on the two points shown in the figure. In this example, the points lie along the *x*-axis, equidistant from the origin. An ellipse is defined by the set of points where the sum of the distances to each point is a constant. For instance, a circle has both points at the same position at the origin. You can physically construct an ellipse by putting two nails into a board and loosely tying a string between the nails. Then stretch the string with a pencil, and trace the curve made by keeping the string taunt. In a sense, the ellipse is being drawn using a slightly more elaborate type of compass. The ellipse is a circle that has been stretched along one direction.

As mentioned in Chapter 1, the equation of an ellipse centered at the origin can be written as:

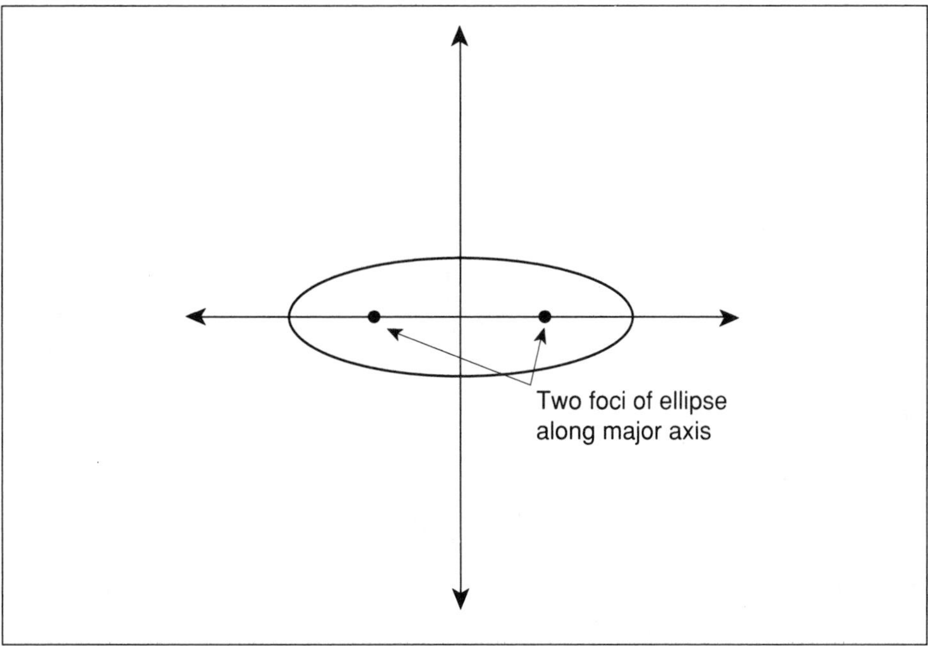

Figure 5-4. An ellipse with a major axis along the x-axis

$$(x/a)^2 + (y/b)^2 = 1 \qquad \text{(Equation 5-6)}$$
$$y = +/- b * sqrt(1 - (x/a)^2)$$

The variables *a* and *b* represent the "radius" of the ellipse along the *x*- and *y*-axes respectively. The structure for storing an ellipse is then:

```
typedef struct gEllipse_struct {
  float a,b;          /* Size of ellipse in x- and y-axes */
  float x,y;          /* Center of ellipse */
} gEllipse;
```

The longer of the two axes is referred to as the *major* axis of the ellipse; the smaller is referred to as the *minor* axis. For the moment, you should assume that the major axis lies along the *x*-axis; that is, that *a* is greater than *b*. You can use the steps shown in Procedure 5-2 to draw the top and bottom halves of the ellipse:

```
float x, y;
int ix, iy, lastx, lasty1, lasty2;
gEllipse ellipse;
gColor color;

lastx = -ROUND(ellipse.a);
lasty1 = 0;
lasty2 = 0;
for(x= -ellipse.a; x <= ellipse.a; x += 1.0) {
 y = ellipse.b*sqrt(1.0 - (x/ellipse.a)*(x/ellipse.a))
 ix = ROUND(x + ellipse.x);
 iy = ROUND(y + ellipse.y);
 gLineDraw(lastx, lasty1, ix, iy, color);
 lastx = ix;
 lasty1 = iy;
 iy = ROUND(ellipse.y - y);
 gLineDraw(lastx, lasty2, ix, iy, color);
 lasty2 = iy;
}
```

Procedure 5-5. Plotting an ellipse

Notice that the you need even more floating-point operations with this method than you did for the circle. Furthermore, you would not want to loop through *x* if the major axis lies along the *y*-axis, since this makes a very poor rendition. This routine must therefore be expanded to check for this condition and loop through the *y*-coordinates instead of the *x*-coordinates. The loop through *y* is in all other respects identical to the one shown previously for *x*.

Just as for the circle, this procedure leaves several things to be desired in terms of overall plotting accuracy. Let's see how you can adapt the midpoint algorithm to the ellipse. As you did for the circle, you can construct a function to determine whether a point is inside or outside the ellipse:

$$F(x,y) = (b * x)^2 + (a * y)^2 - (a * b)^2 \qquad \text{(Equation 5-7)}$$

Note that you multiplied through by $(a * b)^2$ to eliminate any fractional portions. Even though the equation for $F(x,y)$ is very similar to that of the circle, you cannot plug it into procedures 5-2 and 5-3 for drawing the circle. There are two primary reasons for this:

1. Because of the different scale factors in x and y, you no longer have the eight-fold symmetry of the circle.
2. You must determine the point at which incrementing by 1 pixel in the x direction causes more than a 1-pixel change in y.

To handle the first issue, you'll notice that you still have four-fold symmetry; that is, if a point (x,y) is on the ellipse, then the following three points are on it as well:

$(-x, y)$, $(x, -y)$, $(-x, -y)$

You must change your algorithm to plot the upper quadrant of the ellipse rather than just the upper octant. Use the function *gEllipseDrawFour()* to plot the four points for each (x,y) of the upper-quadrant curve. The second issue, however, is a little trickier to deal with.

The main assumption of the midpoint algorithm is that as you moved by 1 pixel in x, you only had two possible choices of the next y-coordinate. This is not true once the curve begins to approach the vertical. The y-coordinate can then change by more than 1 pixel for each step in the y-direction. You must therefore find the point at which this transition occurs and use a different approach to draw the rest of the upper quadrant.

In Figure 5-5, there is a plot of the upper-right quadrant of the ellipse. Recall that for the circle it is easy to identify the point at which y's rate of change would be greater than that of x, namely along the 45-degree axis. So for the portion of the upper-right quadrant below that line, a 1-pixel change in x would cause a more than 1-pixel change in y. You did not have to handle this case for the circle since you used the eight-fold symmetry to plot all other octants. The location of the transition point is shown in Figure 5-5.

If you are familiar with calculus, this would be the point at which the derivative of the portion of the curve corresponding to the upper-quadrant section

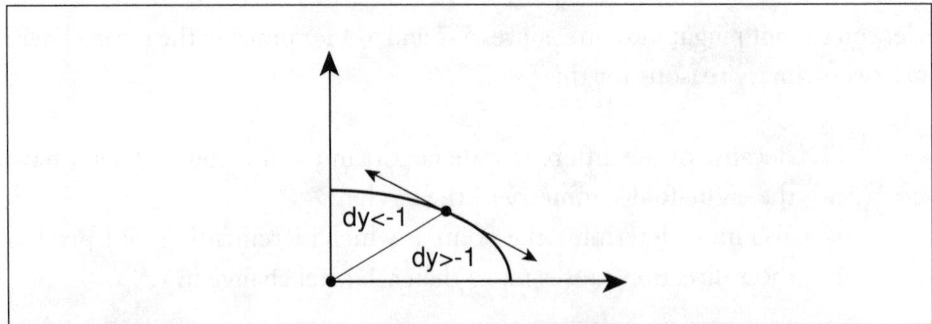

Figure 5-5. Upper-right quadrant of an ellipse. The shift from incrementing in x to incrementing in y occurs at the point where the tangent has slope -1.

of the ellipse is equal to -1. The transition point can be found differentiating Equation 5-6 with respect to *x* and solving to find the point at which it equals -1. You can, however, determine this point without using calculus by looking at Equation 5-6, and considering the change in *y*, referred to as *dy*, for a single pixel change in *x*.

For the incremental algorithm, you evaluate the function $F(x,y)$ at the points $(x + 1, y - 1/2)$. The transition point occurs when *dy* becomes greater than or equal to one. Consider the points $(x,y1)$ and $(x + 1, y2)$ where $y1$ and $y2$ represent the exact value of *y* to be on the ellipse for the given *x*-value. Thus, $F(x,y1) = F(x + 1, y2) = 0$, and $dy = y2 - y1$. You can now evaluate the sum of these two functions as:

$$F(x,y1) + F(x + 1,y2) = b^2 * ((x + 1)^2 - x^2) + a^2 * (y2^2 - y1^2) \quad \text{(Equation 5-8)}$$
$$= b^2 * (2x + 1) + a^2 * ((y2 - y1) * (y2 + y1))$$
$$= 0$$

which can be rewritten as:

$$b^2 * (2x + 1) = -a^2 * (dy * (y2 + y1))$$
$$b^2 * (2x + 1) = -a^2 * (dy * (2 * y1 + dy))$$

By substituting $dy = -1$ into the previous equation, you find the condition for *x* and *y* at the transition point:

$$b^2 * (2x + 1) = a^2 * (2y - 1) \text{ or} \qquad \text{(Equation 5-9)}$$
$$b^2 * (x + 1/2) = a^2 * (y - 1/2)$$

This condition is satisfied when *dy* is exactly -1. Observe that once this condition is satisfied, *dy* becomes increasingly negative as *x* increases; that is, *dy* remains less than -1 for the rest of the quadrant. So you must check for the boundary condition that $b^2 * (x + 1/2) >= a^2 * (y - 1/2)$ for your algorithm. Clearly, this condition will also be satisfied if you use $(x + 1)$ instead of $(x + 1/2)$. You evaluate the previous expression at each midpoint to determine when to switch to the second incremental procedure.

Now that you know how to find the transition point, you must decide what to do at the transition. This is simple because you now increment along *y* instead of *x*. In this second region, you already know that a single pixel change in *y* results in less than a single pixel change in *x*. You can therefore reverse the roles of *x* and *y*, and use the same incremental algorithm as you did for *x*.

Now you need to determine the incremental calculation for $F(x,y)$. You use exactly the same process as you did for the circle evaluation, arriving at:

$$\begin{aligned}
F(x + 2, y - 1/2) &= b^2 * (x + 2)^2 + a^2 * (y - 1/2)^2 - (a * b)^2 \\
&= b^2 * (x^2 + 4 * x + 4) + a^2 * (y - 1/2)^2 - (a * b)^2 \\
&= b^2 * (2 * x + 3 + (x + 1)^2) + a^2 * (y - 1/2)^2 - (a * b)^2 \\
&= D + b^2 * (2 * x + 3)
\end{aligned}$$

$$\begin{aligned}
F(x + 2, y - 3/2) &= b^2 * (x + 2)^2 + a^2 * (y - 3/2)^2 - (a * b)^2 \\
&= b^2 * (x^2 + 4 * x + 4) + a^2 * (y - 3/2)^2 - (a * b)^2 \\
&= b^2 * (2 * x + 3 + (x + 1)^2) - a^2 * (2 * y + 2 + (y - 1/2)^2) - \\
&\qquad (a * b)^2 \\
&= D + b^2 * (2 * x + 3) + a^2 * (2 * y + 2)
\end{aligned}$$

The values for the loop on *y* are found exactly the same way, except now you evaluate $F(x + 1/2, y - 2)$ and $F(x + 3/2, y - 2)$. The final ellipse-drawing procedure is shown in Procedure 5-4. Notice that you compute the starting value for *d* as *F(1, ellipse.b - 1/2)* for the *x*-loop, and $F(x + 1/2, y - 1)$ for the *y*-loop.

```
gEllipse ellipse;
int x, y;
int a2, b2;                     /*Squares of the ellipse axis size */
int ia, ib                      /* Integer values for ellipse.a,
                                 ellipse.b */

float d, testvar;

x = 0;
y = ROUND(ellipse.b);
ia = ROUND(ellipse.a);
ib = ROUND(ellipse.b);
a2 = ia*ia;
b2 = ib*ib;
d = b2 - a2*ellipse.b + 0.25*a2 ;      /* Initial value for d */
gEllipseDrawFour(x, y, ellipse.x, ellipse.y, color);
                                       /* Plot the first point */
while(a2*(y - 0.5) > b2*(x+1)) {       /* Loop in x */
 if(d <= 0) {                          /* We are outside the ellipse
*/
 d += ib*(2*x + 3);
 } else {                              /* We are inside the
                                          ellipse */
 d += ib*(2*x+3) + ellipse.a*(2*y + 2);
 y—;
 }
 gEllipseDrawFour(&ellipse, x, y, color);
 x++;
}

/* Now loop in y instead */
d = b2*(x+0.5) + a2*(y-1.0) - a2*b2;
                                /* Calculate F(x+1/2, y-1) */
gEllipseDrawFour(&ellipse, x, y, color);
                                /* Plot the first point */
while(y >= 0) {                 /* Loop in y */
 if(d <= 0) {                   /* We are outside the ellipse */
 d += ib*(2*x + 2) + ellipse.a*(-2*y + 3);
 x++;
 } else {                       /* We are inside the ellipse */
```

```
        d += ia*(-2*y + 3);
    }
    gEllipseDrawFour(&ellipse, x, y, color);
    y--;
}
```

Procedure 5-6. Midpoint method for drawing an ellipse

You can now solve the problem of plotting correctly displayed circles by treating them as ellipses. You set the *x*-axis coordinate, *a*, equal to the radius of the circle, and set the *y*-axis coordinate, *b*, to the radius * *yfactor*, where *yfactor* is computed using Equation 5-5. When plotted, this ellipse will appear circular on the screen.

Polygons

So far, you have seen three types of objects for representing an area:

- Rectangle
- Circle
- Ellipse

Clearly there are many others that have not been covered, ones that you could easily develop using algorithms of methods similar to those derived for the circle and ellipse.

As you saw in Chapter 1, you can cover a much broader range of objects by adding polygons to your list of graphic objects. A *polygon* is simply a connected set of points in a plane that define some enclosed area of that plane. The points are connected by simple line segments. Each point is referred to as a polygon *vertex*. The main restriction placed on a polygon is that the last point is connected to the first point, which always makes a closed object. Some sam-

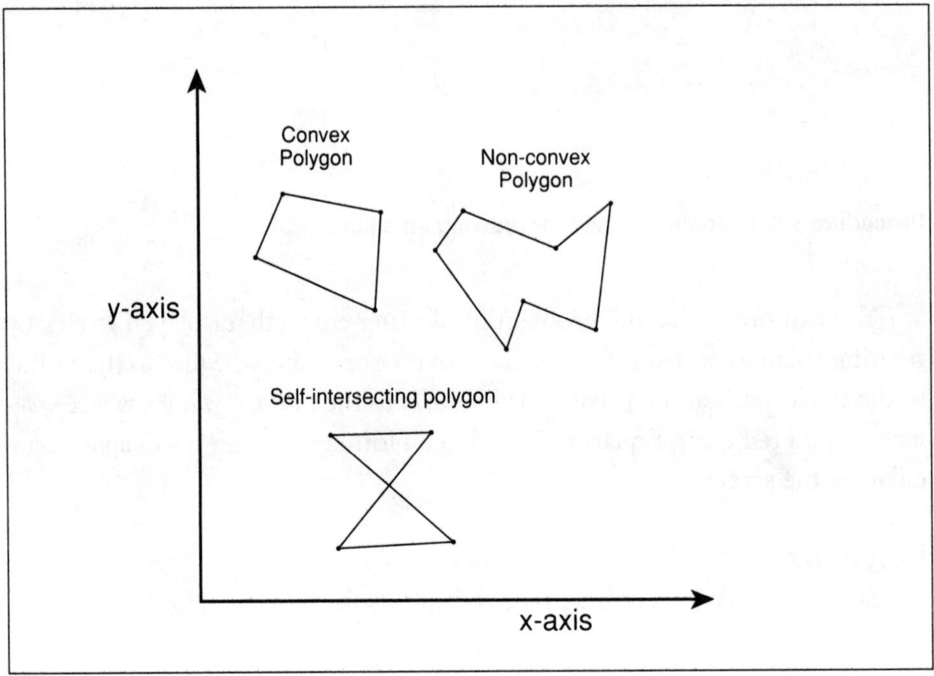

Figure 5-6. Examples of all three types of polygons

ple polygons are shown in Figure 5-6, along with some objects that are not valid polygons. A polygon is represented internally by the following structure:

```
typedef struct gPolygon_struct {
 int npoints;
 int size;
 gPoint *points;
} gPolygon;
```

Note that this structure uses a pointer to an array of points. A single point is defined as:

```
typedef struct gPoint_struct {
 int x, y;
} gPoint;
```

If the variable *poly* is a pointer to a *gPolygon* structure, then *poly->points[n]* is the *(n + 1)*st point of the polygon. (It is *n + 1* since C uses an array index of zero to specify the first element of an array.) The number of vertices of the polygon is stored in the *npoints* element. A triangle would have *npoints* of three. Recall that you included an additional element called *size*. This variable stores the number of currently allocated points in the *points* array of the polygon.

In general, *size* must be greater than or equal to *npoints*. This is provided so that you can freely add and delete points from the polygon without constantly having to reallocate memory. When the polygon is created, you may optionally specify an initial number of points to allocate for the polygon. As new vertices are added or removed, a new *points* array does not have to be allocated unless you attempt to add more points than are currently allocated for the polygon. In that case, a new *points* is allocated that is large enough to store all the points of the polygon. This is discussed in more detail with the polygon-vertex functions.

Since most polygon processing consists of looping through all of the vertices, you must ensure that the edge connecting the last point to the first point is processed. A typical polygon processing section of code is as follows:

```
int i;
gPoint point1, point2;

/* Start with the last point of the polygon */
point1 = poly->points[poly->npoints-1];
for(i=0; i<poly->npoints; i++) {
 point2 = poly->points[i];
 /* Now p1, p2 define an edge of the polygon for further
    processing */
 point1 = point2;      /* Now go on to the next edge */
}
```

As with your other objects, there are the standard set of functions for creating, copying, and deleting polygons. Polygons, however, present a more interesting programming issue because they are not of fixed size, as are circles and ellipses. There may be any number of points in a polygon, subject to the memory limits of your computer. This presents a slight dilemma if you want to create polygons dynamically, for instance, by allowing someone to create polygons using a mouse in a paint program. In this case, your program has no idea how many points a user may enter before finally closing the polygon.

There are two basic choices for solving this problem:

1 Create a polygon with a fixed maximum size
2. Allow a polygon to be created dynamically

The first solution is computationally efficient, but it could potentially waste a lot of memory. You must have your program verify that users do not enter more than the maximum number of points and take appropriate action if they attempt to do so. The second solution provides efficient memory usage at the cost of extra memory management.

Neither C nor C++ provide a means to deallocate "part" of an array. The polygon routines shown here provide the advantages of both methods. You may allocate a polygon of some reasonable initial size and then add vertices to it freely. If you attempt to add more vertices than was initially allocated, the polygon routines will create a new *points* array large enough to hold the additional vertices, copy the old *points* array into the new one, and free the old *points* array.

The *gPolygonCreate(n)* function creates a polygon structure for an *n*-vertex polygon. All the points are initialized to zero. You may then add vertices using the *gPolygonAddPoint( )* function:

```
gPolygon *gPolygonAddPoint(poly, i, x, y);
gPolygon *poly;
int i;
float x, y;
```

This will set the *i*th vertex of the polygon to the passed *x*- and *y*-values. If *i* is less than *poly->size*, then it simply sets the *i*th point to the specified value and returns with the value of *poly*. The number of points in the polygon will then be updated to be the maximum of either *i* or *poly->npoints*. If *i* is greater than or equal to *poly->size*, then the function will allocate a new *points* array large enough to store *i* + 1 points; copy the existing *poly->points* array into this new structure; set the *i*th point to the passed *x*- and *y*-values; destroy the *poly->points* array; set *poly->points* to the newly allocated array; and finally, return the new *gPolygon* structure as its return value. This function also lets you pass a *NULL* value for the *poly* argument. This tells *gPolygonAddPoint* to create a new polygon structure. A typical use of this function would be:

```
int i, npoints;
float x, y;
gPolygon *poly;

poly = NULL;
npoints = 0;
while(still_looping) {
 getPoints(&x, &y);
 poly = gPolygonAddPoint(poly, npoints, x, y);
 npoints++;
}
```

Notice that *gPolygonAddPoint()* also lets you change the value of any vertex, in addition to being able to add new vertices.

This book also provides the function *gPolygonRemovePoint(poly, i)* to remove the *i*th point of a polygon. This function does not free any memory; it simply shifts all the vertices from *i+1* to *poly->npoints* down into the *points* array, effectively removing the point. The only way to free any excess memory is to use *gPolygonCopy()* to copy the polygon into a new structure. *gPolygonCopy()* creates a new polygon with its size *size* equal to the number of points in the polygon.

To further reduce the problem of potential memory fragmentation, the function *gPolygonSetMemoryIncrement()* is provided. If *gPolygonAddPoint* is forced to create a new *points* array, the new *size* will be at least *gPolygonSetMemoryIncrement()* larger than the number of vertices needed. By default, this increment is set to 10. So every time a polygon is extended, at least 10 points are added to the *points* array at a time.

Types of Polygons

In this book, I classify polygons into three basic types, each with increasing complexity:

1. Convex
2. Nonconvex
3. Self-intersecting

Convex polygons

A *convex polygon* is one that has the property that if you connect any two points inside of the polygon by a line segment, then the line segment is also contained within the polygon. Any regular polygon, such as a square, pentagon, or hexagon, is a convex polygon. All triangles are convex. This property will be quite useful when you learn how to fill the polygon interior in Chapter 8. In particular, many graphics hardware polygon-filling algorithms require convex polygons for their methods to work. It is, therefore, often useful to know if a polygon is convex or not.

Nonconvex polygons

A *nonconvex polygon* is one that does not satisfy the previous condition for convexity. Such a polygon is shown in the top-right polygon of Figure 5-6. Although not convex, this type of polygon still describes a single closed area. This is the most common type of polygon to process, and the one that you will use when studying polygon filling in Chapter 8.

Self-intersecting polygons

This is a polygon whose boundary intersects itself. Two examples are shown in the bottom of Figure 5-6. The intersection points effectively divide the area into multiple separate regions. This type of polygon is generally not used in graphics processing because the area that it is supposed to define is ambiguous. For example, the right-hand star polygon of Figure 5-6 could be considered to cover the entire region of the star or to separate the center from each of the points. Self-intersecting polygons are allowed, but the results may not always turn out as you intended. This will be more evident when drawing filled polygons in Chapter 8.

Drawing Polygons

Unlike the circle and ellipse, drawing polygon boundaries are relatively easy. We simply loop through the points and connect the dots with straight lines. This is provided by the function *gPolygonDraw(poly)*. The situation will, however, be reversed when you learn to draw a filled polygon in Chapter 8. Circles and Ellipses are very easy to fill compared to polygons. Polygons, however, can provide more interesting shapes.

Curves and Polylines

The arcs you drew for the circle and ellipse define various types of curves. You can generalize this in a number of ways. The most obvious way is to approximate a particular curve using a *polyline*. A polyline is simply a series of points connected by line segments. The polygon boundary you previously defined is a polyline. Unlike a polygon, a polyline does not have to be closed, and you don't really care if it is self-intersecting or not. A polyline defines a curve through the plane. It does not define a region or area as the polygon does. The structure for a polyline is identical to that of the polygon and, in fact, is simply equated to the *gPolygon* structure using a *typedef*:

```
typedef gPolygon        gPolyLine;
```

As with the polygon, there are exactly *npoints* points in a *gPolyLine* structure. When processing a polyline, the first and last points may or may not be the same point. The function *gPolyLineDraw()* draws the passed polyline. The functions *gPolyLineAddPoint()* and *gPolyLineRemovePoint()* perform the same functions for polylines as their equivalents do for polygons.

There are two primary uses for a polyline:

1. To store a set of externally acquired data for later processing, such as digitizing points from a screen or a map
2. To approximate some mathematically derived function

You have already seen an example of the second use when you devised the "simple" circle- and ellipse-plotting functions. Recall that for the circle, you simply evaluated the function for y for every x from *-circle.radius* to *+circle.radius*. As you saw, this approach has problems, but it makes for a reasonable first pass at plotting a circle.

You can take a similar approach to plotting any function in which you know that y is an explicit function of x. There are many cases in which you cannot write such an explicit function. The circle was a simple example. It had to be broken into two halves, since for every x there are two points ($+y$ and $-y$) that lie on the circle. In general, you cannot guarantee any such symmetry in the functions you may have to plot. Instead, it is better to think of a curve as a path through the plane.

Let's introduce a new parameter, t, and consider both x and y to be functions of t. You can then specify a curve by specifying the two functions $x(t)$ and $y(t)$. This is called a *parametric* representation of a curve because both of our Cartesian coordinates are now functions of this new parameter. This is analogous to specifying the path of a particle in the plane, where you think of t as corresponding to time. The curve is traced by an imaginary pen particle. You can compute (at least in theory) the curve for any time t that you desire. You can also compute the value of y for any particular x by finding the value t that results in the corresponding value of x. This value for t may then be plugged into the expression $y(t)$ to get the corresponding y.

In order to simplify things, if you have a curve that goes from point $p1$ to point $p2$, you generally choose functions so that when $t = 0$, $(x(0), y(0)) = p1$ and when $t = 1$, $(x(1), y(1)) = p2$. For example, you can directly write down the parametric functions for a line segment:

$$x(t) = x1 + t * (x2 - x1) = (1 - t) * x1 + t * x2 \qquad \text{(Equation 5-10)}$$
$$y(t) = y1 + t * (y2 - y1) = (1 - t) * y1 + t * y2$$

Similarly, you can write the parametric equations for an ellipse by having t represent the angle in polar coordinates:

$$x(t) = a * cos(t * 2 * PI) \qquad \text{(Equation 5-11)}$$
$$y(t) = b * sin(t * 2 * PI)$$

The parametric representation has many advantages as opposed to having you find an explicit function for $y(x)$. It neatly handles the problem for shapes, such as circles, that do not have a single-valued function for $y(x)$. In fact, the curve can loop around the plane as many times as you like. As an example, Equation 5-11 can be changed to the plot of a spiral if you multiply both $x(t)$ and $y(t)$ by t. This type of curve would be impossible to specify with y as an explicit function of x.

Parametric representations also neatly avoid the problem of potentially evaluating infinite slopes if the curve becomes nearly vertical over part of its path. You can easily lose calculated precision as the curve approaches the points at which it becomes vertical (or has a vertical tangent). A parametric curve is also easier to transform (translate, scale, and rotate), as you'll see in Chapter 6.

The most important feature, however, is that you can make adjoining curves match up more easily by forcing their respective parametric representations to match the endpoints. You can also impose constraints other than just requiring that the adjoining endpoints of curves have the same point. Conditions, such as matching first- or second-order derivatives, can also be specified with relative ease. You saw a small form of this in the ellipse-plotting procedure. You wanted to plot separate, adjoining curves for the upper quadrant. For the first region, you used x as a parameter, and for the second region, you used y. By the way you constructed the procedure, you automatically enforced the condition that the curves match at the transition between the regions. You will see a more complex example of this later in the chapter, when you learn to match polynomial curves.

Approximating a Curve

Once in parametric form, you can easily make a polyline approximation to the curve by dividing t into n intervals of length $1/n$. You then compute the values of $(x(t), y(t))$ for $i = 0$ to 1, in steps of $1/n$. The problem with this approach is choosing n. You can always make an arbitrarily close approximation by choosing n large, but this can be quite wasteful. You usually cannot make a universal choice of n that will work for all curves. If you know some of the properties of the curve, you can make a fairly intelligent guess. For example, the circumference of a circle of radius r is simply $2 * PI * r$. If you choose n to be the nearest integer greater than $2 * PI * r$, then you should have a sufficiently fine step size to create an accurate rendition of the circle. In general, if you know (or can make an educated guess about) the length of the curve, then your step size should be selected as 1/length.

Throwing a curve

Often, simply connecting points by a straight line does not produce visually pleasing results, especially if the points are spaced far apart. This is because the curve is not smooth at the vertices of the polyline. Analytically, it is because the derivative of the polyline is almost always discontinuous at each of the vertices. You can remedy this by using something other than a straight line to connect the points. Doing this requires that you use the other points along the polyline and fit another type of curve in a smoother way. There are many choices for these types of functions. By far, the simplest method is to fit a polynomial to a set of points. Any set of n points may be exactly fitted by an n-1 order polynomial. Such a polynomial (in t), would look like:

$$x(t) = a_n * t^{n-1} + a_{n-1} * t^{n-2} + \ldots + a_1 \qquad \text{(Equation 5-12)}$$
$$y(t) = b_n * t^{n-1} + b_{n-1} * t^{n-2} + \ldots + b_1$$

You can compute the polynomial coefficients simply by plugging in the n points and solving the resulting set of linear equations in the coefficients, using your favorite linear--equation-solving algorithm. Again, once you have this polynomial representation; you can draw it by simply stepping through the polynomial in small increments of the parameter t. Notice that this is still a polyline approximation, just at a much finer scale than when you simply connect the points.

This technique works well for a small number of points, but it can get very computationally burdensome for large numbers of points. It also means that you must recompute the entire polynomial if any of the points along the polyline are changed. A 1,000-point polyline would require that you invert a (1,000 x 1,000)-element matrix, which is not a pretty picture!

So, instead you should try to approximate several points at a time by polynomials, and then ensure that the endpoints of the polynomials match. These approximated curves are known as *splines*. The mathematics for computing various types of splines is beyond the scope of this book. But there are several good references on the topic, particularly *Computer Graphics: Principles and Practice* (Addision-Wesley, 2nd edition, 1990), listed in the references in Appendix B. We can, however, discuss the basic idea.

Polynomial Curves

Suppose you want to make a point-by-point polynomial approximation to a set of points along a polyline. You begin by taking the first 2 points of the polyline and fitting a third-order polynomial to it. To completely specify this polynomial, you must impose the following four constraints:

1. The polynomial must pass through the two points and the derivative of the curve at the endpoints must equal the specified value as shown in Figure 5-7.
2. The derivative at *p2* is estimated by looking at the slope of the line between *p2* and *p3*. For the first point, the derivative is estimated by the line from *p1* to *p2*.
3. These derivatives are all with respect to the parameter *t*. Each point is then processed in turn with the constraint that the endpoints match and that the derivatives match at each successive point.
4. So, the derivative for any point must be the same at that point in the approximated polynomials on either side of the point.

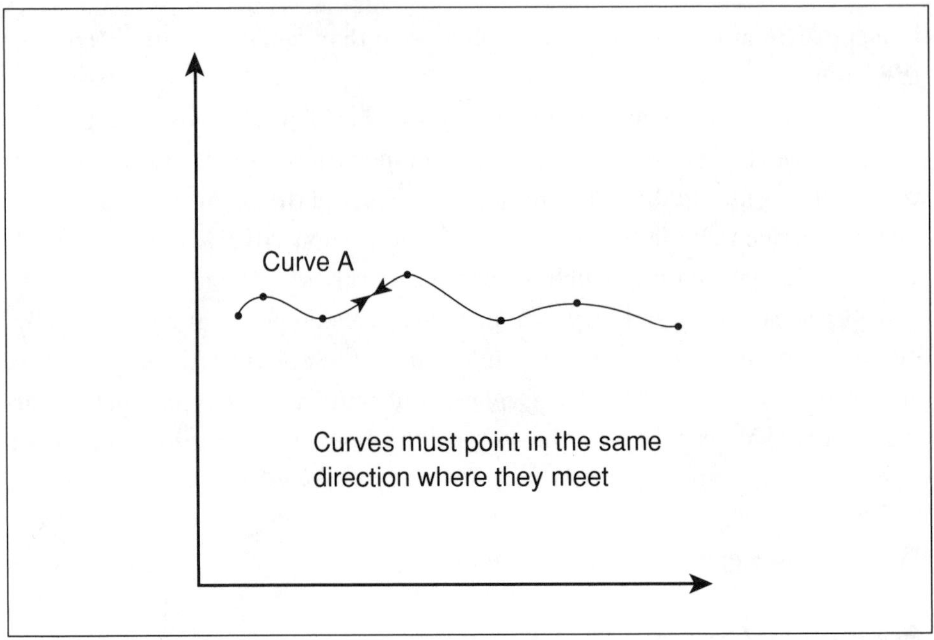

Figure 5-7. To create a smooth joint between two curves, the curves should not only meet, but the tangents at the point of intersection should have the same slope.

Another benefit of using approximated polynomials is that you already know how to incrementally evaluate them. This makes the drawing functions for polynomial curves very efficient, as you saw with the circle- and ellipse-plotting functions. However, this is not the case if you use the parametric representation of the previous ellipse, which involves the use of *sin()* and *cos()*. To use that representation requires that you call those functions for every iteration in *t*, which is computationally expensive on machines without a floating-point coprocessor.

When the connecting polynomials are plotted, it produces a smoother fitting curve than that achieved by simply connecting the dots. The type of approximated polynomials used in this approach are known as *Hermite* polynomials. The general form of these polynomials is:

$$x(t) = a_n * (1 - t)^{n-1} + a_{n-1} * t * (1-t)^{n-2} + \ldots + a_2 * t^{n-2} * (1-t) + a_1 * t^{n-1}$$
$$y(t) = b_n * (1-t)^{n-1} + b_{n-1} * t * (1 - t)^{n-2} + \ldots + b_2 * t^{n-2} * (1-t) + b_1 * t^{n-1}$$

You can see by the form that for $t = 0$, $(x, y) = (a_n, b_n)$ and that for $t = 1$, $(x, y) = (a_1, b_1)$. Note that the parametric form of the line shown in Equation 5-10 is exactly the same form for order n equal to 1.

Another type of polynomial, known as *Bézier*, uses separate control points to specify the slopes at each of the points on the curve, rather than simply estimating from successive points along the polyline. This type of control, however, requires more data than just sample points along a curve, you must specify these control points as well. See the bibliography for books about these and other techniques.

For the purposes of this book, you will use polyline approximations to draw the analytic figures you will be examining. Polylines have the great advantage of computational simplicity. For shapes like circles and ellipses, you can generate a polyline (or polygon for that matter) of sufficient resolution to create the equivalent plot as your fast circle- and ellipse-plotting functions do. You will see the utility of polygons and polylines in the next chapter when you study drawing scaled and rotated circles and ellipses.

Better Drawings

The methods I have described for generating curves, polygons, and polylines provide the basic tools for drawing a wide variety of shapes and figures. You can combine these shapes in many ways to produce elaborate drawings. But you are still missing some important operations that make truly clever drawings. Several obvious questions that are answered by these operations include the following, all of which are answered in the following chapters:

- How do you move, scale, and rotate a given shape to create a new shape?
- How do you draw solid figures?
- How do you draw thick edges (greater than 1-pixel wide)?
- How do you draw using patterns?

Functions Found in This Chapter

Circle functions

```
gCircle *gCircleCreate(float x, float y, float radius);
```

Creates a *gCircle* structure representing a circle centered at *(x,y)* of radius *radius*.

```
gCircle *gCircleCopy(gCircle *dest, gCircle *source);
```

Copies a *gCircle* structure.

```
void gCircleDelete(gCircle *circle);
```

Deletes a *gCircle* structure.

```
void gCircleDrawSimple(gCircle *circle, gColor color);
```

Draws a circle in the color specified by *color* via plotting the function $y = sqrt(r^2 - x^2)$ along the *x*-axis. As the plot progresses, each plotted point is connected with a line segment to the previously plotted point.

```
void gCircleDraw(gCircle *circle, gColor color);
```

Same as *gCircleDrawSimple()* except that this function uses the midpoint algorithm.

```
void gCircleDrawEight(gCircle *circle, int x, int y,
                 gColor color);
```

Used by the circle-drawing routines to plot the eight-symmetric points of the circle in each octant. With this function, the circle-drawing routines only have to plot one octant of the circle.

Ellipse functions

```
gEllipse *gEllipseCreate(float x, float y, float a, float b);
```

Creates a *gEllipse* structure representing an ellipse centered at (*x*,*y*) with an *x*-axis length of *a*, and a *y*-axis length of *b*.

```
gEllipse *gEllipseCopy(gEllipse *dest, gEllipse *source);
```

Copies a *gEllipse* structure.

```
void gEllipseDelete(gEllipse *ellipse);
```

Deletes a *gEllipse* structure.

```
void gEllipseDrawSimple(gEllipse *ellipse, gColor color);
```

Draws an ellipse in the color specified by *color* via plotting the function $y = b * sqrt(1.0 - (x/a)^2)$ along the *x*-axis.

```
void gEllipseDraw(gEllipse *ellipse, gColor color);
```

Same as *gEllipseDrawSimple()* except that this function uses the midpoint algorithm.

```
void gEllipseDrawFour(gEllipse *ellipse, int x, int y,
             gColor color);
```

Used by the ellipse-drawing routines to plot the four-symmetric points of the ellipse in each quadrant. With this function, the ellipse-drawing routines only have to plot one quadrant of the ellipse.

Polygon functions

```
gPolygon *gPolygonCreate(int nvertices);
```

Creates a *gPolygon* structure with enough initial allocated storage for *nvertices* vertices. Additional storage will be allocated as necessary when vertices are added. The polygon is initialized with zero vertices.

```
gPolygon *gPolygonCopy(gPolygon *dest, gPolygon *source);
```

Copies a *gPolygon* structure.

```
void gPolygonDelete(gPolygon *polygon);
```

Deletes a *gPolygon* structure.

```
void gPolygonDraw(gPolygon *polygon, gColor color);
```

Draws a polygon on the screen in the color specified by *gColor*.

```
gPolygon *gPolygonAddPoint(gPolygon *polygon, int i, float x,
                           float y);
```

Adds the *i*th vertex to a polygon (as with all C arrays, the first vertex of a polygon is zero). If necessary, more storage is allocated to accommodate the new point in the polygon. This routine may also be used to set any vertex in the polygon to a new value.

```
gPolygon *gPolygonRemovePoint(gPolygon *polygon, int i);
```

Deletes the *i*th vertex from a polygon.

```
void gPolygonSetMemoryIncrement(int inc);
```

If *gPolygonAddPoint()* must allocate more memory for a polygon, it adds enough storage to hold *inc* more vertices. The default value for *inc* is 10. This helps to prevent your program from making an inordinate number of memory allocation/deallocation calls.

CHAPTER 6

Linear Algebra 101

With tools from the previous chapters, you can now create complex drawings filled with circles, ellipses, polygons, and polylines of all descriptions. But, perhaps, now you want to take part of the drawing and shrink it to fit into a smaller area. Or, maybe, you decide to rotate one of your ellipses to a 45-degree angle. Of course, you may decide to move part of the drawing to a different part of the screen or to move, rotate, and rescale parts of your drawing.

That's where this chapter comes in. You'll learn how to easily perform these types of operations on any of the drawing elements described so far. Using the concept of matrices, you will be able to combine any sequence of these steps without having to perform a huge amount of additional arithmetic.

Affine Transformations

There are four elementary operations you'll typically want to perform on a graphic object:

Translation: Moving an object on the screen
Scaling: Stretching or squashing the object in one or both axes
Reflection: Reflecting an object about a line
Rotation: Rotating the object

These operations are known as *affine transformations*. A general transformation is an operation that takes a point (x,y) and maps it to a new point (x', y'). For notational purposes, I refer to a transformation simply as $T(x,y)$. The term *affine* refers to the property that straight lines remain straight after the transformation. This can be derived from the following mathematical property:

$$T(x1 + x2, y1 + y2) = T(x1,y1) + T(x2,y2) - T(0,0) \qquad \text{(Equation 6-1)}$$

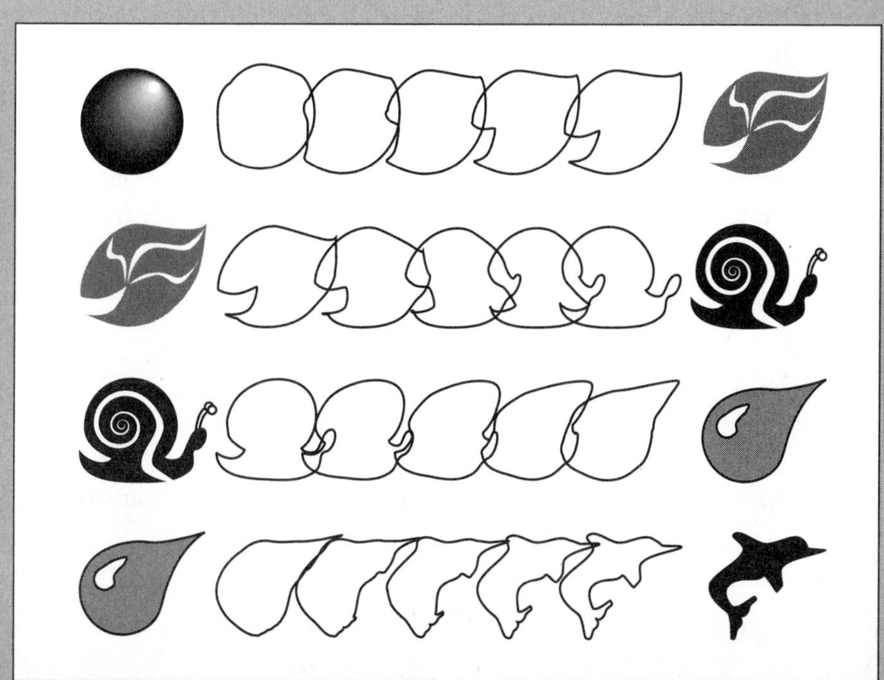

Even though you have only learned how to draw a relatively small number of geometric shapes, you can use these shapes to represent a much wider variety of figures by using transformations. A transformation is a mathematical operation that takes one object and smoothly transforms it into another object, as shown in the picture above.

In this chapter, you'll learn about the class of affine transformations that lets you take a basic shape, such as a rectangle, and perform operations like translation (moving it about the screen), rotation (rotating it about a point), and scaling (stretching or squashing it). With these simple operations, you'll be able to turn a rectangle into a diamond, or change a circle into an ellipse. By combining multiple transformations, you can easily move objects about the screen and transform them however you desire. Throughout the rest of the book, you'll see how transformations are used to represent complex objects in a logical and straightforward manner that would be difficult by other means.

This property is very useful because it means that you only need to transform the endpoints of line segments, and then connect the two new endpoints with a straight line. Thus, a polygon or polyline can be transformed by applying the transformation to each vertex and then replotting the result. For more complex shapes, such as circles and ellipses, you must examine the object's defining equation (or equations) and see which properties the newly transformed object has. You will see how to do this in the next chapter. Let's first see how each transformation is defined.

Translation

A translation is simply:

$$T_{trans}(x,y) = (x + xoff, y + yoff) \qquad \text{(Equation 6-2)}$$

where *xoff* and *yoff* are constants to be added to *x* and *y* respectively. A translation operation lets you move objects freely around the screen.

Scaling

A scaling operation multiplies *x* and *y* by constants:

$$T_{scale}(x,y) = (xscale * x, yscale * y) \qquad \text{(Equation 6-3)}$$

This transformation always scales *(x,y)* relative to the origin at (0,0). This is the basic transformation to change the size of the object being drawn. As you will see, you must be very careful about the position of the object relative to the origin before applying a transformation like scaling. If an object is not centered at the origin, the scaling operation will not only change the object's size, but also move the object center to some other point on the screen. For example, if *xscale* and *yscale* are both equal to two, and you have a circle centered at (100,100), then scaling by two will move the circle center to (200,200). This probably isn't what was desired. In the next section, you'll learn how to combine transformations to avoid this type of problem.

Reflection

A reflection transformation flips an object about the *x*- or *y*-axis:

$$T_{xrefl}\ (x,y) = (-x,y)$$
$$T_{yrefl}\ (x,y) = (x\ -y) \qquad \text{(Equation 6-4)}$$

As with the scaling transformation, the reflection transformation flips the object about the *x*-axis (line $y = 0$) or the *y*-axis (line $x = 0$). The reflection transformation is most useful for handling the problem of the frame-buffer coordinate system having *y* increase from top to bottom. The common Cartesian coordinate system has *y* increasing from bottom to top. The reflection transformation, in combination with the translation transformation, provides a straightforward means of transforming objects.

Rotation

The rotation operation is the most complex affine transformation, and the one that is most confusing. Referring to Figure 6-1, try to transform a point by rotating it through angle A. You can derive the transformation by switching to polar coordinates and using the following angle identities you might recall from high school:

$$cos(A + B) = cos(A) * cos(B) - sin(A) * sin(B) \qquad \text{(Equation 6-5)}$$
$$sin(A + B) = sin(A) * cos(B) + cos(A) * sin(B)$$

As shown in Figure 6-1, the rotation transformation is:

$$\begin{aligned} T_{rot}\ (x,y) &= (r * cos(A + O), r * sin(A + O)) \qquad \text{(Equation 6-6)} \\ &= (r * cos(A) * cos(O) - r * sin(A) * sin(O), \\ &\quad r * sin(A) * cos(O) + r * cos(A) * sin(O)) \\ &= (x * cos(A) - y * sin(A), x * sin(A) + y * cos(A)) \end{aligned}$$

Again, note that rotation is always with respect to the origin. This can cause confusion unless some care is taken to ensure that you are rotating the object about the correct point. This will often mean that an object must be moved (translated),

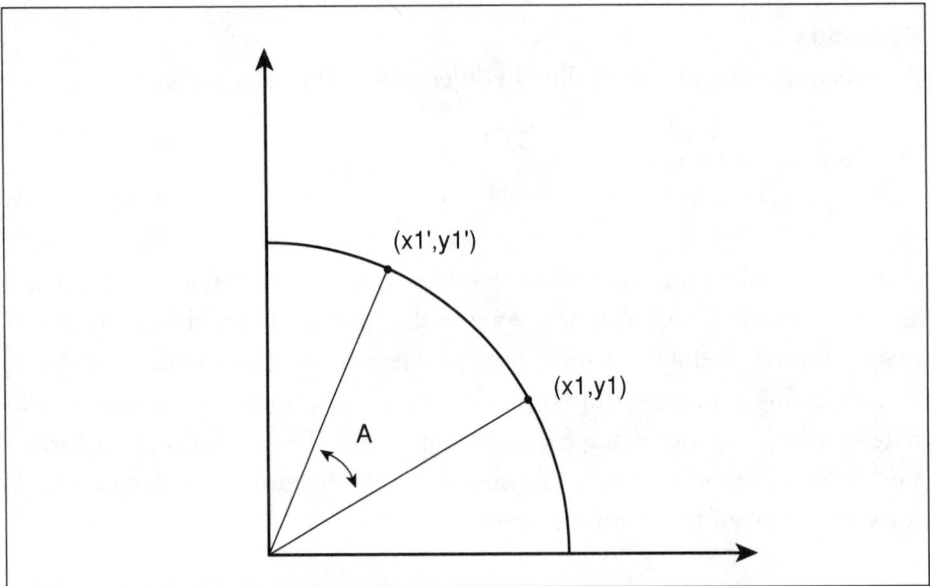

Figure 6-1. Rotating a point through angle A

rotated, and then moved back so that it rotates about the desired point, such as the center of the object. This issue will be covered in more detail later.

Linear Algebra

Before fleeing in panic at the mere thought of algebra, let's calmly consider what needs to be accomplished. You'll want to transform graphic objects, perhaps, by many different transformations. You could develop a set of routines to perform each transformation and then call each function separately to do the total transformation. Using this technique, a sequence of *n* transformations is represented as:

$$T_{total}(x, y) = T_n(T_{n-1}(\ldots T_2(T_1(x, y))\ldots)) \qquad \text{(Equation 6-7)}$$

If you wanted to transform a polygon by T_{total}, you would have to transform the vertices *n* times. This could become quite computationally expensive. Instead, it would be better if you could express the transformation T_{total} in a simpler way, and perform the computation only once per vertex.

Matrix Notation

If you examine each form of the affine transformations previously shown, you'll notice that you can express each of them using the notational convention of a matrix. In particular, each operation can be expressed as:

$$T(x,y) = \begin{pmatrix} x' \\ y' \end{pmatrix} = \begin{pmatrix} m_{00} & m_{01} \\ m_{10} & m_{11} \end{pmatrix} \begin{pmatrix} x \\ y \end{pmatrix} + \begin{pmatrix} xoff \\ yoff \end{pmatrix}$$

(Equation 6-8)

where an *(x,y)* coordinate pair is represented as a *column vector*. The matrix *m* is defined by its coefficients, where each coefficient is identified by the row (first index) and column (second index) of where it is in the matrix. The matrix *m* multiplies the column vector using the standard rules for matrix multiplication:

$$x' = m_{00} * x + m_{01} * y + xoff$$
$$y' = m_{10} * x + m_{11} * y + yoff$$

(Equation 6-9)

Each row of the matrix transforms the column vector by multiplying one element at a time and summing the results. The column vector *(xoff, yoff)* is added to the column vector that resulted from multiplying the matrix using vector addition. *Vector addition* simply means to add the coordinates from the two vectors together. So far, using matrices and vectors is just a notational convention that provides a more succinct way of expressing a transformation. You can express the transformation in Equation 6-8 even more compactly if you use a 3 x 3 matrix instead of a 2 x 2 matrix and add the constant 1 as the third element of all your *(x,y)* column vectors. Equation 6-8 then becomes:

$$T(x,y) = \begin{pmatrix} x' \\ y' \\ 1 \end{pmatrix} = \begin{pmatrix} m_{00} & m_{01} & xoff \\ m_{10} & m_{11} & yoff \\ 0 & 0 & 1 \end{pmatrix} \begin{pmatrix} x \\ y \\ 1 \end{pmatrix}$$

(Equation 6-10)

Notice that now the translation offset is represented by *(xoff, yoff)* in the third column of the matrix. The next step is to find the matrix coefficients for each of the four types of transformations. You can do this directly from each of the definitions. The coefficients of each matrix are determined by identifying the matching terms of the transformation from their respective equations with the terms in Equation 6-9. Once you have determined how to create the appropriate matrices, you'll see how these transformations may be applied to all the graphic objects you have seen so far, creating a far more flexible and comprehensive graphics toolkit.

Translation matrix

The matrix for translating a vector is:

$$T_{trans}(x,y) = \begin{pmatrix} 1 & 0 & xoff \\ 0 & 1 & yoff \\ 0 & 0 & 1 \end{pmatrix}$$

(Equation 6-11)

Scaling matrix

The matrix for scaling a vector is:

$$T_{scale}(x,y) = \begin{pmatrix} xscale & 0 & 0 \\ 0 & yscale & 0 \\ 0 & 0 & 1 \end{pmatrix}$$

(Equation 6-12)

By convention, it is assumed that both *xscale* and *yscale* are greater than zero.

Reflection matrix

The matrix for reflecting coordinates (changing their sign) is:

$$T_{xrefl}(x,y) = \begin{pmatrix} -1 & 0 & 0 \\ 0 & 1 & 0 \\ 0 & 0 & 1 \end{pmatrix}, T_{yrefl}l(x,y) = \begin{pmatrix} 1 & 0 & 0 \\ 0 & -1 & 0 \\ 0 & 0 & 1 \end{pmatrix}$$

(Equation 6-13)

Rotation matrix

The matrix for rotating a vector by an angle A is:

$$T_{rot}(x, y) = \begin{pmatrix} cos(A) & -sin(A) & 0 \\ sin(A) & cos(A) & 0 \\ 0 & 0 & 1 \end{pmatrix}$$

(Equation 6-14)

Multiple Transformations

Now that you have a convenient notation for your transformations, you can look at what happens when two transformations are combined. You can see the results by applying Equation 6-9 twice. This gives you the following equation for combining transformations T_1 and T_2, in which you first apply T_1 followed by T_2 (in order to simplify the notation, you use the symbol b for the matrix coefficients of T_1 and the symbol a for the matrix coefficients of T_2):

$$T_2(T_1(x,y)) = T_2(b_{00} * x + b_{01} * y + xoff_1, b_{10} * x + b_{11} * y + yoff_1)$$

$$= [a_{00} * (b_{00} * x + b_{01} * y + xoff_1) + a_{01} * (b_{10} * x + b_{11} * y + yoff_1) + xoff_2),$$
$$a_{10} * (b_{00} * x + b_{01} * y + xoff_1) + a_{11} * (b_{10} * x + b_{11} * y + yoff_1) + yoff_2)]$$

$$= [(a_{00} * b_{00} + a_{00} * b_{10}) * x + (a_{00} * b_{01} + a_{01} * b_{11}) * y + a_{00} * xoff_1 + a_{01} * yoff_1 + xoff_2,$$
$$(a_{10} * b_{00} + a_{11} * b_{10}) * x + (a_{10} * b_{01} + a_{11} * b_{11}) * y + a_{10} * xoff_1 + a_{11} * yoff_1 + yoff_2]$$

(Equation 6-15)

Notice that the final result represents another matrix transformation:

$$T_{total}(x, y) = T_2(T_1(x, y)) =$$

$$\begin{pmatrix} a_{00} * b_{00} + a_{01} * b_{10} & a_{00} * b_{01} + a_{01} * b_{11} & a_{00} * xoff_1 + a_{01} * yoff_1 + xoff_2 \\ a_{10} * b_{00} + a_{11} * b_{10} & a_{10} * b_{01} + a_{11} * b_{11} & a_{10} * xoff_1 + a_{11} * yoff_1 + yoff_2 \\ 0 & 0 & 1 \end{pmatrix} \begin{pmatrix} x \\ y \\ 1 \end{pmatrix}$$

(Equation 6-16)

The result of the previous equation is very useful. It means that the combination of any two affine transformations is itself an affine transformation. By repeatedly applying this rule, combining any number of affine transformations results in a single affine transformation. The single transformation matrix may then be applied to your coordinates, which gives you the same result as if you had applied each transformation separately. This greatly reduces the amount of computation you have to perform when applying multiple transformations.

Equation 6-16 is exactly what you would expect if you are familiar with the rules of matrix multiplication. In fact, you can easily extend Equation 6-16 by adding a more general bottom row (something other than 0 0 1) to give you the general rule for multiplying matrices: If $C = A * B$, where A and B are matrices, then the element in the ith row and jth column of C is given by the formula:

$$c_{ij} = a_{0i} * b_{j0} + a_{1i} * b_{j1} + a_{2i} * b_{j2}$$

(Equation 6-17a)

$$c_{ij} = \sum_{k=0}^{2} a_{ki} * b_{jk}$$

(Equation 6-17b)

Equation 6-17b is an easier way of expressing how to compute elements of C when the matrices are larger than 3 x 3. In general, k is summed from zero to the number of rows (minus one) in the matrix.

The Matrix and Vector Library

The *glinalg.c* module provides a library of routines for manipulating matrices and column vectors. The two basic data types are *gVector* for column vectors and *gMatrix* for matrices. The library is currently coded only to support 3 x 3 matrices and $(x, y, 1)$ column vectors, but it can be easily generalized for other applications.

In addition to the basic *Create*, *Copy*, and *Delete* functions for both types, there are functions that correspond to each transformation type and to transforming vectors by matrices. The function *gVectorCreate()* takes two arguments, x and y, and returns a pointer to the created *gVector* structure. The *gMatrix-*

Create() function takes no arguments; it returns an *identity* matrix. The identity matrix transforms *(x,y)* into *(x,y)*; that is, it has no effect when used as a transformation. The identity matrix has the same effect on matrices and vectors that multiplying by one does on scalar numbers.

Vector functions

The basic transformation function is *gTransformVector*:

```
gVector *gTransformVector(gMatrix *matrix,
                                    gVector *vecin, gVector *vecout);
```

As you can see, this function takes a vector as input and puts the transformed vector into *vecout*. This function, as do many others throughout the package, allows the output vector to be the *NULL* pointer. If *vecout* is *NULL*, then a new vector is created and returned. Otherwise, the passed argument *vecout* is the return value.

Additionally, these functions are designed to work *in place*, meaning that *vecin* and *vecout* may be pointers to the same vector. The code for this function uses a *static* temporary vector to copy *vecin* before performing any other calculations. In this manner, *gTransformVector()* avoids having to create temporary vector storage every time it is called. This makes *gTransformVector* more efficient, which is quite important since you'll be using it frequently.

To make this function even more all-purpose, you should let the *matrix* pointer be *NULL*. In this case, *vecin* is simply copied to *vecout*. You will make use of this property later to avoid having to constantly check whether or not you are passing a *NULL* pointer to the function.

In addition to the transformation call, vectors may be explicitly set using the following function:

```
gVector *gVectorSet(gVector *vec, float x, float y);
```

If the passed pointer *vec* is *NULL*, then a new vector is created and its elements are set to the values *(x, y, 1)*, just as in *gVectorCreate()*. If *vec* is not *NULL*, then the passed vector is set and the returned value is the same as *vec*. So, *gVectorSet()* can be used to create new vectors, just as *gVectorCreate()* is.

The converse to *gVectorSet()* is:

```
void    gVectorGet(gVector *vec, float *x, float *y);
```

This function sets the variables *x* and *y* to the values stored in the vector *vec*.

Vectors may be added together using:

```
gVector *gVectorCombine(gVector *vec1, gVector *vec2,
                        float a, float b, gVector *vecout);
```

where the resulting vector, *vecout*, is equal to *a * vec1 + b * vec2*. This function allows for a weighted combination of two vectors, but it can be used for simple addition by simply passing *a = 1* and *b = 1*. If either *vec1* or *vec2* is *NULL*, then the function simply does not add the vector. This produces the same effect as if either scale factor is zero. So, a vector may be scaled by a constant simply by passing the vector as *vec1* and *NULL* for *vec2*. To illustrate this, a macro is supplied to negate a vector (multiply each element of the vector by -1) as follows:

```
#define gVectorNegate(vec)    (gVectorCombine((vec), NULL,  \
                                    -1.0, 0.0, vec))
```

As with *gTransformVector()*, *vecout* may be the same as *vec1* or *vec2* if desired.

Matrix functions

The following four functions correspond to the basic transformations:

```
gMatrix *gMatrixTranslate(gMatrix *matrixIn,
                          gMatrix *matrixOut,
                          gVector *offset);
gMatrix *gMatrixScale(gMatrix *matrixIn,
                          gMatrix *matrixOut,
                          gVector *scale_factors);
```

```
gMatrix *gMatrixRotate(gMatrix *matrixIn,
                               gMatrix *matrixOut,
                               float angle);
gMatrix *gMatrixReflect(gMatrix *matrixIn,
                               gMatrix *matrixOut,
                               int xreflect, int yreflect);
```

As with the vectors, each function takes an input matrix, multiplies it by the appropriate transformation matrix, and stores it in the matrix pointed to by *matrixOut*. Any of these functions may be passed a *NULL* pointer for *matrixIn*; in which case, the function creates an identity matrix and applies the specified transformation to that matrix. Additionally, any of the functions may be passed a *NULL* pointer for *matrixOut*. If that happens, a new matrix is created, set to the result of the operation, and the pointer of the newly created matrix is returned. A complex transformation is created by making an initial matrix (usually the identity) and calling the appropriate functions from the previous sequence.

The functions *gMatrixTranslate()* and *gMatrixScale()* use vectors to pass their arguments. The first element of the vector sets the *x*-offset while the second sets the *y*-offset. This makes these functions easier to generalize to vectors and matrices with dimensions greater than three. For instance, if you want to translate an object and then rotate it, you can create the necessary matrix with a program segment such as:

```
gMatrix *matrix;
gVector *offset;
float  xoff,yoff,angle;

offset = gVectorSet(NULL, xoff, yoff);
matrix = gMatrixTranslate(NULL, NULL, offset);
gMatrixRotate(matrix, matrix, angle);
```

Notice that you do not need to use the return value of *gMatrixRotate()* in this example because you are performing an in-place operation. You also did not need to create the matrix explicitly; *gMatrixTranslate()* did that when you passed a *NULL* for both the *matrixIn* and *matrixOut* arguments.

The *angle* passed to *gMatrixRotate()* is specified in degrees. The rotation angle is positive for counter-clockwise rotation, corresponding to the normal mathematical definition of an angle. The arguments *xreflect* and *yreflect* of *gMatrixReflect()* are either zero or one, depending on whether the matrix should be reflected about the *x*- or *y*-axis respectively.

The previous functions let you create a new matrix from a series of transformation steps. You will, however, need to combine two matrices using matrix multiplication. This is provided by the cleverly named function *gMatrixMultiply()*:

```
gMatrix *gMatrixMultiply(gMatrix *matrix1,
                         gMatrix *matrix2,
                         gMatrix *matrixOut);
```

This function multiplies the passed matrices in the order *matrix1* * *matrix2*. As with the transformation functions, if *matrixOut* is *NULL*, then a new matrix is created. Otherwise, the contents of *matrixOut* are replaced by the results of the multiplication. If either argument is *NULL*, then the non-*NULL* matrix is simply copied to the output matrix. If both *matrix1* and *matrix2* are *NULL*, *gMatrixMultiply()* creates and returns an identity matrix.

Matrix utilities

In addition to the previous functions, you'll also learn several functions that will be useful later. The function *gMatrixSetTranslation()* sets the translation offsets of the passed matrix to the values of the passed vector. It has arguments and functions similar to those of *gMatrixTranslate()* except *gMatrixSetTranslation()* forces the translation offset (third column) to the values in the passed vector. In effect, it removes any previous translation transformations and replaces them with the one specified by the vector argument.

Similarly, the function *gMatrixGetTranslation()* creates and returns a vector corresponding to the third column of the transformation matrix. Its only argument is the matrix with the translation offset that is needed. This function is useful with other functions that try to remove any translation offset before applying and then resetting the matrix using *gMatrixSetTranslation()*.

There are occasions when you may need to transform all the points in a polygon or polyline. The function *gTransformPoints()* does this. It takes a pointer to a matrix, a pointer to an array of *gPoint* elements, and the number of elements of the array as arguments. This function takes each point, transforms it using the passed matrix, and then puts the transformed values back into the array. The values in the passed *gPoint* array are overwritten; so you must remember to copy the polygon or polyline and use *gTransformPoints()* on the copied object if you want to save the original polygon. *gTransformPoints()* is often used by other polygon processing functions that must process all the vertices multiple times. It saves computation time by only performing the transformation once for each vertex and saving the results rather than transforming each vertex several times.

Matrices and Objects

If you examine the header files for each of the geometric objects defined in the previous chapters (rectangle, circle, ellipse, polygon, and so on), you'll notice that they all possess a *gMatrix* pointer. This has not been needed until this point since the *gMatrix* data type has not been introduced yet. This pointer is used by the various drawing and manipulation routines to define a transformed object.

When an object is initially created, a *gMatrix* pointer is set to *NULL*. If the pointer remains *NULL*, then there is no transformation to apply. But if the pointer is not *NULL*, then the object is to be transformed using the matrix before any other processing, such as drawing, is performed. This provides a powerful means of transforming objects in an all-purpose way. Using this approach, you do not need to provide separate types like *rotatedEllipse* or *rotatedPolygon* for each geometric object. Instead, you use a matrix to specify a transformation that is applicable to any type.

For example, you can create a rotated ellipse by creating a normal ellipse centered at the origin, and then by creating a suitable rotation matrix. The ellipse may then be positioned anywhere on the screen. You then apply a translation matrix to the rotation matrix using the function *gMatrixTranslate*. As you'll see in the next section, it is quite important to apply the matrices in the

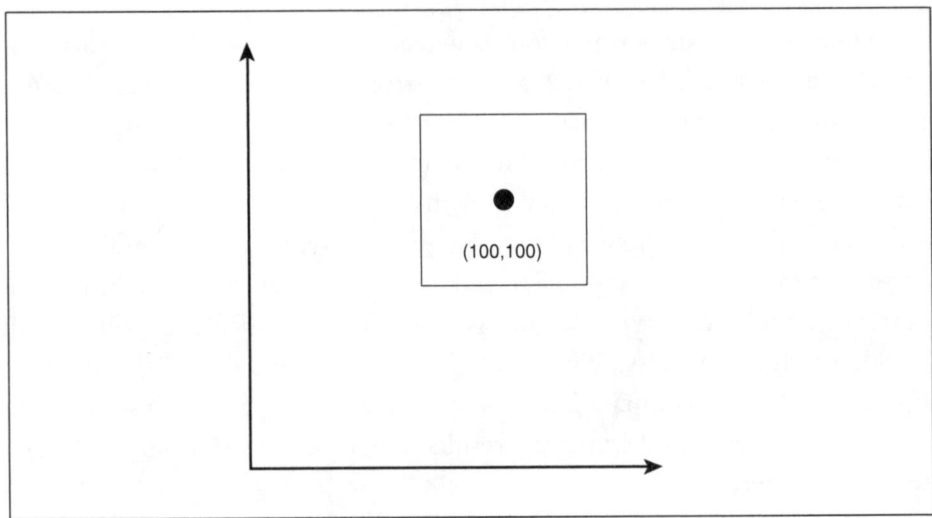

Figure 6-2. A square centered around point (100, 100)

proper order. If the translation were used first, followed by the rotation matrix, the ellipse would end up in a totally different part of the screen.

As previously mentioned in this book, you've implemented most of the algorithms to, as much as possible, try and create an object-oriented environment. The inclusion of the matrix pointer with each geometric type you define is a good example of how *class inheritance* is used. In an object-oriented language, such as C++, you define a base class *gObject*, and derive each of your types from this class. The base class would contain the matrix pointer and methods for manipulating it. These methods could then be used automatically with any of the derived classes. With C, you simply include the matrix pointer as part of each new object you create.

Rotation about The Center of an Object

As mentioned earlier, the three transformations of scaling, reflection, and rotation are all relative to the origin. You usually want to transform an object relative to some other point, for example, its center. Figure 6-2 shows a simple square that can be rotated 45 degrees to make a diamond shape. As the figure illustrates, the center is at (100, 100). If you transform the object directly using the appropriate rotation matrix, you'll create the figure shown in Figure 6-3.

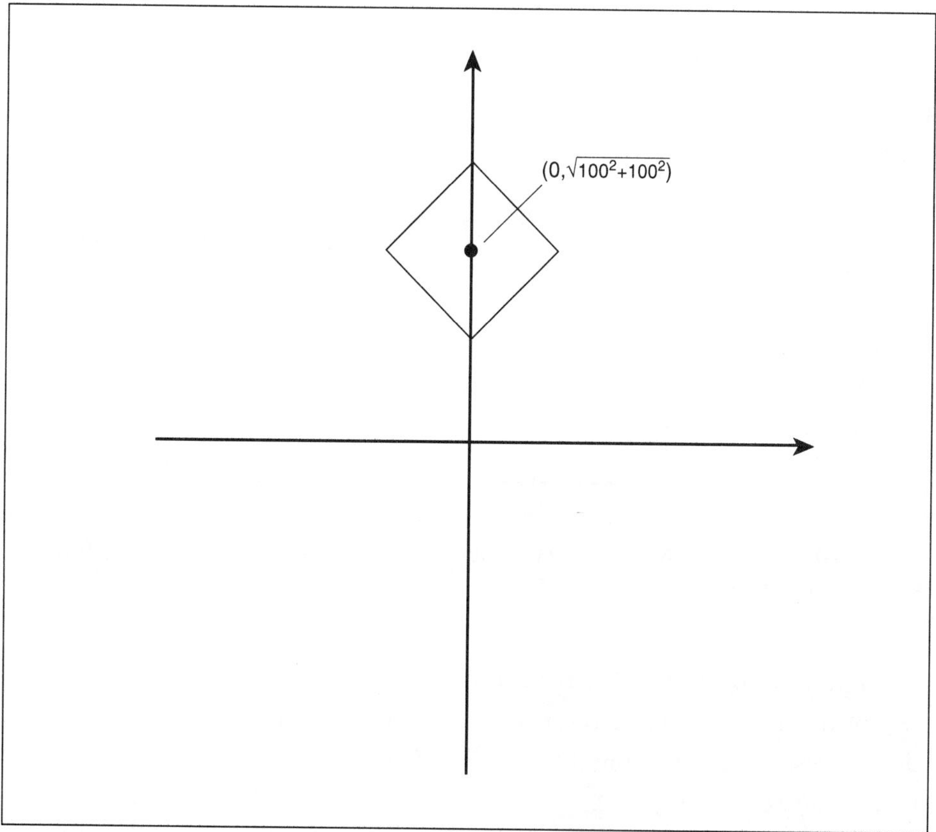

Figure 6-3. Same square rotated by 45 degrees with respect to (0,0). Note that the center of the square has moved as well.

Although the object is correctly oriented, it has now moved because the center of the object has also rotated by 45 degrees with respect to the origin. To correct this problem, you must perform the following three transformations:

1. Translate the object so that its center is at the origin. In the previous example, this corresponds to applying offsets of (-100, -100).
2. Rotate the object by 45 degrees.
3. Translate the object back to its original position by applying the opposite translation from the first transformation. You apply a translation of (100, 100) for the previous example.

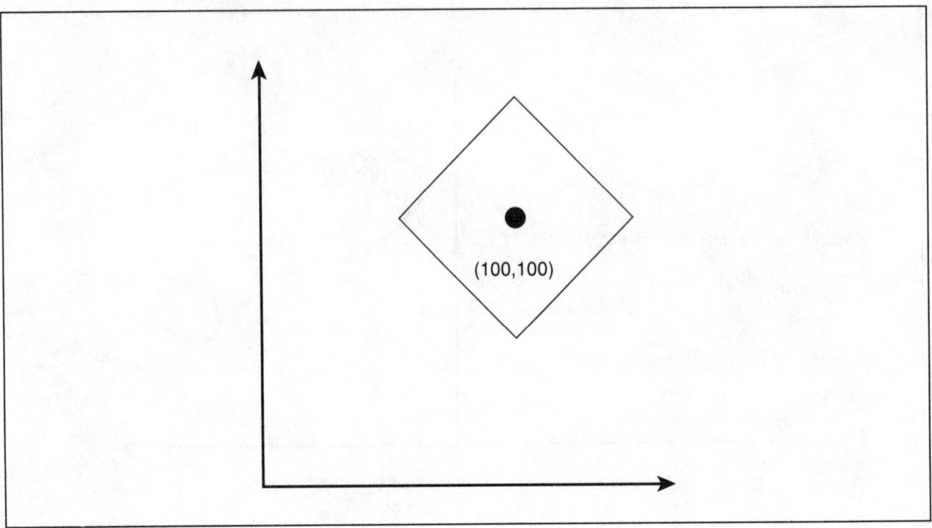

Figure 6-4. Square rotated about its center at (100,100) using the combined three-step transformation

You need to create these three transformations, combine them in the *correct* order, and then apply the resulting transformation to the object for the desired result as shown in Figure 6-4. The C segment that generates the appropriate transformation is:

```
gMatrix *matrix;

matrix = gMatrixTranslate(NULL, NULL, -100, -100);
gMatrixRotate(matrix, matrix, 45.0);
gMatrixTranslate(matrix, matrix, 100, 100);
```

The exact same steps apply to the scaling and reflection operations. The object must be translated so that whichever axis you want to scale or reflect about (*x* or *y*, or both), passes through the object's center point (or whichever point you want to scale the object around).

A Question of Scale

Scaling is only one of the three transformations that can actually affect the shape of an object. If both *x* and *y* are identically scaled, then the shape will remain the same. For example, if you scale a circle by two in both axes, you will get a circle with a radius twice as large. However, if you scale the circle in just one axis, you create an ellipse.

Combining rotation and scaling can also distort the object so it no longer has the same properties as the original object. For instance, if you take a square and rotate it 45 degrees, you create a diamond. If the diamond is then stretched horizontally, the new shape no longer has right angles at the four corners. As with the rotation, you must be careful about the order in which transformations are applied in order to create the desired result. Suppose you have a rotated square that you would like to convert into a rotated rectangle. The transformations to accomplish this are:

1. Rotate the square by the *negative* rotation angle to realign it with the *x*- and *y*-axes
2. Scale the square horizontally (or vertically)
3. Rotate the object back to its original position by applying the opposite rotation from the first step

You'd get a very different shape if you skipped the first and third steps. Instead of a rotated rectangle, you get a squashed diamond! As with rotating an object about its center point, you can easily create a single transformation matrix to accomplish the previous actions:

```
gMatrix *matrix;
gVector *scale;

matrix = gMatrixRotate(NULL, NULL, -angle);
scale = gVectorSet(NULL, xscale, yscale);
gMatrixScale(matrix, matrix, scale);
gMatrixRotate(matrix, matrix, angle);
```

Figuring the order of transformations is often quite confusing, and it is even more confusing when dealing with more than two dimensions. The demonstration program at the end of this chapter explains some of the effects that changing the order of the operations will have. But even if you get the order wrong, it is usually an easy program bug to find because the results will be obviously wrong when drawn to the screen!

Drawing Transformed Objects

Now that you have the appropriate matrix tools, you can look at how to draw transformed objects. The simplest ones to transform are those consisting only of straight-line segments or points. So far, you've seen points, rectangles, polygons, and polylines. Drawing transformed versions of these objects is quite straightforward. The drawing procedure for a transformed polygon is:

```
gVector *vertex;                /* Stores current vertex */
gPolygon *poly;
float x, y, lastx, lasty;
int i;
gColor color;

/* Get first point */
vertex = gVectorSet(NULL, poly->points[0].x,
                     poly->points[0].y);
gTransformVector(poly->matrix, vertex, vertex);
gVectorGet(vertex, &lastx, &lasty);
for(i=1; i<=poly->npoints; i++) {
 /* Get ready to transform the next vertex */
 vertex = gVectorSet(vertex, poly->points[i].x,
                     poly->points[i].y);
 /* Transform it */
 gTransformVector(poly->matrix, vertex, vertex);
 gVectorGet(vertex, &x, &y);
 gLineDraw(ROUND(lastx), ROUND(lasty),
                ROUND(x), ROUND(y), color);
 lastx = x;
 lasty = y;
}
```

This procedure works even if *poly->matrix* is *NULL* since *gTransformVector()* is defined to simply copy the vector in that case. This procedure loops through all the points in the polygon, transforming each point, and drawing the line segment between the current point and previous (transformed) point. For polygons, you must loop through *poly->npoints + 1* points to make sure that you draw the connection between the first and last vertices.

You use an almost identical procedure to draw transformed points, rectangles, and polylines. Now, what about drawing transformed curves as found with the circles and ellipses from Chapter 5? There are several alternatives, but let's first see how the four basic affine transformations affect a curve.

The three transformations translation, rotation, and reflection all possess the property that they will not affect the size of the object. The object's size and shape remains the same after the transformation; it's just at a different location and/or orientation on the screen. As mentioned earlier, only the scaling operation can affect the actual shape of an object. The object generally retains the same basic properties, even after it has been scaled. An ellipse is still an ellipse, even after it has been stretched in one or both directions. A circle, however, becomes an ellipse if it is scaled differently in the x- and y-axes. That is why the ellipse is described as a generalization of the circle and has a similar structure to the circle.

Unfortunately, our efficient drawing algorithms developed in Chapter 5 only work with circles and ellipses that are aligned with the x- and y-axes. They typically won't work for an arbitrarily transformed ellipse. But fear not, recall how you developed both a polyline-approximation method and a parametric-approximation method for creating these curves. The parametric method is a powerful and compact means of representing any type of shape. Let's see how you can draw a transformed, parametrically defined shape.

Drawing Parametric Curves

Recall that a parametric curve is represented by two functions of an intermediate variable, t. The two functions are referred to as $x(t)$ and $y(t)$. As you saw in Chapter 5, many types of commonly drawn curves may be represented as parametric curves. The circle, ellipse, and even the line segment can be represented very compactly in a parametric format. In fact, many types of curves can only be represented parametrically, as illustrated by the circle and the ellipse in Chapter 5.

But a parametric curve need not be smooth like the circle and ellipse. The polygon and polyline are parametric curves as well, defined as a sequence of connected line segments. It is often necessary to compute a polygonal approximation to a curve in order to draw it. It is therefore worth some effort to consider performing this kind of conversion and, in general, how to draw parametric curves efficiently.

You can assume that the complete curve is defined by plotting values of *t* ranging from zero to one. You can plot the curve by choosing a small increment, *tinc* for *t*, and step from zero to one in increments of *tinc*. For each point, you can compute a new coordinate (*x(t)*, *y(t)*) and connect the current point with the previous one. The following procedure shows how this is implemented. Note that in this procedure, the parametric functions for *x* and *y* are shown as *xcurve(t)* and *ycurve(t)* respectively.

```
gVector *vertex;                /* Stores current vertex */
gMatrix *matrix;                /* Transform matrix */
float x, y;
int newx, newy, lastx, lasty;
float t, tinc;
gColor color;

/* Get first point */
vertex = gVectorSet(NULL, xcurve(0), ycurve(0));
gTransformVector(matrix, vertex, vertex);
gVectorGet(vertex, &x, &y);
lastx = ROUND(x); lasty = ROUND(y);
for(t=0.0; t <= 1.0; t += tinc) {
 vertex = gVectorSet(vertex, xcurve(MIN(t, 1.0),
                     ycurve(MIN(t, 1.0)));
 /* Transform it */
 gTransformVector(matrix, vertex, vertex);
 gVectorGet(vertex, &x, &y);
 newx = ROUND(x); newy = ROUND(y);
 /* Only draw it if this point is different */
 if(newx != lastx || newy != lasty) {
```

```
    gLineDraw(lastx, lasty, newx, newy, color);
    lastx = newx;
    lasty = newy;
  }
 /* Make sure last point is drawn */
 vertex = gVectorSet(vertex, xcurve(1.0), ycurve(1.0));
 gTransformVector(matrix, vertex, vertex);
 newx = ROUND(x); newy = ROUND(y);
 if(newx != lastx || newy != lasty) {
  gLineDraw(lastx, lasty, newx, newy, color);
 }

 }
```

This procedure is very similar to the one you just examined for drawing polygons. You must ensure that t does not exceed one; otherwise, you would overshoot the end of the curve. You must also make certain that the curve is always drawn to the endpoint at $t = 1$. Depending on the value of *tinc* and the particular curve you are drawing, you may get a lot of duplicate points due to integer rounding. That's why you have placed an *if* statement to see if the next transformed point is different from the last point in either the x- or y-coordinate. If it is, then you draw a new line segment between the two points. This type of check often avoids unnecessary drawing.

In order to make an accurate representation of the object, you must find a suitable value for *tinc*. It is somewhat like the children's story "Goldilocks and The Three Bears." If *tinc* is too small, you'll perform a lot of unnecessary calculations; if it is too large, your smooth curve will look too polygonal (too many sharp corners). You want to find the value that is just right.

As mentioned in the previous chapter, you can choose a reasonable value for *tinc* if you know or can estimate the length of the curve. For simple curves like the circle and ellipse, this is easy since you have simple formulas available to find the length of the curve. The trick is to figure out how a transformation affects the length of the curve. A simple way to do this is to use your initial value of *tinc* and process the curve as shown in the previous procedure. Instead of drawing the curve, you compute the length of each line segment you would draw. Summing all the lengths gives you a reasonable estimate of the trans-

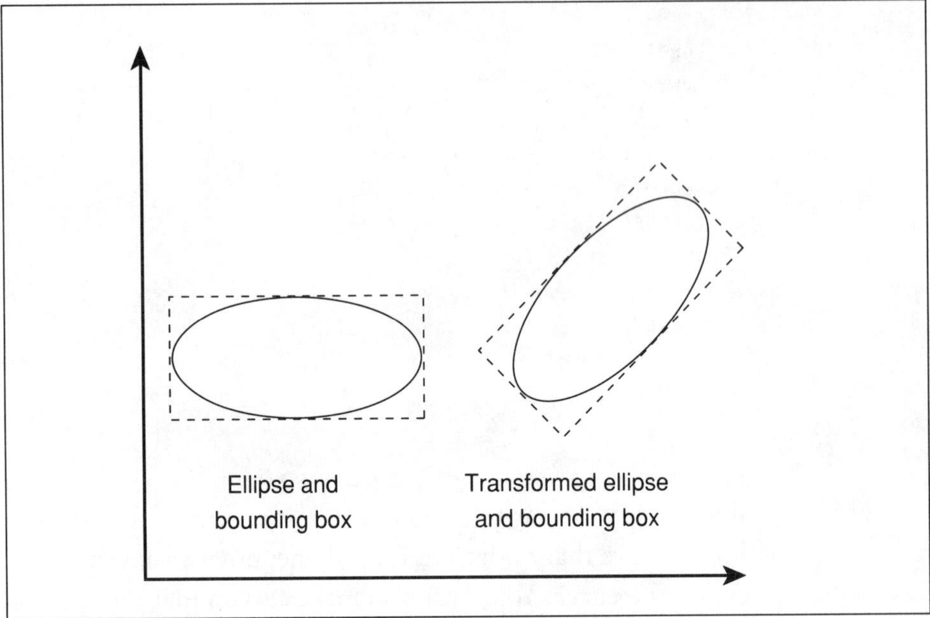

Figure 6-5. On the left, a nonrotated ellipse and its corresponding bounding box. On the right, the same ellipse rotated 45 degrees and the transformed bounding box.

formed curve's length. You can then compute a new value of *tinc* suitable for drawing the curve using *1.0/transformed_length*. This approach has the drawback that it requires processing the curve twice, which may be an expensive computational process. You can, however, estimate how the length will change by transforming a much simpler object that is related to the desired curve, or boundary of a graphic object known as the bounding box.

In Figure 6-5, a sample ellipse with its bounding box is shown on the left side of the figure and a typical transformation of the same ellipse and bounding box is shown on the right. The transformed ellipse always remains within the transformed bounding box. Because you are using affine transformations, you can look at how the transformation affects the size of the bounding box and then compare the size of the original box to the transformed box.

The ratio of the length of the box perimeter will be very close to (and in many cases, exactly the same as) the ratio of the corresponding curve lengths. It is not necessary to transform the actual bounding box of the curve. Again, since the transformation is affine, you can look at how the transformation affects any box that is convenient, such as a simple unit square.

The ratio of the original perimeter length to the transformed length will be the same as comparing the transformed bounding boxes. So now you must determine how the unit square is transformed by a given matrix. A rectangle is transformed just like any other polygon. To compute the transformed perimeter length, you should transform all four vertices of the rectangle, compute the lengths of each side, and sum them. The ratio between the original length to the transformed length is called the *scaling ratio*. Listing 6-4 shows a function for finding this ratio given a transformation matrix.

```
float FindScalingRatio(gMatrix *matrix)
{
gVector *vertex[4];
float x1, y1, x2, y2, length, ratio;

/* Check for NULL matrix; assume it is the identity */
if(matrix == NULL)
 return 1.0;

/* Transform the 4 corners of the unit square */
vertex[0] = gVectorSet(NULL, 0.0, 0.0);
gVectorTransform(matrix, vertex[0], vertex[0]);
vertex[1] = gVectorSet(NULL, 0.0, 1.0);
gVectorTransform(matrix, vertex[1], vertex[1]);
vertex[2] = gVectorSet(NULL, 1.0, 1.0);
gVectorTransform(matrix, vertex[2], vertex[2]);
vertex[3] = gVectorSet(NULL, 1.0, 0.0);
gVectorTransform(matrix, vertex[3], vertex[3]);

gVectorGet(vertex[0], &x1, &y1);
length = 0.0;
for(i=1; i<=3; i++) {
 gVectorGet(vertex[i], &x2, &y2);
 /* Now add to the length */
 length += sqrt( (x2-x1)*(x2-x1) + (y2-y1)*(y2-y1));
 x1 = x2; y1 = y2;
```

```
}

/* Now compute the scaling ratio */
/* Unit square has perimeter length of 4 */
ratio = 4.0 / length;
gVectorDelete(vertex);

return ratio;
}
```

Listing 6-4. Finding the scaling ratio using a bounding box

Once the scaling ratio is found, modify the value of *tinc* used in drawing the transformed curve by multiplying it by the scaling ratio. The larger the object becomes, the smaller the scaling ratio will be and the finer the increment *tinc* should be. If you don't rescale the increment, the curve would look more and more polygonal as it is scaled larger.

Drawing Transformed Circles and Ellipses

Given this approach, you can now create a procedure for drawing transformed circles and ellipses. You should note that a circle can be transformed into an ellipse by simply scaling the circle. In fact, you can think of any ellipse as just a transformation of the unit circle. You only need one drawing routine that can be applied to transformed circles or ellipses. So first, let's look at the function for drawing a transformed circle, shown in Listing 6-5.

```
void gCircleDrawTransformed(gCircle *circle)
{
gMatrix *matrix;                    /* Transform matrix */
float x, y;
int newx, newy, lastx, lasty;
float t, tinc;
gColor color;

ratio = FindScalingRatio(circle->matrix);
/* Get first point */
```

```
tinc = (1.0 / circle->radius) * ratio;
vertex = gVectorSet(NULL, circle->radius + circle->x, circle->y);
gTransformVector(circle->matrix, vertex, vertex);
gVectorGet(vertex, &x, &y);
lastx = ROUND(x); lasty = ROUND(y);
/* t represents an angle in radians, running from 0 to 2 * PI */
for(t=0.0; t <= 2.0*PI; t += tinc) {
 xp = circle->radius * cos(MIN(t, 2*PI));
 yp = circle->radius * sin(MIN(t, 2*PI));
 vertex = gVectorSet(vertex, xp, yp);
 /* Transform it */
 gTransformVector(matrix, vertex, vertex);
 gVectorGet(vertex, &x, &y);
 newx = ROUND(x); newy = ROUND(y);
 /* Only draw it if this point is different */
 if(newx != lastx || newy != lasty) {
  gLineDraw(lastx, lasty, newx, newy, color);
  lastx = newx;
  lasty = newy;
 }
}
/* Make sure last point is drawn */
vertex = gVectorSet(vertex, circle->radius + circle->x, circle->y);
gTransformVector(circle->matrix, vertex, vertex);
newx = ROUND(x); newy = ROUND(y);
if(newx != lastx || newy != lasty) {
 gLineDraw(lastx, lasty, newx, newy, color);
}
```

Listing 6-5. Drawing a transformed circle by parametric approximation

You can use this same routine to draw a transformed ellipse by creating a circle with a transformation matrix that is the product of two matrices, or the transformation of the ellipse multiplied by the transformation that converts a circle into an ellipse, which is simple scaling. The completed drawing routine is shown in Listing 6-6.

```
void gEllipseDrawTransformed(gEllipse *ellipse)
{
gCircle *circle;
gMatrix *matrix;
gVector *scale;

/* Get the scaling for the ellipse */
scale = gVectorSet(NULL, ellipse->a, ellipse->b);
/* Now create a scaling matrix. This converts a unit circle into
   the ellipse */
matrix = gMatrixScale(NULL, NULL, scale);
/* Now combine with whatever transformation the ellipse has */
matrix = gMatrixMultiply(ellipse->matrix, matrix, matrix);
/* Finally, create a unit circle with this transformation */
circle = gCircleCreate(NULL, 1.0, ellipse->x, ellipse->y);
circle->matrix = matrix;

gCircleDrawTransformed(circle);
gVectorDelete(scale);
gCircleDelete(circle);

return;
}
```

Listing 6-6. The function gEllipseDrawTransformed() for drawing a transformed ellipse

An application does not use either of these routines directly. Instead, it simply uses *gCircleDraw()* or *gEllipseDraw()* as appropriate. These routines then verify if a transformation should be applied by checking if the *matrix* pointer in these structures is *NULL* or not. If they are *NULL*, then you can use the drawing routines from the previous chapter. Otherwise, you must use the drawing routines for transformed objects shown previously.

Although you have not done so, these routines could also be modified to check if the transformation does not involve a rotation. If it doesn't, then you could use our ellipse-drawing routine from Chapter 5. Scaling an ellipse just scales the parameters *a* and *b*. Translation and reflection of a circle or an ellipse moves the center. So, you could create a new, transformed ellipse that is still aligned with the *x*- and *y*-axes. This would be faster to draw, but it is less general than the transformed ellipse-drawing procedure already discussed.

Drawing Other Parametric Curves

With only small modifications, the previous procedure can be used for any parametrically defined curve, such as polynomials and the various types of splines. The name *spline* is derived from the long flexible strips of metal used by draftpersons to lay out curved surfaces on cars, airplanes, and ships. Small weights, called *ducks* are used to pull the spline in various directions.

By analogy, a graphics spline is a curve in which a series of *control points* are used to pull the curve in a particular direction. The parametric-curve drawing techniques that you have used so far are generally not used in drawing splines. Instead of transforming each point along the curve, as you did for the previous parametric curves, only the control points are transformed. The equation of the curve can then be directly derived from the transformed control points. This is a more efficient means of transforming these types of curves. However, drawing the curve based on the control points is considerably more complicated than any of the examples you have seen so far. Several of the references listed in the bibliography provide more detailed descriptions for drawing splines and other types of polynomial curves.

You'll be studying the method for drawing transformed objects that suffers from requiring considerably more floating-point arithmetic than the integer algorithms of the previous chapter. But what you lose in speed, you'll gain in flexibility. As floating-point processing becomes more comparable to integer-processing speed, this becomes much less of an issue. It is important to note that the specialized algorithms of the previous chapter were developed specifically to maximize the drawing efficiency of the most common geometric objects, because a lot of drawings use those objects all the time.

When it becomes worth the effort, you will be able to create speciality routines to more efficiently draw the objects that you need, using similar approaches as those derived for the circle and ellipse. This will always be the trade-off between efficiency and generality.

The Power of Transformations

While the types of transformations you have explored let you manipulate geometric objects in a number of ways, it is not really clear why this is especially useful. True, you can now rotate, rescale, and move an object around the screen, but this could have been accomplished directly, without resorting to matrices. You could have simply created the *rotatedEllipse* and *rotatedPolygon* types and be done with it. You've already examined one reason why not to do this: namely it creates a lot of unnecessary duplication of effort when defining new geometric objects. Let's look at some of the other significant advantages.

Rescaling a drawing

Suppose you have some complicated architectural or engineering drawing that consists of many circles, arrows, polygons, and objects too numerous to mention. You have plotted it full scale on the screen and now you want to zoom in on a particular section, say by a factor of five. It would be most undesirable to have your program go in and actually rescale all the objects that make up the drawing. Instead, let's create a transformation that can do the work for us.

The user selects a point in the drawing to zoom in on, say at the point *(x,y)*. The zoom by five can be accomplished using the following three steps:

```
gMatrix *zoom_matrix;
gVector *offset, *scale;
float         x, y, xc, yc;

offset = gVectorSet(NULL, -x, -y);
/* First, center the drawing around (x, y) */
zoom_matrix = gMatrixTranslate(NULL, NULL, offset);
/* Now, zoom by 5 */
scale = gVectorSet(NULL, 5.0, 5.0);
zoom_matrix = gMatrixScale(zoom_matrix, zoom_matrix, scale);
```

```
/* Now put this in the center of the screen */
xc = GetMaxX() / 2;
yc = GetMaxY() / 2;
offset = gVectorSet(offset, xc, yc);
zoom_matrix = gMatrixTranslate(zoom_matrix, zoom_matrix,
                               offset);
```

The first step sets the center of the transformation to be about the point *(x, y)*. The second step then scales everything by a factor of five, with the scaling centered about the point *(x, y)*. The last step puts the point *(x, y)* in the center of the screen. Now, what if you want to zoom in again? To do this, you can use the previous algorithm, except you must change the first *gMatrixTranslate()* call to use *zoom_matrix* instead of *NULL*:

```
zoom_matrix = gMatrixTranslate(zoom_matrix, zoom_matrix,offset);
```

Our application simply retains the current *zoom_matrix*, representing the magnification and centering of the whole drawing at any one time. Initially, *zoom_matrix* is simply the identity matrix, so no transformations are in effect and the drawing is at full scale. A complete *zoom-in* function is shown in Listing 6-1. You can zoom out in exactly the same manner and by any desired factor via factors less than one when the vector *scale* is created and set, as shown in the function *zoom_in*.

```
/* Create the transformation to zoom into a drawing */
/* Note that zoom_factor is greater than 1.0 to zoom in
   and less than 1.0 to zoom out */
/* The position (x,y) is always in screen coordinates */

gMatrix *zoom_in(gMatrix *current_zoom,
                 float zoom_factor, float x, float y);
{
float                xc, yc;
gMatrix         *zoom_matrix;
static gVector *offset = NULL,
               *scale = NULL;
offset = gVectorSet(offset, -x, -y);
```

```
/* First, center the drawing around (x, y) */
zoom_matrix = gMatrixTranslate(current_zoom,
                                current_zoom, offset);
/* Now, zoom by zoom_factor */
scale = gVectorSet(scale, zoom_factor, zoom_factor);
zoom_matrix = gMatrixScale(zoom_matrix, zoom_matrix,
                           scale);
/* Now put this in the center of the screen */
xc = GetMaxX() / 2;
yc = GetMaxY() / 2;
offset = gVectorSet(offset, xc, yc);
zoom_matrix = gMatrixTranslate(zoom_matrix, zoom_matrix, offset);

return zoom_matrix;
}
```

Listing 6-1. Listing for the procedure to create a transformation to zoom into or out of a drawing

Given *zoom_matrix*, you can set the transformation matrix for all your objects equal to the zoom matrix and redraw the objects. For example, you can draw all the polygons using the following procedure:

```
gPolygon        *poly, *polylist[100];
gColor   color, polycolors[100];

for(i=0; i<numpolygons; i++) {
 poly = polylist[i];
 color = polycolors[i];
 poly->matrix = zoom_matrix;
 gPolygonDraw(poly, color);
}
```

This works fine as long as the none of the polygons themselves have transformations. But to handle this case, you must modify the procedure as follows:

```
gPolygon       *poly, *polylist[100];
gColor   color, polycolors[100];
gMatrix  *temp_matrix = NULL, *save_matrix;

temp_matrix = gMatrixCreate();
for(i=0; i<numpolygons; i++) {
 poly = polylist[i];
 color = polycolors[i];
/* Save the original polygon matrix */
 save_matrix = poly->matrix;
 poly->matrix = gMatrixMultiply(zoom_matrix, poly->matrix,
                              temp_matrix);
 gPolygonDraw(poly, color);
 poly->matrix = save_matrix;
}
```

Listing 6-2. Procedure for applying a transformation to a list of polygons

Note that because of the way you defined *gMatrixMultiply()*, this function works whether or not the polygons have a transformation. If *poly->matrix* is *NULL*, then it simply copies *zoom_matrix*, which is the desired action in this case.

Changing coordinate systems

Another very common need in drawing objects is to change coordinate systems and/or the units in which you are drawing. For example, you may have an architectural drawing where the units are specified in meters and you want to draw this on the screen. Perhaps, you may want to fit the drawing into a small rectangular window on the screen. Or, the drawing was done in normal Cartesian coordinates with y increasing from bottom to top and you must convert it to screen coordinates. You can perform all these tasks, simultaneously if desired, by constructing the proper transformation matrix.

Suppose you know that a drawing was created in units of inches. This means that all the coordinates will be specified that way, including the centers and radii of circles, polygon vertices, and so on. To fit the drawing onto the screen, you must know the extent of the drawing; that is, how far the drawing extends both vertically and horizontally in inches. This is usually specified using a *bounding box*, which is just a rectangle that contains the entire drawing. Given such a rectangle, how do you fit the drawing to the screen? You can use the procedure shown in Listing 6-3 to construct an appropriate transformation matrix that does the work for you.

```
/* Find the transformation to fit a drawing tothe screen */
gMatrix *FitToScreen(gRectangle *box)
{
gMatrix *tmatrix;
gVector *offset, *scale;
float xlength, ylength, scale;

/* First, move the corner (xmin, ymin) to the origin */
offset = gVectorSet(NULL, -box->xmin, -box->ymin);
tmatrix = gMatrixTranslate(NULL, NULL, offset);
/* Now, scale the two sides to fit onto the screen */
/* Be careful, you must preserve aspect ratio */
/* For simplicity, this assumes the aspect ratio of
   the screen to be 1.0 */
xlength = box->xmax - box->xmin;
ylength = box->ymax - box->ymin;
if(xlength > ylength) {
 scale = GetMaxX() / xlength;
} else {
 scale = GetMaxY() / ylength;
}
scale = gVectorSet(NULL, scale, scale);
tmatrix = gMatrixScale(tmatrix, tmatrix, scale);
/* Assuming the drawing is in a "bottom-up" coordinate
   system, you must flip it in y */
tmatrix = gMatrixReflect(tmatrix, tmatrix, 0, 1);
/* Finally, translate the drawing so that (xmin, ymin)
   is in the lower-left corner of the screen, which is
```

```
    coordinate (0, GetMaxY()-1) */
offset = gVectorSet(offset, 0, (float)(GetMaxY() - 1));
tmatrix = gMatrixTranslate(tmatrix, tmatrix, offset);

return tmatrix;
}
```

Listing 6-3. Procedure for fitting a drawing to a screen using a bounding box. This procedure assumes that y increases from bottom to top for the drawing. If this is not the case, then the call to gMatrixReflect() along with the last call to gMatrix-Translate() should be removed.

The procedure in Listing 6-3 solves several problems simultaneously. It preserves the aspect ratio of the drawing, computes the necessary offset to center the drawing on the screen, and then reflects the coordinates to handle the two different coordinate systems. Furthermore, you accomplish this using very little additional computation. Once the matrix is generated, you apply it to each object in your drawing, just as you did before.

Hierarchical objects

This is a fancy name for the simple operation of grouping objects together and then treating them as a single object. For instance, suppose you wanted to move several circles as one object. Or, you want to spin it about the center of the center circle. Just as in the previous examples, you can do this simply by creating a single rotation matrix (with the appropriate translation to center the rotation in the center circle) and applying this matrix to all of the objects. The procedure is the same as in Listing 6-2. This gives you the flexibility to group objects together any way you wish. All the objects that make up the larger group object may then be manipulated as one, solely by specifying a common matrix that is applied to all of them.

Although you have not done so, it is an interesting extension to the library to add an object type that is, for example, a list of polygons. This object should have its own matrix pointer, just like any other object. The drawing routine for this object is almost identical to that of Listing 6-2. Most advanced drawing programs provide this capability to arbitrarily group objects together. Using affine transformations make this an incredibly easy thing to do.

Multi-dimensional objects

While you will not deal with multiple dimensions explicitly in this book, you can easily extend your matrices to handle any number of dimensions, rather than just the two you are concerned with. In particular, you can manipulate three-dimensional objects in the same manner. All of the rules work the same. Instead of 3 x 3 matrices, you use 4 x 4 matrices. The matrix equations and functions are nearly identical. The exception is rotation, where instead of specifying a single rotation angle, you must specify up to three different rotation angles for rotation around any of the three axes.

As you can see, affine transformations provide the means for performing the elementary graphics operations of translation, scaling, rotation, and reflection in any combination. By using the matrix representation and creating a suitable library, you provide a convenient and efficient means for manipulating objects in a variety of ways. You can also see how many objects are intrinsically related, such as the circle and ellipse, via an affine transformation. By exploiting these relationships, you greatly reduce the number of different functions needed to draw all of the different types of objects you might want to create.

Transformations In Action

The demonstration program *dxform.exe* shows a continuously animated sequence of transforming a polygon. The screen is divided into four separate windows on the screen. The first three windows dynamically show the effects of translation, rotation, and scaling as applied to a simple polygonal object. The last window shows all three operations being combined simultaneously.

From the keyboard, you can select the order in which the three transformations are applied. Try it, and observe how big of a difference in appearance the order of applying transformations makes. You should also observe how complex motion can be derived by combining the individually simple transformations in various orders. An interesting modification to this program is to replace the example polygon with circles, ellipses, or other polygons and see how they transform. You will find that a floating-point coprocessor greatly improves the performance of the demonstration.

Off-Screen Behavior

One common effect of transforming objects is that they can often move off the screen. For example, when you magnify a drawing, presumably much of the drawing is not actually drawn on the screen any more. So far, your drawing algorithms have not dealt with this. In the next chapter, you will see how various *clipping* algorithms can be used to gracefully handle off-screen objects.

Functions Found in This Chapter

Demonstration program

`dxform.exe`

This program shows how individual transformations affect a shape and then how the combination of transformations distort an object in several ways.

Vector functions

```
gVector *gVectorCreate(float x, float y);
```

Creates a vector with initial values *x* and *y*.

```
gVector *gVectorCopy(gVector *dest, gVector *source);
```

Copies a *gVector* object.

```
void gVectorDelete(gVector *vector);
```

Deletes a *gVector* object.

```
void gVectorSet(gVector *vector, float x, float y);
```

Sets the elements of a vector to the passed *x*- and *y*-arguments.

```
void gVectorGet(gVector *vector, float *x, float *y);
```

Returns the *x*- and *y*-coordinates of the passed vector.

```
gVector *gVectorCombine(gVector *vec1, gVector *vec2,
                        float a, float b, gVector *vecout);
```

Computes a linear combination of two vectors as: *vecout* = *a* * *vec1* + *b* * *vec2*. The result is stored in *vecout*. If *vecout* is *NULL*, then a new vector is created. If either *vec1* or *vec2* is *NULL*, then they are treated as a zero vector.

Matrix functions

```
gMatrix *gMatrixCreate(void);
```

Creates an identity matrix.

```
gMatrix *gMatrixCopy(gMatrix *dest, gMatrix *source);
```

Copies a *gMatrix* object.

```
void gMatrixDelete(gMatrix *matrix);
```

Deletes a *gMatrix* object.

```
gMatrix *gMatrixTranslate(gMatrix *matrixIn, gMatrix *matrixOut,
                          gVector *offset);
```

Translates a matrix by the offset specified in the vector *offset*. If *matrixIn* is *NULL*, then it is treated as if an identity matrix were passed. If *matrixOut* is *NULL*, then a new matrix is created and the result is stored in this new matrix. Otherwise, the result overwrites the entries in *matrixOut*.

```
gMatrix *gMatrixScale(gMatrix *matrixIn, gMatrix *matrixOut,
                      gVector *scale_factors);
```

Scales the matrix using the scale factors specified in the vector *scale_factors*.

```
gMatrix *gMatrixRotate(gMatrix *matrixIn, gMatrix *matrixOut,
                       float angle);
```

Rotates the matrix by the angle *angle*, expressed in radians. The rotation is positive for counter-clockwise rotation.

```
gMatrix *gMatrixReflect(gMatrix *matrixIn,gMatrix *matrixOut,
                        int xreflect, int yreflect);
```

Reflects the matrix about the *x*-axis if *yreflect* is nonzero, and reflects the matrix about the *y*-axis if *xreflect* is nonzero.

```
gMatrix *gMatrixMultiply(gMatrix *matrix1, gMatrix *matrix2,
                         gMatrix *matrixOut);
```

Multiplies two matrices together and stores the result in *matrixOut*. The matrices are multiplied in the order *matrix1* * *matrix2*. If either *matrix1* or *matrix2* is *NULL*, then they are treated as if they were identify matrices.

```
gVector *gTransformVector(gMatrix *matrix, gVector *vecin,
                          gVector *vecout);
```

Performs the basic matrix-multiplication function on vectors. The result is stored in *vecout*, unless it is *NULL*, in which case a new output vector is created and returned.

```
gMatrix *gMatrixSetTranslation(gMatrix *matrixIn, gMatrix
                               *matrixOut, gVector *offset);
```

Operates in the same manner as *gMatrixTranslate()* except that it forces the translation offset for *matrixIn* to the passed vector *offset*, putting the result into *matrixOut*. In effect, any offset in the passed matrix is removed and replaced with the offset in *offset*.

```
gVector *gMatrixGetTranslation(gMatrix *matrix);
```

Creates and returns a vector with the current translation offset of the passed matrix.

```
void gTransformPoints(gMatrix *matrix, gPoint *points, int
                      npoints);
```

This function transforms an array of *gPoint* elements containing *npoints* entries. This function is quite useful when transforming polygon or polyline coordinates. The *points* array is overwritten so you must be careful to make a copy of the *points* array prior to calling this function if you need to keep the original.

CHAPTER 7

Clipping and Windowing

In the previous chapter, you learned how to move, resize, and reshape graphic objects. One problem with using these operations is that they can often cause part or all of an object to appear off screen. But what do the drawing routines do if you attempt to draw an object off screen? Clearly, you would like to have the drawing program create the part of the object that is within the screen boundaries and simply ignore the part that is off the screen.

In a windowing system, such as MS-Windows, you must do more than just check if an object is off screen; you must draw only the portion of an object that appears within the window that the graphics program is using. The drawing must not intrude upon other windows, even if the window is resized or is only partially visible because of overlapping windows. To simplify this discussion, I'll refer to the visible region of the screen that your drawing occupies as the *drawing region*. For MS-DOS applications, this will be some portion of the screen, usually the whole screen. For a windowing system, the drawing region corresponds to the screen's active window, although it can be just a subportion of a window. Since windows can overlap each other, the visible area of the drawing region is usually only some subset of the window that is left visible by the overlapping windows.

To solve the problem of this limited viewing area, you must restrict objects to only be drawn on the desired area of the screen, a process known as *clipping*. There are two basic ways to implement clipping:

1. Check each pixel as it is drawn to see if it falls within the drawing region
2. Take an object and create a new object that is entirely contained within the drawing region by including only those portions of the object within the drawing region, as shown in Figure 7-1.

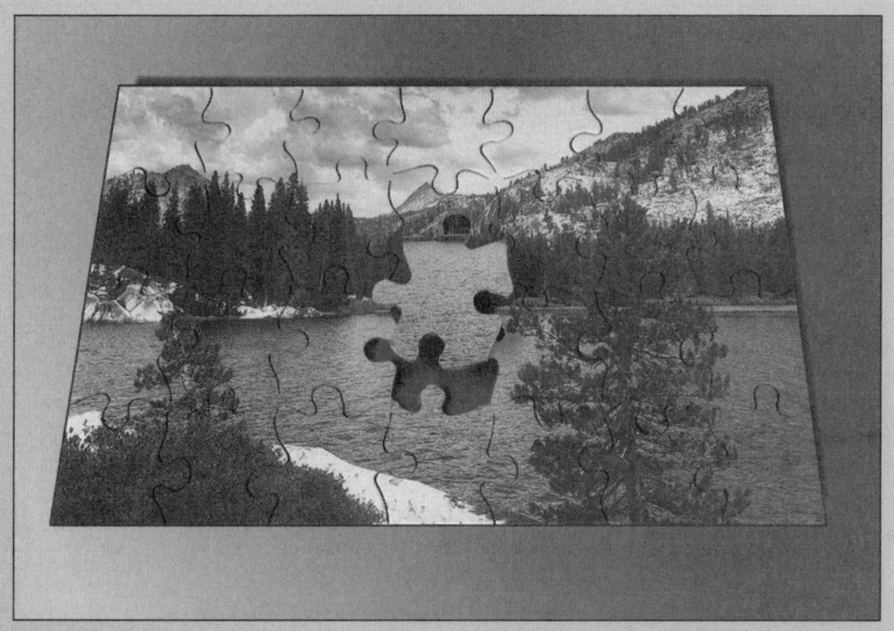

Often your drawing is only a piece of what's on the entire screen. If you work in a windowing environment, such as MS-Windows, your drawing is confined within a window that is usually not the whole screen. Even in a non-windowed environment, you will often need to restrict your drawing to just a portion of the screen, such as plotting a function without overwriting the axes of the plot.

Restricting a drawing to just one portion of the screen is a process known as clipping. This chapter shows a number of different ways to implement clipping for your drawings. You will also learn how the process of windowing works to keep several different drawings on the screen simultaneously, without the drawings interfering with one another. Finally, you will see how to create very complex clipping regions, such as the pieces of the puzzle above, for fancy special effects that would otherwise be quite difficult to perform.

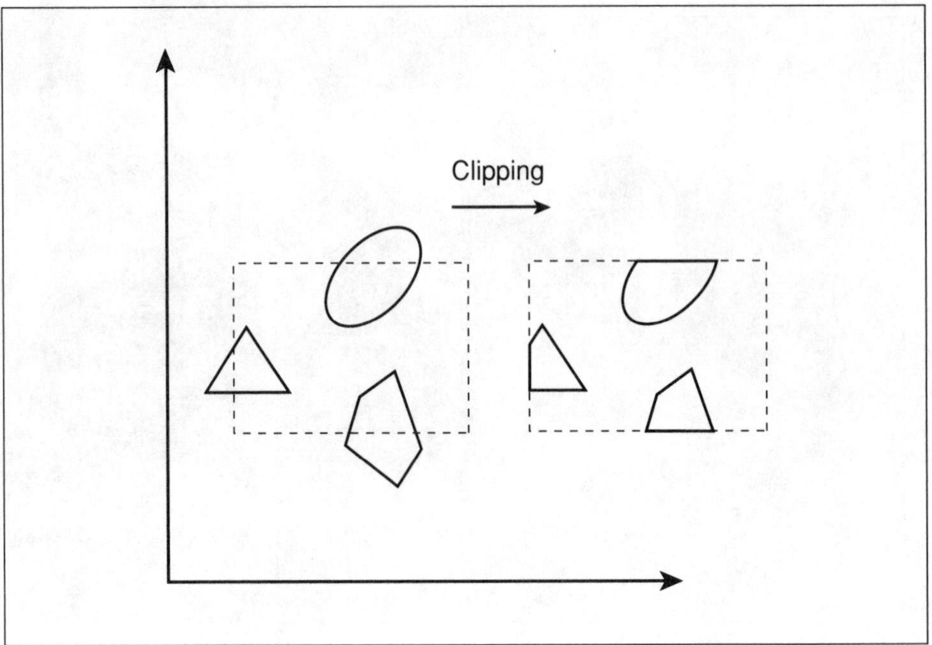

Figure 7-1. Creating a clipped object from an object and a clipping rectangle

The first method is referred to as *pixel-based clipping*, and it is the easiest to implement. Pixel-based clipping is performed by having *gPlotPixel()* check if both the *x*- and *y*-coordinates are inside the drawing region and by ignoring any request to draw a pixel outside the drawing region. For certain compute-intensive applications, this approach has the following drawbacks:

- It requires a comparison of every pixel, whether the pixel is drawn or not.
- Each pixel is checked, even if the object is wholly contained within or totally outside the drawing region. So, a drawing will take nearly the same amount of time to draw even if 90 percent of the objects are not in the drawing region.
- This method only works on raster devices, such as frame buffers. A device, such as a pen plotter, requires that the drawing be analytically clipped (the second method) to the drawing region.

Despite these drawbacks, there are two main advantages of pixel-based clipping:

1. It is an elegant solution that works for all objects
2. There are many graphics-hardware devices that directly support this method

The first advantage results because all the drawing routines ultimately call *gPlotPixel()* to write pixels to the screen. Any clipping operation that is part of *gPlotPixel()* will be applied to every object drawn. In the section covering bounding-box checking, you'll learn how to improve the efficiency of pixel-based clipping by explicitly checking if objects are entirely within or outside the drawing region.

The second clipping method, or *analytic clipping*, is generally more complicated. The term *analytic* refers to how you'll compute a new shape that results from clipping the original unclipped shape to the drawing region for this method. This new shape is the exact representation of the portion of the object that fits within the drawing region. For even relatively simple shapes, such as circles, the clipping operation produces an object that is partially the original shape and partially a polygon, as shown in Figure 7-2. Because of the potential complexity of clipped objects, I restrict the use of analytic clipping to only clipping polygons and polylines to a drawing region. Any other objects, such as circles and ellipses, must be approximated by a polygon or a polyline and the approximated shape is then clipped.

Analytic clipping is used in two primary cases:

1. When using an analog-plotting device, such as a pen plotter
2. When using special hardware to perform some of the drawing operations at high speed, including drawing polygons

For the first case, there is no real choice except to analytically clip all the objects to the desired drawing region. The second case is becoming increasingly more common as sophisticated graphics hardware becomes more affordable.

Instead of using the routines you have developed for drawing objects, such as the circle- and ellipse-drawing algorithms, you should pass the object descrip-

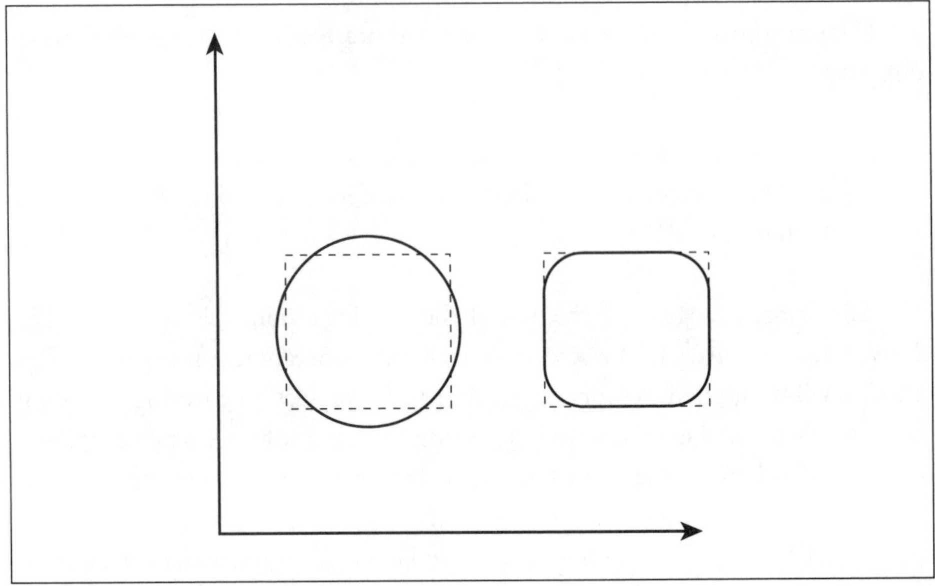

Figure 7-2. Clipping a circle by a rectangle. Note that now the object is partially a circle and partially a corner of the rectangle.

tion directly to the graphics card and let it do the work. Such hardware devices perform much of the computational work of drawing objects far more efficiently than the PC can. This is especially true when objects must be drawn as solid-filled objects.

Such hardware implementations, however, often place restrictions on the types of objects on which they will operate. For instance, most graphics-hardware implementations only work with integer coordinates. Furthermore, they may represent the coordinates using only 16-bit words. This allows integer coordinates ranging from -32768 to +32767, which is more than adequate for any resolution frame buffer. But you can easily exceed this range if you were to, for example, zoom into a drawing with a high enough magnification.

Additionally, the filling algorithms used by the hardware may further restrict the maximum width or height of the object. For instance, the hardware may only allow a maximum fill width equal to the width of the frame buffer. If you have an object like a rectangle that happens to be larger than the frame-buffer width when magnified, then you are out of luck. The graphics card may not draw the rectangle at all; or worse, it may attempt to draw the rectangle but instead generate strange artifacts on the screen. Analytic clipping guarantees that a polygon or polyline passed to the hardware is within the constraints of the hardware.

Rectangular Drawing Regions

By far, the vast majority of drawing regions are defined as either simple rectangular regions or, in the case of windows, as intersections of rectangular regions. In the following section, you'll solve the problem of analytically clipping objects to a simple rectangular drawing region. This region will be stored in the variable *rect*, which is a *gRectangle* data type. After solving the rectangular clipping problem, you'll then show several methods for dealing with more general types of drawing regions.

Checking the Bounding Box

With either clipping method, you can save yourself a lot of trouble if you determine whether or not an object is either completely within or outside the drawing region. If it is outside, then you can simply skip drawing the object. If it is completely contained within the drawing region, then you need not perform any further clipping. Ideally, there should be a simple test that can be performed on an object to determine whether it is inside, outside, or partially clipped by a drawing region. The simplest means is to use the *bounding box*. This is the smallest rectangle that completely contains the object. For a polygon, you can compute the bounding box with a simple procedure:

```
gPolygon *polygon;
gRectangle bbox;

bbox.xmin = bbox.xmax = poly->points[0].x;
bbox.ymin = bbox.ymax = poly->points[0].y;
for(i=1; i<polygon->npoints; i++) {
 bbox.xmin = MIN(polygon->points[i].x, bbox.xmin);
 bbox.ymin = MIN(polygon->points[i].y, bbox.ymin);
 bbox.xmax = MAX(polygon->points[i].x, bbox.xmax);
 bbox.ymax = MAX(polygon->points[i].y, bbox.ymax);
}
```

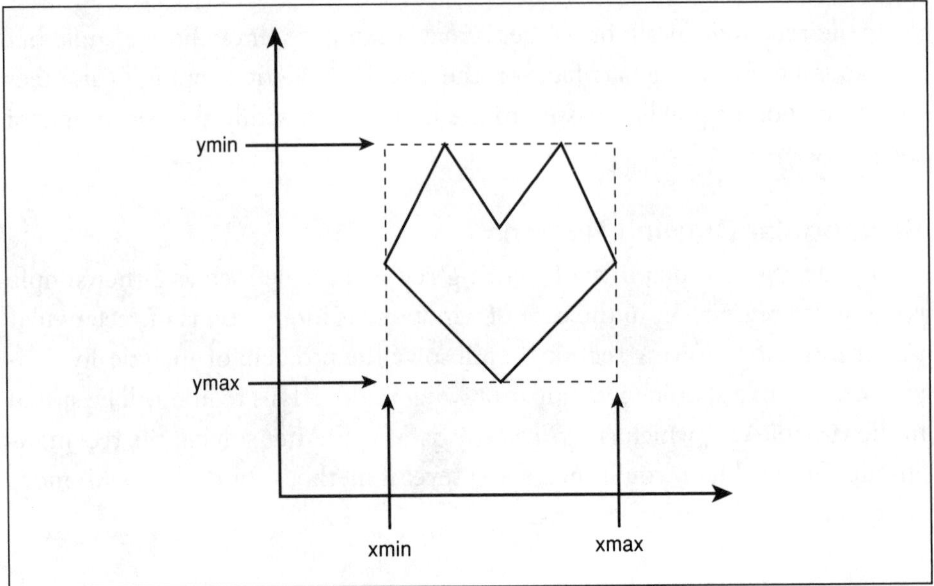

Figure 7-3. Bounding box for a polygon

The rectangle *bbox* represents the smallest, nonrotated rectangle that completely encloses the polygon. This is shown in Figure 7-3. You now must determine whether *bbox* intersects the drawing region, *rect*. To do this, you construct a function, *gBoundingBoxCheck()*, that returns zero if the bounding box is outside *rect*, one if the rectangles partially overlap, and two if *bbox* is completely within *rect*. These values are best defined as *enum* data types:

```
typedef enum {
     gBBOX_OUTSIDE = 0,
     gBBOX_OVERLAP = 1,
     gBBOX_INSIDE = 2
} gBBOX_STATE;
```

Constructing *gBoundingBoxCheck()* is considerably simpler than checking the overlap of arbitrary polygonal regions since you only have to deal with rectangles. To begin, you split the problem into two separate parts, one testing the *x*-coordinates and the other testing the *y*-coordinates. The tests are identical in each case. Next, you define a C macro, *gCLIP_CHECK()*, that tests a value to see if it is between two other values. This function returns one of three values, defined by the *enum* type *gCLIP_STATE*:

```
typedef enum {
     gCLIP_LEFT   = -1,
     gCLIP_MIDDLE = 0,
     gCLIP_RIGHT  = 1
} gCLIP_STATE;
```

These conditions correspond to the three possibilities that the test coordinate is less than the minimum, between the minimum and maximum, or greater than the maximum. Since *gCLIP_CHECK()* is implemented as a macro to maximize its efficiency, it works if the values to be tested are integer or floating point. *gCLIP_CHECK()* is defined as:

```
#define        gCLIP_CHECK(xmin, x, xmax)     \
               ((x) < (xmin) ? gCLIP_LEFT : \
                ((x) > (xmax) ? gCLIP_RIGHT : gCLIP_MIDDLE));
```

Let's look carefully at this macro. If *x* is less than *xmin*, then it returns *gCLIP_LEFT*. Otherwise, it performs the second test to see if *x* is greater than *xmax*. If so, it returns *gCLIP_RIGHT*, otherwise *gCLIP_MIDDLE*. Looking at Figure 7-4, *bbox* will be outside *rect* if *bbox.xmax* is less than *rect.xmin* or *bbox.xmin* is greater than *rect.xmax*, as shown in the first two cases of the figure. For *bbox* to be entirely within *rect* (at least as far as the *x*-coordinate is concerned), *bbox.xmin* must be greater than or equal to *rect.xmin* and *bbox.xmax* must be less than or equal to *rect.xmax*, as shown in the third case. Otherwise, *bbox* partially overlaps *rect* in the *x*-coordinate, as shown in the fourth case.

If the first two cases occur, you do not need to proceed further since *bbox* must lie outside *rect*. *gBoundingBoxCheck()* can immediately return with a value of *gBBOX_OUTSIDE*. Similarly, if the fourth case occurs, *bbox* cannot lie entirely within *rect*, and again, you can have *gBoundingBoxCheck()* return immediately with a value of *gBBOX_OVERLAP*. So, only in the third case do you continue

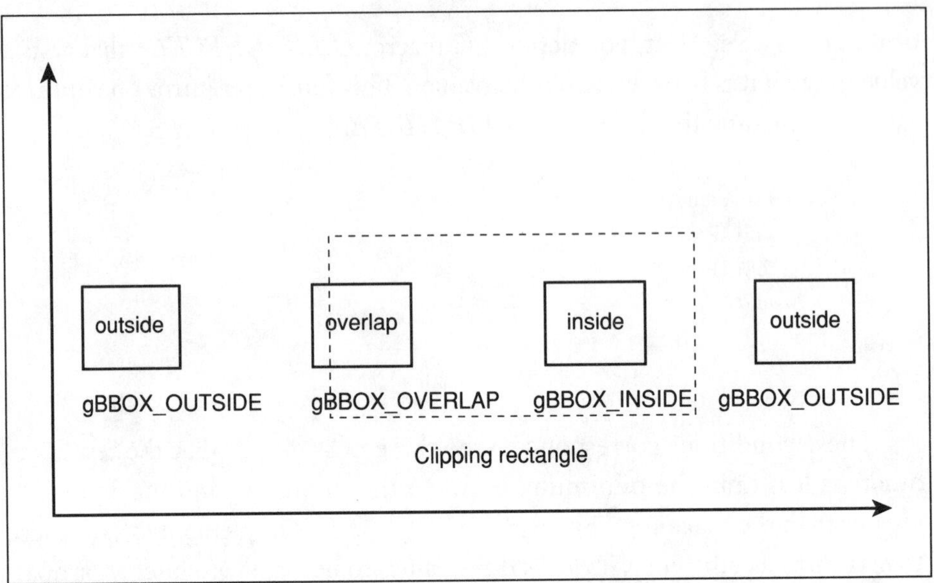

Figure 7-4. The four basic cases for a bounding box to overlap with a clipping rectangle. These illustrate the cases in the x-axis only. Similar cases can occur for the y-coordinate as well.

with checking the *y*-coordinate. In this case, you already know that *bbox* lies within *rect* as far as the *x*-coordinate is concerned, so you perform the exact same check on *y* as you did for *x*. If either of the first two cases occur, then *bbox* is outside, and *gBoundingBoxCheck()* returns with a value of *gBBOX_OUTSIDE*. If the third case occurs, then *bbox* is inside, and the function returns with *gBBOX_INSIDE*. Otherwise, the function returns with *gBBOX_OVERLAP*. The entire function is shown in Listing 7-1.

```
gBBOX_STATE gBoundingBoxCheck(gRectangle *bbox,
                              gRectangle *rect)
{
gCLIP_STATE xmin_check, xmax_check;
gCLIP_STATE ymin_check, ymax_check;

xmax_check = gCLIP_CHECK(rect->xmin, bbox->xmax,
                         rect->xmax);
if(xmax_check == gCLIP_LEFT)          /* Case 1 */
```

```
  return gBBOX_OUTSIDE;

 xmin_check = gCLIP_CHECK(rect->xmin, bbox->xmin,
                          rect->xmax);
 if(xmin_check == gCLIP_RIGHT)         /* Case 2 */
  return gBBOX_OUTSIDE;

 /* Now check for case 3, both inside */
 if(xmin_check == gCLIP_MIDDLE && xmax_check == gCLIP_MIDDLE) {

  ymax_check = gCLIP_CHECK(rect->ymin, bbox->ymax,
                           rect->ymax);
  if(ymax_check == gCLIP_LEFT)         /* Case 1 in Y */
   return gBBOX_OUTSIDE;

  ymin_check = gCLIP_CHECK(rect->ymin, bbox->ymin,
                           rect->ymax);
  if(ymin_check == gCLIP_RIGHT)        /* Case 2 in Y */
   return gBBOX_OUTSIDE;

  if(ymin_check == gCLIP_MIDDLE &&
    ymax_check == gCLIP_MIDDLE)        /* Case 3 in Y */
    return gBBOX_INSIDE;
 }

 /* If you made it here, then the boxes must overlap */
 /* It doesn't matter whether it's in x, y or both */
 return gBBOX_OVERLAP;
 }
```

Listing 7-1. Function that determines to what extent two rectangles overlap

With *gBoundingBoxCheck()*, you can now quickly determine if any clipping needs to be applied by checking the returned value for *gBBOX_OVERLAP*. If the returned value is *gBBOX_OUTSIDE*, then the object is not visible within the drawing region and need not be drawn at all. If the returned value is *gBBOX_INSIDE*, then there is no need to clip the object at all.

As shown in Listing 7-1, *gBoundingBoxCheck()* uses bounding boxes that are aligned with the *x*- and *y*-axes. If you use transformations to position objects, you must take the transformation into account in computing the bounding boxes of the transformed object. As mentioned in Chapter 6, you can apply the same transformation to an object as you can apply to its bounding box. The transformed rectangle will still enclose the object. However, it may no longer be aligned with the coordinate axes if the transformation contains a rotation.

A correctly aligned bounding box is generated by treating the transformed bounding box as a four-sided polygon. The procedure previously shown for computing the bounding box of a polygon is then used to find the new, aligned bounding box. This new bounding box will also contain the object, but it may be much larger than the actual object. This is especially true if the object is long and skinny and then rotated 45 degrees. This is shown in Figure 7-5.

As you'll see in the next section, you can generalize *gBoundingBoxCheck()* to work with a transformed rectangle, that is, to check the transformed rectangle directly against the drawing region. In this case, you treat the transformed rectangle as a polygon. The polygon-clipping algorithm, developed in the following section, can then be used to determine if the polygon is within *rect*. However, this involves considerably more computation and is usually not worth the trouble for the relatively small number of cases in which it improves the drawing performance.

For complex drawings, the bounding-box test provides significant improvements to the drawing speed. This can be quite important for all types of CAD (computer-aided design) drawings, such as electronics schematics, architectural drawings, and mechanical diagrams. A typical drawing sequence for a list of polygons might be:

```
gRectangle bbox, rect;
gPolygon  *poly;
gPolygonList *polygons[100];
int i, numpolygons;
gBBOX_STATE bstate;

for(i=0; i<numpolygons; i++) {
 poly = polygons[i];
```

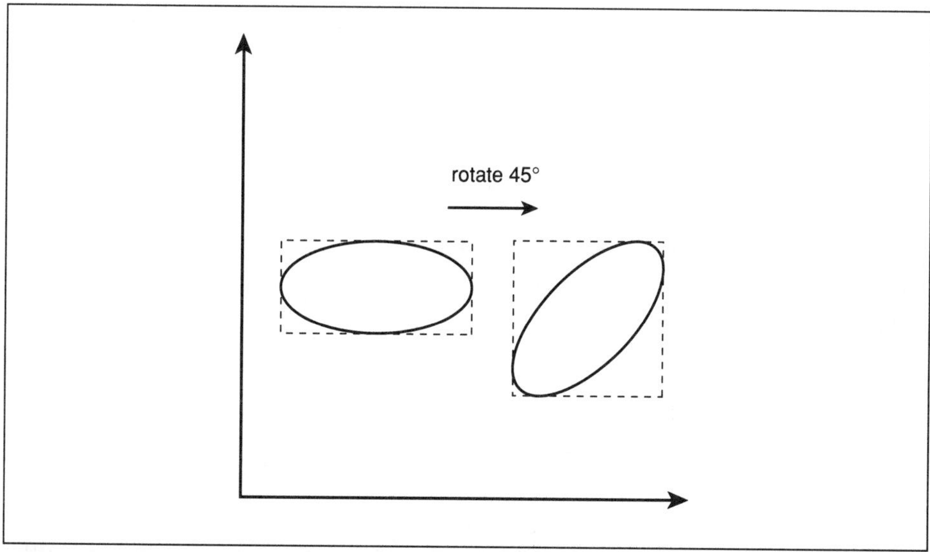

Figure 7-5. Bounding box for a rotated object. Note that depending on the rotation angle, the new bounding box can be much larger than the bounding box of the unrotated object.

```
    gPolygonFindBoundingBox(poly, &bbox);
    bstate = gBoundingBoxCheck(&bbox, &rect);
    if(bstate == gBBOX_INSIDE) {
     /* Turn clipping off; draw the polygon */
    } else if (bstate == gBBOX_OVERLAP) {
     /* Turn clipping on; draw the polygon */
    } /* Polygon is outside; skip it */
}
```

Of course, there is additional computational overhead in generating the bounding box for each polygon. Instead, you may want to compute the bounding box for an entire group of polygons and just test this one bounding box against the drawing region.

Analytic Line Clipping

The goal of using the analytic-clipping algorithm is that when you are given a polyline or polygon, you can produce a new polygon or polyline that represents just the portion of the object inside the drawing region. But before you

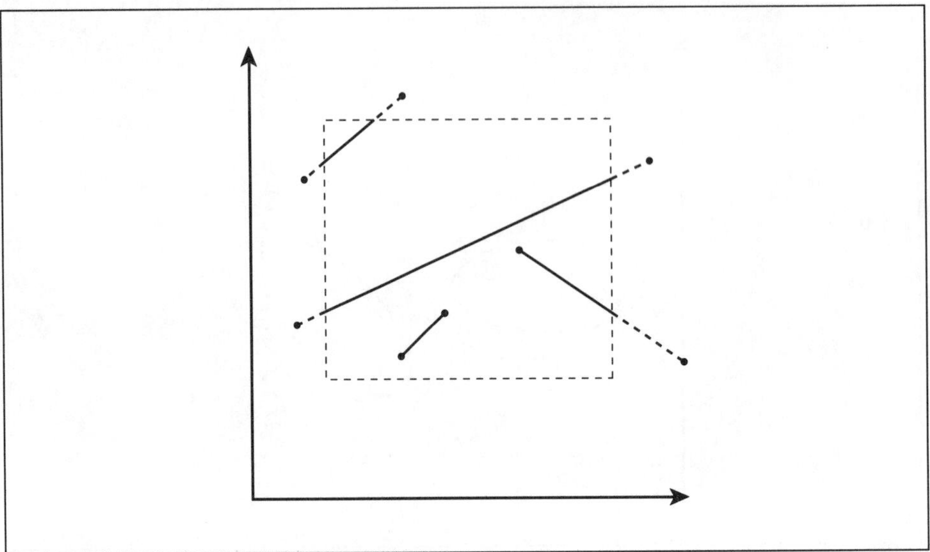

Figure 7-6. Examples of clipping line segments by a clipping rectangle

develop the complete algorithm, you should consider the simpler problem of clipping a single line segment against the drawing region. This situation is shown in Figure 7-6 for several different line segments. As you can see from the figure, even if both endpoints of the line segment are outside the rectangle, part of the line segment may still be inside.

Your job is to produce the line segment that intersects the drawing region. The line-clipping procedure developed here is a variation of the most widely used algorithm, originally developed by E. Cohen and I. E. Sutherland. They are two computer graphics pioneers who developed many of the original and most widely used graphics algorithms. Sutherland was especially interested in high speed graphics methods and applications, eventually cofounding the premier flight simulator visuals company, Evans & Sutherland.

The fundamental calculation to perform is clipping a line segment against one of the edges of *rect*. To do this, you determine which sides of the rectangle the line segment crosses (if any). For each edge it crosses, you then find the intersection point of the line segment and the edge. The computed intersection point then replaces the endpoint that is outside the rectangle. The new line segment is then completely on one side of the edge that you clipped against.

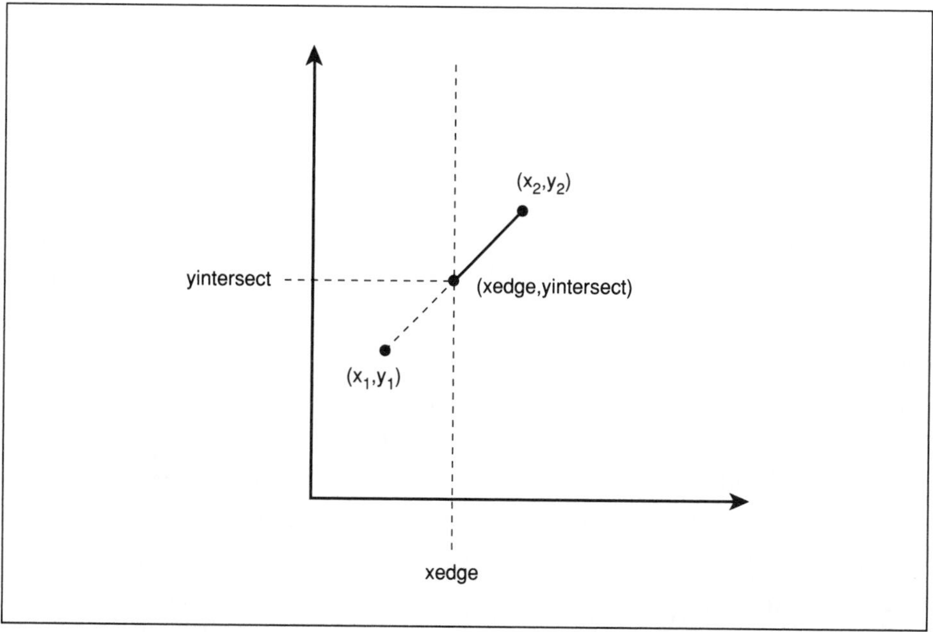

Figure 7-7. Clipping a line segment against a single vertical edge. This is assumed to be the left edge of the clipped rectangle. So, the clipped line segment replaces (x1, y1) with the point (xedge, yintersect).

By successively clipping the line segment against all four sides of the rectangle, a fully clipped line segment is obtained. This clipped line segment is guaranteed to be completely contained by the rectangle.

Clipping a line segment against a single vertical line is shown in Figure 7-7. The vertical line represents the equation $x = xconst$, where *xconst* is either *rect.xmin* or *rect.xmax*, depending on which side of *rect* you are testing. The intersection is found by using the parametric form for the equation of the line segment:

$$x(t) = t * x1 + (1 - t) * x2 = x1 + t * (x2 - x1)$$
$$y(t) = t * y1 + (1 - t) * y2 = y1 + t * (y2 - y1)$$

You find the value for t at the intersection point, and then you substitute this into the equation to determine, in this case, y. For a vertical-line intersection, you already know the *x*-value, namely *xconst*. Substituting this into the equation for *x(t)* and solving for *t* gives you:

$$t = (xconst - x1) / (x2 - x1) \qquad \text{(Equation 7-1)}$$

Substituting this value of *t* into the equation for *y* provides the value of *y* at the intersection point. You should perform the same procedure when clipping against a horizontal line, except now *t* is determined by solving the equation *y(t) = yconst*, where *yconst* is either *rect.ymin* or *rect.ymax*. Once you have the value of *t*, it is substituted into the equation for *x(t)* to find the *x*-coordinate of the intersection point. The only remaining issue is to decide which of the two endpoints actually changed, which creates a new line segment that is clipped against the edge. Referring to Figure 7-7 again, if you are clipping against the edge corresponding to *rect.xmin*, then the point *(x1, y1)* becomes the point (*rect.xmin*, *y*), where *y* is the *y*-coordinate at the intersection point. Similarly, if you are clipping against the edge for *rect.xmax*, then the point *(x2, y2)* is changed. So clipping a line segment generates a new line segment.

The procedure for clipping the line segment against the entire drawing region is to clip the line segment against each of the four sides. So, you could simply clip against each edge separately, passing the clipped line segment on to be tested against the next drawing region edge in sequence. Furthermore, it doesn't really matter what order you step through the sides, as long as you test against all four edges. You can, however, make your algorithm a little smarter by adopting some of the methods shown in the *gBoundingBoxCheck()* function.

In order to simplify your clipping computations, let's examine the final formula for *y* in the case of clipping against a vertical edge. If the computed value of *t* is substituted back in, you get:

$$y = y1 + (xconst - x1) * [(y2 - y1) / (x2 - x1)] \qquad \text{(Equation 7-2)}$$

The bracketed quantity is simply the slope of the line. When clipping against a horizontal line, the computed value for *x* is:

$$x = x1 + (yconst - y1) * [(x2 - x1) / (y2 - y1)] \qquad \text{(Equation 7-3)}$$

where the bracketed quantity is the inverse of the slope. These are the formulas you will use in the actual line-clipping procedure. Note that because of the division, you must not attempt to compute the slope if the line segment is vertical or horizontal.

First, note that as with *gBoundingBoxCheck()*, there are a number of cases that can be quickly rejected by checking the line-segment endpoints against *rect*. As before, a line segment can be immediately rejected if the maximum x-coordinate of the line segment is less than *rect.xmin* or the minimum x-coordinate is greater than *rect.xmax* (the first two cases of *gBoundingBoxCheck()*). If both endpoints are within *rect* (the third case), then you proceed with clipping the line segment in y. For the fourth case, you must clip against one or possibly both vertical edges of *rect*. Furthermore, for either the third or fourth case, the line segment must be clipped against the top and bottom edges of the clipping rectangle. The complete clipping algorithm is shown in Listing 7-2.

The function *gClipLine()* is passed the addresses of the two endpoints of the line and is passed a pointer to the rectangular clipping region. The coordinates are then clipped to the rectangle, which changes the passed coordinates. The return value of the function is either zero, indicating that the line segment is completely outside the rectangle, or one, indicating that the segment was successfully clipped. If the line segment is completely outside, then the passed line-segment endpoints are not changed.

There are several important observations you should note about the implementation of *gClipLine()*. The function begins by clipping against the left and right edges of the clipping rectangle. It first checks to see if you have either the first or second case. If you have either of these cases, then *gClipLine()* returns with a value of zero to indicate that the line segment is completely outside the rectangle. It then uses the *gCLIP_CHECK()* function to determine on which side of the these edges each endpoint is.

If, for example, either endpoint is to the left of the rectangle, *gClipLine()* proceeds to determine the intersection point of the line segment with the left edge of the rectangle. Recall that you have already ruled out the possibility that both endpoints are on the left side when you screened for the first case. The formula shown in Equation 7-2 is then used to determine the clipped value of y at the intersection point.

One convenient aspect of using the parametric equation of the line is that it does not matter which of the two endpoints is on the left. Whether the line segment is drawn left to right or right to left, Equation 7-2 always applies. However, you do need to know which of the two endpoints was on the left side in order to determine which one to change to the newly computed intersection point. If the first endpoint was to the left of the rectangle, then it is changed. Otherwise, the second endpoint is changed.

Once the line is clipped against the left side, *gClipLine()* then performs the identical procedure to clip against the right side. The way the procedure is structured avoids the problem of computing the slope of the line segment if it is vertical (the *x*-coordinate of both endpoints are the same). The slope is only computed when the endpoints are on opposite sides of a rectangle.

Now that the line segment has been clipped against the left and right sides, the function proceeds with clipping the top and bottom. This entire procedure is identical to the one for the left and right edges, except that now *y* is fixed, and Equation 7-3 is used to determine *x* at the intersection points. Note that as each edge is tested, *gClipLine()* uses the clipped line segment for processing, not the original line segment passed to it. This is important since clipping against the left and right edges may have eliminated the need for any clipping against the top or bottom edges, as shown in Figure 7-8.

```
/* This function clips a line segment against the
   rectangle passed in rect */

int gClipLine(int *x1, int *y1, int *x2, int *y2,
              gRectangle *rect)
{
int xc1, yc1, xc2, yc2;
int xnew, ynew;
float slope;
gCLIP_STATE check1, check2;

xc1 = *x1;
yc1 = *y1;
xc2 = *x2;
yc2 = *y2;
```

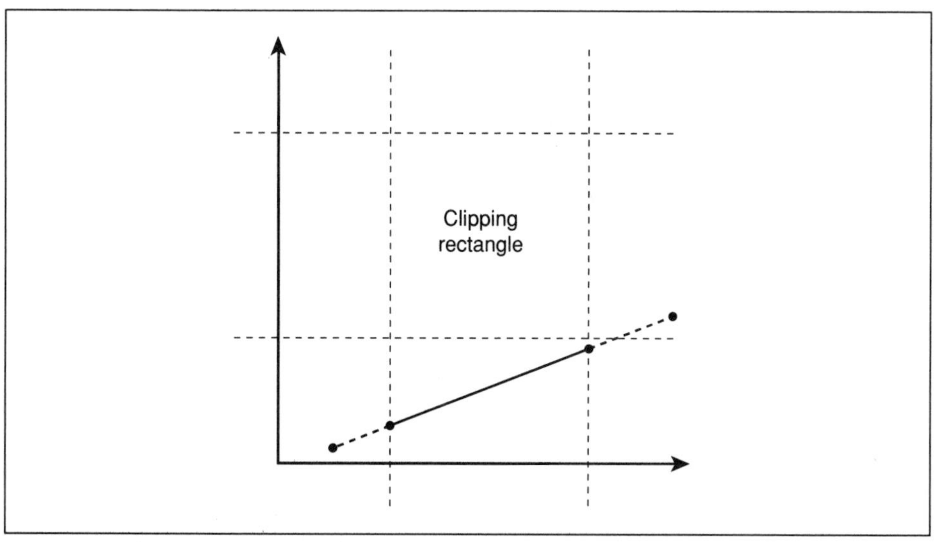

Figure 7-8. Clipping against left and right edges may eliminate the need to clip against the top and bottom edges.

```
/* Check for cases 1 and 2 */
if(xc1 < rect->xmin && xc2 < rect->xmin)
 return 0;
if(xc1 > rect->xmax && xc2 > rect->xmax)
 return 0;

/* Now start checking against the left and right sides */
check1 = gCLIP_CHECK(rect->xmin, xc1, rect->xmax);
check2 = gCLIP_CHECK(rect->xmin, xc2, rect->xmax);
if(check1 == gCLIP_LEFT || check2 == gCLIP_LEFT) {
 /* One is on the left; so clip against rect->xmin */
 /* xc2 cannot equal xc1,since your previous test
   for cases 1 and 2 ruled it out */
 slope = (float)(yc2 - yc1) / (float)(xc2 - xc1);
 ynew = ROUND(yc1 + (rect->xmin - xc1)*slope);
 if(check1 == gCLIP_LEFT) {
  xc1 = rect->xmin;
  yc1 = ynew;
 } else {
  xc2 = rect->xmin;
```

```
      yc2 = ynew;
     }
    }
    if(check1 == gCLIP_RIGHT || check2 == gCLIP_RIGHT) {
     /* One is on the right; so clip against rect->xmax */
     slope = (float)(yc2 - yc1) / (float)(xc2 - xc1);
     ynew = ROUND(yc1 + (rect->xmax - xc1)*slope);
     if(check1 == gCLIP_RIGHT) {
      xc1 = rect->xmax;
      yc1 = ynew;
     } else {
      xc2 = rect->xmax;
      yc2 = ynew;
     }
    }

    /* Now handle clipping against the top and bottom edges */
    /* Check for cases 1 and 2 */
    if(yc1 < rect->ymin && yc2 < rect->ymin)
     return 0;
    if(yc1 > rect->ymax && yc2 > rect->ymax)
     return 0;
    /* Now start checking against the two sides */
    check1 = gCLIP_CHECK(rect->ymin, yc1, rect->ymax);
    check2 = gCLIP_CHECK(rect->ymin, yc2, rect->ymax);
    if(check1 == gCLIP_LEFT || check2 == gCLIP_LEFT) {
     /* One is on top; so clip against rect->ymin */
     /* yc2 cannot equal yc1, since your previous test
        for cases 1 and 2 would have ruled it out */
     slope = (float)(xc2 - xc1) / (float)(yc2 - yc1);
     xnew = ROUND(xc1 + (rect->ymin - yc1)*slope);
     if(check1 == gCLIP_LEFT) {
      xc1 = xnew;
      yc1 = rect->ymin;
     } else {
      xc2 = xnew;
      yc2 = rect->ymin;
     }
    }
    if(check1 == gCLIP_RIGHT || check2 == gCLIP_RIGHT) {
```

```
        /* One is on the bottom; so clip against rect->ymax */
        slope = (float)(xc2 - xc1) / (float)(yc2 - yc1);
        xnew = ROUND(xc1 + (rect->ymax - yc1)*slope);
        if(check1 == gCLIP_RIGHT) {
          xc1 = xnew;
          yc1 = rect->ymax;
        } else {
          xc2 = xnew;
          yc2 = rect->ymax;
        }
      }

      *x1 = xc1;
      *y1 = yc1;
      *x2 = xc2;
      *y2 = yc2;

      return 1;
    }
```

Listing 7-2. Procedure for clipping a line segment against a rectangular region

gClipLine() may be easily extended to work entirely in floating point by changing all the *int* variables to *float* and eliminating the use of the *ROUND()* macro. The integer version shown in Listing 7-2 can cause slight shifts in position of the line because of the *ROUND()* macro.

Polygon Clipping

Having learned how to analytically clip a line segment, you can now turn to the slightly more complicated problem of clipping a polygon to a rectangle. This is shown in Figure 7-9. As you'll recall, when clipping the line segment, you simply threw away the portions of the line outside the rectangle. You cannot do that with the polygon edges. Instead, you'll want to include the portions of each edge from the point where the polygon goes outside the rectangle to the point where the polygon comes back. This process is illustrated in Figure 7-10 for a vertical edge. As with the line segment, you'll clip the polygon against each side of the rectangle separately. Once all four sides have been processed,

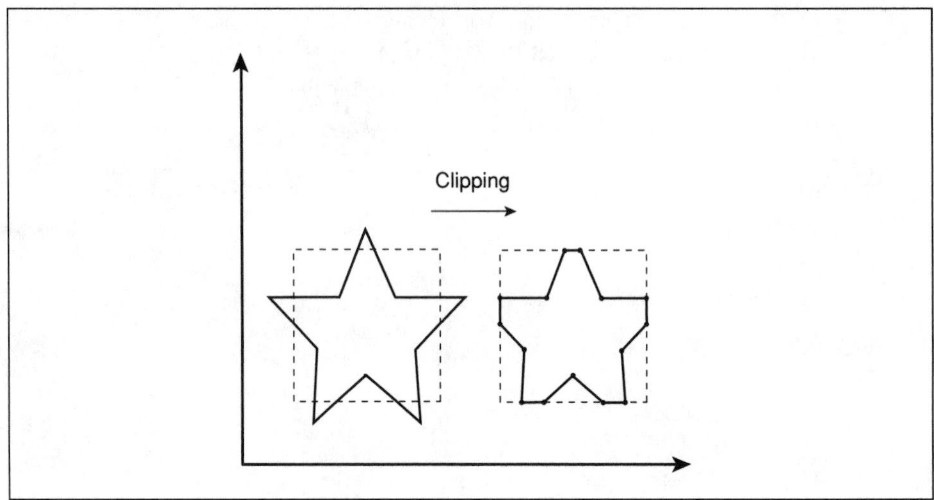

Figure 7-9. Clipping a polygon against a rectangle. Note that the clipped polygon includes parts of the rectangle edge.

the fully clipped polygon is ready for use.

The polygon clipping function is called *gClipPolygon()*. The clipping process begins by first clipping the passed polygon, *poly*, against the left side of the clipping rectangle. This creates a new polygon that represents the original polygon clipped against this edge. The variable *clip_poly* refers to this clipped polygon. This new polygon is then clipped against the right, top, and bottom sides of the clipping rectangle. Each of these four steps operate in exactly the same way, just as they did for the line-clipping algorithm.

To simplify the analysis, I have provided four separate functions that individually clip a polygon against a particular side of the clipping rectangle. The four functions are as follows:

- *gClipPolygonLeft()*
- *gClipPolygonRight()*
- *gClipPolygonTop()*
- *gClipPolygonBottom()*

gClipPolygonLeft() examines each polygon edge in search of the first vertex that is on the right side of the clipping rectangle. If no such vertex is found,

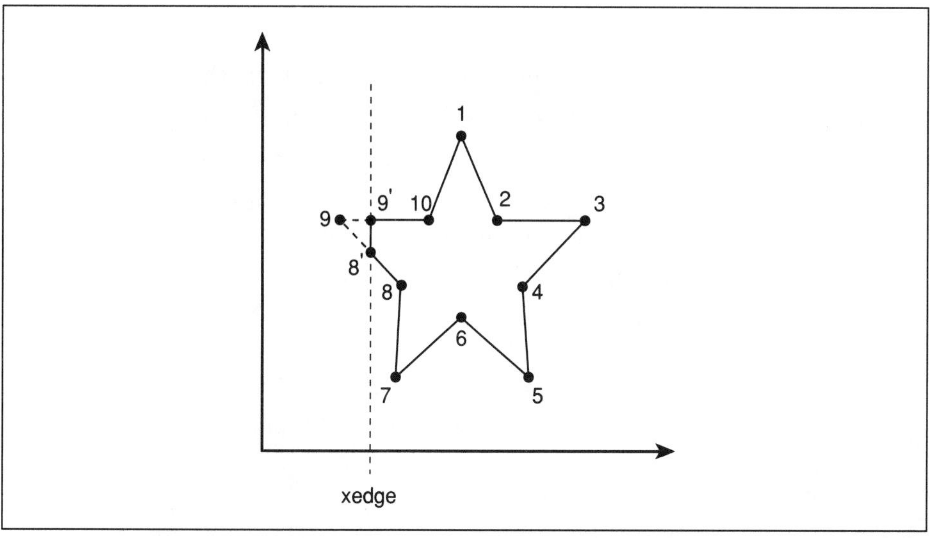

Figure 7-10. Clipping a polygon against a single vertical edge

then the polygon is completely to the left of the clipping rectangle and no further processing is necessary. If, however, a vertex is found, it is added as the first point of *clip_poly*. Starting at this first vertex, *gClipPolygonLeft()* then examines each edge of the polygon in sequence. The *i*th edge of the polygon is defined by the *i*th and (*i+1*)st vertex of the polygon. For each edge, the clipping function must decide whether to add the (*i+1*)st vertex to *clip_poly*, ignore it, or if the edge crosses the clipping line, to clip the edge and add the intersection point. Thus, *gClipPolygon()*, looks for one of the following three conditions:

1. Both vertices defining the edge are on the right side of the line, inside the clipping rectangle. In this case, the (*i+1*)st vertex is added to *clip_poly*.
2. Both vertices defining the edge are on the left side of the line, outside the clipping rectangle. No vertices are added to *clip_poly*.
3. The edge crosses the line. You must find the intersection point and add that point to *clip_poly*. Additionally, you may have to add the (*i+1*)st point as well, depending on whether the polygon edge is entering or exiting the clipping rectangle.

For the third case, there are two separate situations to handle when the edge crosses the line. If the *i*th point is on the right side, then only the computed intersection point needs to be added to *clip_poly*. The *i*th point will have already been added by the time the previous edge is processed. However, if the *i*th point is on the left side, then the polygon is reentering the clipping rectangle. In this case, you must add both the computed intersection point of the edge to the clipping line and the *(i+1)*st polygon vertex. The complete code for *gClipPolygonLeft()* is shown in Listing 7-3.

```
/* Clip against the left side of a clipping rectangle */
gPolygon *gClipPolygonLeft(gPolygon *poly, gRectangle *rect)
{
gPoint  point1, point2;
float   slope, xnew, ynew;
int i;

/* As a guess, allocate the same number of points
   in clip_poly that you have in poly */

clip_poly = gPolygonCreate(poly->numpoints);
point1 = poly->points[poly->numpoints-1];
if(point1.x > rect->xmin)
 gPolygonAddPoint(clip_poly, point1.x, point1.y);

/* Loop through all of the vertices */
for(i=0; i<poly->numpoints; i++) {
 point2 = poly->points[i];
 /* Now check for each possible combination */
 if(point1.x >= rect->xmin) {
  /* point1 is to the right */
  if(point2.x >= rect->xmin) {
   /* Both points are on the right side; go ahead and add point2 */
   clip_poly = gPolygonAddPoint(clip_poly, point2.x, point2.y);
  } else {
   /* Point1 is inside; point2 is outside; find the
      intersection and add it */
   slope = (point2.y - point1.y) /
           (point2.x - point1.x);
```

```
      ynew = point1.y + (rect->xmin - point1.x) * slope;
      xnew = rect->xmin;
      clip_poly = gPolygonAddPoint(clip_poly, xnew, ynew);
     }
   } else {
    /* point1 is outside */
    if(point2.x >= rect->xmin) {
      /* point2 is inside; point1 is outside; find the
         intersection and add it */
      slope = (point2.y - point1.y) /
              (point2.x - point1.x);
      ynew = point1.y + (rect->xmin - point1.x) * slope;
      xnew = rect->xmin;
      clip_poly = gPolygonAddPoint(clip_poly, xnew, ynew);
      /* Also must add point2 since you came back inside */
      clip_poly = gPolygonAddPoint(clip_poly,
         point2.x, point2.y);
    }
   }

   point1 = point2;
  } /* Loop through all the vertices */

  return clip_poly;
  }
```

Listing 7-3. Procedure for clipping a polygon against the left-hand edge of a clipping rectangle

As stated previously, the other three clipping functions are the same except for the edge of the rectangle that the polygon is clipped against. The completed version *gClipPolygon()* is shown in Listing 7-4. Notice that you must toggle between two separate polygons. One polygon holds the most recently clipped version, and the other receives the output after the next clipping operation. After each clipping operation, *gClipPolygon()* tests to see if the number of points in the polygon is zero. This indicates that the passed polygon was entirely on the outside of the clipping edge. In this case, a *NULL* pointer is returned, which indicates to the calling program that no further processing of this polygon is required.

```
gPolygon *gClipPolygon(gPolygon *poly,
  gRectangle *rect)
{
gPolygon *clip_poly1, *clip_poly2;

clip_poly1 = gClipPolygonLeft(poly, rect);
if(clip_poly1->numpoints == 0) {
 gPolygonDelete(clip_poly1);
return NULL;
}
clip_poly2 = gClipPolygonRight(clip_poly1, rect);
gPolygonDelete(clip_poly1);
if(clip_poly2->numpoints == 0) {
 gPolygonDelete(clip_poly2);
 return NULL;
}
clip_poly1 = gClipPolygonTop(clip_poly2,
rect);gPolygonDelete(clip_poly2);
if(clip_poly1->numpoints == 0) {
 gPolygonDelete(clip_poly1);
 return NULL;
}
clip_poly2 = gClipPolygonBottom(clip_poly1, rect);
gPolygonDelte(clip_poly1);
if(clip_poly2->numpoints == 0) {
 gPolygonDelete(clip_poly2);
 return NULL;
}

return clip_poly2;
}
```

Listing 7-4. Complete function for clipping a polygon against a clipping rectangle. Note that gClipPolygon() must hold two polygons at any one time. One polygon holds the current polygon to be clipped, while the other receives the output of the clipping operation.

The polygon-clipping algorithm can also be applied to the drawing methods of the previous chapter for transformed rectangles, circles, and polygons. Recall that the transformed objects were drawn essentially the same way as polygons are, by drawing a series of connected vertices. To use the clipping algorithm, you would need to store the transformed coordinates into a polygon and then use *gClipPolygon()* to generate the clipped polygon. If you have the appropriate graphics hardware, the clipped polygon can then be passed directly to it for rendering.

While analytic clipping can provide significant performance improvements on specialized hardware, it is still a time-consuming operation, especially for drawings containing thousands of polygons. Since most PC graphics cards do not currently have this kind of on-board capability, most software resorts to the pixel–based-clipping method. This is especially true for various windowing environments, such as MS-Windows.

Windowing

The most common type of drawing region you are likely to run into is a window, even if you aren't running MS-Windows. A window is a rectangular drawing area that can be dynamically moved or resized by either a user or by another program.

In an operating environment, such as MS-Windows, an application uses a window as a local display device. In the DOS environment, it is useful to be able to divide the screen into separate areas to allow multiple independent drawings to be displayed at the same time. For instance, the line–drawing-demonstration program in Chapter 4 divides the screen into two halves, so you can observe the two different line-drawing methods. In either case, all the graphics output from the application reside within the window and may not intrude on other parts of the display.

The program usually can't tell that a program is writing to a window. The program works as if the window were the entire screen. For instance, if your graphics library is implemented on a window-based system, then the screen coordinate (0,0) would refer to the upper-left corner of the window, but not necessarily the upper-left corner of the screen. The operating system translates your coordinates to wherever the window happens to be on the screen. Drawing to a window that can vary its size requires the ability to rescale and move a drawing anywhere on the screen and make sure that drawing to one window does not spill into another one.

You saw in Chapter 6 how transformations are used to scale and transform drawings to fit anywhere on the screen. However, this does not solve the problem of how to keep a transformed drawing from writing over other parts of the screen. Clipping solves that problem. So far, though, you have only dealt with rectangular clipping regions. In a true windowing environment, you must also handle the situation of overlapping windows. When windows overlap, the drawing region of the bottom window should not intrude upon the drawing region of the top window. This requires the ability to clip against a more complex clipping shape. Figure 7-11 shows an example of the type of clipping region required for multiple overlapping windows.

A windowing environment must be able to clip any type of object so that only part of the object is drawn on the visible portion of the window. As I pointed out in the beginning of this chapter, analytic-clipping methods are not suitable for many types of objects, especially complex curves and text, because of speed constraints. Furthermore, most graphics cards do not support analytic clipping in the hardware. Instead, windowing systems usually perform clipping at the pixel level. Since operating systems like MS-Windows must check each pixel before it is written to the screen, they are slower than graphics in DOS. However, if the hardware supports clipping directly, then much of the performance drain due to clipping can be removed.

Clipping Functions

Most graphics packages, such as the one provided in Borland C++, let you specify rectangular clipping regions only. In addition, they let you explicitly enable or disable the clipping operation, depending on whether you need it or not. With the *gBoundingBoxCheck()* function, you may determine that an object (or, perhaps, a whole group of objects) is completely within the drawing area, meaning that clipping can be safely disabled. I have extended this idea to provide a more general approach to implement pixel-level clipping.

Instead of specifying a region in which to clip, you provide a function to perform the clipping test. Just as data can be passed as arguments, C lets you

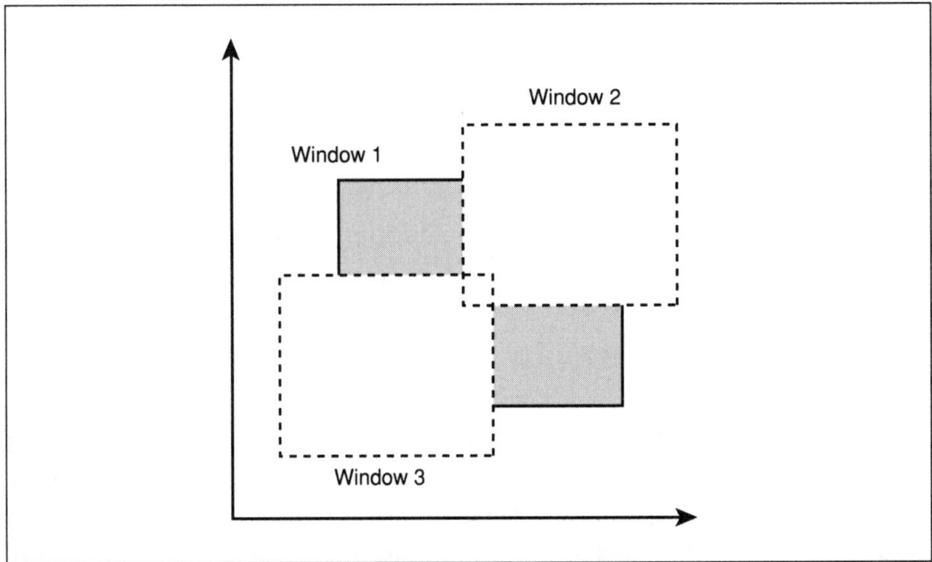

Figure 7-11. Clipping region required to support multiple overlapping windows

pass pointers to functions as well. A function pointer lets a C function call another user-defined function. You'll want to define a clipping function that can be called by *gPlotPixel()*. The clipping function is passed the *x*- and *y*-screen coordinates of a pixel to be drawn as arguments. The clipping function returns either zero, indicating that the pixel should not be drawn, or one indicating that it is alright to draw that pixel. An example function for clipping to a rectangle is:

```
int gRectangleClipTest(int x, int y, void *clip_data)
{
gRectangle *rect;

rect = (gRectangle *)clip_data;
if(gCLIP_CHECK(rect->xmin, x, rect->xmax) != gCLIP_MIDDLE)
 return 0;
if(gCLIP_CHECK(rect->ymin, y, rect->ymax) != gCLIP_MIDDLE)
 return 0;

return 1;
}
```

Note that the function is supplied an additional argument, *clip data*, as a *void* pointer. This pointer may be a pointer to any structure you may need inside of the clipping function. It is set when the clipping function is established by a call to *gAddClipFunction()*. In this example, *clip data* is a pointer to the rectangle to clip against. You do not have to use this pointer; it is there to provide a way to pass additional data that defines the clipping region. For instance, to use the previous rectangle clipping function, you would make a call like:

```
gAddClipFunction(&gRectangleClipTest, (void *)&rect);
```

The passed rectangle pointer is saved along with the pointer to the clipping function in a linked list of clipping-function structures. Each structure in the linked list contains the pointer to a clipping function and a pointer to the passed data. The function is called *gAddClipFunction()* because you may have more than one clipping function. Each subsequent call to *gAddClipFunction()* adds an additional clipping function to the list of clipping functions. A clipping function is removed from the list by a call to *gRemoveClipFunction()*, which passes the same arguments as *gAddClipFunction()*.

By allowing multiple clipping functions, you can write functions that add their own clipping regions and then remove them before returning to the calling program, without affecting any clipping that was in effect before your function was called. For instance, suppose you have the function *drawrect()* to draw into a small rectangle on the screen. This function is called by another routine that is drawing into a larger window that contains the small rectangle. *drawrect()* can add a clipping function to restrict drawing to the rectangle, draw whatever it wants, and then remove the clipping function once it is completed. So, *drawrect( )* does not affect any other clipping that the calling routine set up; it only adds the clip region necessary for *drawrect()*. This type of modular programming makes it easier to use your code in an application because it does not interfere with the environment established by the calling program.

Whenever a pixel is to be drawn, *gPlotPixel()* checks to see if a clipping function has been defined by a call to *gAddClipFunction()*. If so, then before the pixel is written, the clipping function is called. If the function returns a one, the pixel is then drawn. If it returns a zero, *gPlotPixel()* immediately returns, and the pixel is not drawn. Using this approach, you can create clipping regions of any shape or combination of shapes. For example, the following function defines a circular clipping region:

```
int gCircleClipTest(int x, int y, void *clip_data)
{
gCircle *circle;

circle = (gCircle *)clip_data;
if(SQUARE(x - circle->x) + SQUARE(y - circle->y) <=
   SQUARE(circle->radius))
 return 1;

return 0;
}
```

To disable clipping completely, simply call *gRemoveClipFunction()* with the same function pointer and data argument you used to add the clip function:

```
gRemoveClipFunction(&gCircleClipTest, circle);
```

Often, however, you may want to turn off clipping only for the duration of the function and then restore it after your function is completed. The function *gSetClipEnable()* provides this capability. It has a single *int* argument, *enable*. If *enable* is zero, clipping is disabled. If *enable* is one, then clipping is reenabled to use the current clipping function.

While the clipping function may not define a rectangular clipping region, it is still useful for many other functions (especially the filling functions in Chapter 8) to be able to find the bounding box of the clipping region that your clipping function defines. For example, the circular clipping region of *gCircleClipTest()* has a bounding box defined by:

(xmin, ymin) = (circle->x - circle->radius, circle-> y - circle->radius)
(xmax, ymax) = (circle->x + circle->radius, circle-> y + circle->radius)

The function *gSetClipBoundingBox()* lets you pass a rectangle that represents the bounding box for your clipping function. The function *gGetClipBoundingBox()* returns a pointer to this bounding box. Typically, *gGetClipBoundingBox()* is used within a function that needs to know how much of the screen it should even consider for an operation. The *gPolygonFill()* of Chapter 8 takes advantage of this in order to avoid trying to fill parts of a polygon that are off the screen. If no bounding box is set, then the bounding rectangle is the entire screen. The bounding box is also reset to the entire screen whenever *gAddClipFunction()* is called with a *NULL* argument, or the clipping is disabled with *gSetClipEnable()*.

The complexity of the clipping function will determine how fast the clipping operation is. Using a clipping function similar to the one for rectangular clipping, you can handle multiple overlapping windows. For the bottom window, the *clip data* pointer is a list of rectangles corresponding to each of the windows that are on top. You then decide to draw the pixel only if it is inside the bottom window, but outside all the other windows above it. Using clipping functions is a very compact way of defining a clipping region. While it is the most flexible, it is not the fastest.

The most common method of pixel clipping uses a *bitmap* to define which pixels can be written to. A *bitmap* is a two-dimensional memory array that you use in much the same way as you would use the frame buffer. In a sense, a bitmap is simply a frame buffer in main memory. Each element of the array is used like a frame-buffer pixel. A special kind of bitmap called a *clip mask* is used for pixel-based clipping. Each element of the bitmap is either one or zero, indicating that a pixel can (one) or cannot (zero) be written to. This provides a convenient means for defining complex clipping regions, such as overlapping windows.

In a windowing system, each window has an associated clip mask. Whenever a window is moved on top of another window, the clip mask for the lower window is zeroed out for the overlapping portions. One disadvantage of this technique is that the clip mask must be at least as large as the window with which it is used. This is one of the many reasons why window-based systems use more memory. The primary advantage of this technique is speed, especially since many of the newer graphics cards support this type of masking operation directly in the hardware. Deciding whether or not to write a pixel is just a matter of checking the corresponding element of the clip mask. You'll learn more about bitmaps in Chapter 9.

Clipping In Action

The demonstration program *dclip.exe* provides an interactive means of seeing how clipping affects performance. This program lets you view several animated figures moving about the screen. Using the numeric keys, you can switch between various types of clipping regions, including a rectangle, a circle, and various combinations of the two. In addition, the arrow keys let you move the clipping regions around the screen. This program uses clipping functions to implement the clipping. If you examine the source code, provided on the disk accompanying this book, you'll see that the clipping regions may be changed quite easily using the clipping functions. For example, moving the clipping rectangle around the screen only requires adding offsets to the clip rectangle that is passed to *gRectangleClip( )*. It doesn't require any additional graphics calls. You'll see in Chapter 9 how bitmaps can help speed up the clipping operations, especially for complex clipping regions.

A Solid Start

At this point, you have the tools to draw the outlines of various graphics objects. You can transform the shapes using matrices while keeping the drawing in a localized part of the screen using any of the clipping methods described in this chapter. In fact, you can now develop applications that divide the screen into multiple separate windows without the graphics of one spilling into the graphics of the other. However, the techniques presented so far only let you draw the outline or boundary of the object. In the next chapter, you'll see how to turn your drawing outline into a solid collection of filled objects.

Functions Found in This Chapter

Demonstration program

`dclip.exe`

Demonstrates multiple combinations of clipping regions, and how they can be dynamically altered and moved about the screen.

Clipping functions

```
gCLIP_STATE gCLIP_CHECK(x1, x, x2)
```

A macro that returns one of three values: *gCLIP_LEFT* if $x < x1$, *gCLIP_RIGHT* if $x > x2$, or *gCLIP_MIDDLE* otherwise (x is between $x1$ and $x2$).

```
gBBOX_STATE gBoundingBoxCheck(gRectangle *bbox, gRectangle *rect);
```

Returns one of three values: *gBBOX_INSIDE* if *bbox* is completely contained inside *rect*; *gBBOX_OUTSIDE* if *bbox* is completely outside *rect*; or *gBBOX_OVERLAP*, which indicates that the two boxes overlap.

```
int gClipLine(int *x1, int *y1, int *x2, int *y2,
              gRectangle *rect);
```

Clips the line segment from *(x1, y1)* to *(x2, y2)*. The return value is zero if the line segment does not intersect the rectangle. Otherwise, the passed values are changed to represent the clipped line segment.

```
gPolygon *gClipPolygon(gPolygon *poly, gRectangle *rect);
```

Clips the passed polygon to the passed rectangle. A new clipped polygon is created by this call. If the number of points in the result is zero, then the polygon was completely outside the rectangle.

```
void gAddClipFunction(int *clip_func(int x, int y,
                      void *clip_data),
                      void *clip_data);
```

Adds a clipping function to a global list of clipping functions used by *gPlotPixel()* to determine if a pixel can be drawn or not. The clipping function must return an *int* result of one if the pixel can be drawn, or zero otherwise.

```
void gRemoveClipFunction(int *clip_func(int x, int y,
                          void *clip_data),
                          void *clip_data);
```

Removes a clipping function from the global list of clipping functions added by *gAddClipFunction()*.

```
int gRectangleClipTest(int x, int y, void *clip_data)
```

A clipping function that clips *x* and *y* to a passed rectangle.

```
int gCircleClipTest(int x, int y, void *clip_data)
```

A clipping function that clips *x* and *y* to a passed circle.

```
void gSetClipBoundingBox(gRectangle *bbox);
```

Sets the bounding box for the clip function set with *gAddClipFunction()*. It is up to you to ensure that the passed rectangle really is the bounding box for the object. By default, this bounding box is set to the entire screen, (0,0) to (*gGetMaxX()-1*, *gGetMaxY()-1*).

```
gRectangle *gGetClipBoundingBox(void)
```

This function returns a pointer to the current bounding box for the clip region. This pointer is just the address of the global static variable where the bounding box is stored when set by *gSetClipBoundingBox()*. Your program must not use *free()* on this pointer.

```
void gSetClipEnable(int enable);
```

Turns clipping on (*enable* = 1) or off (*enable* = 0). This determines whether *gPlotPixel()* looks for a clip function or not.

CHAPTER 8

Making a Solid Picture

The previous chapters dealt with representing and drawing a variety of geometric shapes. However, the drawing routines developed thus far only draw the outlines or boundaries of the objects. The ability to draw filled, or solid, objects is a necessary requirement for every graphics package.

Twenty years ago, before raster frame buffers were readily available and those that existed were quite expensive, it was quite acceptable to only draw object outlines. Now, however, the inexpensive frame buffer and CRTs make it easy to represent solid, filled shapes. All computer graphics applications from business bar charts to three dimensional drawings require drawing filled objects. Your mission, if you choose to accept it, is to create functions that find and fill all of the pixels inside each of the geometric shapes presented so far. You begin by learning to fill the interior of an object with a constant color. Once that is accomplished, you will see how this can easily be turned into the filling of the interior with any desired pattern of colors.

Scan Conversion

All of the geometric objects discussed so far, with the exception of the point and the polyline, define closed areas, or regions, of the screen. The process of determining all of the pixels in the interior of that region is traditionally called *scan conversion*. The reason for this name is that a typical color-filling algorithm works by processing one row of pixels at a time. For each row, you find the pixels along the row that are in the interior of the object and set those pixels to the desired fill color. Each row corresponds to a single *scan line* on the CRT. Once a scan line is completed, the fill function proceeds to work on the next scan line until all of the scanlines which intersect the object have been processed.

Most scan conversion algorithms begin by determining the minimum and maximum Y coordinate that bound the object, as shown in Figure 8-1. If the bounding box for the object has already been computed, then this information is readily available. The *ymin* and *ymax* of the bounding box are the values you

Most complex drawings, such as the one shown above, require objects composed of lines and solid-filled objects. Filling an object via a computer follows the same basic process as if you were to do it by hand. You must find the boundary of the object and fill in the middle portion, being careful not to go outside the boundary.

In this chapter, you'll learn how to fill virtually any type of graphic object. In addition to filling an object with a solid color, you'll also see how to fill the interior with a repeated pattern of any size, shape, and color combination, to create dazzling images.

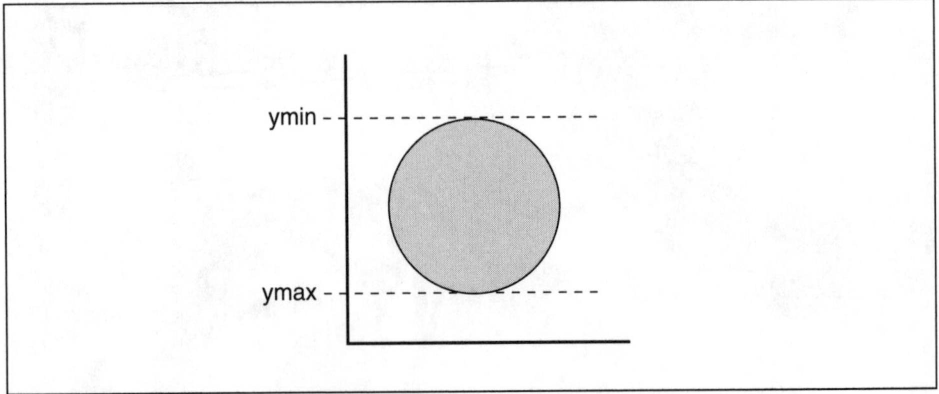

Figure 8-1. Bounding y-values for a circle

want. If this is not readily available, then you can either: (a) derive it from the geometric properties of the object or (b) compute the minimum and maximum *y*-coordinates of the bounding box. For example, the first technique may be used for circles. A circle of radius r and centered at (*x1*, *y1*) has a minimum *y*-coordinate of *y1* - *r*, and a maximum *y*-coordinate of *y1* + *r*. For a polygon, you must use the second technique and simply scan the vertices to find the minimum and maximum *y*-values, as you did in Chapter 7. Once the minimum and maximum *y*-values are found, the object is scanned from *ymin* to *ymax*:

```
int y;
for(y=ymin; y <= ymax; y++) {
 /* Find interior pixels for row y */
 /* Fill the pixels */
}
```

For most of the objects you will have to draw, the interior pixels usually occur as sequential groups of pixels, called *spans*, as shown in Figure 8-2. For row *y1* in the figure, there are two spans of pixels that must be filled. For row *y2*, there is only one. A span is specified by a starting *x* and an ending *x*-coordinate. A simple way to fill a span of pixels is to create a span-filling function based on *gPlotPixel()*:

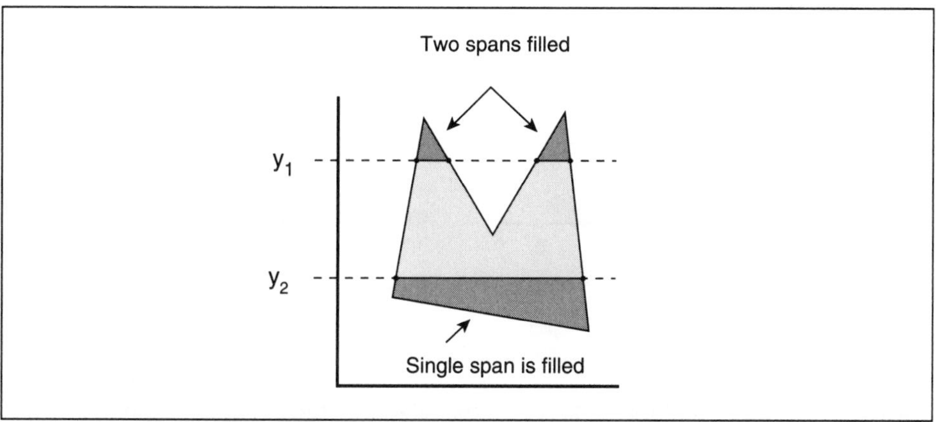

Figure 8-2. Filling spans of pixels for different scanlines that intersect a polygon

```
void gPlotSpan(int y, int x1, int x2, gColor color)
{
 int x, xmax, xmin;

 xmin = MIN(x1, x2);
 xmax = MAX(x1, x2);
 for(x = xmin; x <= xmax; x++) {
  gPlotPixel(x, y, color);
 }
}
```

Note that this does not require that you pass the endpoints of the span in increasing order. *gPlotSpan()* automatically finds the minimum and maximum values and loops through for each one to fill in the pixels. This implementation of *gPlotSpan()* works just fine but is not very efficient because you call *gPlotPixel()* for every pixel along the row. Many graphics cards provide special span-drawing functions that can greatly improve the drawing performance for filling objects by filling spans very quickly. The graphics package in this book provides a version of *gPlotSpan()* that has been optimized for DOS, but does not include any support for custom graphics cards. *gPlotSpan()* is a device-dependent function that you may want to customize to take advantage of any special graphics capabilities of your hardware. However, you must take care

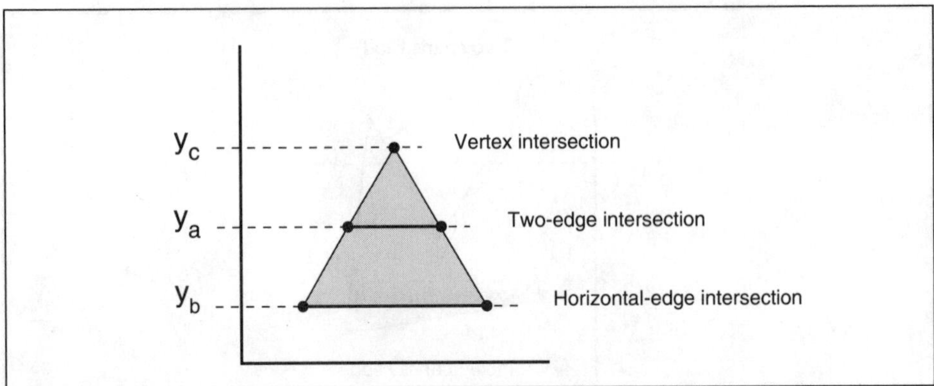

Figure 8-3. Scanlines intersecting a convex polygon intersect at two points, along a horizontal edge, or at a vertex of the polygon.

when making such a change to *gPlotSpan()*. By using *gPlotPixel()*, the *gPlotSpan()* function correctly takes pixel-based clipping into account when drawing spans. I will discuss some of the implementation issues for custom versions of *gPlotSpan()* in the following sections.

Filling Convex Objects

The simplest types of objects to fill are *convex*. Recall from Chapter 5 that a convex object is mathematically defined as one in which a line drawn between any two points in the interior is entirely contained within the object. Rectangles, circles, ellipses, and triangles are all examples of convex objects. Generally, finding all of the pixels in the interior of a convex object is much simpler than for a non-convex object. Convexity also implies that any line which intersects a convex object intersects it in either: a) two points, b) is exactly lined up with one of the edges, or c) exactly intersects a vertex. All three cases are shown in Figure 8-3 for a triangle. The scan conversion algorithm requires that you find the intersection points of each raster scan line with an object. If you know the object is convex, then you only need to find the two points of intersection; the entire span between these points is also inside of the object. Later, when scan-converting polygons are discussed, we will deal with the problem encountered when the scan line is lined up with a horizontal edge or intersects a single vertex of the polygon. Let's see how to fill several of the convex object types you have looked at so far.

Rectangles

Filling rectangles is quite easy, as you undoubtedly already guessed. The rectangle-filling procedure is just:

```
void gRectangleFill(gRectangle *rect, gColor color)
{
int x1, y1, y;

x1 = ROUND(rect->xmin);
x2 = ROUND(rect->xmax);
for(y=ROUND(rect->ymin); y <= ROUND(rect->ymax); y++) {
 gPlotSpan(y, x1, x2, color);
}

        }
```

This procedure will not work on a rotated rectangle, however. The edges of the rectangle may no longer be strictly horizontal and vertical, which is the basic assumption of *gRectangleFill()*. A transformed rectangle is still convex, though, and may be filled using the convex polygon-filling routine discussed in the next section.

Circles

Recall that circles are drawn by computing points along a single octant and using *gCircleDrawEight()* to plot the eight points of each octant. You can modify this approach to fill the circle by noting that for each computed point (x,y) along the upper octant, four sets of spans can be generated for the scanlines at x, y, $-x$, and $-y$:

$(-x,y)$ to (x, y)
$(-y,x)$ to (y,x)
$(-x,-y)$ to $(x, -y)$
$(-y,-x)$ to $(y, -x)$

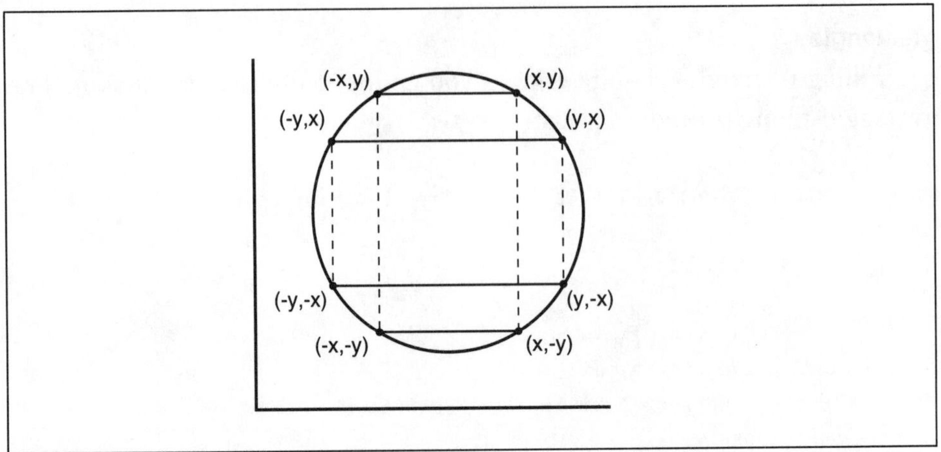

Figure 8-4. The four spans used in filling a circle. Just as the circle-drawing algorithm can plot 8 points at a time, the fill algorithm can connect them to create four spans at a time.

The four scanlines are shown in Figure 8-4. The function *gCircleFill()* is exactly the same as *gCircleDraw()* except that it uses *gCircleFillFour()* to fill in the four spans instead of *gCircleDrawEight()* to plot the points along the sides.

Ellipses

Ellipses are filled in much the same way as circles. Instead of creating four spans per computed point, we can only create two:

$(-x,y)$ to (x,y)
$(-x,-y)$ to $(x,-y)$

In all other respects, *gEllipseFill()* is exactly the same as *gEllipseDraw()* except that *gEllipseFillTwo()* is used to draw the two spans instead of *gEllipseDrawFour()* to plot the four points.

Just as you did for transformed rectangles, you must use the convex polygon-filling routine, described in the next section, to draw a rotated or transformed ellipse. However, a transformed ellipse is still convex, so the assumptions made for convex polygon scan conversion are still valid.

Convex polygons

Convex polygons are the most general type of convex object. They are generated in a number of ways such as by transforming rectangles, circles, or ellipses. For all of those object types, even when transformed, they still remain convex, as noted before. This is a general property of convex objects. Any affine (matrix) transformation of a convex object generates another convex object. It is easy to see that this is true for each of the fundamental transformation operations of translation, rotation, reflection, and scaling. Since each of these operations preserves object convexity, any combination of them will preserve convexity as well. Given this property, you can proceed with developing a method for filling a convex polygon, knowing that it will apply to any transformation you care to use. Specifically, this function will work for filling transformed rectangles, ellipses, and circles. The function *gPolygonConvexFill()* in the *gscan.c* module performs this function.

First, *gPolygonConvexFill()* checks for the trivial cases of 0 vertices (empty polygon), 1 vertex (a single point), and 2 vertices (a line segment). In these cases, the function either returns for 0 points, plots the single point for one vertex, or draws the line segment for 2 vertices. For the non-trivial cases, *gPolygonConvexFill()* loops through the vertices and finds the minimum and maximum *y*-coordinates, *ymin* and *ymax* respectively, for scan conversion. It then sets up a loop from *ymin* to *ymax* and for each scan line, finds which edges the scan line intersects. When an intersecting edge is found, the *x*-coordinate of the intersection point is determined and saved. When two different intersection points (intersections with different *x*-coordinates) are found, the span between these two points is drawn, and *gPolygonConvexFill()* continues to the next scan line. The process can be summarized as follows:

Find the minimum and maximum *y*-values for the polygon.

For each scan line do the following:

1. Determine which edges a scan line intersects.
2. Given an intersecting edge, find the *x*-coordinate of the intersection point.
3. Once two different intersection points are found, draw the span between them.

Let's examine each step of this process. Finding *ymin* and *ymax* is straightforward:

```
gPolygon poly;
int i;
int ymin, ymax;

ymin = poly->points[0].y;
ymax = ymin;
for(i=1; i < poly->npoints; i++) {
 ymin = MIN(ymin, poly->points[i].y); ymax = MAX(ymax, poly-
>points[i].y);
        }
```

Once these limits are found, *gPolygonConvexFill()* processes each scan line by looping for *y* from *ymin* to *ymax*. For each *y*, you must find all of the polygon edges that the scan line intersects. It's easy to determine this, as shown in Figure 8-5. Simply check to see if *y* is between the *y*-coordinates of the two endpoints of the edge. If so, then the scan line must intersect the polygon edge. To perform this check, use the variation of the *gCLIP_CHECK()* macro from Chapter 7, *gEDGE_CHECK()*:

```
#define gEDGE_CHECK(y1, y, y2) \
                ((y) < MIN(y1, y2) ? gCLIP_LEFT : \
                ((y) > MAX(y1, y2) ? gCLIP_RIGHT : \
  gCLIP_MIDDLE));
```

There is only one difference between this macro and *gCLIP_CHECK()*, namely, that it does not require *y1* to be less than *y2*. It finds the minimum and maximum between *y1* and *y2* and does the comparison using those values. This avoids having to check to see which of the two *y*-coordinates defining an edge is the minimum and which is the maximum.

Using *gEDGE_CHECK()*, you can check to see if the *i*th edge intersects with the scan line for row *y* using the following:

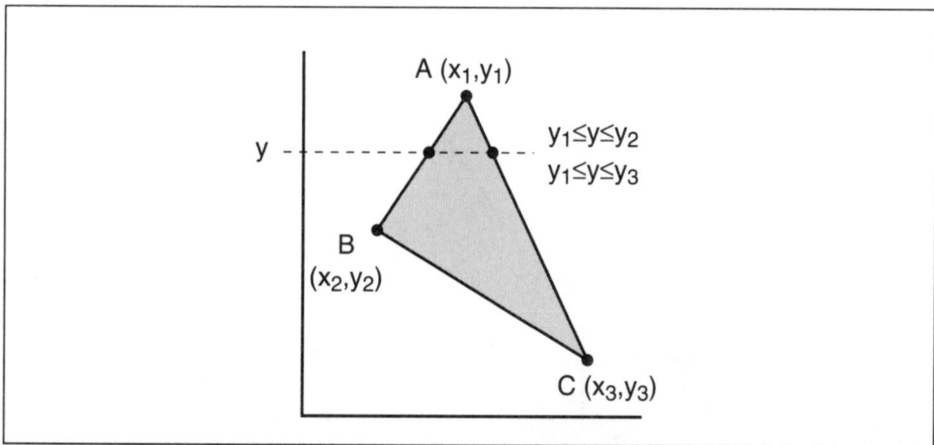

Figure 8-5 Determining if a scan line intersects an edge by comparing y-coordinates. For the scan line shown, y1 <= y <= y2, so the scan line intersects edge AB. Also, y1 <= y <= y3, so the scan line also intersects edge AC.

```
if(gEDGE_CHECK(lastpoint.y, y, poly->points[i].y) ==
  gCLIP_MIDDLE) {
 /* Find the intersection with this edge */
}
```

If the scan line intersects the edge, you must find the intersection point. Fortunately, you already know how to do this from the last chapter. Recall that the x-coordinate of the intersection point may be found by using Equation 8-1 in which $(x1,y1)$ and $(x2,y2)$ are the two vertices defining an edge:

$$x = x1 + (y-y1)*(x2-x1)/(y2-y1) \qquad \text{(Equation 8-1)}$$

The intersection point (x, y) is then one end of the span to be filled. In the special case where $y2$ is equal to $y1$, that is, the line is horizontal, you cannot use Equation 8-1 because of the division by $(y2-y1)$. So, your algorithm must check for this case. But when this occurs, the horizontal edge is the span to be filled, so you can simply use the two endpoints of the horizontal edge to define the span. No further processing is necessary.

In general, because the polygon is convex, you can terminate the loop that looks for scan line intersections with edges as soon as two *unique* intersection

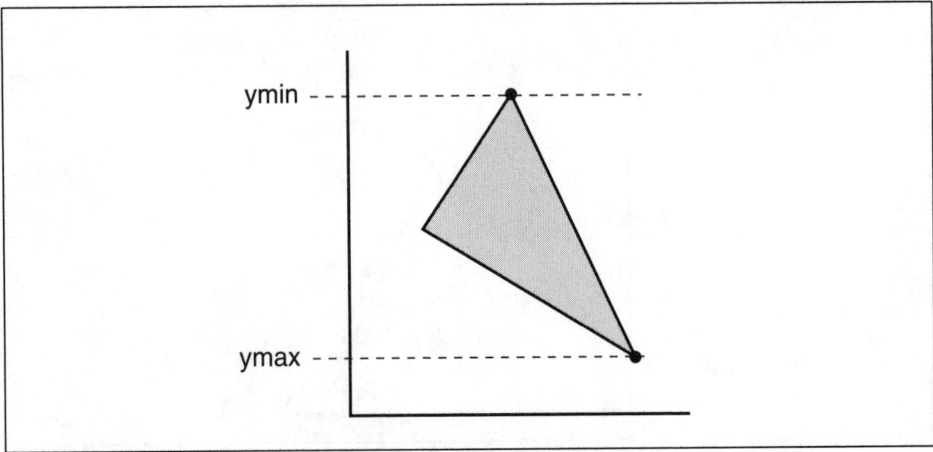

Figure 8-6. A scan line intersecting only a single vertex. For convex polygons, this will only occur on the top and bottom of the polygon.

points are found. Figure 8-6 shows the one case in which only one unique intersection is found, namely, when the scan line intersects a single vertex of the polygon. In this case, the function only needs to plot the single intersection point; the span is just a single pixel wide. The complete listing for *gPolygonConvexFill()* is shown in Listing 8-1.

```
void gPolygonConvexFill(gPolygon *poly, gColor color)
{
gPoint point1, point2;
int i, nfound, xintersect[2];
int x, y, ymin, ymax;

/* Check for trivial cases of 1 or 2 points */
if(poly->npoints == 0) {
 return;
} else if(poly->npoints == 1) {
 gPlotPixel(poly->points[0].x, poly->points[0].y, color);
 return;
} else if (poly->npoints == 2) {
 gLineDraw(poly->points[0].x, poly->points[0].y,
         poly->points[1].x, poly->points[1].y, color);
 return;
```

```
}
/* Find the min and max y */
ymin = poly->points[0].y;
ymax = ymin;

for(i=1; i < poly->npoints; i++) {
 ymin = MIN(ymin, poly->points[i].y);
 ymax = MAX(ymax, poly->points[i].y);
}

for(y = ymin; y <= ymax; y++) { /* Loop over scan lines */
 point1 = poly->points[(poly->npoints) - 1
 nfound = 0;
 for(i=0; i < poly->npoints; i++) {
  point2 = poly->points[i];
  if(gEDGE_CHECK(point1.y, y, point2.y)
     == gCLIP_MIDDLE) {
   /* First, is this edge horizontal? */
   if(point1.y == point2.y) {
    /* Great, you're done! */
    xintersect[0] = point1.x;
    xintersect[1] = point2.x;
    break;     /* Gets out of the edge loop */
   }
   /* Okay, now find the intersection point */
   slope = (point2.x - point1.x) /
          (point2.y - point1.y);
   x = ROUND(point1.x + (y - point1.y)*slope);
   if(nfound == 0) {
    xintersect[0] = x;
    xintersect[1] = x;
    nfound = 1;
   } else {
   /* Make sure it's different from the first point */
    if(x != xintersect[0])
     xintersect[1] = x;
     break;    /* Found two points, you're done! */
    }
   }
```

```
        }                  /* End of checking this edge */

        point1 = point2; /* Go on to next edge */

       } /* Finished this scan line, draw the span */

       gPlotSpan(y, xintersect[0], xintersect[1], color);
      }  /* End of scan line loop */

      }  /* End of gPolygonConvexFill */
```

Listing 8-1. Listing for gPolygonConvexFill(), the function to fill convex polygons.

There are several interesting features in the implementation of *gPolygonConvexFill( )*. The two-element array, *xintersect* ,holds the *x*-coordinate of the two intersection points for plotting the span. The variable *nfound* is used to keep track of how many intersections have been found. Whenever an intersection is found, *nfound* is checked to see if a previous one had been found. If not (*nfound* = 0), then both elements of *xintersect* are set to the computed intersection *x*-coordinate, *x*, and *nfound* is set to 1 to indicate that an intersection has been found. This automatically takes care of the case where the scan line intersects one of the vertices on the top or bottom of the polygon. If another intersection point is found, it will simply overwrite the value in *xintersect[1]*.

Also, note the use of the *break* function. Once the second, unique, intersection point is found, you do not need to process any more of the edges. By using *break*, the function immediately breaks out of the edge processing loop and draws the span. This helps speed up the filling process.

As implemented above, this function is not terribly efficient. First, the slopes of the edges, (shown as the slope variable in the listing), need to be recomputed every time an intersection is found. This computation may be performed many times for each edge during the filling process. The computation of edge slope should be done during the filling process but it should be done only once. In order to do this, allocate space to store the slopes of all of the edges and then compute these slopes in the loop that finds the minimum and maximum values. Unfortunately, allocating memory always takes extra time, so an extra step is added to avoid always having to allocate an array to store the slope data. A local array of float is allocated of a fixed length, in this case 10. If there are 10 or fewer vertices, then the already allocated local array is used. If the polygon has more than 10 vertices, then a temporary array is allocated, and then freed after the polygon is filled. Thus, memory is only allocated and freed whenever the polygon being filled has more than 10 vertices. In most applications, you typically work with polygons of only 3 or 4 vertices, so this approach saves some processing time. The first section of gPolygonConvexFill( ) changes when you add the precalculated slope array: to it

```
#define MAX_FIXED_SLOPE_SIZE  10

float *slope, fixed_slope[MAX_FIXED_SLOPE_SIZE];

/* Find the min and max Y */
ymin = poly->points[0].y;
ymax = ymin;
point1 = poly->points[(poly->npoints) - 1];>
if(poly->npoints > MAX_FIXED_SLOPE_SIZE)
 slope = gcalloc(poly->npoints, sizeof(float));
else
 slope = fixed_slope;

for(i=0; i < poly->npoints; i++) {
 point2 = poly->points[i];
 if(point1.y == point2.y)
  slope[i] = 0.0;
 else
  slope[i] = (point2.x - point1.x) /
       (point2.y - point1.y);
 ymin = MIN(ymin, point1.y);
 ymax = MAX(ymax, point2.y);
}

/* Fill polygon */
...
if(poly->npoints > MAX_FIXED_SLOPE_SIZE) free(slope);

return;
```

Instead of computing *slope* each time an intersection point is found, use *slope[i]*, the already computed value, instead to speed up the computation. The value of *slope* needed in the intersection calculation has already been computed for each edge. For horizontal edges, *slope[i]* is set to zero, since *slope* is not used for these edges. If there are more than *MAX_FIXED_SLOPE_SIZE* vertices, the function *gcalloc()* is used to allocate the array. *gcalloc()* is our version of the C function *calloc()*. It performs basically the same function of allocating memory and initializing the array to zero. However, *gcalloc()* will also check to see if the allocation fails, and if so, prints an error message on the screen and terminates the program. This makes it considerably easier to debug a program, especially since you can then put a breakpoint in *gcalloc()* at the point where the memory allocation fails. The calling syntax for *gcalloc()* is often more convenient than that of *malloc()*, although it does introduce extra computational overhead by initializing the memory. The function *gmalloc()* is also provided as an equivalent to the C *malloc()* function. It also checks to see if the allocation fails, and if so, terminates the program. The two arguments for *gcalloc()* specify the number of array elements and their size, respectively. The single argument for *gmalloc()* specifies the number of bytes of memory to allocate. Since the *slope* array is allocated from memory, you must remember to de-allocate it using *free()* before returning from the function.

Non-Convex Polygons

The *gPolygonConvexFill()* is reasonably efficient and is quite useful for drawing filled versions of known convex objects. It is especially useful for drawing such objects as transformed rectangles, circles, and ellipses. As noted in Chapter 6, the only way to draw arbitrarily transformed circles and ellipses is to approximate them with polygons. The procedure for drawing filled versions of these objects is to generate their polygonal approximation and then use *gPolygonConvexFill()*.

However, you will often need to draw filled objects that are not convex. You must therefore extend the scanning procedure to handle this case. The general method used will be the even-odd rule. Looking at Figure 8-7, all of the scan line intersections with polygon edges are found, sorted from left to right, (that is, in increasing order), and every pair of intersections is used to define a span. In the figure, intersection points AB form one span, CD a second, and EF a third. The term *even-odd* refers to the fact that if the intersections are numbered 1, 2, 3, and so forth, and you start processing at intersection 1, then pixels are drawn until you reach intersection 2. You continue to scan until intersection 3 is reached, and then start filling again. This process continues until you run out of intersections. One consequence of this rule is that their must always be an even number of intersections. This will be true for any closed figure, such as a polygon.

At first glance, it seems that filling a non-convex polygon is an easy extension of the convex polygon-filling algorithm. Instead of terminating after finding two intersections, keep scanning to find all of the scan line intersections with all of the edges. Once these are found, you then draw the spans defined by pairs of intersection points. However, you must now handle certain special cases, such as horizontal edges and vertex intersections, a little more carefully than was necessary in the convex case. The first change to the algorithm is to simply ignore horizontal edges. This may seem strange, but bear with me. The second change handles the case in which the scan line exactly intersects a polygon vertex. The two possibilities for vertex intersection are shown in Figure 8-8. In either case, the test for the scan line intersecting an edge would be true for both edges AB, and BC. For scan line *ya* in the figure, you only want to count the intersection once. This corresponds to the rule in the convex case of finding two *unique* intersection points. For scan line *yb*, you must count the intersection twice because it intersects with both of the edges containing the vertex. Based on this, the general rule for determining whether a vertex intersection is added to the list of intersections is: if a scan line intersects a vertex and the vertex is the first point of the edge (as in edge BC of Figure 8-8), then that vertex is added to the list of intersections only if the previous edge is aligned, as in case (b) of Figure 8-8. The alignment can be checked by seeing if *(C.y - B.y)* has the same sign as *(B.y - A.y)*. If the sign is the same, then you have case (a), and the vertex should only be added once, when edge AB is processed. The

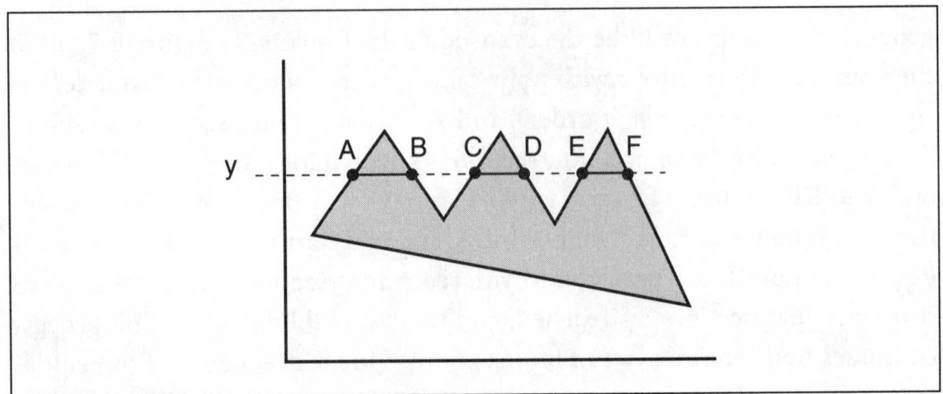

Figure 8-7. Intersections of a scan line with a non-convex polygon. Note that each pair of intersections defines a span to be filled.

test condition is only evaluated when the scan line intersects the first point of the edge, edge BC in this case. In the second case for the scan line at y_b, you evaluate *(E.y - D.y)* and compare it with *(D.y - C.y)*. In this case, the signs are different, and the vertex D must be added twice, once when edge CD is processed and once when edge DE is processed.

The comparison of *(C.y - B.y)* with *(B.y - A.y)*, which is only done when processing edge BC, must also check for the condition that AB could be horizontal. In this case, you must scan backwards through the polygon to find the first non-horizontal edge. The first such edge is used in the test, just as you would have used AB if it had not been horizontal. The complete test of whether the first point of an edge should be added can be performed by evaluating the product *(C.y - B.y)*(B.y - A.y)*. If this product is greater than 0, then the signs are the same and the vertex should be added as an intersection. Otherwise, the vertex is not added.

Unfortunately, this rule can still lead to problems with horizontal edges. Consider Figure 8-9, in which you evaluate the scan line that intersects the horizontal edge BC. By the vertex counting rule, you would add the point B, skip the edge BC, ignore the point C (because *(D.y - C.y)*(B.y - A.y)* is positive) and add the intersection point *i* along DA. You only get one span to fill in from B to *i*. To be correct, you should also fill in the span from *i* to C. This can be accomplished in one of two ways. All intersected horizontal edges can be added

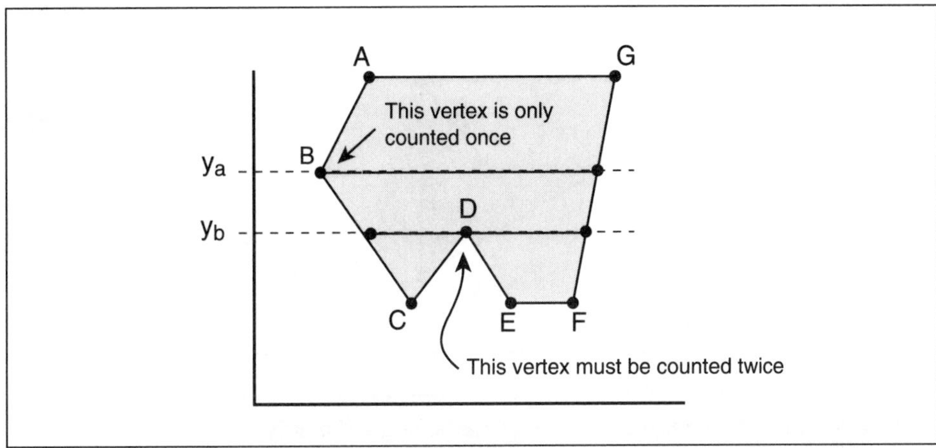

Figure 8-8. The two basic cases of a scan line intersecting with a vertex

to the list of intersections *after* sorting, to ensure that they get filled in. Some areas will be filled in twice, but the number of horizontal edges will usually be small. The second method is to simply draw the horizontal edges in after the rest of the scan conversion. Either method will work, so that, in the end, horizontal edges are correctly filled in.

The complete listing for *gPolygonFill( )*, (which, of course, works on convex polygons as well), is shown in Listing 8-2. There are now two additional allocated arrays, the array *xintersect* which contains all of the potential edge intersections for a scan line, and the array *horiz* which identifies each edge as either horizontal (*horiz[i]* = 1) or non-horizontal (*horiz[i]* = 0). The *horiz* array is set at the same time the *slope* array is, when the edges are scanned for the minimum and maximum values. Note that the same trick is used for allocating these arrays that was used in *gPolygonConvexFill( )*, namely, that if the polygon has less than a preset number of vertices (10 in this case), you use pre-allocated arrays for *slope*, *horiz*, and *xintersect*. Otherwise, the arrays are explicitly allocated and freed at the end.

The *xintersect* array must hold up to *poly->npoints* intersections for any one scan line. The method developed so far for adding intersections ensures that the maximum number of possible intersections with a scan line is at most the number of edges in the polygon. The intersection values are in no particular

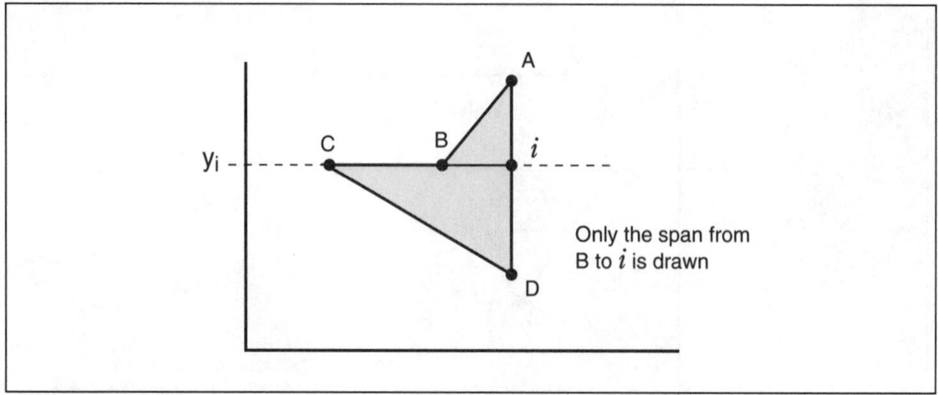

Figure 8-9. Scan line intersecting a horizontal edge of a polygon. As shown by the marked intersection points, the horizontal edge may not always be completely included as a span.

order after all of the edges have been processed, so the *xintersect* array must be sorted into increasing order of *x*-coordinates before you can pair up the intersection points into spans. To do the sort, you use a sorting method known as a *bubble-sort*. The *xintersect* array is scanned, an element at a time, and if two sequential elements are in the wrong order, that is, if *xintersect[i]* is greater than *xintersect[i+1]*, then they are swapped. The variable *wrong_order* is used to indicate whether a swap was necessary or not during the scan. The scan is repeated until no elements need to be swapped, indicating that the array is completely sorted. The variable *pass* counts the number of times you have scanned the array. Each time the array is scanned, you are assured that the last *pass* elements are in the correct order, so they do not need to be checked again.

Note that *gPolygonFill()*, uses *SWAP()*, a macro not discussed before. The *SWAP()* macro simply swaps the contents of the variables passed as the first two arguments. The last argument is a temporary variable used to hold the value of one of the variables while it is set to the value of the other variable. Again, since it is defined as a macro, it can work on any data type. It will even work on structures such as *gPoint*, swapping all of the structure members.

```
#define MAX_FIXED_SIZE 10

void gPolygonFill(gPolygon *poly_passed, gColor color)
```

```
{
gPolygon *poly;
gPoint point1, point2, testpoint1, testpoint2;
int i, j, nfound, temp, sign, pass;
int x, y, ymin, ymax, wrong_order;
int *horiz,fixed_horiz[MAX_FIXED_SIZE];
int *xintersect, fixed_xintersect[MAX_FIXED_SIZE];
float *slope, fixed_slope[MAX_FIXED_SIZE];

/* Allocate slope and horizontal detection arrays */
if(poly->npoints > MAX_FIXED_SIZE) {
 slope = (float *)gcalloc(poly->npoints, sizeof(float));
 horiz = (int *)gcalloc(poly->npoints, sizeof(int));
 /* Since a maximum of only one intersection is added per
    edge, there can only be at most poly->npoints
    intersections per scan line */
 xintersect = (int *)gcalloc(poly->npoints, sizeof(int));
} else {
 slope = fixed_slope;
 horiz = fixed_horiz;
 xintersect = fixed_xintersect;
}


/* Make a copy, transform the points */
poly = gPolygonCopy(NULL, poly_passed);
gTransformPoints(poly->matrix, poly->points, poly>npoints);

/* Find the min and max y */
ymin = poly->points[0].y;
ymax = ymin;
point1 = poly->points[(poly->npoints) - 1;
for(i=0; i < poly->npoints; i++) {
 point2 = poly->points[i];
 if(point1.y == point2.y) {
  horiz[i] = 1;
  slope[i] = 0.0;
 } else {
  horiz[i] = 0;
```

```
    slope[i] = (point2.x - point1.x) /
              (point2.y - point1.y);
  }
  ymin = MIN(ymin, point1.y);
  ymax = MAX(ymax, point2.y);
 }

 for(y = ymin; y <= ymax; y++) {        /* Loop over scanlines */
  point1 = poly->points[(poly->npoints)-1];
  nfound = 0;
  for(i=0; i < poly->npoints; i++) {
   point2 = poly->points[i];
   if(gEDGE_CHECK(point1.y, y, point2.y)
       == gCLIP_MIDDLE) {
    /* First, is this edge horizontal? */
    if(horiz[i]) {
     /* skip it */
     continue;  /* Goes to end of the edge loop */
    }
    /* Did you intersect the first vertex point? */
    if(y == point1.y) {
     /* Yes, must find first non-horizontal edge */
     j = i-1    if(j < 0) j = poly->npoints - 1;
     while(horiz[j]) {
      j—;
      if(j < 0) j = poly->npoints - 1;
     }
     /* Now perform sign test */
     if(j > 0)
      testpoint1 = poly->points[j-1];
     else
      testpoint1 = poly->points[poly->npoints-1];
     testpoint2 = poly->points[j];
     sign = (testpoint2.y - testpoint1.y) *
            (point2.y - point1.y);
     if(sign < 0)
      xintersect[nfound++] = point1.x;
     /* All done for vertex matching case */
    } else {
```

```
    /* Not at the first vertex, find the intersection*/
    x = ROUND(point1.x + (y - point1.y)*slope[i]);
    xintersect[nfound++] = x;
   }
  }          /* End of checking this edge */

  point1 = point2; /* Go on to next edge */

 } /* Finished this scan line, draw all of the spans */

 /* First, sort the intersections */
 pass = 0;
 do {
  wrong_order = 0;
  for(i=0; i < nfound-1-pass; i++) {
   if(xintersect[i] > xintersect[i+1]) {
    wrong_order = 1;
    SWAP(xintersect[i], xintersect[i+1], temp);
   }
  }
  pass++;
 } while(wrong_order);

 /* Great, now you can draw the spans */
 for(i=0; i < nfound; i += 2) {
  gPlotSpan(y, xintersect[i], xintersect[i+1], color);
    }
} /* End of scan line loop */
/* Finally, draw all of the horizontal edges */
point1 = poly->points[poly->npoints - 1];
for(i=0; i < poly->npoints; i++) {
 point2 = poly->points[i];
 if(horiz[i])
  gPlotSpan(point2.y, point1.x, point2.x, color);
 point1 = point2;
}

if(poly->npoints > MAX_FIXED_SIZE) {
 free(horiz);
```

```
        free(slope);
        free(xintersect);
    }
    gPolygonDelete(poly);  /* Delete our copy */

}                          /* End of gPolygonFill */
```

Listing 8-3. The function gPolygonFill() for filling non-convex polygons

Clipping and Filling

Just as with drawing the objects, you need to consider what happens when an object being filled must be clipped against some clipping region. If the object is analytically clipped, there is no problem, you simply fill the clipped object as you would any other object. Likewise, for pixel-based clipping, there is no problem if you use the *gPlotSpan()* function as it was defined previously. However, our approach, as currently implemented, may not be a very efficient algorithm for several reasons. First, when you compute *ymin* and *ymax*, you find the limits for the polygon. These may be well outside of the clipping region, as shown in Figure 8-10. So, the first improvement is to restrict *ymin* and *ymax* to be within the clipping region. To do this, use the function *gGetClipBoundingBox()* described in Chapter 7. Note that if you supply your own clipping functions, you must set the bounding box using *gSetClipBoundingBox()*. By default, *gGetClipBoundingBox()* returns a rectangle which bounds the entire screen. Thus, even if you don't do anything else, you will at least be clipping against the screen. Once you have the bounding box, the search for *ymin* and *ymax* is changed slightly. Instead of initializing *ymin* and *ymax* to the first point of the polygon, they are set to the minimum and maximum *y*-coordinates of the returned bounding box, as shown in the following code segment:

```
gRectangle *bbox;

/* Find the min and max y */
bbox = gGetClipBoundingBox();
ymin = bbox->ymin;
ymax = bbox->ymax;
```

By using the bounding box, you avoid the problem of processing scanlines that are outside of the clipping region. The bounding box may also be used to keep from processing spans that are outside of the clipping region. You cannot simply reject intersection points that are outside of the clipping region, as the other endpoint defining the span may be within the clipping region, or on the other side of the clipping region. Instead, change *gPlotSpan()* to check spans to see if they are outside of the bounding box as shown in Listing 8-4.

```
void gPlotSpan(int y, int x1, int x2, gColor color)
{
 int x, xmax, xmin;
 gRectangle *bbox;

 bbox = gGetClipBoundingBox();
 /* First, is y within the clipping region? */
 if(gCLIP_TEST(bbox->ymin, y, bbox->ymax) !=
      gCLIP_MIDDLE)
  return;

 xmin = MIN(x1, x2);
 xmax = MAX(x1, x2);
 /* If the left endpoint is greater than bbox.xmax or if the right
    endpoint is less than bbox.xmin, then the span is outside of
    the clipping region, don't draw it */
 if(xmin > bbox->xmax || xmax < bbox->xmin)
  return;

 for(x = xmin; x <= xmax; x++) {
  gPlotPixel(x, y, color);
 }
}
```

Listing 8-4. Modifed version of gPlotSpan() that avoids drawing spans that are completely outside of the clipping region.

As stated earlier, you do not really have to check the span against the clipping region if *gPlotSpan()* is defined using *gPlotPixel()* because *gPlotPixel()* will

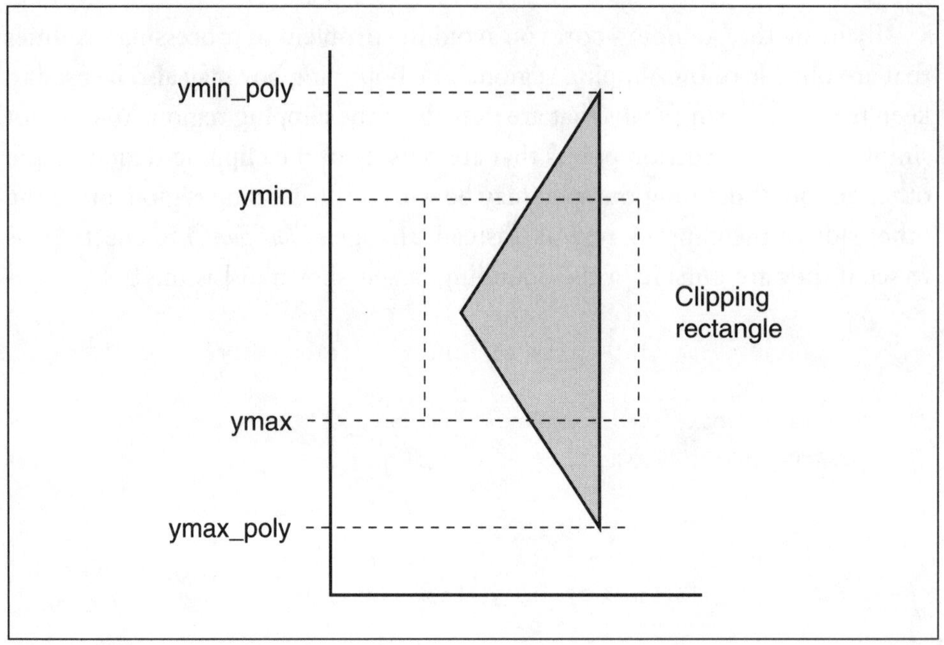

Figure 8-10. Finding ymin and ymax for a polygon. These may be outside of the clipping region, so both ymin and ymax are first clipped to the limits of the clipping region to speed up the fill operation.

do the clipping. However, rejecting spans that are completely outside of the clipping region can significantly improve the performance of span drawing. Testing every drawn pixel with *gPlotPixel()* is slower than rejecting the entire span with one test. Furthermore, if you define *gPlotSpan()* to take advantage of some fast drawing capabilities of the graphics hardware, then it is even more important to check against the clipping region. Note that this method only rejects spans that are outside of the bounding box of the clipping region. *gPlotPixel()* will take care of those pixels that are inside of the bounding box, but not necessarily inside of the clipping region, such as in the case of overlapping windows described in Chapter 7.

A Pattern for Filling

Filling an object with a solid color is quite useful. However, much more can be done. One of the most common ways to create more interesting images is to fill the interior with a repeated pattern. If you use MS-Windows, you see this technique all of the time in the background image of the displays. A single pattern is stored in a bitmap as simply a two-dimensional rectangular array of pixel values. The pattern is repeated until the entire screen is filled in. With a slight addition to *gPolygonFill()*, you can add pattern drawing capability to our scan conversion routines.

Instead of writing a single color out to the screen in *gPlotSpan()*, you create a new function called *gPlotSpanWithBitmap()*. Instead of a *gColor* variable for the last argument, this function takes two pointers to *gBitmap* structures. (*gBitmap* is defined in Chapter 9; for the moment you just need to know that it contains an two-dimensional array of *gColor* values that define the bitmap.) The drawing color for each pixel is selected from the bitmap as a function of the (*x*,*y*) screen coordinate being drawn. The bitmap element is selected by taking the *x*- and *y*-coordinates passed to *gPlotPixel()* and computing an *x* and *y* bitmap index using modulo arithmetic. For instance, if the bitmap has *nx* columns and *ny* rows, you take the *x* coordinate and compute (*x* mod *nx*), using the macro *gMod*(*x*, *nx*). The *mod* operator "wraps" *x* around to always return a value between 0 and *nx*-1 Ordinarily, you would just use the C percent operator, but this operator does not produce the desired result if *x* is negative. The following is the definition for *gMod()*:

```
#define gMod(a, b) ((a) >= 0) ? ((a) % (b)) :
            ((b) - ((-(a)) % (b))))
```

The computed index value (*gMod(x, nx)*) specifies the column of the bitmap to access. You perform exactly the same calculation with the *y* -coordinate to find the row of the bitmap. Note that the coordinates are offset by the quantities *bitmap->x0* and *bitmap->y0* respectively. This provides the capability to position the bitmap relative to the screen. If the polygon is moved, you can use these two values in the *gBitmap* structure to keep the bitmap in the same location relative to the polygon. The two computed bitmap indices specify which bitmap element to plot on the screen at this position. The second bitmap passed to the function determines whether or not the pixel should be written. If a *NULL* is passed for this argument, then all values from the bitmap will be used.

You will see in Chapter 9 how the second argument may be used to overlay a bitmap image over a drawing. The completed version of *gPlotSpanWithBitmap()* is shown in Listing 8-5.

```
void gPlotSpanWithBitmap(int y, int x1, int x2,
                gBitmap *bitmap, gBitmap *clip){
 int x, xmax, xmin, xbitmap, ybitmap;
 gRectangle *bbox;

 bbox = gGetClipBoundingBox();
 /* First, is y within the clipping region? */
 if(gCLIP_TEST(bbox->ymin, y, bbox->ymax) !=
          gCLIP_MIDDLE)
  return;

 xmin = MIN(x1, x2);
 xmax = MAX(x1, x2);
 /* If the left endpoint is greater than bbox.xmax or  if
    the right endpoint is less than bbox.xmin, then the span
    is outside of the clipping region, don't draw it */
 if(xmin > bbox->xmax || xmax < bbox->xmin)
  return;

 ybitmap = gMod((y - bitmap->x0), (bitmap->ny));
 for(x = xmin; x <= xmax; x++) {
  xbitmap = gMod((x - bitmap->x0), (bitmap->nx));
  if(!clip) {
   /* No clipping, go ahead and draw */
   gPlotPixel(x, y, bitmap->data[xbitmap][ybitmap]);
  } else if(clip && clip->data[xbitmap][ybitmap]) {
   /* Checked clipping, OK to draw */
   gPlotPixel(x, y, bitmap->data[xbitmap][ybitmap]);
  }
 }
}
```

Listing 8-5. The function gPlotSpanWithBitmap() lets us fill an object with a pattern.

Drawing and filling with bitmap patterns is discussed in more detail in Chapter 9. Another method of creating a fill pattern is to call a function instead of indexing into a bitmap. Just as with the clipping functions, you can define a function which, given an x- and y-coordinate to be plotted, returns the color to plot at that pixel. Generally, however, it is much faster to simply create a precomputed bitmap in which the function is evaluated at every pixel ahead of time. Therefore, I have not provided the option for generating patterns based on evaluating functions in the current package.

More Drawing Techniques

Being able to draw filled versions of objects vastly expands the number and types of drawings you can create. With this capability, you can begin to tackle more advanced graphics problems such as drawing text, animating objects, and creating useful charts and graphs. The next few chapters explore these various applications. But first, you need one other basic drawing type which I have already mentioned several times, the bitmap. Bitmaps have quite a number of uses, two of which you have already seen. In the next chapter, the bitmap structure and associated manipulation functions are defined. In addition, I discuss a number of ways they can be used to create even more elaborate drawings using thick lines and patterned edges.

Functions Found in This Chapter

Demonstration programs

`dfill.exe`

This program first demonstrates filling the various object types with solid colors. It then demonstrates dynamic polygon filling using the same display as *dxform.exe* from Chapter 6. A polygon is shown in the four quadrants of the screen using various affine transformations. *dfill.exe* fills each polygon rather than simply drawing them in outline form.

Filling functions

```
void gPlotSpan(int y, int x1, int x2, gColor color);
```

Fills in the span of pixels for row *y* from *x1* to *x2* using the color *color*.

```
void gRectangleFill(gRectangle *rect, gColor color);
```

Fills a rectangle with the color specified by *color*.

```
void gCircleFill(gCircle *circle, gColor color);
```

Fills a circle with the color specified by *color*.

```
void gCircleFillFour(gCircle *circle, int x, int y,
                gColor color);
```

Draws the four spans connecting the eight symmetric points along the circle. This does the same operation for filling that *gCircleDrawEight()* does for drawing the boundary.

```
void gEllipseFill(gEllipse *ellipse, gColor color);
```

Fills an ellipse with the color specified by *color*.

```
void gEllipseFillTwo(gEllipse *ellipse, int x, int y,
                gColor color);
```

Draws the four spans connecting the four symmetric points along the ellipse. This does the same operation for filling that *gEllipseDrawFour()* does for drawing the boundary.

```
void *gmalloc(unsigned int nbytes);
```

Allocates a block of memory suitable to hold an array *nbytes* long. The calling syntax is exactly the same as the standard C function *malloc()*. *gmalloc()* checks to see if the allocation fails, and if so, prints an error message on the screen and terminates the program.

```
void *gcalloc(unsigned int nelements, unsigned int nbytes);
```

Allocates and initializes a block of memory suitable to hold an array of *nentries*, each element of which is *nbytes* long. The calling syntax is exactly the same as that of the standard C function *calloc()*. *gcalloc()* checks to see if the allocation fails, and if so, prints an error message on the screen and terminates the program.

```
void gPolygonConvexFill(gPolygon *poly, gColor color);
```

Fills a convex polygon with the color specified by *color*. This is faster than calling *gPolygonFill()* if you know that the polygon is convex.

```
gCLIP_STATE gEDGE_CHECK(x1, x, x2)
```

A macro that does the same thing as *gCLIP_CHECK()* except that it does not require that *x1* is less than *x2*. This is useful for scanning polygon edges, where the vertices may be in any order.

```
void gPolygonFill(gPolygon *poly, gColor color);
```

Fills an arbitrary polygon with the color specified by *color*.

```
void gPlotSpanWithBitmap(int y, int x1, int x2,
                         gBitmap *bitmap);
```

Same as *gPlotSpan()*, except that it uses a bitmap instead of a single color. The pattern is repeated across the span so that an object filled with a bitmap appears to be tiled with the pattern.

CHAPTER 9

Drawing Bitmaps

In the previous chapters I developed a set of routines for drawing geometrically defined objects. These types of objects are defined by a small set of parameters, such as the center and radius for a circle or two corners for a rectangle, and can be easily resized or reshaped using the affine transformations. Such objects are also commonly referred to as *vector* objects, since their boundary can be drawn as a line drawing. However, many types of objects that you might need to draw or manipulate are not easily representable by collections of simple geometric objects. For example, you might want to use a scanned photograph as a backdrop for your drawing. Or you might want to create a logo using a paint program. The output of the paint program is a raster version of your logo image, that is, a rectangular array of pixels that define the image.

No matter how an image is created, all that is ultimately saved on the screen is the raster image. Drawing the raster image to the screen simply requires copying pixels from the array to the screen. The raster array of pixels is stored in a structure known as a *bitmap*, which, along with other information, contains the width and height of the stored bitmap image as well as the pixel data comprising the image. In this chapter, you will see how bitmaps are created, manipulated, and used in a variety of different graphics operations, including drawing objects with thick boundaries, filling regions with patterns, and defining and maintaining complex clipping regions. I then discuss some of the limitations of bitmaps and how to efficiently use them in a graphics application.

Bitmaps

The term *bitmap graphics* is often used to describe graphics programs that display images using bitmaps. Any image that can be represented in a frame buffer, can also be stored in a bitmap. In effect, a bitmap is a "pre-drawn" image that can be quickly copied to the screen every time it is needed. In many respects, you can think of a bitmap as a frame buffer stored in your computer's local memory. A bitmap is considerably more flexible in the types of images that can

A graphic image can be constructed in many different ways. Until this point, you have only seen how to create a drawing by combining simple geometric objects, such as lines, ellipses, and polygons. Complex, photographic pictures, like the one shown above, are difficult to describe in such a geometric manner.

The advent of low cost scanning equipment has made it possible to capture photographs in a digital form that can be directly manipulated by a computer. A digital image stored in this manner, referred to as a bitmap, lets you represent any pattern or image. Essentially, a bitmap is a small frame buffer stored in your computer's memory rather than on its graphics card. With such a bitmap, you can easily create elaborate pattern-filled objects or draw shapes using the pattern as a glorified paint brush. With the methods shown in this chapter, you'll have the flexibility to include digitized photographs in your drawing or to create your own drawing patterns in a myriad of combinations, sizes, and colors.

be represented since a bitmap can contain whatever a frame buffer can, including scanned photographs or painted images. However, changing a bitmap's size or orientation is not as easy as doing so for the geometric objects. In fact, this is the main distinguishing characteristic of bitmap graphics. Normally, a bitmap is used to represent a relatively small graphics object (usually less than 50 x 50 pixels) that can be freely moved about the screen, but whose size and orientation remains fixed.

Bitmaps are an essential element of every graphics package and for any windowing system. For instance, in MS-Windows, the main cursor arrow is defined by a special type of bitmap called an *icon*. The cursor icon is simply a bitmap that is drawn just as any other bitmap is, by copying the pixels of the bitmap to the screen. Instead of having to redraw a complicated arrowhead shape every time the cursor is moved, the windowing system simply copies pixels from the cursor bitmap to wherever the cursor happens to be on the screen. This is much faster than redrawing the cursor from its geometric description would be. Similarly, the cursor shape can be immediately switched to create special effects, such as changing from an arrow to an hourglass, just by changing which bitmap is used. As long as the cursor bitmaps are the same size (have the same number of pixels in the bitmap), the bitmaps always take the same amount of time to draw, regardless of the complexity of the image. Copying pixels from a bitmap to the screen is often referred to as a *bitblt* (pronounced "bit-blit") operation. Bitmaps provide many benefits for graphics applications:

- Reading and writing to your computer's local memory is usually much faster than accessing the frame buffer on the graphics card. If you can create your drawing in a bitmap, then you only need to copy the drawing from the bitmap to the screen when the drawing is complete.

- It is generally much easier to animate objects (move them around) that are drawn with bitmaps. Whenever the object moves, the bitmap is erased from the old position of the screen and redrawn in the new position. The speed of this operation depends only on the number of pixels being copied from the bitmap, not on the complexity of the image stored in the bitmap.

- Many types of images, such as those created by paint programs or by scanning in photographs, cannot be usefully represented as a collection of geometric shapes. The only reasonable way to store them is as a raster image, that is, as a bitmap.

- Many types of graphics hardware support very fast pixel-copying operations. In fact, providing faster *bitblt* functions in hardware is the main way that the new crop of fast graphics cards for the PC speed up MS-Windows. Additionally, the development of the local bus for the PC allows pixels in the frame buffer to be accessed at the same speed as normal memory. This provides very fast pixel operations.

Bitmaps are used for many purposes, two of which were mentioned in the previous chapters. The first use was to define a clipping region. The second was to define a pattern for filling a polygon. In the following sections, you will see how bitmaps are used for these and other operations such as drawing thick boundaries for any of the geometric shapes shown so far, as well as learn how to draw arbitrarily shaped regions (not just rectangular) using clipping masks.

Bitmap terminology

The *bit* in bitmap originally meant that only one bit per pixel was stored. In the old days of computing, memory was expensive and the maximum amount available on a particular machine was usually quite low. Since only two values can be represented by one bit (0 or 1), any bitmap image could only contain two colors. While this may seem quite limiting (and it is), it does save a lot of memory by using only two colors; you save a factor of 8 for 256-color VGA images. Later on you will see that clipping regions represented by bitmaps still only use two values per pixel, and thus can be represented by a single bit per pixel. When used as an image, the default color assignment of the two possible values is black for the 0 bits, and white for the 1 bits. However, this color assignment can be overridden and you may assign any color you like to the two possible values. By convention, the color of the 0 pixels is called the *background* color, and the color of the 1 pixels is called the *foreground* color.

Now that memory is much cheaper, and larger quantities are readily available, you do not have to try to compress the bitmap as much. Instead, you will store a bitmap as a two dimensional array of *gColor* values (8 bits per pixel for VGA display). In some graphics environments, such as X-Windows for UNIX, this type of structure is called a *pixmap* (abbreviation for pixel map), to distinguish it from the "classic" 1 bit per pixel bitmap. Throughout this book, the term bitmap is used when referring to any rectangular array of pixels, no matter how many bits per pixel are actually used. The implementation of bitmaps, the *gBitmap* structure, is defined as:

```
typedef struct gBitmap_struct {
 int wide, tall;         /* Width and height */
 int x0, y0;             /* Hot spot of bitmap */
 gColor **data;
} gBitmap;
```

The variables *wide* and *tall* represent the width and height of the bitmap, respectively. The declaration of *data* is a double pointer, the C equivalent of a pointer to a two-dimensional array. The variables *x0* and *y0* define the hot spot, or selection point, of the bitmap. A bitmap is drawn by a call to *gBitmapDraw()*. This specfies the (*x*,*y*) location at which to draw the bitmap. The ***hot spot*** represents the element of the bitmap that is plotted at (*x*,*y*). For example, if the hot spot is (*0*,*0*), then the upper-left corner of the bitmap will be drawn at (*x*,*y*) on the screen. To center the bitmap around (*x*,*y*), set *x0* to *wide*/2 and *y0* to *height*/2. While *x0* and *y0* are usually meant to be within the bitmap, they are not required to be. In effect, the hot spot simply represents where the bitmap should be drawn relative to the (*x*,*y*) coordinate passed to *gBitmapDraw()*.

The name hot spot was coined for bitmaps that are used to represent a cursor. In all windowing systems and in many graphics applications, such as paint and draw programs, the cursor is drawn using a bitmap, usually representing an arrow shape of some sort. For the arrow shape, the tip of the arrow should define the pixel being selected. After creating the bitmap containing the desired arrow shape, you must then set the tip of the arrow as the hot spot for the bitmap. This provides the flexibility of not always having to use the center or corner of the bitmap as the selection point.

Bitmap basics

As with every other structure in the graphics package, there is a *gBitmapCreate()*, *gBitmapCopy()*, and *gBitmapDelete()* function. The *gBitmapCreate()* function has four arguments:

```
gBitmap *gBitmapCreate(int wide, int tall, int x0, int y0);
```

It creates a bitmap of the specified width and height, with a hot spot at (*x0*, *y0*). The value for *x0* must be between *0* and *wide-1*. The value for *y0* must be between *0* and *tall-1*. The *data* field is a pointer to an allocated two-dimensional array of *gColor* pixels. All of the bitmap pixels are initialized to *0*. *gBitmapCopy()* and *gBitmapDelete()* do the usual copying and deleting operations. The main drawing function for bitmaps is *gBitmapDraw()*, which draws the passed bitmap positioned such that the hot spot coordinate (*x0*, *y0*) is located at the (*x*,*y*) coordinate passed to *gBitmapDraw()*. Similarly, the function *gBitmapRead()* copies a specified area of the screen from the frame buffer into the passed bitmap. Thus, one way to create a bitmap is to draw an image to an area of the screen and copy this area into the bitmap. However, this is often not convenient and is certainly not the fastest method because it requires using the frame buffer for the drawing operations. Instead, you can create a bitmap using more direct approaches.

Creating a Bitmap

In many ways, you can treat a *gBitmap* object just as you would treat the frame buffer. Just as the pixels in a frame buffer are accessed using the *gPlotPixel()* and *gReadPixel()* functions, elements of a bitmap may be accessed using the two-dimensional array subscripting of C. As with the frame buffer, the upper left corner of the bitmap is at address (*0*,*0*). To access the pixel at location (*x*,*y*) of the bitmap, pointed to by the pointer *bitmap*, simply refer to element *bitmap->data[x][y]*. Note that this means that a bitmap is stored in column-order. The pointer, *bitmap->data[x]*, is a pointer to the data in row *x*.

Creating a bitmap by setting each pixel individually using array indexing is not a very convenient method, just as plotting a picture point by point with *gPlotPixel()* is not. It would be very useful to create a bitmap using the same drawing tools that are available for the frame buffer. To that end, *gPlotPixel()* is set up to draw directly into a bitmap, instead of onto the screen.

The function *gSetOutputBitmap()* sets the output destination for *gPlotPixel()*, that is, where the pixel is actually drawn. *gSetOutputBitmap()* is passed a single argument, a pointer to a *gBitmap*. If the pointer is *NULL*, then the output is sent to the frame buffer. If the pointer is not *NULL*, then all subsequent calls to *gPlotPixel()* will write pixels to the passed bitmap. Since all of the graphics drawing routines are ultimately based upon *gPlotPixel()*, all of those routines can now be used to write images to a bitmap.

In order to ensure that no illegal memory accesses are attempted when writing to the output bitmap, a rectangular clipping region of the same dimensions as the bitmap is automatically set and enabled for the bitmap. You may, of course, add any additional clipping regions that you wish with *gAddClippingFunction()*. Whenever writing to the bitmap is disabled with a call to *gSetOutputBitmap(NULL)*, the rectangular clipping region for the bitmap is removed.

As was done for the clipping functions, there is also a function to specifically enable or disable writing to a bitmap, forcing the output to the screen. The function *gOutputBitmapEnable()* is passed a single *int* argument, which, if 0, forces *gPlotPixel()* to write to the screen. If the argument is not 0, and a bitmap has been set by *gSetOutputBitmap()*, then the output will be written to the bitmap. By default, writing to the bitmap is enabled whenever you call *gSetOutputBitmap()* with a non-*NULL* bitmap pointer. *gOutputBitmapEnable()* provides a way for your graphics functions to temporarily disable output to a bitmap, for instance, if you want to see what is being drawn into the bitmap, without having to know whether a bitmap is even in use.

Creating Geometric Bitmaps

As mentioned earlier, the method of output redirection lets us use all of the drawing functions for rectangles, circles, elllipses, and polygons to create a bitmap. You do not have to have special versions of any of the drawing routines specifically designed to write into bitmaps. This means a lot less code, and only one version of each drawing routine to debug. Additionally, any and all objects that you develop drawing routines for can also be drawn into bitmaps, without any extra effort on your part. The implementation of the output redirection is quite efficient. *gPlotPixel()* checks to see if a bitmap pointer has been set and, if so, then checks to see if writing to a bitmap has been enabled by a call to *gBitmapEnable()*. These kinds of simple conditional checks execute very quickly compared to the speed of actually writing a pixel to the screen, so the speed of drawing to a bitmap or to a screen is not significantly affected.

As an example, you can create a bitmap of the universal *NO* symbol (circle with a slash through it) using the following code:

```
gBitmap *no_sign
gRectangle rect;
gCircle *circle;

/* Create an 11 x 11 bitmap, center pixel is “hot” */
no_sign = gBitmapCreate(11, 11, 5, 5);
gSetBitmapOutput(no_sign);
rect.xmin = rect.ymin = 0.0;
rect.xmax = rect.xmax = 10.0;         /* Whole rectangle */
gRectangleDraw(&rect, gWHITE);        /* White background */
circle = gCircleCreate(5.0, 5.0, 5.0);
gCircleDraw(circle, gBLACK);          /* Black circle */
gLineDraw(0, 0, 10.0, 10.0, gBLACK); /* Slash */
gCircleDelete(circle);
gSetBitmapOutput(NULL);
/* All finished, no_sign is ready for use */
```

Creating Bitmaps From Arrays

While creating bitmaps using the drawing algorithms is quite useful, it is not always suitable. Occasionally you will want to create bitmaps by specifying each individual pixel entry in a table. In C this is best accomplished by creating an initialized array, that is, one in which the inital values of each entry is defined in the declaration of the array. This technique lets you hand code special symbols like text characters. For example, you can create an array for a 5 x 5 bitmap of a plus sign with a declaration like:

```
gColor plus_sign[25] =
    {
      0, 0, 1, 0, 0,
      0, 0, 1, 0, 0,
      1, 1, 1, 1, 1,
      0, 0, 1, 0, 0,
      0, 0, 1, 0, 0
    }
```

The function *gBitmapSetFromArray()* copies the data from an array such as *plus_sign* into a bitmap. It is up to you to make sure that the size and dimensions of the array are the same as those of the bitmap. In this example, you must have previously created a 5 x 5 bitmap before calling *gBitmapSetFromArray()*, with a code segment such as the following:

```
gBitmap *bitmap;

bitmap = gBitmapCreate(5, 5, 0, 0).
gBitmapSetFromArray(bitmap, plus_sign, NULL);
```

If there is a size mismatch, disastrous results can occur, so its worth checking to make sure the sizes match. Furthermore, as shown for *plus_sign*, the array must specify the bitmap in columnar order, that is, a row at a time. As shown in the example of *plus_sign*, the basic structure of the bitmap can be seen by laying out the data in the same order, specifying each row of the bitmap as a separate data line. The plus sign can be clearly seen by the arrangement of the ones. The calling syntax for *gBitmapSetFromArray()* is

```
gBitmap *gBitmapSetFromArray(gBitmap *map, gColor *data,
                             gColor *lookup_table);
```

The return value is just the value of the *map* variable you pass to the function. The last argument is an optional pointer to a lookup table for the data in the array. If this argument is *NULL*, then the data is simply copied from the array directly to the bitmap. If the pointer is not *NULL*, then the data is mapped through the lookup table using the following method:

```
for(j=0; j < map->tall; j++) {
 for(i=0; i < map->wide; i++) {
   map->data[i][j] = lookup_table[*(data++)];
 }
}
```

The optional lookup table lets you easily create bitmaps with different sets of colors without having to create multiple copies of the source array. For example, if you wanted to create separate red, green, and blue plus signs, you could use the following code sequence:

```
gBitmap *red_plus, *green_plus, *blue_plus;
gColor lookup[2];

lookup[0] = gBLACK;            /* Background is always black */

red_plus = gBitmapCreate(5, 5, 2, 2);
lookup[1] = gRED;
gBitmapSetFromArray(red_plus, plus_sign, lookup);
green_plus = gBitmapCreate(5, 5, 2, 2);
lookup[1] = gGREEN;
gBitmapSetFromArray(green_plus, plus_sign, lookup);
blue_plus = gBitmapCreate(5, 5, 2, 2);
lookup[1] = gBLUE;
gBitmapSetFromArray(blue_plus, plus_sign, lookup);
```

As with matching the bitmap and array sizes, it is very important that the lookup table be large enough to map the maximum color value in the array. One way to ensure this is to create the lookup table dynamically using code such as the following:

```
gColor *lookup, max_value;

max_value = plus_sign[0];
for(i=1; i < 25; i++)
 max_value = MAX(max_value, plus_sign[i]);
lookup = (gColor *)calloc(max_value + 1, sizeof(gColor));
/* Now initialize the array */
for(i=0; i <= max_value; i++)
 lookup[i] = i;
```

This code segment creates a default lookup table that leaves values unchanged. The table size is *max_value+1*, since all of the color entries are between 0 and *max_value*. Once the table is created, you can then assign values to the lookup table entries that you wish to remap.

The companion function to *gBitmapSetFromArray()* is *gBitmapCopyToArray()*. This function takes the same arguments as its counterpart. It performs the reverse operation, copying pixels from a bitmap to an array, which may be further manipulated or saved for later use.

Clipping and Bitmaps

One problem with bitmap drawing, as I have currently defined it, is that the bitmap only represents a rectangular region. When copied to the screen, the entire rectangular region that the bitmap represents will be overwritten. This is clearly not the way objects such as the cursor arrow work in a windowing system. Only the arrow portion overwrites the screen; the rest of the pixels in the bitmap are not written. One way to provide this feature would be to adopt a convention that any bitmap pixel of value 0 (or some other fixed value) is not written to the screen. This is a perfectly reasonable approach, but has the drawback that value 0 cannot be part of the bitmap image. Instead of this method, you define the region to be drawn by using another bitmap, called a clip mask. A *clip mask* is a bitmap with the same dimensions as the bitmap being drawn. A nonzero entry in the clip mask means that the corresponding value in the drawing bitmap should be drawn on the screen. A 0 entry means that the entry is not to be drawn. In many cases, you may use the same bitmap for both the drawn bitmap and the clip mask.

In order to draw using clip masks, the bitmap drawing function, *gBitmapDraw()*, takes four arguments:

```
void gBitmapDraw(int x, int y, gBitmap *map, gBitmap *mask);
```

As previously mentioned, the *x* and *y* arguments represent the point of the screen where the hot spot of the bitmap is drawn. The *map* argument specifies the bitmap to be drawn. The *mask* argument specifies which pixels of the *map* bitmap should actually be copied to the screen. If *mask* is *NULL*, then all pixels of *map* are copied. Otherwise, only the selected pixels are copied. In the *plus_sign* example, you would use the *plus_sign* bitmap for both arguments, so only the pixels defining the cross are mapped to the screen. Note that even with the various color copies of the *plus_sign*, you can still always use the original *plus_sign* bitmap as the clip mask.

Using such a clip mask, you can define any type of shape to a drawn bitmap that you need. The example of the *no_sign* is a good example. In that example, the symbol was drawn in black with the background in white. Since black is usually value 0 in the color palette, you cannot use the *no_sign* bitmap as a clip mask (otherwise, you would see through the circle and slash). Instead, you must create a new bitmap as a clip mask. This can be accomplished in one of two ways. In the first method, the new clip mask is created just as the original was, by drawing into a new clip mask using zeros for the background and ones for everything else. This however, might require a lot of extra processing if the drawn bitmap required many drawing operations to create. The second method provides a more general approach when there are certain color values in the drawn bitmap that should not be drawn. For the *no_sign*, you want the background color, drawn in the color *gWHITE*, to not be drawn. All of the other pixels should be drawn. The function *gBitmapCreateClipMask()* shown in Listing 9-1 creates a clip mask using this approach. *gBitmapCreateClipMask()* is passed a bitmap, an array of background colors, and the number of elements contained in the array. It returns with a pointer to the new clip mask. Normally, there is only one background color that needs to be remapped, but this function lets you assign multiple ones if desired.

```
gBitmap *gBitmapCreateClipMask(gBitmap *map,
      gColor *back_colors, int numcolors);
{
gColor *lookup, *array;
gBitmap *clip_mask;
int i;

if(!map)
 return NULL;

clip_mask = gBitmapCopy(map, NULL);

for(i=0; i < clip_mask->wide; i++) {
 for(j=0; j < clip_mask->tall; j++) {
  color = clip_mask->data[i][j];
  for(k=0; k < numcolors; k++) {
   if(color == back_colors[k])
    clip_mask->data[i][j] = 0;/* Make transparent*/
   else
    clip_mask->data[i][j] = 1;/* Make visible */
  }
 }
}

return clip_mask
}
```

Listing 9-1. Function for creating a clip mask from an existing bitmap by making the bitmap colors you pass transparent, all other pixels are drawn

You can use this function to create a clip mask for the *no_sign* bitmap as follows:

```
gBitmap *clip_mask, *no_sign;
gColor back_colors;
```

```
back_colors = gWHITE;
clip_mask = gBitmapCreateClipMask(no_sign, &back_colors, 1);
```

Defining a Clipping Region

As mentioned in Chapter 7, one way to represent an arbitrary clipping region is with a bitmap, and this is exactly the clip mask structure previously defined. Recall that a clipping region defines the areas of the screen (or window) to which your program can write. A clip mask can define any arbitrarily shaped clipping region. The function *gClipMaskClipTest()*, provided as a standard clipping function, serves as an example of how to use a clip mask as a clipping region. To use this function, you must create a bitmap and set the pixels that define the clipping region to 1. For instance, the following code defines a circular clipping region:

```
gBitmap *map;
gCircle *circle;
int xleft, ytop;

/* Define a 128 x 128 clipping region */
map = gBitmapCreate(128, 128, xleft, ytop);
circle = gCircleCreate(63.5, 63.5, 63.5);
/* Now redirect the output */
gSetOutputBitmap(map);
/* Draw the circle */
gCircleFill(circle, 1);        /* Enable all in the circle */
gSetOutputBitmap(NULL);
gAddClippingFunction(gClipToClipMask, map);
gCircleDelete(circle);
```

Notice that two parameters, *xleft* and *ytop*, define where to position the upper left corner of the bitmap on the screen. Normally, these values are used in the bitmap to define the hot spot of the bitmap. However, since You are not actually going to draw this bitmap, You can instead use those values to inform *gClipMaskClipTest()* where to place the clip mask on the screen. For instance, to center this bitmap on the screen, you would set *xleft* to *gGetMaxX()/2 - 64* and *ytop* to *gGetMaxY()/2 - 64*. Once the clip mask is create and set, it is then passed in a call to *gAddClippingFunction()*:

```
gAddClippingFunction(&gClipMaskClipTest, map);
```

The complete listing for *gClipMaskClipTest()* is shown in Listing 9-2. This version works under the assumption that pixels outside of the bitmap cannot be drawn. It uses the *gRectangleClipTest()* function from Chapter 7 to make this test. You can easily change *gClipMaskClipTest()* to allow pixels outside of the bitmap simply by returning a 1 instead of a 0 when *gRectangleClipTest()* returns a zero (indicating the point was outside of the bitmap).

```
int gClipMaskClipTest(int x, int y, void *data)
{
gBitmap *mask;
gRectangle rect;

mask = (gBitmap *)data;
if(!mask)
 return 1;     /* Must be ok */

/* Check to see if the pixel is outside of the bitmap */
rect->xmin = mask->x0;
rect->xmax = mask->x0 + mask->wide - 1;
rect->ymin = mask->y0;
rect->ymax = mask->y0 + mask->tall - 1;

/* Use the rectangle test function */
if(!gRectangleClipTest(x, y, &rect))
 return 0;

/* Okay, its in the clip mask, see if its okay */

        if(mask->data[x - mask->x0][y - mask->y0])
         return 1;
        else
```

```
        return 0;

    }
```

Listing 9-2. The clipping function gClipMaskClipTest( ). This function determines if a pixel can be drawn based on a passed bitmap.

Generally, this function will be much faster than checking for individual clipping regions, especially for complex regions. Other than checking against the clipping rectangle, no floating point operations are required, as they are in *gCircleClipTest()*. Many of the newer graphics cards also provide hardware support for clip masks, making the bitmap drawing operation even faster.

In Chapter 7, I mentioned how complex clip regions are generated by overlapping windows. The clip mask provides a simple way to keep track of the visible portion of a window. A clip mask is maintained for each window, and is initially set to allow writing on any part of the window. Anytime another window covers a piece of the current window, the clip mask is updated to reflect the overlap by simply writing a rectangle of zeroes into the clip mask for the overlapping window. Whenever a part of the window is made visible again, the newly visible part of the clip mask is again set to 1 (enabled for writing).

One way to create an elaborate clipping region that cannot be created geometrically is to use a scanned photograph. Scanners are now available inexpensively to scan photographs yourself. You can also acquire any number of images by downloading images from bulletin boards such as CompuServe. Once an image is loaded as a bitmap, you may use the *gBitmapCreateClipMask()* function to create a clip mask. Any set of color values in the photograph may be set to opaque, while all of the others are set so that they can be overwritten. Then, you can fill in the enabled regions of the photograph with your graphics. You see this effect often in television where a technique known as *chroma-keying* is used. For example, the weatherperson is shown standing in front of an weather map by overlaying two separate images: one of the weatherperson standing against a blue screen and one of the weather map. The weatherperson image is used as a clip mask for the weather map. Any part of the blue screen behind the weatherperson is enabled for writing, and is overwritten by the weather

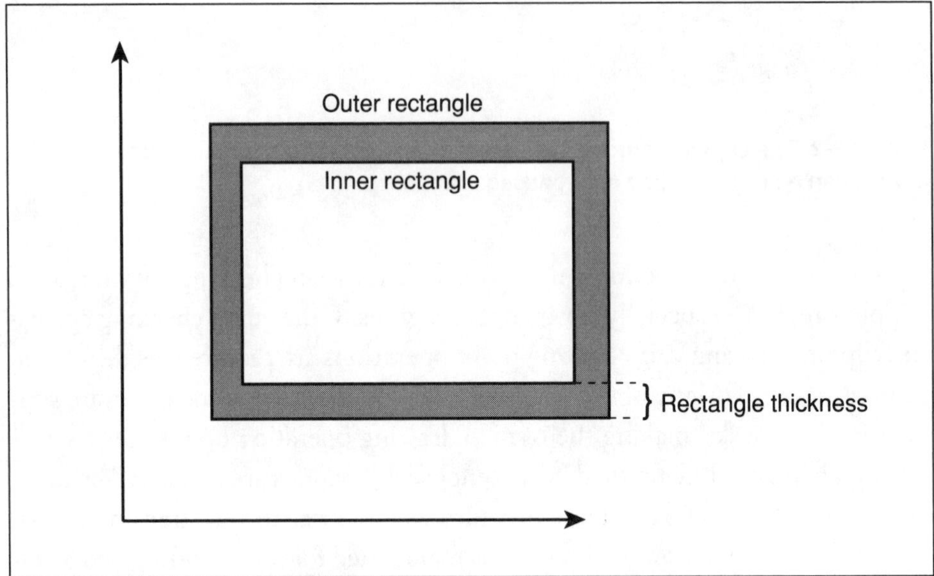

Figure 9-1. Creating an inner and outer rectangle to create a thick boundary

map image. Using this same technique with your graphics provides a good way to create interesting and elaborate combinations of images.

A Brush with Bitmaps

All of the outline drawing routines, such as *gRectangleDraw()*, *gCircleDraw()*, and *gPolygonDraw()*, draw the boundaries as just one pixel wide. In many cases, you want to draw thicker lines for the borders of objects. One method for doing this is to create an inner and outer version of the object and fill in the space between the two objects. For instance, a thick rectangle can be created by defining two rectangles, as shown in Figure 9-1. You can then fill in the region between the two rectangles using, for instance, the polygon fill routine. A similar method can be used to draw thick boundaries for any of the other shapes. A thick line can be drawn by creating a rectangle around the line of appropriate thickness, as shown in Figure 9-2. However, doing a fill operation requires a lot more calculation, and time, than simple line drawing.

Another method for creating thick lines is to use bitmaps. Instead of drawing a single pixel at each point along a line (or a circle, or an ellipse, or what-

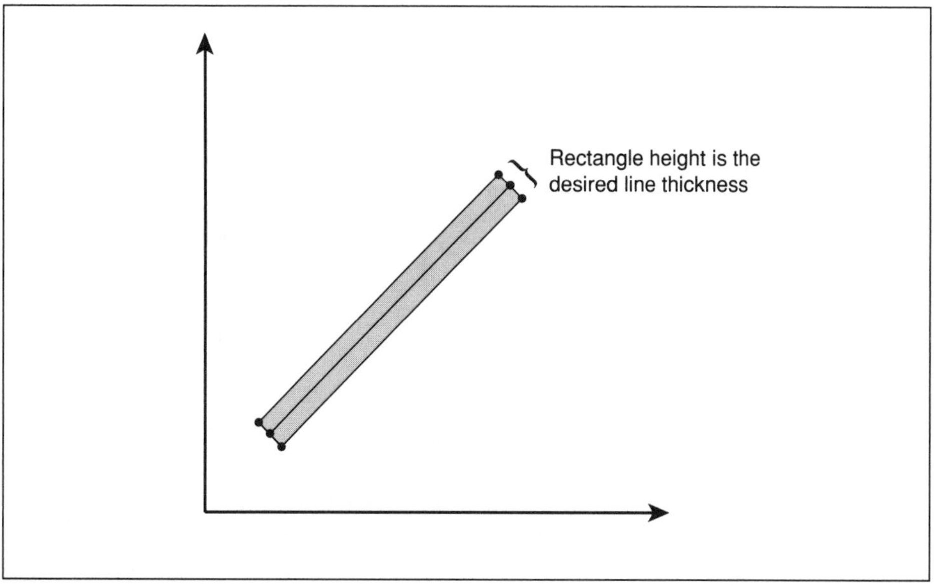

Figure 9-2. Creating a thick line by defining, and then filling in, a rectangle around the line

ever shape), you plot an entire bitmap, usually centered around the pixel being plotted. For instance, you can create a thick rectangle with a line width of 5 pixels by plotting a solid 5 x 5 bitmap for all of the points along each edge. This process is illustrated in Figure 9-3. The bitmap and a clip mask used to draw thick lines are collectively known as a *brush*. All paint programs provide many different brush styles to create various special effects.

A bit of nomenclature is in order here. As I previously stated, the combination of a bitmap and an optional clip mask is called a brush when it is used in line drawing. By selecting different size and shape brush bitmaps, you can create many different special effects just as a painter can with different brushes. The bitmap/clip mask combination is called an *icon* when used in a windowing system to represent some interactive symbol, like the cursor pointer or a graphic button that can be selected with the mouse. When used in a function plot to mark certain special points in the plot, the bitmap/clip mask combination is simply referred to as a symbol, because it is not an interactive part of the drawing (the user cannot select it). When used to define the fill pattern of a polygon, it is referred to as a pattern. All of these items: a brush, icon, symbol, or

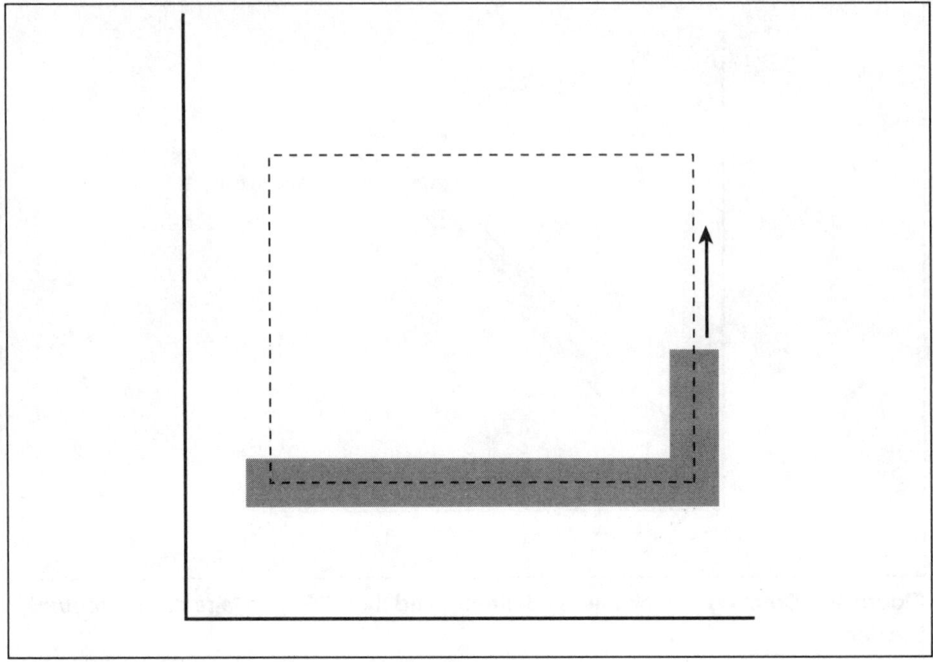

Figure 9-3. A thick rectangle drawn by plotting a bitmap brush around the rectangle. The brush is drawn centered around each pixel along the edges of the existing rectangle. As the brush is moved around the edges, it fills in all of the adjacent pixels, creating a thick edge.

pattern, are the same thing. The different names refer to the particular use of the bitmap and associated clip mask.

Applying brushes to your line drawings is easy. Once again, there is a function which determines whether *gPlotPixel()* plots a single pixel as usual or draws a brush, centered around the point (*x*, *y*), using a variation of *gBitmapDraw()*, called *gBrushDraw()*. Both functions take the same arguments and operate in a very similar manner. *gBrushDraw()* uses the same algorithm as *gPlotSpanWithBitmap()* does to fill a polygon with a pattern. Imagine that the screen has been filled with the pattern represented by the brush. Drawing a line using *gBrushDraw()* "uncovers" the pattern underneath, making it visible on the screen. When you see it in action in the demonstration program, or in your favorite paint package, a line or curve drawn using a brush makes it appear as if you are erasing the screen to reveal the bitmap pattern underneath. The only coding difference between *gBitmapDraw()* and *gBrushDraw()* is that *gBrushDraw()* adds the *x* and *y* screen coordinates of *gPlotPixel()* to the bitmap indices (using the *gmod()* function to compute each index modulo to the bitmap size). The bitmap is then copied to the screen using the shifted bitmap indices.

A brush is activiated by a call to *gSetBrush()*, which takes two arguments, a bitmap and a clip mask. As usual, if the clip mask argument is *NULL*, then the entire bitmap is copied to the screen. Once the brush is set, each call to *gPlotPixel()* will draw a brush with the hot spot centered at (*x*,*y*). As with *gPlotSpanWithBitmap()*, the hot spot offset may be used to shift the pattern on the screen. By incorporating the brush drawing as part of *gPlotPixel()*, all of the object outlines may be drawn with any desired brush shape without developing any new plotting routines.

Drawing with a brush is generally slower than drawing without one because more pixels must be drawn for each plotted point. However, the effects you can create with a brush can be quite impressive and would be difficult to create otherwise.

There are also times when you might want to disable the use of the brush temporarily and then re-enable it without having to reset the bitmap. The function *gSetBrushEnable()* serves this purpose by either disabling (pass a zero for the argument) or enabling (pass a nonzero value) the current brush. The function *gSetBrushEnable()* returns as its value the current setting of the brush enable flag. This lets you enable or disable the brush for the duration of your function, and then restore the brush to its previous setting before your function was called. If you examine the code for *gBrushDraw()*, you will observe that it must disable the brush with a call to *gSetBrushEnable(0)* before copying the bitmap pixels to the screen. *gBrushDraw()* uses *gPlotPixel()* to draw the bitmap pixels to the screen. If the brush was not disabled, the calls to *gPlotPixel()* would attempt to call *gBrushDraw()* again, leading to an endless recursive loop. Once the entire bitmap is copied, the enable flag is set to its previous value, before *gBrushDraw()* was called by invoking *gSetBrushEnable(prev_value)* just before the function returns.

The most effective brush for drawing thick lines is a circular one. Using a circular brush gives the line the proper thickness no matter what angle it is drawn at. Using a circular brush will make the endpoints of a line segment appear rounded. The circular brush can also be used to create rounded corners on objects such as rectangles and polygons, as shown in Figure 9-4. Rectangular brushes may be used to create sharp edges when drawing horizontal and vertical lines, such as in drawing a thick rectangle.

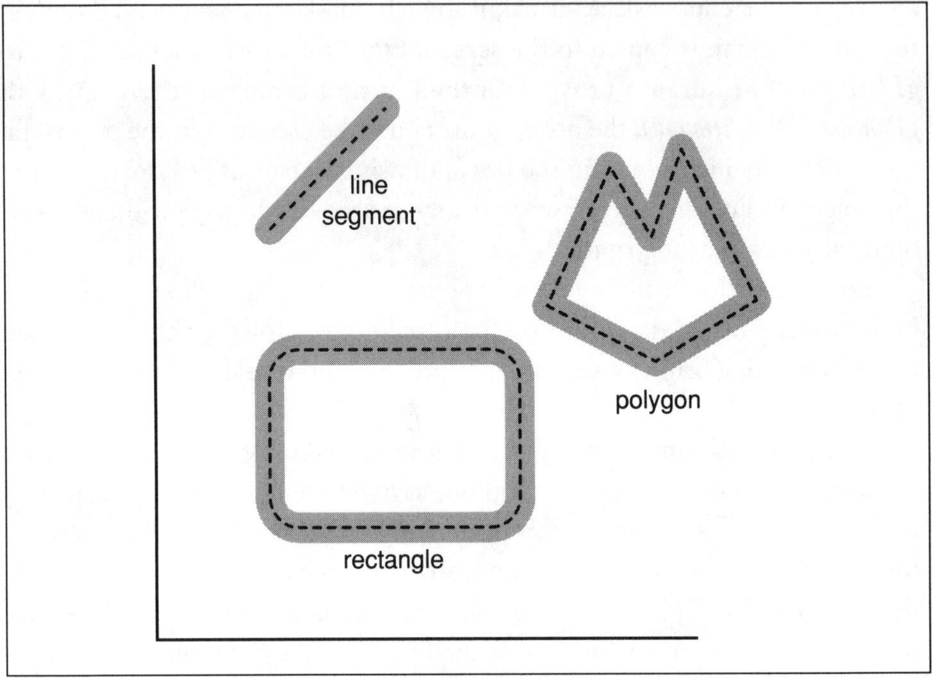

Figure 9-4. Using a circular brush to create rounded corners for rectangles and polygons

Bitmap Patterns

In Chapter 8, you learned how bitmaps can be used to specify patterns for filling polygons. The function *gPlotSpanWithBitmap()* is the main function providing this capability. Unlike the brush drawing, you do not want to draw an entire bitmap for every pixel along the span. Instead, you want to determine which pixel to plot from the bitmap based on the *(x,y)* coordinates along the span. You saw in Chapter 8 how using modulo arithmetic on the coordinates repeats the pattern across the entire span. By using a clip mask in combination with the bitmap, you can plot symbols on top of a background image, with the background image showing through the transparent (where the clip mask is 0) portions of the symbol. For instance, you can first fill the polygon in red. Then you can fill the polygon again, using the bitmap pattern, where red would show through the transparent parts of the symbol.

The *gSetBrush()* function is also used to affect how polygon filling occurs. If a bitmap (and possibly a clip mask) have been set with *gSetBrush()*, and the brush has been enabled, then *gPlotSpan()* calls *gPlotSpanWithBitmap()* with the brush that has been set. Once again, note that all of the fill routines can now automatically support pattern filling with bitmaps, since they all use *gPlotSpan()* to plot pixels. If you examine the code for *gPlotSpanWithBitmap()*, you will see that it disables the brush with a call to *gSetBrushEnable(0)* before calling *gPlotPixel()*, otherwise *gPlotPixel()* would draw the entire bitmap at each pixel along the span, a very undesireable result!

Just as bitmaps are used to draw thick lines in boundaries, bitmaps may also be used to fill with some of the more common fill patterns. For instance, to create a hatched fill pattern, as shown in Figure 9-5, you can use a pattern defined by the array *hatch_map*:

```
gColor hatch_map[16]=
{
 0, 0, 0, 1,
 0, 0, 1, 0,
 0, 1, 0, 0
 1, 0, 0, 0
}
```

The following pattern, also shown in Figure 9-5, creates a cross-hatch pattern:

```
gColor cross_hatch_map[16]=
{
 0, 1, 0, 1,
 1, 0, 1, 0,
 0, 1, 0, 1,
 1, 0, 1, 0,
}
```

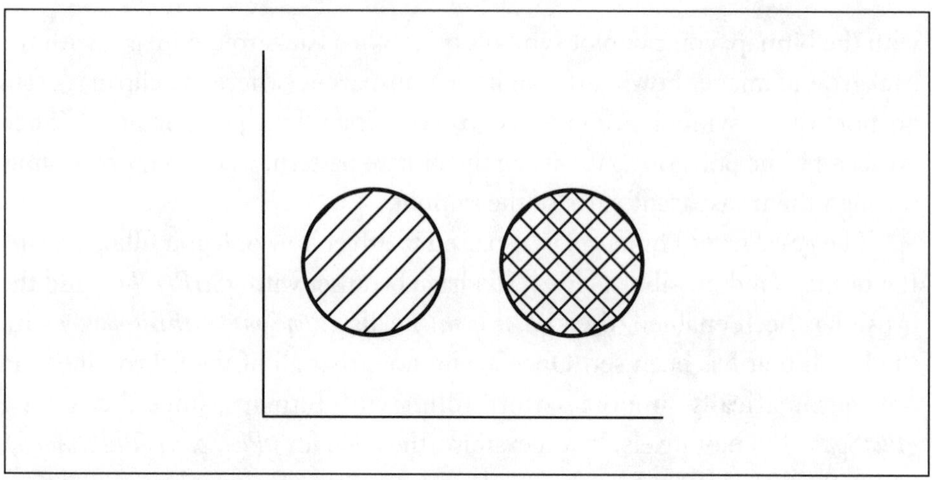

Figure 9-5. Filled circles with a single hatch pattern on the left and a cross-hatch on the right

The variety of possible patterns is endless. Note that the types of pattern definitions for the *hatchmap* and *cross_hatch_map* may also be used as clip masks, making it possible to fill a shape without entirely overwriting the image underneath. Similarly, by using *gBitmapSetFromArray()* with an appropriate lookup table, you can create hatching patterns with alternating colors by assigning one color to the 0 values, and one to the 1 values. The following pattern creates an even more colorful pattern cross-hatch:

```
gColor cross_color_map[16]=
{
 1, 2, 3, 4,
 2, 3, 4, 3,
 3, 4, 3, 2,
 4, 3, 2, 1,
}
```

I recommend that you experiment with different patterns and see the effects for yourself. The demonstration program, *dbitmap.exe*, provides an example of how multiple patterns can be combined.

Bitmap vs. Vector Graphics

While bitmaps provide the ability to represent and draw many types of images that would be impossible to represent with a geometric description, they still have two principle drawbacks. First, they can take up considerably more memory to represent an object. For instance, a circle with a radius of 100 pixels would require a bitmap of 200 x 200 pixels to store, as opposed to just storing the radius and location of the *gCircle* structure. A 200 x 200 bitmap corresponds to 40,000 *gColor* elements, which, at a minimum, corresponds to 40,000 bytes of storage. If you have a 24-bit system, the *gColor* type is represented by a *long*, and would require 160,000 bytes of memory to represent a 200 x 200 bitmap.

The second major problem is the inability to transform bitmaps, especially to resize them. For any object that can be approximated by a polygon, you can transform the object is easily. The vertices are transformed and then the new object drawn and/or filled. The same operation on a bitmap is not quite so simple to perform.

The problem of bitmap storage is one that has lessened with the decreasing cost and increasing availability of memory, both in the computer RAM and in disk storage space. Also, many compression programs that can significantly reduce the amount of storage required for a given bitmap are now available. However, if you have enough bitmaps, the memory needs can become untenable. As I discuss in Chapter 10, most printers describe text characters as collections of bitmaps called *fonts*. The number of different character fonts you can keep in memory at one time depends on how much memory your printer and computer have. In general, bitmaps should be used for small graphic symbols such as text or symbols.

Large bitmaps can also take longer to draw than their geometric counterpart. A 100 x 100 bitmap must always copy 10,000 pixels to the screen, regardless of the complexity of the image. If the image contained only a few unfilled shapes, the figure can be drawn much more quickly by just drawing the geometric objects directly. Again, the method to use will depend on how many pixels comprise the bitmap and the complexity of the image.

Resizing a bitmap is more difficult. A bitmap can be easily doubled in size by duplicating every row and every column and copying the result to another

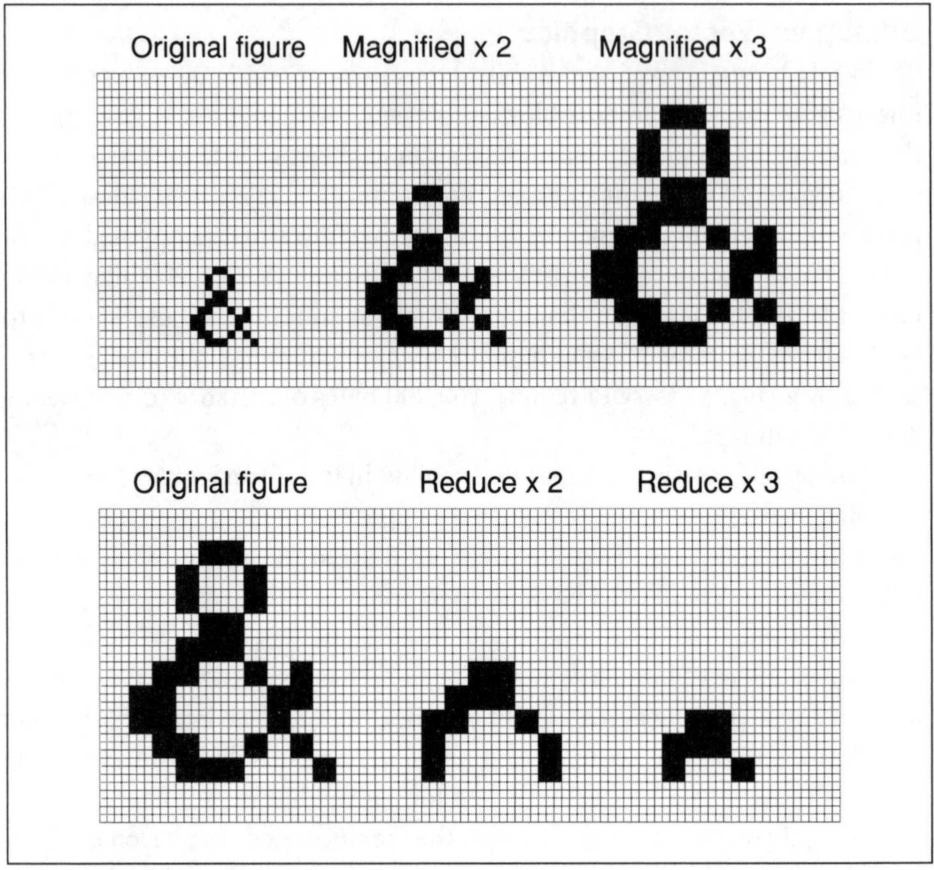

Figure 9-6. Resampling a bitmap to create different sizes. The top row shows a magnified bitmap, resulting in a blocky image. The bottom shows a reduced bitmap, resulting in a coarse image.

bitmap. Similarly, you can increase the size by any integer multiple by duplicating rows and columns *n* times. However, the problem with this approach is that, as the bitmap size is increased, it starts looking quite blocky, as shown in Figure 9-6. A bitmap can be reduced in size using a similar approach, by taking every *n*th row and every *n*th column of the larger bitmap. The problem with this is that the resulting bitmap will look too coarse, as also shown in Figure 9-6. In Chapter 13, I will discuss some methods to get around these problems for black and white bitmaps. In general, though, rescaled bitmaps almost always look worse than the original, whether they are magnified or shrunk down. This problem has led to the widespread availability of geometric text fonts that can be easily resized and look proper at all scales. I will examine the pros and cons of bitmap and vector text in Chapter 10.

Bitmap Demonstration

The demonstration program *dbitmap.exe* shows several examples of how complex figures with interesting patterns can be created. It starts with a simple unfilled circle, and then steps through various stages of drawing the outline with different brush types and filling the interior with multicolored patterns. It then shows how other objects can be overlaid and filled with pattern, with, and without, disturbing the underlying image using clip masks. This is an excellent program to tinker with to explore your own patterns and combinations.

Bitmap Graphics

While this chapter introduces bitmap-based graphics, it has only covered a few of the many possible applications of bitmaps. In the succeeding chapters, I will show how bitmaps are used to place text on the screen, to plot symbols on a function plot, and one of the most important uses, to generate animated symbols and characters for fun, games, and even some serious work. So, for more graphic fun, read on!

Functions Found In This Chapter

Demonstration Program

dbitmap.exe

This program demonstrates how brushes and multiple fill patterns can be combined to create elaborate images.

Bitmap manipulation functions

```
gBitmap *gBitmapCreate(int wide, int tall, int x0, int y0);
```

Function for creating a bitmap. The created bitmap is *wide* pixels in width and *tall* pixels in height. The "hot spot" for the bitmap is set to *(x0, y0)*, representing what pixel the bitmap is centered on.

```
gBitmap *gBitmapCopy(gBitmap *src, gBitmap *dest);
```

Copies a *gBitmap* structure.

```
void gBitmapDelete(gBitmap *map);
```

Deletes a *gBitmap* structure.

```
void gBitmapSetFromArray(gBitmap *map, gColor *data,
                         gColor *lookup);
```

Sets the elements of *map* using the data stored in *data*. *data* must be a *gColor* array containing at least as many entries as there are pixels in *map*. If lookup is non-*NULL*, then the elements of *data* are mapped through *lookup* before being copied into *map*.

```
void gBitmapCopyToArray(gBitmap *map, gColor *data,
                        gColor *lookup);
```

Copies the pixels from the bitmap *map* to the array *data*. *data* must be a *gColor* array containing at least as many entries as there are pixels in *map*. If *lookup* is non-*NULL*, then the elements of *map* are mapped through *lookup* before being copied into *data*.

Bitmap drawing functions

```
void gBitmapDraw(int x, int y, gBitmap *map, gBitmap *mask);
```

Draws the bitmap passed in *map* on the screen. The bitmap is positioned on the screen so that the hot spot of the bitmap, stored as *map->x0* and *map->y0* is drawn at *(x,y)*. If *mask* is non-*NULL*, it must be a bitmap of the same dimensions as *map*. Only the pixels of *map* where the corresponding element of *mask* is nonzero will be drawn.

```
void gBrushDraw(int x, int y, gBitmap *map, gBitmap *mask);
```

Similar to *gBitmapDraw()*, except that it does not place the bitmap hot spot around the point *(x,y)*. Instead, it uses the same algorithm as *gPlotSpanWithBitmap()* to offset the bitmap indices by *x* and *y*. This routine is used by *gPlotPixel()* if you enable a brush with *gSetBrush()*.

```
void gSetOutputBitmap(gBitmap *map);
```

Redirects *gPlotPixel()* to either write to the screen (*map* is *NULL*), or to the bitmap specified by *map*. If *map* is not-*NULL*, then a rectangular clipping region the same dimensions as *map* is created to ensure that no pixels are written outside of *map*.

```
void gSetOutputBitmapEnable(int enable);
```

Enables (*enable* = 1) or disables (*enable* = 0) writing to a bitmap. If *enable* is 0, then output always goes to the screen, whether a bitmap has been set or not with *gSetOutputBitmap()*. If *enable* is 1, then writing to bitmaps can occur if one has been set.

```
gBitmap *gBitmapCreateClipMask(gBitmap *map,
                               gColor *back_colors, int numback);
```

Creates a clip mask from the passed bitmap *map*. The array *back_colors* represents all of the colors that should be enabled for writing, that is, the colors that should be transparent for the bitmap. Any pixel in *map* that is one of the colors in *back_colors* will be enabled in the clip mask. All other pixels are disabled (set to 0 in the clip mask).

```
int gClipMaskClipTest(int x, int y, void *mask);
```

A clipping function that may be added using *gAddClipFunction()*. The data argument must be a valid clip mask. This function will only allow writes for *(x,y)* coordinates that correspond to nonzero values in the clip mask. The clip mask is positioned on the screen by setting the hot spot coordinates (*x0*, *y0*) of mask to where the upper-left corner should be positioned.

```
void gSetBrush(gBitmap *map, gBitmap *mask);
```

Sets a bitmap and clip mask pair (collectively called a brush) to create thick, or patterned, line drawings. Once set, all subsequent calls to *gPlotPixel()* will draw the bitmap (centered on the hot spot) at the passed *(x,y)* coordinate, rather than setting the pixel to the passed color.

```
int gSetBrushEnable(int enable);
```

Enables (*enable* = 1) or disables (*enable* = 0) the brush in *gPlotPixel()*. If *enable* is 0, then *gPlotPixel()* will work as always, drawing a single pixel. If *enable* is 1, and a drawing bitmap has been set with *gSetBrush()*, then the bitmap is drawn instead. The return value is the current setting of the brush-enable flag. This lets your function reset the flag to the same value it had before your function was called.

Drawing Text

Except for purely artistic drawings, text will be an essential part of the graphics you are likely to see and create. Whether you need to label a plot, annotate a drawing, or just sign your name to your masterpiece, text-drawing functions are a vital part of any software graphics package.

Text drawing is also one of the more complicated features in a graphics package because there are so many options. Text can be drawn in hundreds of styles, in a wide range of sizes, and enhanced with features, such as boldface, italics, and underlining. Letting the user work with a wide range of different text styles, sizes, and attributes is an essential part of any desktop publishing, graphic design, or printing software.

One of the principal attractions to window-operating systems, such as MS-Windows, in addition to their windowing and multitasking capabilities, is in their ability to draw text on the screen in exactly the same manner as it is drawn on paper. In this chapter, you'll learn how to add text easily to your drawings by introducing a new set of text-drawing routines that use the graphic primitives from the previous chapters. You'll see how many visible text attributes, such as text size, can be implemented using the affine transformations from Chapter 6. Finally, you'll learn other issues and features of drawing text that is incorporated into more sophisticated graphics packages.

Graphic Text

Drawing characters on the screen is the most fundamental drawing operation on your PC. Without it, you could not type on the keyboard. The normal text mode of DOS uses bitmaps stored on the graphics display card to draw characters typed on the screen. The bitmaps for each character are stored in a special ROM (read-only memory) on the video card of the graphics hardware. As the ASCII code for each character is written to the screen, the graphics card uses the code as an index to select the right bitmap for that character. The bitmap representing that particular character is then drawn on the screen.

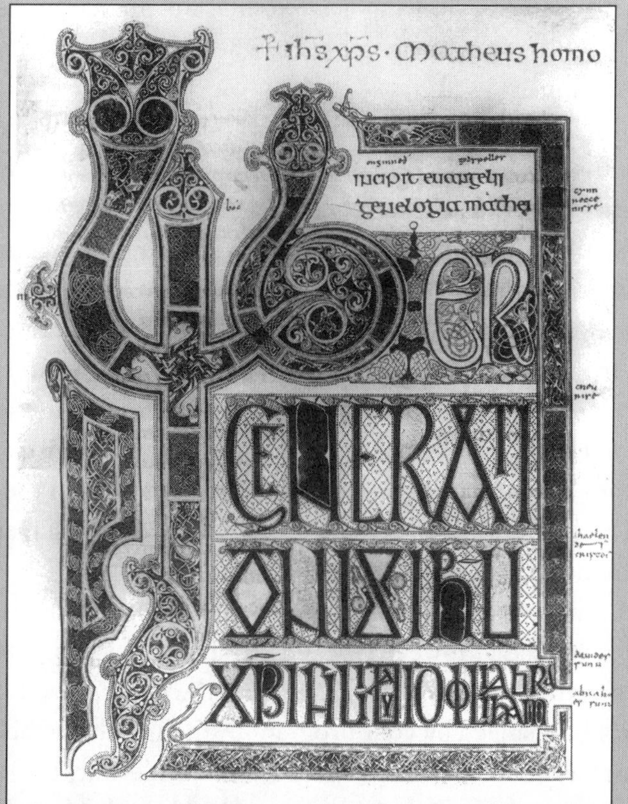

PHOTO COURTESY OF MARBURG/ART RESOURCE, N.Y.

The printed word is, of course, one of the principal means of communicating with others; this book is just one small example. An essential part of any graphic drawing is the ability to annotate and label it with the desired text. But like any other graphic object, you want the ability to draw text in a variety of styles, shapes, sizes, colors, and modes.

As desktop publishing has become more and more popular, people have demanded more capability in drawing text. A drawing, such as the one shown above, may have taken days or weeks to create by hand. Even with a computer, the process of creating the individual characters may still take weeks for an artist to perfect. But once the characters are created, the computer can instantaneously create a page of text in the desired style with the correct size and spacing between characters.

The techniques shown in this chapter provide a strong basis for learning how to create elaborate text on the screen. By using the transformations from the previous chapter, text may be easily translated, scaled, rotated, and enhanced with such features as italics and boldface. You now have the tools to create your own illuminated text and to recreate medieval manuscripts for yourself!

The character drawing is simplified for the hardware by dividing the screen into an array of character cells, where the size of a character cell is the size of the bitmaps used.

The standard screen configuration is usually 80 columns by 24 rows. Most graphics cards support other configurations, such as 80-characters wide by 50 rows (VGA) or 132-characters wide by 50 rows, but the number of options is usually quite limited. A character is always drawn into one of the cells, and therefore cannot be drawn to an arbitrary pixel location on the screen, as can be done using the *gBitmapDraw()* function. To draw a string of characters, the hardware keeps track of the position on the screen of the last character. Once a character is drawn, the next character is drawn in the next cell to the right of the last character, unless a special character, such as linefeed (go to the next line) or carriage return (return to the beginning of the current line) is received. The hardware also handles scrolling text off the screen when text is written to the bottom line of display.

Since the bitmap-drawing operation is performed entirely by the hardware, it is very fast. However, for most graphic drawings, using bitmaps on the graphics card is seriously limited because the bitmap size is fixed and because it cannot be changed by your program. Although characters can be enhanced in several ways, for instance, with bold and underline, the character size, shape, and orientation on the screen cannot be altered. Many DOS programmers have gone to great lengths to use the basic text mode as creatively as possible, but ultimately it is just not possible to work with many types of drawings in the DOS text mode.

All drawing software uses the VGA graphics mode of the display, which lets you write to any pixel on the screen. You cannot use the bitmaps stored on the hardware to draw text in the graphics mode. As with all your other graphic objects, characters are drawn by plotting the pixels that make up the character. Since there is no hardware drawing assistance, you sacrifice drawing speed. But as you will see, having your software do all the text drawing provides tremendous flexibility for displaying text in ways impossible in DOS text mode.

Text With Style

There are two distinct aspects to drawing text. The first is defining the style in which to draw the text, and the second is implementing the actual mechanics of drawing a character at a particular location on the screen with a certain style. The text style specifies how a character should look on screen by setting various drawing attributes (character size and orientation) and any enhancements (boldface and italics). In your software, a style is stored in a *gStyle* structure. The *gStyle* structure serves the same purpose for drawing graphics text as style guides do in a word processor. Once the style is created and set with the desired attributes, you can draw strings in that style using *gTextDraw()*. The *gStyle* structure is defined as:

```
typedef struct gStyle_struct {
 gBitmapFont *bfont;     /* Bitmap font for this string */
 gPolyFont  *pfont;      /* Polyline font for this string */
 int xfont, yfont;       /* X and y dimensions of the font */
 float xscale, yscale;   /* X and y scale factors */
 float angle;  /* Angle of string on screen */
 float charAngle;        /* Angle of individual characters
                            with respect to the string */
 int italicsFlag;        /* = 1 if should be italicized */
 int boldFlag;           /* = 1 if should be boldface */
 gBitmap *brush, *clip_mask;
} gStyle;
```

As with all your other graphics data types, there are the *gStyleCreate()*, *gStyleCopy()*, and *gStyleDelete()* functions. The elements *gBitmapFont* and *gPolyFont* are pointers to structures that contain the graphical descriptions of the characters. These are discussed in detail in the following section, "Drawing Characters."

Displaying a string on the screen is quite easy with the *gTextDraw()* function. For example, you may display a string on the screen using the default style with code, such as the following:

```
gStyle *mytext;

mytext = gStyleCreate();
gTextDraw(mytext, 100, 100, "My String", gWHITE);
```

This code draws the string "My String" on the screen in white starting at location (100, 100), using the default style. The default style uses a simple 8 x 8-pixel bitmap font of block letters. Since you have not set any other text drawing attributes for the given text style, the string is drawn using default values for all the other parameters. There are several different attributes of a style that determine such things as the string's angle on the screen, the characters' sizes, what font to use, and whether to italicize or apply boldface to the string. Each of the drawing attributes of a style may be set using the functions listed in Table 10-1.

Table 10-1. Functions for setting the various style attributes

Function	Description
*void gStyleSetBitmapFont(gStyle * style, gBitmapFont * font)*	Sets a bitmap character font for the style
*void gStyleSetPolyFont(gStyle * style, gPolyFont * font)*	Sets a polyline character font for the style
*void gStyleSetAngle(gStyle * style, float angle)*	Sets the angle at which to draw text for the style. The entire string is rotated by this angle.
*void gStyleSetCharRotation(gStyle * style, float angle)*	Sets the angle of each character's rotation with respect to the string direction

Table 10-1. *continued*

Function	Description
*void gStyleSetScale(gStyle * style, float xscale, float yscale)*	Sets the x- and y-scale factors for the characters. Each character will now be xscale * font->wide by yscale * font->tall pixels
*void gStyleSetPixelScale(gStyle * style, int width, int height)*	Sets the x- and y-scales so that the resulting characters are the specified width and height in screen pixels
*void gStyleGetPixelSize(gStyle * style, int * width, int * height)*	Retrieves the pixel width and height of the characters drawn using this style
*void gStyleSetItalicsEnable(gStyle * style, int enable)*	Enables or disables drawing in italics
void *gStyleSetBoldEnable(gStyle * style, int enable)*	Enables or disables drawing in boldface
void *gStyleSetBrush(gStyle * style, gBitmap * bitmap, gBitmap * clip_mask)*	Sets an optional brush for use in drawing the characters. Useful for enhancing polyline characters.

The *gStyle* structure provides the significant advantage of letting you create several different text styles for drawing at one time, and later letting you use whichever one is appropriate. For instance, you can create three different types of strings for large character labels, normal text, and small annotation text as follows:

```
gStyle *big_label, *normal_text, *small_label;

big_label = gStyleCreate();
/* Big labels are three times larger */
```

```
gStyleSetScale(big_label, 3.0, 3.0);

normal_text = gStyleCreate();

small_labels = gStyleCreate();
/* Small labels are half size and italicized */
gStyleSetScale(small_labels, 0.5, 0.5);
gStyleSetItalicsEnable(small_labels, 1);
```

Styles make it easy for you to treat a text drawing in a very modular fashion. By passing a style pointer to any of your specialized text drawing functions, you can change the appearance of your images simply by changing which style is used. There are several examples of using styles in this manner for labeling plots described in the next chapter.

Drawing Characters

Now that you know how to define a style, you must learn how to draw a character on the screen with the appropriate style characteristics. A character is drawn on the screen in one of two ways:

1. As a bitmap representing the character
2. As a collection of graphics objects, such as polylines, polygons, or higher-order curves like the splines described in Chapter 5.

A simple block letter *A* is shown in Figure 10-1 using both methods. To draw arbitrary strings of ASCII text, a graphical definition of each letter (either bitmap based or geometrically based) must be created and stored in a structure known as a font. A *font* is an array of structures where each element of the array is the graphical description of a single character. The ASCII character set supports up to 256 characters, so a font needs to contain at most 256 character definitions. There are two basic data types for fonts, the *gBitmapFont* type, discussed in the next section, and the *gPolyFont* type, discussed in the section called "Vector Characters."

A font is normally associated with a character set. However, it is more accurate to think of a font as an array of symbols. For drawing text, the index into the font array is generated from the value of the character. However, you can

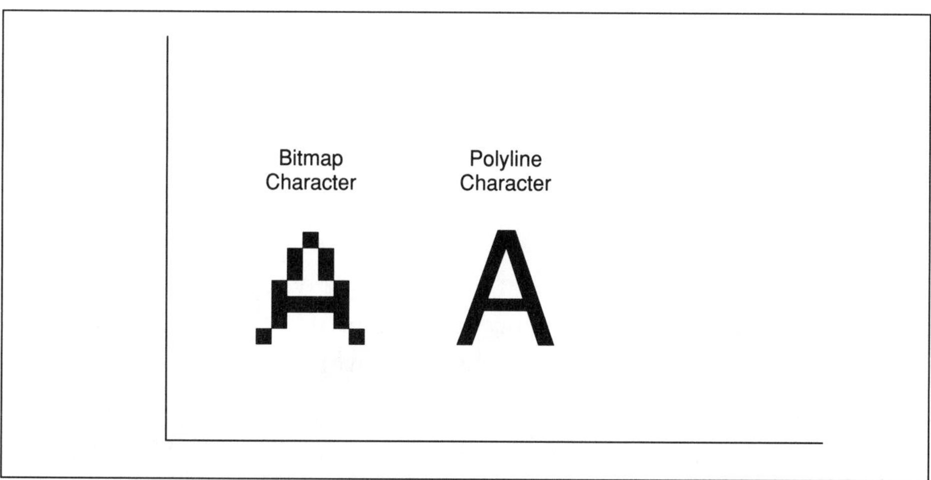

Figure 10-1. Two different ways to draw the letter A

store any collection of symbols in a font and use whatever indexing scheme you like. The *gTextDraw()* function expects a valid string to be passed, so the element zero cannot be used in a font (zero terminates a string and so is ignored by *gTextDraw()*) and the number of symbols in a font must be less than or equal to 256. Other than these restrictions, you can design whatever arcane symbols you want, store them in the appropriate font type, and then draw them using any style attributes by using *char* arrays to select the appropriate symbol. The following code illustrates how you might use a font in this manner:

```
gBitmapFont *bizarre_font;
gStyle *style;
char bizarre_string[10];

/* Create and load the bizarre font */
/* And then draw the symbol */
bizarre_string[0] = 2;      /* Use symbol 2 */
bizarre_string[1] = 10;     /* Use symbol 10 */
bizarre_string[2] = 0;      /* Terminate string */

style = gStyleCreate();
gStyleSetBitmapFont(style, bizarre_font);
gTextDraw(style, 100, 100, bizarre_string, gWHITE);
```

A font is a useful structure for storing and managing any set of symbols. Let's first look at the *gBitmapFont* data type, which stores bitmap character definitions.

Bitmap Fonts

The most common way to store a character representation is a bitmap. You can draw bitmap-based fonts using a variation of the bitmap-drawing functions described in Chapter 9. Recall that the *gBitmap* data type stores bitmaps as two-dimensional arrays of *gColor* elements with each pixel of the bitmap represented by a *gColor* value. Bitmap fonts are one case in which using 1 byte per bitmap element, as *gBitmap* does, wastes a lot of memory because you need at lot of bitmaps (one for each character). To avoid using quite as much memory, you should use the *gBitmapFont* data type, defined as:

```
typedef gBitmapFont_struct {
 int wide, tall;     /* Width and height of each character */
 int nchars;         /* Number of characters in font */
 int nbytes;         /* Number of bytes per font character */
 char **font_array; /* Array of data for the font */
 /* Each element of this array is a pointer to the
    data for an individual character */
} gBitmapFont;
```

The *font_array* is a pointer to an array of *char* pointers. Unlike the *gBitmap* data type, the bitmap definition of each character is stored using 1 bit per pixel. Then a single *char* can represent 8 pixels of the bitmap. The default bitmap font that I have provided defines characters using an 8 x 8 bitmap. So, only 8 bytes of storage are used for each character, rather than the 64 bytes required if you used the *gBitmap* data type. For example, a plus sign may be defined with the definition:

```
char plus_sign[8] = {0x14, 0x14, 0x14, 0x36, 0x36,
                     0x14, 0x14, 0x14};
```

Each *char* element in this definition corresponds to one row of the bitmap, since you are using bitmaps 8-pixels wide. To make it convenient to define and access the bitmap definition, there is always an integer number of bytes per row. So, to define a bitmap font using 10 x 10-pixel bitmap, you would use two *char* elements for each row, since a single *char* can only store 8 bits. For the case of a 10-pixel wide character definition, the last 6 bits are ignored.

To create a bitmap font, you use the *gBitmapFontCreate()* function with the following arguments:

```
gBitmapFont *bfont;

bfont = gBitmapFontCreate(wide, tall, nchars);
```

This call creates the *gBitmapFont* structure, and allocates *font_array* with bitmaps that are all zero. Once the font is created, you must then load each character definition into the font array. The function *gBitmapFontLoadChar()* provides this service. The definition of the *plus_sign* can be loaded in the following manner:

```
gBitmapFont *bfont;

/* Create an 8 x 8-bitmap font of 256 characters */
bfont = gBitmapFontCreate(8, 8, 256);
gBitmapFontLoadChar(bfont, (int)'+', plus_sign);
```

This code copies the definition of *plus_sign* into the proper location of *font_array*. The same procedure is then used to load all of the character definitions you have created. You do not necessarily have to define all the characters. Any characters that are not loaded have bitmaps of all zeroes, which means the character will not be drawn on the screen.

Note that the previous method for loading the character definitions produces the proper results no matter what integer value the character '+' actually has on your particular hardware. While most machines now use the standard ASCII character set, some still do not. By explicitly casting the value of '+', you'll always correctly look up the character definition, even if the compiler or machine you are using has a different numeric value for the character.

The graphics package automatically creates and loads a default bitmap font of 8 x 8 block letters the first time *gInitDisplay()* is called. Whenever a style is created with *gStyleCreate()*, it is automatically assigned this default font. You may get the pointer to this default font using the function *gGetDefaultBitmapFont()*. This pointer must *not* be freed by a call to *gBitmapFontDelete()*. If necessary, you can make a copy of the font using *gBitmapFontCopy()*. For a complete example of how to create and load a bitmap font, examine the function *gInitDefaultBitmapFont()* in the *gfont.c* module found on the disk that accompanies this book.

Drawing bitmap characters

Drawing a string horizontally across the screen using bitmap characters is straightforward. The hot spot for a bitmap-based character is the upper-left corner of the bitmap. You cannot use *gBitmapDraw()* directly since the bitmap font stores each character using 1 bit per pixel. Instead, you should follow the same basic procedure as in *gBitmapDraw()*, except you must unpack the character definition one bit at a time. The basic drawing procedure is shown in Listing 10-1 for the function *gTextDrawSimpleBitmap()*.

```
void gTextDrawSimpleBitmap(int x, int y, char *ch,
                           gBitmapFont *bfont, gColor color);
{
char letter, *bits, rowbits;
int row, col, bitcount;

/* Create a static array that can be used to test
   if individual bits are turned on */
static char mask[8] = {0x80, 0x40, 0x20, 0x10,
                       0x08, 0x04, 0x02, 0x01};

/* Loop through all characters of the string */

while(*ch) {
 letter = *ch++;                /* Get the next letter */
 bits = bfont->font_array[(int)letter];
 for(row=0; row < bfont->tall; row++) {
  bitcount = 0;
  for(col=0; col < bfont->wide; col++) {
   /* Once all 8 bits are processed, go to the next one */
   if(bitcount == 8) {
```

```
        /* Reset bitcount; get the next byte */
        bitcount = 0;
        rowbits = *bits++;
       }
       if(rowbits & mask[bitcount]) /* Is this bit set ? */
        gPlotPixel(x + col, y + row, color);
       bitcount++;
      }                             /* End of column loop */
      bits++;                       /* Go to the next row */
     }                              /* End of row loop */

     x += bfont->wide;              /* Move over one bitmap wide */
    }                               /* End of string processing loop */

    return;
    }
```

Listing 10-1. The function gTextDrawSimpleBitmap() draws a horizontal string across the screen using a bitmap font.

In this drawing procedure, the variables *x* and *y* represent the position of the upper-left corner of each bitmap. As each character is drawn, the next character is drawn directly adjacent to the previous character horizontally across the screen. This is accomplished by incrementing *x* by the width of the bitmap-character size as each character is processed. The variable *bitcount* is used in the main drawing loop to count the number of horizontal pixels that have been drawn. If the bitmap width is greater than 8 pixels, this variable is used to decide when to get the next byte of the character definition. Every time 8-horizontal pixels are drawn, the next byte of the bitmap is retrieved by incrementing the data pointer *bits*.

Drawing bitmap characters using this procedure is fine as long as the bitmap is not scaled or rotated. Transforming bitmaps using an affine transformation requires considerably more computation than transforming geometric objects, such as polylines and polygons. Furthermore, a rescaled bitmap often does not appear as smooth and uniform as the original. The ability to transform a character and have it look basically the same at all scales, is the major motivation for representing text using a different method. In the software, I provide an alternative font that defines characters by a collection of individual polylines. Before investigating how to transform bitmap-based characters, let's first see how the simpler polyline-based characters are defined, drawn, and transformed, and then we'll return to the problem of resizing and rotating bitmap-based characters.

Vector Fonts

Vector, or polyline, fonts define characters using a line-drawing format. You define the characters by specifying the individual lines that make up the character. Figure 10-2 shows the line definitions for several different characters. The font-data structure is very similar to the bitmap-font structure. The font structure *gPolyFont* is defined as:

```
typedef gPolyFont_struct {
 int wide, tall;          /* Dimensions of each character */
 int nchars;              /* Number of characters in font */
 gPolychar **font_array; /* Array of data for the font */
 /* Each element of this array is a pointer to the
    data for an individual character */
} gPolyFont;
```

The *font_array* pointer, on the other hand, points to a very different structure than the bitmap-font pointer does, as you might expect. The *gPolychar* structure is defined as:

```
typedef struct gPolychar_struct {
 gPolyline **polys;
 int numpolys;
} gPolychar;
```

A character may be defined by any number of separate polylines. The polyline definition of a character is created by thinking of how to draw the character with a pen. A new polyline is created each time you "lift" the pen from the paper. For instance, a *gPolychar* definition for the letter *T* uses two polylines, one to define the vertical portion, and one to define the horizontal portion.

Figure 10-2. Polyline definition of several different characters

The function *gPolycharLoad()* simplifies the process of creating a *gPolychar* structure. *gPolycharLoad( )* expects a *char* array containing the following information:

- Number of polylines, *npolys*
- Definition of each polyline
- Number of points in the polyline, *npoints*
- *npoints* pairs of *(x,y)* points defining the polyline

For instance, the letter *T* is defined with the following declaration:

```
char polyT[] = {2,   /* Number of polylines */
        2,           /* First polyline point count */
        0, 0,        /* First point on 1st polyline */
        100, 0,      /* Second point on 1st polyline */
        2,           /* Npoints in second polyline */
        50, 0,       /* First point in 2nd polyline */
        50, 100      /* Second point in 2nd polyline */
        };
```

The coordinate system for a *gPolychar* is oriented in the same manner as the frame-buffer coordinate system. (0, 0) is the upper-left corner of the character and (*wide*, *tall*) is the lower-right corner of the character. In this example and in the default polyline font provided on the disk accompanying this book, the characters are defined using a (0, 0) to (100, 100) range. As you will see shortly, the actual units used for defining the character are irrelevant as it can easily be rescaled to any size by applying affine transformations.

We can now create and set characters in a polyline font with code, such as the following:

```
gPolyFont *pfont;

/* Create an 100 x 100-polyline font of 256 characters */
bfont = gPolyFontCreate(100, 100, 256);
gPolyFontLoadChar(pfont, (int)'T', polyT);
```

A default polyline font is provided on the disk accompanying this book, which you may use for your text strings in the module *gfont.c.* A pointer to this default font may be retrieved with the function *gGetDefaultPolyFont().* This pointer must *not* be freed by your program with a call to *gPolyFontDelete().* For a complete example of how to create and load a polyline font, examine the function *gInitDefaultPolyFont()* in the *gfont.c* module.

Drawing a Vector Font

Drawing a vector font is easy. You simply use *gPolyLineDraw()* for each polyline that makes up the character. The main interest in using a *gPolyFont*-character definition is to scale character strings to any size and to draw them in any orientation. But transforming polylines is also easy by using the affine transformations described in Chapter 6. The only tricky part is drawing successive characters in a string next to one another. The character spacing must be adjusted to account for any scaling applied to the characters.

A *gStyle* structure defines the screen size of the characters drawn on the scale using two scale factors, *xscale* and *yscale*. The scale factors may be set using one of two functions: *gStyleSetScale()* and *gStyleSetPixelScale().* The first function simply specifies *x*- and *y*-scale factors for the basic character size. If the font size is 8 x 8 pixels, and both scale factors are set to 2, then the characters will be drawn twice their normal size, as 16 x 16-pixel characters. Similarly, if scale factors of 0.5 are specified, then characters are drawn half their normal size, or as 4 x 4-pixel characters.

The function *gStyleSetPixelScale( )* is a more convenient alternative. With this function, you specify the desired *x*- and *y*-pixel size at which to draw the characters. This function makes the size of the characters drawn on the screen independent of the particular font used. For instance, the default-polyline font uses characters defined as 100 x 100-pixel characters. These characters can be drawn as 10 x 10-pixel fonts by calling *gStyleSetPixelScale(style, 10.0, 10.0).*

If the font is changed to the default bitmap font, the characters are still drawn as 10 x 10-pixel fonts, even though the font dimension is now 8 x 8, not 100 x 100. In either case, the scale factors are used to generate a matrix for transforming characters using the function *gMatrixScale( )*. The scale factors also affect the spacing between characters. The drawing function must therefore compute the spacing between characters and offset each character by the spacing size as each character is drawn.

In addition to scaling, you also need to be able to draw the text on the screen at any angle. As you already know, you can rotate any object using the affine transformations and the *gMatrixRotate( )* function. Rotating an individual character is easy, but you must also determine where to draw each successive character. Figure 10-3 shows the basic method.

When a character string is scaled and rotated, you can see where each successive character is drawn by applying the transformation to the vector *(pfont->wide, 0.0)*. Call this transformed vector *spacing*, with *x*- and *y*-elements of *xspacing* and *yspacing* respectively. The transformed vector lies along the top edge of the transformed character. The first character is drawn with the upper-left corner at (*x*, *y*). The next character is drawn with its upper-left corner at position (*x* + *xspacing*, *y* + *yspacing*). The starting position for each successive character is found by offseting the previous position by the *spacing* vector.

Using this approach, any type of affine transformation may be applied to the string, including reflection, which draws the string as a mirror image. I have also provided the capability to rotate the individual characters with respect to

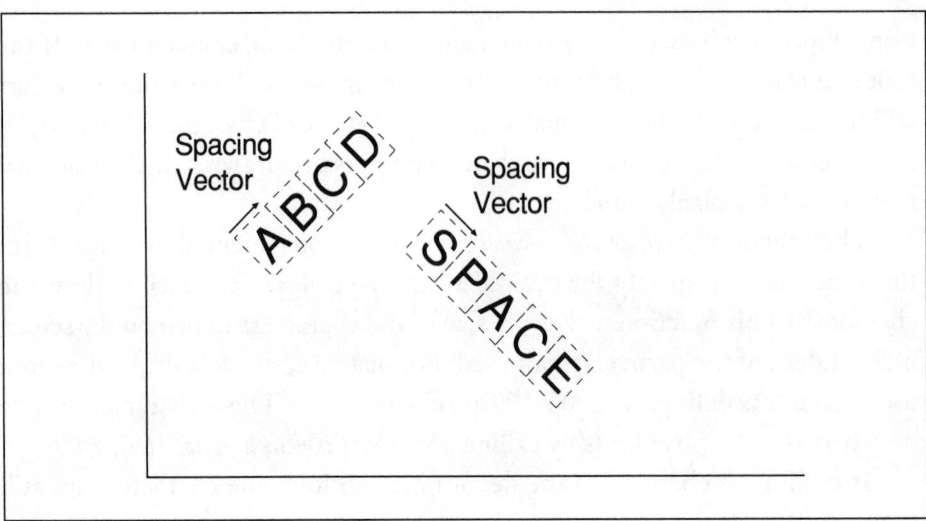

Figure 10-3. When a string is transformed, the position of each successive character can be determined by transforming the spacing vector.

the string. So, you can draw strings, such as the ones shown in Figure 10-4, where the characters are spaced in one direction, but rotated in another.

This provides a convenient way to create vertical labels. To create such a vertical label, the string is rotated by -90 degrees (the string now draws from top to bottom). However, rotating the string also rotates the characters. So, a character rotation of 90 degreees is applied to make the characters horizontal. The drawing procedure for a transformed-polyline string of characters is as follows:

```
/* The drawing procedure is passed a string,
   starting x and y, and a color */

gMatrix *smatrix;
gVector *vtemp, *spacing;
gStyle *style;
gPolyFont *pfont;
gPolychar *pchar;
char letter;

/* Get the polyline font */
```

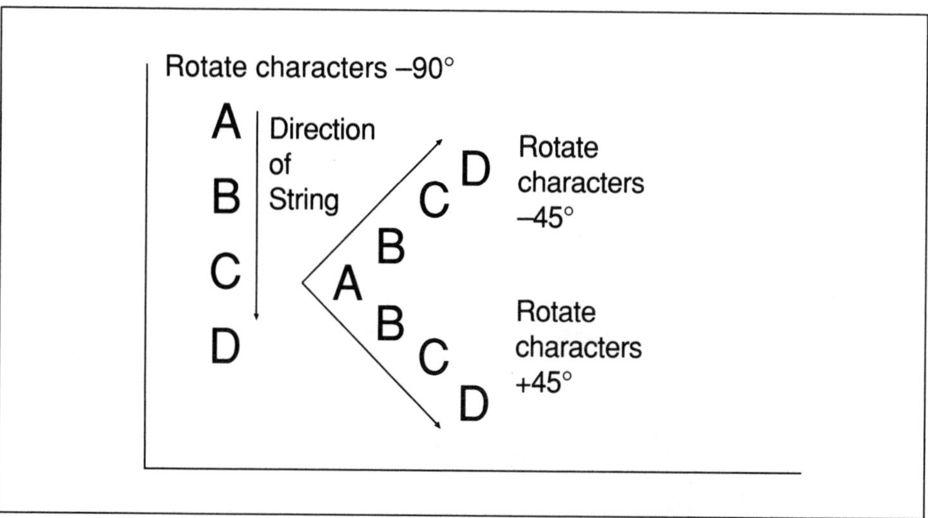

Figure 10-4. Strings in which the characters are rotated in a different direction from the direction the string is drawn

```
pfont = style->pfont;
/* Get the scale factors */
vtemp = gVectorCreate(style->xscale, style->yscale);
smatrix = gMatrixScale(NULL, NULL, vtemp);
/* Now apply the rotation */
gMatrixRotate(smatrix, smatrix, style->angle);

/* Find spacing vector */
spacing = gVectorCreate((float)pfont->wide, 0.0);
gTransformVector(smatrix, spacing, spacing);

/* Now apply character rotation */
gMatrixRotate(smatrix, smatrix, style->charAngle);

/* Set matrix to initial position */
gVectorSet(vtemp, (float)x, (float)y);
gMatrixTranslate(smatrix, smatrix, vtemp);

/* Now draw the characters */
while(*ch) {
 letter = *ch++;        /* Get the next letter */
```

```
    pchar = pfont->font_array[(int)letter];
    for(i=0; i < pchar->npolys; i++) {
     poly = pchar->polys[i];
     /* Set the matrix transformation to use smatrix */
     poly->t = smatrix;
     gPolylineDraw(poly, color);
     /* Now reset it back to NULL */
     poly->t = NULL;
    }
    gMatrixTranslate(smatrix, smatrix, spacing);
   }

   gMatrixDelete(smatrix);
   gVectorDelete(vtemp);
   gVectorDelete(spacing);
```

Procedure 10-1. Drawing procedure for transforming polyline character strings

The previous procedure draws a text string across the screen at any angle using any desired scale factor. The vector *spacing* contains the translation offset to apply for each successive character. The use of affine transformations makes drawing polyline strings of any size and any angle very simple, as the previous procedure shows.

Transforming Bitmap Characters

Drawing transformed-bitmap characters uses exactly the same approach as drawing transformed-polyline characters. The only difference is in how to draw each character as a rescaled and rotated bitmap. For polyline characters, the function *gPolylineDraw()* handles all transformations for you. You do not have the equivalent capability in *gBitmapDraw()*. So, you'll just have to handle this problem yourself.

The matrix *smatrix* in the polyline–character-drawing routine represents the transformation from a character in its normal size and orientation to a scaled and rotated shape on the screen. This is called a *forward* transformation because it takes an untransformed figure and distorts it. Figure 10-5 shows a typical character transformation, using rectangles to show how the bitmap boundaries transform.

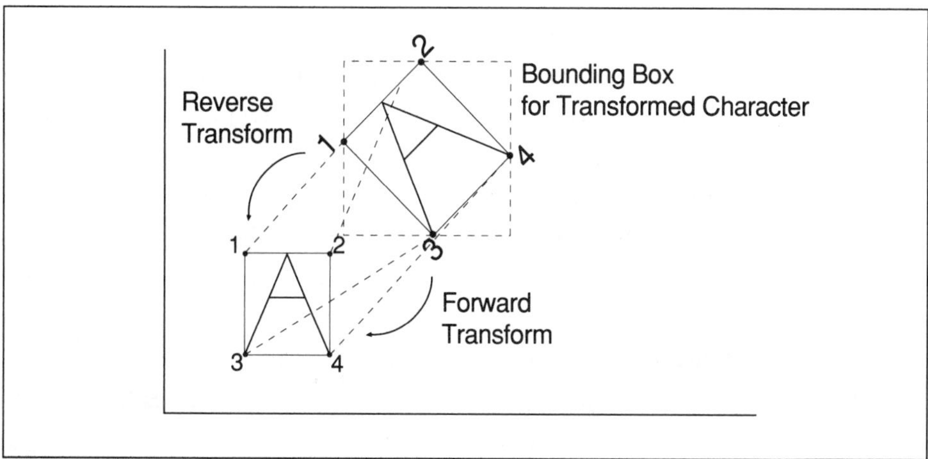

Figure 10-5. Forward and inverse transformations for a bitmap. The inverse transformation maps pixels from the rotated bitmap back to the original bitmap.

Your goal should be to fill in the transformed rectangle with the appropriate pixels from the character bitmap. You can do this by creating the *inverse transformation*, which takes the transformed bitmap and converts it back to its original size and orientation. Referring to Figure 10-5, the inverse transformation takes *(x,y)* coordinates inside the rotated and scaled rectangle and transforms them into *(x,y)* coordinates inside the original, nontransformed bitmap. So, you can fill in the rotated and scaled bitmap by using the inverse transform to tell you which pixels to read from the nontransformed-character bitmap.

An inverse transformation can be constructed simply by reversing the process used to construct the forward transformation. Listing 10-2 shows the function *gTextDrawUsingBitmap()*, which draws a text string of any size or orientation using a bitmap-character font. The matrix *inverse* is constructed as the inverse to *smatrix*. The transformations used to create *smatrix* are applied in the reverse order, using the opposite values. For instance, whereas *smatrix* is scaled by *style->xscale* and *style->yscale*, the inverse matrix is scaled using *1.0/style->xscale* and *1.0/style->yscale*. Similarly, the rotation is inverted by using the negative rotation angle.

Once the inverse matrix is constructed, you must then find the bounding box for the transformed character. To draw each transformed character, you scan the bounding box of the transformed character and fill it with pixels from the original bitmap, as shown in Figure 10-5. The *(x,y)* coordinates within the original bitmap are the values *bcol* and *brow.* The bit at location *(bcol, brow)* is then located in the bitmap to see whether or not the pixel in the transformed character should be plotted.

As you'll see in Listing 10-2, this routine is not very efficient because it takes every pixel in the bounding box of the transformed character and uses the inverse transformation to find the corresponding pixel in the character bitmap. For instance, if a character is magnified by a factor of three, you must perform this operation for nine times as many pixels as there are in the input bitmap. But you'll have avoided the more onerous calculation of calling *gTransformVector()* for every output pixel.

By taking advantage of the linearity of affine transformation, you can compute the horizontal and vertical increments for each affine transformation to apply to every output pixel.These precalculated quantities are then used to increment the bitmap address inside the main output-pixel plotting loop. This process eliminates the need to perform a matrix multiply for each output pixel. Instead, you add an offset to each pixel coordinate, which is considerably less arithmetic.

The main disadvantage of using transformed bitmap characters is that they generally produce characters that appear blocky if the font is scaled too much. In fact, even a factor of three is noticeably blocky. But bitmap characters can be more elaborate than polyline characters since the bitmap does not require that all lines are drawn with the same width. The choice of whether to use bitmap or polyline fonts depends on the particular drawing needs you have and what fonts you may have available.

```
void gTextDrawUsingBitmap(gStyle *style, int x, int y,
            char *ch, gColor color);
{
gMatrix *smatrix, *inverse;
gVector *vtemp, *spacing, *offset;
gStyle *style;
gBitmapFont *bfont;
char letter;
float xt, yt, xoff, yoff;
```

```
float xhadd, yhadd, xvadd, yvadd, xcorner, ycorner;
int xmin, xmax, ymin, ymax, xscreen, yscreen;
int bcol, brow;       /* X and y offset into character bitmap */
int bytes_per_row;    /* Number of chars per row of bitmap */
char *bits, rowbits;

if(!style || !style->bfont || !ch)
 return;

/* Get the bitmap font */
bfont = style->bfont;
/* Get the scale factors */
vtemp = gVectorCreate(style->xscale, style->yscale);
smatrix = gMatrixScale(NULL, NULL, vtemp);
/* Now apply the rotation */
gMatrixRotate(smatrix, smatrix, style->angle);

/* Find spacing vector */
spacing = gVectorCreate((float)bfont->wide, 0.0);
gTransformVector(smatrix, spacing, spacing);

/* Now apply character rotation */
gMatrixRotate(smatrix, smatrix, style->charAngle);

/* Find bounding box of transformed character by transforming all
   corners */
gVectorSet(vtemp, (float)bfont->wide, 0.0);
gTransformVector(smatrix, vtemp, vtemp);
gVectorGet(vtemp, &xt, &yt);
xmax = xmin = xt; ymax = ymin = yt;
gVectorSet(vtemp, (float)bfont->wide, (float)bfont->tall);
gTransformVector(smatrix, vtemp, vtemp);
gVectorGet(vtemp, &xt, &yt);
xmax = MAX(xmax, xt);
xmin = MIN(xmin, xt);
ymax = MAX(ymax, yt);
ymin = MIN(ymin, yt);
gVectorSet(vtemp, 0.0, (float)bfont->tall);
gTransformVector(smatrix, vtemp, vtemp);
```

```
gVectorGet(vtemp, &xt, &yt);
xmax = MAX(xmax, xt);
xmin = MIN(xmin, xt);
ymax = MAX(ymax, yt);
ymin = MIN(ymin, yt);
gVectorSet(vtemp, 0.0, 0.0);
gTransformVector(smatrix, vtemp, vtemp);
gVectorGet(vtemp, &xt, &yt);
xmax = MAX(xmax, xt);
xmin = MIN(xmin, xt);
ymax = MAX(ymax, yt);
ymin = MIN(ymin, yt);

/* Construct inverse matrix by following steps in reverse */
inverse = gMatrixRotate(NULL, NULL, -style->charAngle);
gMatrixRotate(inverse, inverse, -style->angle);
gVectorSet(vtemp, 1.0 / style->xscale,
                  1.0 / style->yscale);
gMatrixScale(inverse, inverse, vtemp);

/* Offset is now used to determine where to draw the character */
offset = gVectorCreate((float)x, (float)y);
bytes_per_row = (bfont->wide + 7) / 8;

/* Set affine increments */
/* Here, you use the properties of affine transforms to avoid using
   gTransformVector() for every pixel. You find the vertical and
   horizontal increments and use these in the inner loop */
gVectorSet(vtemp, 0.0, 0.0);
gTransformVector(inverse, vtemp, vtemp);
gVectorGet(vtemp, &xt, &yt);
gVectorSet(vtemp, 1.0, 0.0);
gTransformVector(inverse, vtemp, vtemp);
gVectorGet(vtemp, &xhadd, &yhadd);
xhadd -= xt; yhadd -= yt;
gVectorSet(vtemp, 0.0, 1.0);
gTransformVector(inverse, vtemp, vtemp);
gVectorGet(vtemp, &xvadd, &yvadd);
xvadd -= xt; yvadd -= yt;
```

```
/* Now draw the characters */
while(*ch) {
 letter = *ch++;                  /* Get the next letter */
 bits = bfont->font_array[(int)letter];
 /* Find current offset on screen */
 gVectorGet(offset, &xoff, &yoff);
 yscreen = floor(yoff);
 gVectorSet(vtemp, (float)xmin, (float)ymin);
 gTransformVector(inverse, vtemp, vtemp);
 gVectorGet(vtemp, &xcorner, &ycorner);
 /* Now process all pixels in the loop */
 for(row=ymin; row <= ymax; row++) {
  xt = xcorner - xhadd;
  yt = ycorner - yhadd;
  xscreen = floor(xoff) - 1;
  for(col=xmin; col <= xmax; col++) {
   xt += xhadd;
   yt += yhadd;
   xscreen++;
   /* Now you have point in original bitmap; is it inside ? */
   if(gCLIP_CHECK(-0.5, xt, bfont->wide-0.5) !=
     gCLIP_MIDDLE ||
     gCLIP_CHECK(-0.5, yt, bfont->tall-0.5) !=
     gCLIP_MIDDLE)
     continue;
   brow = ROUND(yt) * (bytes_per_row);
   rowbits = bits[brow];
   bcol = ROUND(xt);
   rowbits = bits[brow + bcol/8];
   if(rowbits & mask[bcol % 8]) /* Is this bit set ? */
    gPlotPixel(xscreen, yscreen, color);
  }                               /* End of column loop */
  xcorner += xvadd;
  ycorner += yvadd;
  yscreen++;
 } /* End of row loop */
 /* Move to next character position */
gVectorCombine(offset, spacing, 1.0, 1.0, offset);
}
```

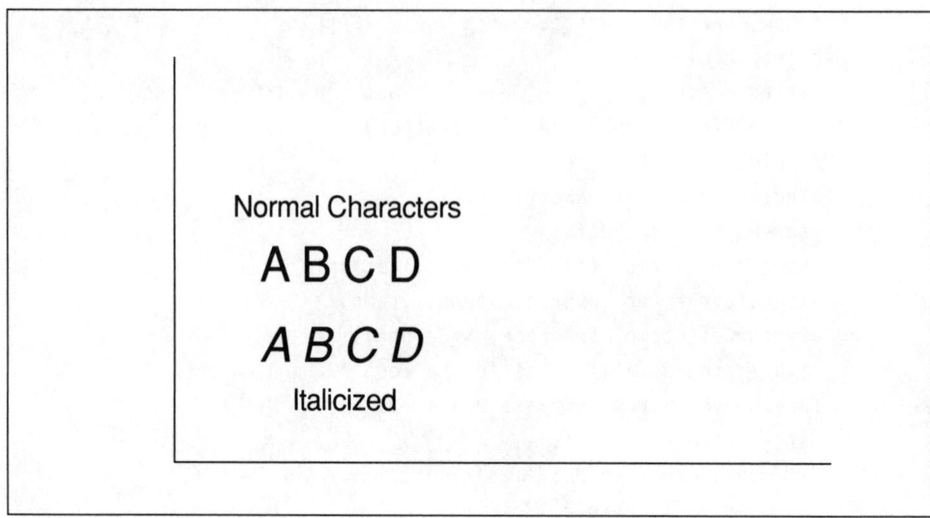

Figure 10-6. Italicizing characters skews them to the right

```
gMatrixDelete(smatrix);
gMatrixDelete(inverse);
gVectorDelete(vtemp);
gVectorDelete(spacing);
gVectorDelete(offset);

return;
}
```

Listing 10-2. The gTextDrawUsingBitmap() function draws transformed-bitmap characters.

Enhancing Text

Affine transformations provide a powerful means of transforming characters in a variety of ways other than just simple scaling. For instance, you can italicize text by constructing a matrix that skews the characters to the right, as shown in Figure 10-6. To create a skew, you first rotate the rectangle, scale the rectangle horizontally by a small amount, and then rotate the rectangle back so that the top and bottom edges are once again horizontally aligned. This process is shown in Figure 10-7. The procedure for generating the skew matrix is:

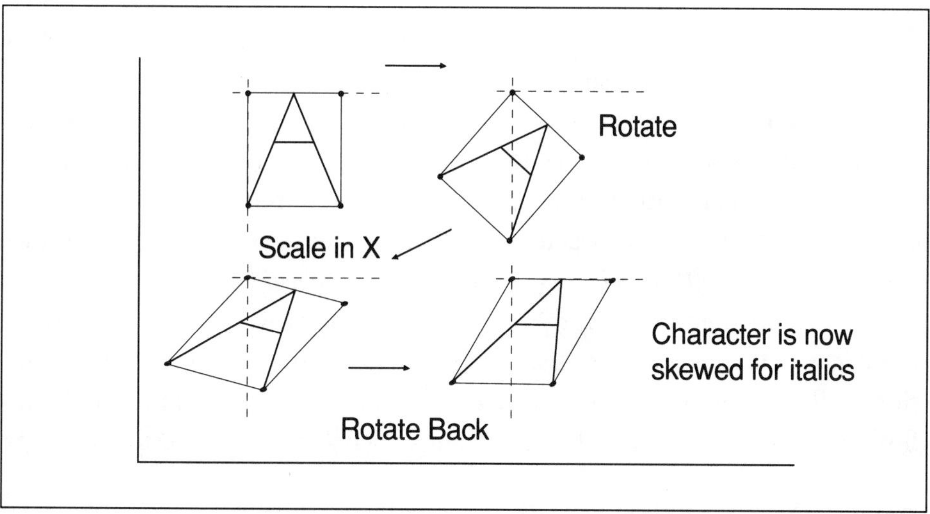

Figure 10-7. Generating the transformation to italicize characters

```
gMatrix *italics;
gVector *scale;
float angle;

italics = gMatrixRotate(NULL, NULL, -20.0 * DEGREES_TO_RAD);
scale = gVectorCreate(1.2, 1.0);
gMatrixScale(italics, italics, scale);
angle = atan(tanD(20.0)/1.2);
gMatrixRotate(italics, italics, angle);
```

The *italics* matrix is then applied to the *smatrix* just as the character rotation is. You can vary the rotation amount and scaling to create extreme italics if desired.

You can create a boldface effect by drawing polyline characters with a brush. When the boldface option is set with *gStyleBoldEnable()*, *gTextDraw()* creates a temporary 3 x 3-bitmap brush that is passed to *gSetBrush()*. The polylines that make up the characters are then drawn with the brush, creating a boldface effect. The boldface option is not supported for bitmap fonts. You can draw polyline characters using any type of brush you wish by using *gStyleSetBrush()*, instead of enabling the boldface option. By using your own brushes, you can draw characters with any type of pattern. Patterned characters can produce interesting and colorful results.

The ability to draw characters using brushes is a good example of the benefits of modular software. Since the brushes are part of *gPlotPixel()*, you did not have to add any other code to turn your simple polyline characters into elaborate pattern-filled characters. All the work has been done already since *gTextDraw()* calls *gPolylineDraw()*, which in turn calls *gPlotPixel()*, which automatically plots the brushes for you. Brush drawing is available for any graphics objects you may add to this software package, without requiring any additional effort on your part. It is always nice to have some of the work already finished for you, so you can do other things, such as create interesting bitmaps.

Demonstration Time

To illustrate the variety of text types that you can draw with this software, the program *dtext.exe* is provided on the disk accompanying this book. This program draws text strings with random orientations in random locations and in random sizes. *dtext.exe* also draws examples of italicized and boldface text as well as patterned text using the polyline font and various bitmap patterns. There is virtually an unlimited number of text styles that can be created using the tools presented in this chapter, and *dtext.exe* shows only a few of the possibilities.

Almost The Last Word

You now have a complete set of tools for drawing text on the screen. Text may be drawn in any size and in any orientation by, once again, using matrices to specify how to transform characters. The transformations can be used to create special effects, such as italicizing. The *gStyle* structure provides a convenient means of setting a number of different text styles that may be used in any combination throughout your drawing. This is quite useful for elaborate drawings, such as maps, that use text of several different sizes and orientations.

You have seen that characters may have two completely different representations, either as bitmaps or as polylines. In more advanced graphics systems, characters are represented by more complex curves, such as the splines described in Chapter 5. The advantage of bitmap characters is their drawing speed when they do not need to be scaled or rotated, and that the characters can be a little more elaborate since you can draw anything as a bitmap. The disadvantage of bitmap characters is their much slower drawing speed when they are scaled or rotated and their blocky appearance if they are magnified too much.

The polyline representation provides a completely different means of drawing characters. Polylines are easily transformed and look consistent at all scales. The disadvantage of a polyline representation is that the lines are always drawn 1-pixel thick at all scales, though this can be somewhat compensated via an appropriate bitmap brush. Even with a brush, the polylines will be drawn with the same thickness, which is not always desirable for all types of characters.

There are, of course, many attributes of drawing text that are not covered by this software. For instance, all of your text is drawn in a uniformly spaced manner; that is, each character is separated by the same number of pixels on the screen. Drawing proportionally spaced text requires that the *spacing* vector used to position the next character depends on the character being drawn. Drawing lowercase characters in which part of the character descends below the line that the text is drawn on also has not been dealt with, though this may be added by storing a hot spot with each character definition and positioning the character based on the hot spot. There are some cases where you might want each character within a string to be resized differently. This program also does not dealt with drawing more than one line at a time and automatically spacing the strings vertically as well as horizontally.

All these extra features are available in more advanced graphic packages and, certainly, they can be added to this package using the tools provided in this book. The important point to remember about this software is that drawing text is not as complex as it might seem at first. By using the affine transformations, most of the work in scaling, rotating, and enhancing the text is done for you with the routines from the previous chapter. As I can attest, the only real work is in creating the bitmaps and polylines for the fonts. Once they are there, using them is simple.

Applications Ahead

Now that you have assembled an extensive collection of drawing tools, it's time to do something useful with them. In the next chapter, you will combine all the graphics routines developed in this and the previous chapters to create fully labeled and annotated function graphs. In the succeeding chapters, you'll study several other types of applications that are both fun to watch and easy to create now that you have the routines for drawing any type of figure. So, read on, and find out how you can impress your friends and family, and even do something practical.

Functions Found in This Chapter

Demonstration programs

`dtext.exe`

This program displays text on the screen using various styles and both types of fonts. Strings are displayed at different scales, at various angles, and using brushes to create patterned text.

Text style functions

```
gStyle *gStyleCreate(void);
```

Creates a new style structure. The default style draws text using an 8 x 8-bitmap font horizontally across the screen.

```
gStyle *gStyleCopy(gStyle *dest, gStyle *src);
```

Copies a style structure.

```
void gStyleDelete(gStyle *style);
```

Deletes a style structure. Deleting a style does not delete any font that is defined for the style.

```
void gStyleSetBitmapFont(gStyle *style, gBitmapFont *font);
```

Sets a bitmap font for a text style. If a polyline font is set, it is disabled and the bitmap font will be used in future calls to *gTextDraw()*.

```
void gStyleSetPolyFont(gStyle *style, gPolyFont *font);
```

Sets a polyline font for a text style. If a bitmap style is set, it is disabled and the polyline font will be used in future calls to *gTextDraw()*.

```
void gStyleSetAngle(gStyle *style, float angle);
```

Sets the rotation angle for drawing strings. This rotates the entire string by the specified angle.

```
void gStyleSetCharRotation(gStyle *style, float angle);
```

Sets the rotation angle of each character with respect to the string direction.

```
void gStyleSetScale(gStyle *style, float xscale, float yscale);
```

Sets the *x*- and *y*-scale factors for the style. The effective width of each character is *xscale*font->wide* and the effective height is *yscale*font->tall*.

```
void gStyleSetPixelScale(gStyle *style, int width, int height);
```

Sets the scale factors so that the resulting characters are the specified width and height in screen pixels, independent of the font size.

```
void gStyleGetPixelSize(gStyle *style, int *width, int *height);
```

Retrieves the pixel width and height of the characters drawn using this style. This is useful for figuring out how much space on the screen a given character string is going to take.

```
void gStyleSetItalicsEnable(gStyle *style, int enable);
```

Enables or disables drawing in italics.

```
void gStyleSetBoldEnable(gStyle *style, int enable);
```

Enables or disables drawing in boldface. Boldface will only work for polyline fonts.

```
void gStyleSetBrush(gStyle *style, gBitmap *bitmap,
              gBitmap *clip_mask);
```

Sets an optional brush for use in drawing the characters. This lets you draw polyline characters using patterned brushes for some very creative effects.

Font functions

```
gBitmapFont *gBitmapFontCreate(int wide, int tall, int n);
```

Creates a bitmap font of *n* characters where each font is *wide*-pixels across and *tall*-pixels high.

```
gBitmapFont *gBitmapFontCopy(gBitmapFont *dest, gBitmapFont *src);
```

Copies a bitmap font.

```
void gBitmapFontDelete(gBitmapFont *font);
```

Deletes a bitmap font.

```
void gBitmapFontLoadChar(gBitmapFont *font, int i, char *data);
```

Loads a bitmap definition for element *i* into the bitmap font. The bitmap definition is a *char* array defining the bitmap row by row with a single bit per pixel.

```
void gInitDefaultBitmapFont(void);
```

Initializes the default 8 x 8-bitmap font.

```
gBitmapFont *gGetDefaultBitmapFont(void);
```

Retrieves the pointer to the default bitmap font. This pointer must *not* be freed by your program.

```
gPolyFont *gPolyFontCreate(int wide, int tall, int n);
```

Creates a polyline font of *n* characters where each font is *wide*-pixels across and *tall*-pixels high.

```
gPolyFont *gPolyFontCopy(gPolyFont *dest, gPolyFont *src);
```

Copies a polyline font.

```
void gPolyFontDelete(gPolyFont *font);
```

Deletes a polyline font.

```
void gPolyFontLoadChar(gPolyFont *font, int i, char *data);
```

Loads a polyline character definition for element *i* into the polyline font. The *data* array defines the character by specifying the number of polylines and then defines the character for each polyline, along with the number of points in the polyline and the *(x,y)* coordinates of the points in the polyline.

```
void gInitDefaultPolyFont(void);
```

Initializes the default 100 x 100-polyline font.

```
gPolyFont *gGetDefaultPolyFont(void);
```

Retrieves the pointer to the default polyline font. This pointer must *not* be freed by your program.

Text-drawing functions

```
void gTextDraw(gStyle *style, int x, int y, char *ch,
    gColor color);
```

Draws the passed string, starting at location *(x,y)* on your screen. The string will be drawn in the color specified by *color* using the text style *style*. If *style* is *NULL*, then the default text style is used.

Plotting Functions

So far, an extensive set of drawing tools has been developed but no particularly practical tasks have been performed with this resource. In this, and the next several chapters, you will see how to put these drawing tools to good use creating useful, informative, and fun graphics. In this chapter, you will see how to plot functions on the screen in a variety of different ways. Graphs and charts are some of the most common and aesthetically pleasing ways of presenting data to others, as is evident from the great variety of graphics drawing tools available as standard parts of spreadsheet, database, and word processing software packages. There are also many commercial software packages, such as Mathematica from Wolfram Research and MathCad from MathCad, Inc., which specialize in providing creative ways to plot and graph sets of data. This chapter provides a beginning set of software tools for plotting functions and examines some of the problems you might encounter when creating your own graphs. And while this chapter describes a number of different methods for creating plots, it only provides a starting point. In many ways, creating informative plots is as much an art as a science. By combining the tools from the previous chapters with the ones developed in this one, you can create exactly the type of plots you need.

Graphical History

Plotting, or graphing, functions continues to be one of the principal means of communicating scientific and mathematical information. The graph of a function is a visually intuitive way of showing the relationship (or possibly the lack thereof) between two quantities. Historically, creating an accurate graph has been a very precise and tedious art, requiring meticulous care by the person creating the graph. Before the advent of mechanically-assisted plotting, a scientist or engineer would create a plot by manually plotting selected points along the curve and then connecting the points using a straight edge. Any num-

One of the most common uses of graphics is plotting functions. A function can be a mathematical function or a function derived from measuring data or performing calculations. In this chapter, you'll learn some of the basic issues of function plotting, including how to properly scale and label a plot, and how to choose the particular style of plot for a specific application.

There are many types of graphs, from line plots and scattergrams to bar charts and pie charts, and no single type is suitable for all situations. In this chapter, you'll learn how to create a flexible set of plotting tools that can be adapted to virtually any plotting problem that you might encounter.

ber of things can go wrong with this process. If the scale of the plot is incorrect, or if not enough measured data points are available, or if some points are incorrectly plotted, then the entire plot might have to be drawn again. Creating plots for some scientific disciplines became easier as mechanical devices, such as the moving needles in a seismograph, were developed to help automate the plotting process. Even with such mechanical assistance, many plotting problems were, and still are, difficult to overcome. For instance, with a seismograph, there is always a trade-off between *sensitivity*, setting how small a signal can be measured, and *dynamic range*, the maximum signal that can be measured before the needles go off of the scale. If the sensitivity is increased to measure faint signals, then any large signal will quickly saturate the device, producing an incorrect plot for the large signal, (that is, the plot either goes off of the paper or the needles reach their maximum extent). Conversely, if the dynamic range is increased to accommodate large variations in the measured signal, then small fluctuations in the signal may not be measured very precisely, and may not show up at all in subsequent plots of the data. As you will see in the next section of this chapter, setting an appropriate scale for a plot still presents a significant problem. The computer, however, provides a much wider range of options for dealing with scaling and other plotting problems in a more timely and flexible manner than can be hoped for using manual techniques.

Computers have completely changed the process of graphing, mostly for the better. The computer can create plots much more quickly, accurately, and repeatedly than a person can. The computer can also work with many more data points than any one person (or even a team of people) could possibly cope with. And, as you will see, the computer can easily embellish a plot to provide even more information by adding such features as labels and symbols for critical points, error bars to show how accurately a given point is measured, and overlays of other plots to see how various functions might be related to one another. Additionally, the computer can process data as it is generating the plot of that data.

In many experiments, the directly measured data may not be what winds up being graphed. Often, the data needs to be processed before it can be meaningfully plotted. For example, in an experiment to measure how much braking force a car's brakes are applying to stop a car traveling at different speeds, the braking force may be derived from measurements of how long it takes to stop the car. The direct quantity being measured is the total braking time (the time needed to bring the car to a halt) as a function of the speed of the car. The effective braking force is then computed, based on the initial speed of the car and the braking time. The braking force may then be plotted against the different car velocities to see the relationship between braking force and initial car speed. The braking force measurement is a derived quantity, based on the time measurement. Many experiments require these kinds of computations to produce what actually needs to be plotted. This type of processing can take a long time by hand. But the computer can process raw data quickly, and, even process the data as it is being measured. By providing instantaneous feedback to the scientist of the progress of the experiment, the experimental parameters can be adjusted to compensate for observed anomalies. This is far different from the turn of the century when experimental results could take days or weeks to be processed, plotted, and then reviewed.

Also of great importance in experimental work, is the fact that the computer can help the researcher compensate for variations in the measuring equipment, for instance, to account for some instrument flaw or loss of instrument calibration. This is how astronomers are able to get around many of the limitations caused by the optical flaws in the Hubble space telescope. The unprocessed images supplied by the Hubble are processed through a computer model of how the optics distort the "true" image and the process inverted to yield the image that the undistorted Hubble should produce. Just as the computer may be used to correct erroneous data (if you know the source of the error), the computer can also be used to perform additional processing to generate more useful or meaningful information. For instance, in studying stock market prices, you might not be interested in the absolute price of a given stock, but rather in what the percentage change in the stock value is over time. Or you might want to correct the price to take into account inflation over time. Without a computer to do this type of work, there is considerable additional work to compute these derived data sets and then to plot the results. However, it is just as easy to corrupt the data as it is to enhance it. Any type of additional data processing must be done carefully, otherwise computer processing of data can easily be overdone, resulting in data that is less useful than, and possibly even distorted from, the original data.

After a discussion of the most commonly used plots, you begin by creating a plot of a typical function with the tools developed in the previous chapters. The steps I will discuss include: where the different parts of the graph will go on the screen, how to scale the graph to ensure that the points plotted actually fit on the screen, and how to label the graph. Then, the section on "Creating a Complete Plot" will show you how to combine each of these steps to generate a plot. Additionally, at the end of the chapter, there is a discussion on how to create several other kinds of plots.

The Plot Begins

A two-dimensional graph shows the relationship between two variables, one variable represented by the x coordinate, and the other represented by the y-coordinate. The simplest types of graphs are plots of functions, in which for each x coordinate, there is a corresponding y-value, derived by evaluating $y = f(x)$. The function $f()$ may be a mathematical function or it may represent measurements taken by some instrument for different values of x. By plotting pairs of points, $(x, f(x))$, you can visually see the relationship between the two variables. In this type of graph, the variable x is called the *independent* variable and the y-coordinate is called the *dependent* variable, since the value of y depends on x. In some disciplines, such as economics, the relationships are reversed for historical reasons, and x becomes the dependent variable and y, the independent variable. There are several other types of functions that can be plotted, among them the parametric curves shown in Chapter 5. For a parametric curve, both x and y depend on a third parameter, t. The five basic types of functions that will be considered in this chapter are the following:

1. Mathematical functions, like $y = sin(x) + cos(x)$.
2. Recorded measurements, where one variable is some measured quantity as a function of another variable. With this type of function, you may only know the value of the function for a small set of measured points. For example, if you run an experiment and measure some

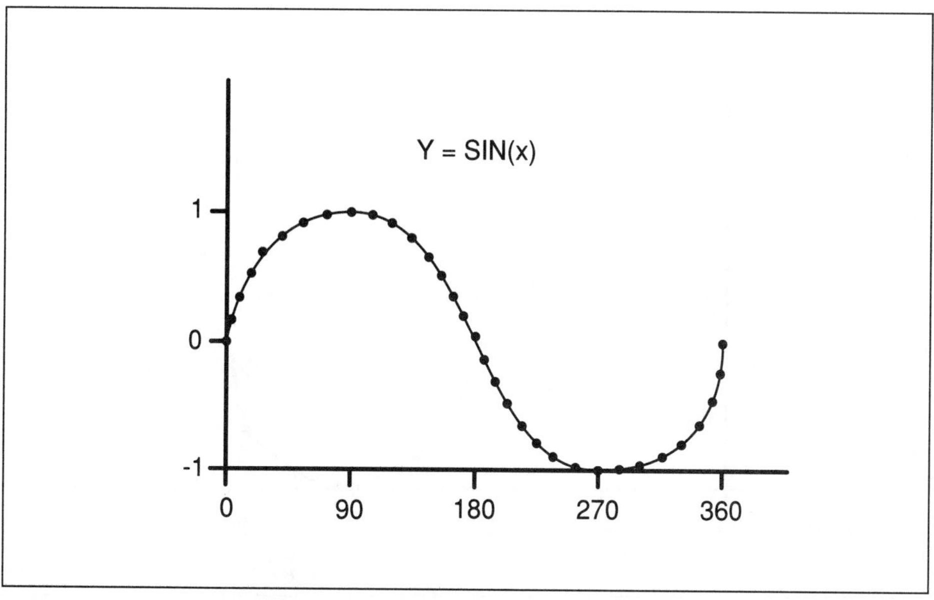

Figure 11-1. Plot of y=sin(x) with x ranging from 0 to 2*PI using 40 sample points

quantity at one-second intervals, then you must estimate the value of the function for the times between measurements, like at time $t = 2.5$ seconds.

3. Parametrically defined data in which both the x and y coordinates are functions of a third independent parameter t. In this case, both x and y are dependent variables. Any parametrically defined curve, such as the circle and ellipse from Chapter 5, fit into this category.
4. Two-dimensional data in which both x and y separately measured quantities. An example of this type of data is astronomical measurements of various properties of stars, such as mass and brightness. Measurements of both quantities might be taken for hundreds of stars and then plotted as (x,y) coordinate pairs to see if there is some correlation between the two quantities.
5. Discrete functions in which only a relatively small number of data points are used. For instance, plotting the closing Dow Jones Industrial Average for the last 7 days only has 7 data points. These types of functions are normally presented as bar chart type graphs.

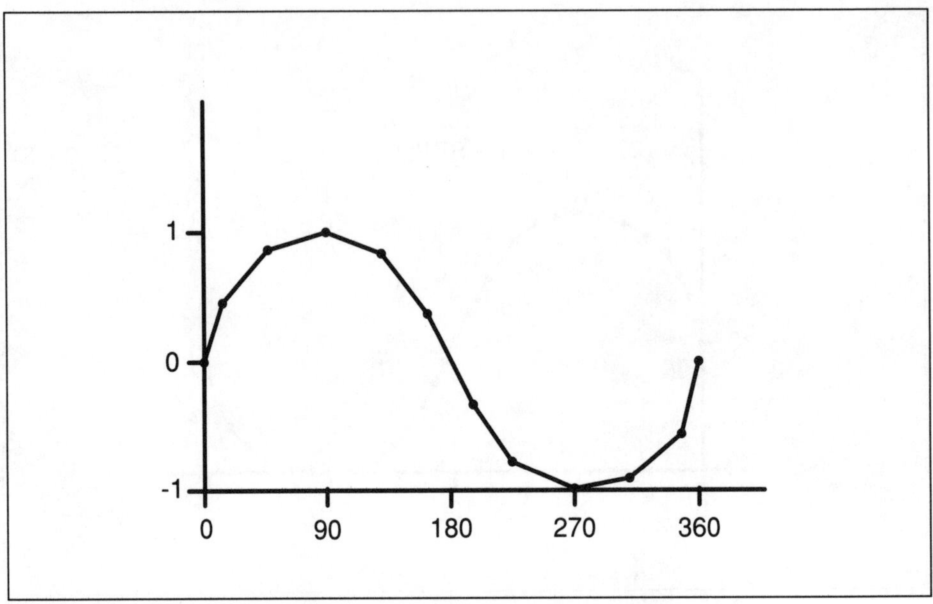

Figure 11-2. Same as Figure 11-1, except now only 12 sample points are used

The first two types of functions are usually plotted in a "connect-the-dot" type fashion, often referred to as a *line plot*. The function is evaluated at regularly spaced intervals along the *x*-axis. This creates a coordinate pair $(x, f(x))$, which can then be plotted as a point on the screen. Each plotted point is referred to as a *sample point*. Each sample point is connected to its neighbor sample point with, most commonly, a straight line. This process is shown in Figure 11-1 for the function $y=sin(x)$. In the first case, the *x*-values range from 0 to $2^*\pi$, using 40 equally-spaced points along the *x*-axis. Figure 11-2 shows the resulting plot if only 12 points are used. As can be seen by comparing the two plots, using fewer sample points produces a less accurate plot of the function.

The third type of data is plotted in a very similar fashion to the first two. Instead of evaluating a single function at regular intervals along the *x*-axis, the two parametric functions are evaluated for evenly spaced values of the parameter *t*. This is how the circle- and ellipse-plotting functions worked. As each new point $(x(t), y(t))$ is computed, it is connected with the previous point by a straight line, exactly the same as with the first two types of functions.

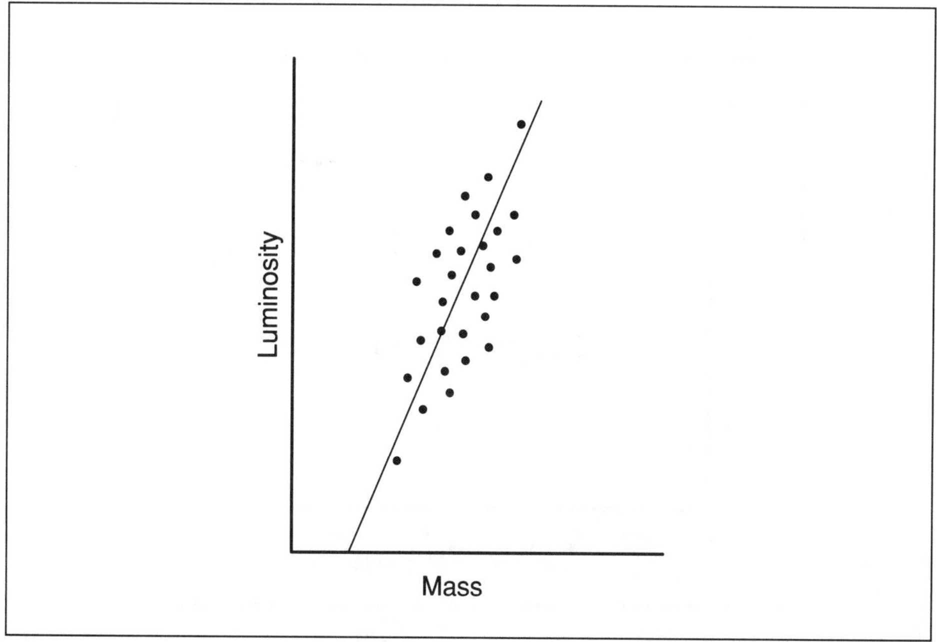

Figure 11-3. Scattergram plot for two measured variables, star mass and brightness. The line through the points represents a "best-fit" to the data, showing that the two variables are strong related. If the data were more widely scattered around the plot, then there would be no reasonable way to draw a line, and the variables would be considered independent of one another.

The fourth type of function is plotted simply as a collection of points, as shown in Figure 11-3. This kind of plot is sometimes referred to as a *scattergram*, due to the apparent scattering of points around the plot. This type of plot is used to see if there is some visible relationship between the quantities represented by the x and y variables. In Figure 11-3, there is an approximate linear relationship between the variables, that is, a line can be drawn through the plot that all of the points are relatively near. With this type of data, one can make a reasonable case that the two quantities being plotted are closely, though not completely, related.

The fifth type of function is usually plotted as a *bar chart*. For each point along the x-axis, a rectangle of some pre-determined width is plotted. The height of the rectangle corresponds to the data value for this point along the x-axis. An example is shown in Figure 11-4. The bars may be adjacent to one

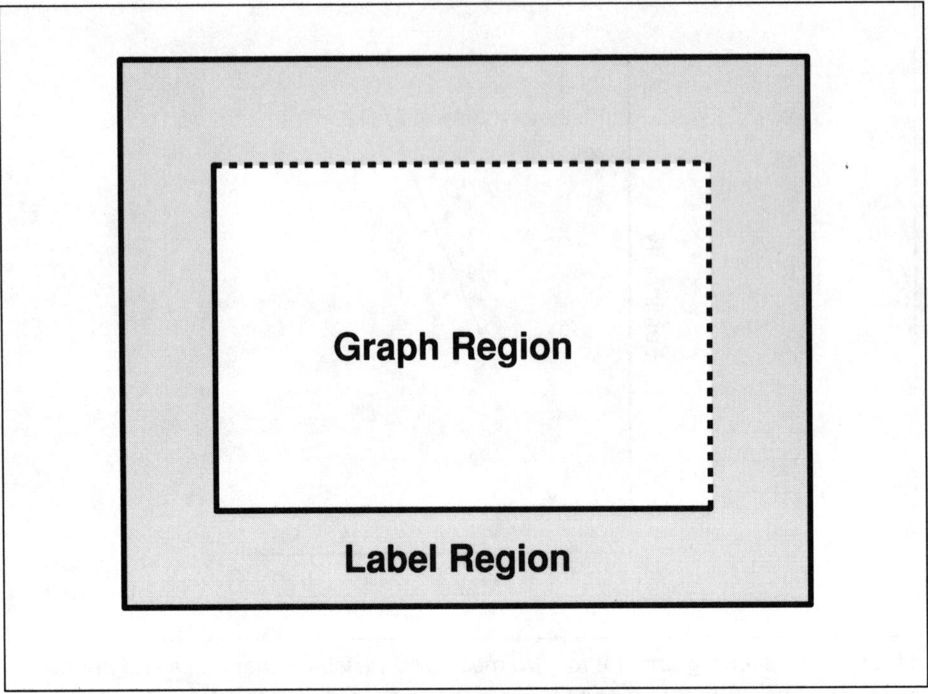

Figure 11-4. A plot is divided into two regions. The graph region is where the drawing actually occurs. The label region contains all of the tick marks and labeling.

another, or separated by any amount of space deemed appropriate. The bars are usually filled with a solid color, or if the image must be printed in black and white, with some suitable pattern, such as the cross-hatch pattern presented in Chapter 9.

Diagram of a Plot

Plots can vary greatly in appearance depending on what type of data is being plotted, what features of the data should be emphasized, and personal preference. The entire area of the screen that a plot occupies is referred to as the *plot region*. For general purposes, the plot region is usually the entire screen. The plot region is subdivided into two separate regions as shown in Figure 11-4. The *graph region* is the portion of the plot region that the function graph actually occupies. Any part of the graph that would be drawn outside of the graph region is not drawn. The second region of the plot is called the *label* region.

All coordinate axes, tick marks, labels, and plot titles are drawn in the label region. The plot is divided into these two areas to ensure that there is sufficient room for all of the labeling that may be applied and to keep the graph of the function from overwriting the labels.

The plot region and the graph region are specified using *gRectangle* structures. The plot region for the entire screen can be easily created using the following code segment:

```
gRectangle *plot_region;

plot_region = gRectangleCreate();
plot_region->xmin = 0.0;
plot_region->ymin = 0.0;
plot_region->xmax = gGetMaxX() - 1.0;
plot_region->ymax = gGetMaxY() - 1.0;
```

Generating the graph region rectangle, however, can be a little more difficult since you may want to leave room for a label region around the sides of the graph region. The function *gCreateGraphRegion()*, described in the following section, creates a graph region rectangle from a passed plot region rectangle, leaving enough room for labels using the default character sizes.

Drawing Coordinate Axes

There are many different types of plots, as mentioned earlier, but all share some common features. To be useful, a plot must have coordinate axes to identify the scale of the data being plotted. A coordinate axis is drawn as a single line with two or more tick marks and, optionally, numeric labels drawn under the tick marks to indicate the value they represent. A *tick mark* is simply a marker to indicate a specific coordinate along the axis, just as the marks on a ruler indicate every inch along the length of the ruler. Tick marks are drawn as a small vertical line segment (7 pixels tall) along the x-coordinate axis, and as a small horizontal line segment (7 pixels wide) along the y-coordinate axis. To make a readable plot, the tick marks should be labeled to identify the coordinate the tick mark represents, just as a ruler is labeled. However, it is not always necessary to label every tick mark, just as every subdivision on a ruler is not labeled.

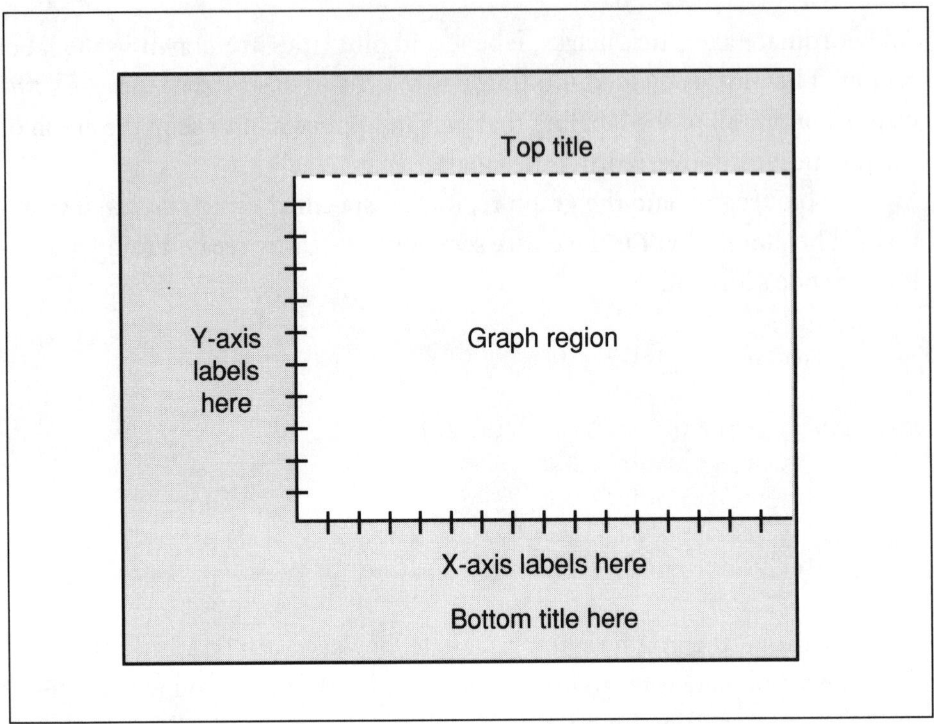

Figure 11-5. Graph and label regions for a lower-left coordinate axes plot

The spacing, and number, of tick marks depends on the type of function being plotted. Several tries are usually required before you arrive at the desired number, spacing, and labeling of tick marks. Figure 11-5 shows a typical set of coordinate axes with appropriate tick marks and labeling.

There are two basic types of *x*- and *y*-coordinate axes that may be drawn using the software provided in this book. The first is the usual set of coordinate axes in which the two axes intersect in the lower-left corner of the graph region. This is the type used in most of the figures of this book. The graph region usually extends from where the coordinate axes intersect up to the upper-right corner of the plot region, as shown in Figure 11-5. If, however, a title is placed on the top of the graph, the graph region muse be shrunk to accommodate the title string. The label region for this type of plot consists of the area between the coordinate axes and the plot region, extending to the left and down, as shown in Figure 11-5.

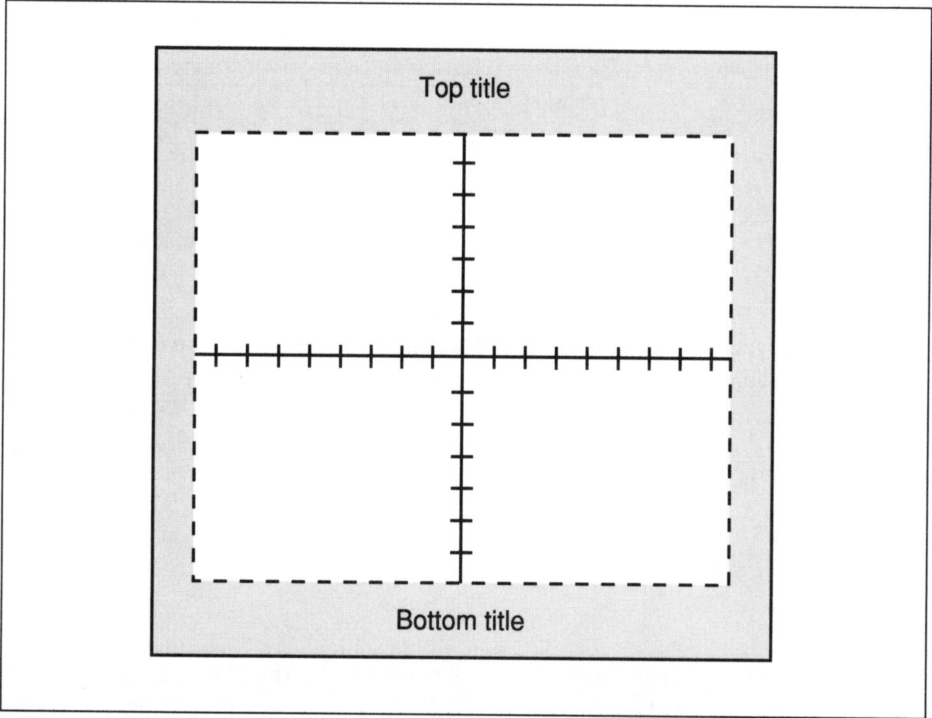

Figure 11-6. Graph region for a centered-coordinate axes plot

The second type of coordinate axes are centered in the plot region. These are quite useful for drawing functions, such as *y=sin(x)* which exhibit symmetry about one or both of the axes. For these types of functions, it is often desirable to demonstrate the symmetry by plotting centered coordinate axes. For this type of plot, the graph region may be the entire plot region, or a slightly reduced area if there are extra labels on the sides of the plot. The label region is almost always the same as the entire plot region, since the coordinate axes with appropriate tick marks must be drawn inside the graph region. Figure 11-6 shows an example of a coordinate axis centered type plot.

The *enum* type *gAXES_TYPE* is used to identify the various types of coordinate axes for the various plot drawing routines. The following code defines *gAXES_TYPE*:

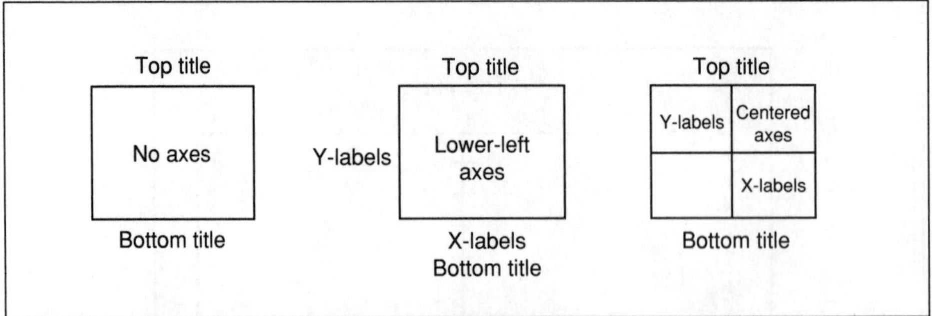

Figure 11-7 Layout for the three different coordinate axes types. The dotted line indicates the entire plot region for each type.

```
typedef enum {
 gAXES_NONE = 0,
 gAXES_LOWERLEFT,
 gAXES_CENTER
} gAXES_TYPE;
```

The function *gCreateGraphRegion()*, shown in Listing 11-1, creates a graph region from a passed plot region and passes an argument of type *gAXES_TYPE* indicating the desired type of coordinate axes. If a coordinate axes type of *gAXES_NONE* is passed, then no axes will be drawn in the final plot, and the graph region is set equal to the plot region minus an area on the top and bottom for plot titles. For the type *gAXES_LOWERLEFT*, the graph region is created with sufficient room for tick marks and labels up to 5 characters long and room for a top and bottom plot label. For a coordinate axes type of *gAXES_CENTER*, the graph region is set to leave room along the bottom and top of the plot for any desired labeling. Tick marks and labeling for the tick marks are drawn inside of the graph region, and so do not need any extra space. The layout of these three types of plots is shown in Figure 11-7.

```
/* Create an appropriate graph region for a given plot
  region */

gRectangle *gCreateGraphRegion(gRectangle *plot_region,
                                gAXES_TYPE ctype,
                                gStyle *text_style);
```

```
{
gRectangle *graph_region;
float xsize, ysize, xleft, ytop, ybott;

/* What is the current size of text */
gStyleGetPixelSize(text_style, &xsize, &ysize);
graph_region = gRectangleCopy(plot_region, NULL);
if(!graph_region)
 return NULL;

switch(ctype) {
case gAXES_NONE:
 /* Leave room for 3 lines (space and titles) */
 graph_region->ymin += 3*ysize;
 graph_region->ymax -= 3*ysize;
 break;
case gAXES_LOWERLEFT:
 /* On the left, leave room for tick marks, a space,
    5 chars, and another space */
 xleft = 4 + xsize + 5*xsize + xsize;
 /* On the bottom, leave room for tick marks, a space,
    1 char, a space, 1 char (title), and a space */
 ybott = 4 + 5*ysize;
 /* On top, leave room for a space, 1 char, space */
 ytop = 3*ysize;

 graph_region->xmin += xleft;
 graph_region->ymin += ytop;
 graph_region->ymax -= ybott;
 break;
case gAXES_CENTER:
 /* Leave room on top and bottom for 3 lines */
 graph_region->ymin += 3*ysize;
 graph_region->ymax -= 3*ysize;
 break;
} /* End switch */

/* Is this a valid region or was plot region too small? */
if(graph_region->xmax <= graph_region->xmin ||
```

```
     graph_region->ymax <= graph_region->ymin) {
    free(graph_region);
    graph_region = NULL;
  }

  return graph_region;
}
```

Listing 11-1. gCreateGraphRegion() creates a graph region appropriate to the type of coordinate axes being drawn, leaving enough room for standard labeling.

The function *gCoordinateAxesDraw()* draws the coordinate axes of the specified type. This function takes eight arguments:

```
void gCoordinateAxesDraw(gAXES_TYPE ctype,
                         gRectangle *graph_region,
                         int nxticks, int nyticks,
                         gStyle *text_style,
                         char **xlabels, char **ylabels);
```

The first argument sets the type of coordinate axes being drawn and the second sets the region of the screen corresponding to the graph region. The arguments *nxticks* and *nyticks* set the number of evenly spaced tick marks to draw along the *x* and *y* axes, respectively. If either of these is 0 or 1, then no tick marks are drawn. If the number of tick marks is greater than 1, then that many evenly spaced tick marks are drawn along the corresponding axis. A tick mark is always drawn at both ends of the axis, so a value of 3, for instance, would cause a tick mark to be drawn at both ends and in the middle of the axis. A value of 4 would divide the axis into thirds, and so forth. Of course, *nxticks* and *nyticks* can be different numbers since the *x* and *y* axes may be scaled differently.

In addition to drawing the axes and plotting tick marks, *gCoordinateAxesDraw()* can also add labels for the tick marks. The arguments *xlabels* and *ylabels* are each a pointer to an array of strings that are used to label each of the tick marks. If *xlabels* is *NULL*, then no labels are drawn for the *x*-axis, and similarly if *ylabels* is *NULL*. If either label pointer is not *NULL*, then it points to an array of strings. Each element of the array is a pointer to a string that labels the corresponding tick mark. The *xlabels* array must have at least *nxticks* pointers, and the *ylabels* array must have at least *nyticks* pointers. Each string in the *xlabels* array is centered beneath the tick marks on the *x*-axis, and each string in the *ylabels* array is centered vertically and to the left of the tick mark for the *y*-axis. If any of the pointers in either the *xlabels* or *ylabels* array is *NULL*, then the label in that postion is not drawn. Thus, there is no need to have a label for every tick mark, only the ones that you wish to label. The variable *text_style* determines the text style used for the labels. Creating the individual label strings is easy using the C function *sprintf()*. For example, suppose that you wish to label a plot in which both *x* and *y* range from 0 to 10. This requires 11 tick marks for each axis and each tick mark should be labeled with the number 0 through 10. A sample code segment to create the necessary labels is shown in the following:

```
char **labels;
char string[10];
int i;

/* Allocate labels array of char pointers */
labels = (char **)gcalloc(11, sizeof(char *));
for(i=0; i < 11; i++) {
 string[0] = 0;
 /* Write appropriate label */
 sprintf(string, "%2d", i);
 labels[i] = (char *)gcalloc(strlen(string) + 1, sizeof(char));
 strcpy(labels[i], string);
}

gCoordinateAxesDraw(gAXES_LOWERLEFT, graph_region,
                    11, 11, NULL, labels, labels);
```

A temporary *char* array, *string*, is used to contain the result of each *sprintf()* operation. Each label is then created as a copy of the contents of *string*. This method ensures that each label is large enough to contain the result of the *sprintf()* operation. For instance, if the *%2d* is changed to *%3.1f*, to print labels like 1.0, 2.0, etc., each resulting string needs to be one character larger. The method shown requires no code changes; it automatically creates label strings of the correct length as long as the *sprintf* format statement does not use more than 9 characters. In general, tick mark labels should be kept to 5 or less characters to ensure that they will fit into the plot region and to make the plot more readable. The graph region may always be resized, however, to allow longer labels to fit.

The line drawing for both of the coordinate axes and the tick marks use any currently set options for line drawing, including any brushes set with *gSetBrush()*. This provides the ability to draw the axes and tick marks as thicker lines to give emphasis or to go with special styles. The tick mark labels are drawn using the font and text size specified by the style passed to *gCoordinateAxesDraw()*. This allows the plot to be labeled in any desired text style or size. As with most text drawing options, any brush drawing option set by *gSetBrush()* is disabled prior to drawing the labels. The brush is then re-enabled when *gCoordinateAxesDraw()* returns.

As with a ruler, you may want to draw more tick marks than labels. This can be accomplished in one of two ways. You can either create as many tick marks as necessary and only provide labels for the appropriate tick marks, setting the pointers for the other tick mark labels to *NULL*, or you can call *gCoordinateAxesDraw()* multiple times using different tick mark spacing. For instance, in the previous example, a tick mark can be placed midway between each integer coordinate using the following:

```
gCoordinateAxesDraw(gAXES_LOWERLEFT, graph_region,
                    21, 21, NULL, NULL, NULL);
gCoordinateAxesDraw(gAXES_LOWERLEFT, graph_region,
                    11, 11, NULL, labels, labels);
```

By using these two calls, the coordinates axes and some of the tick marks will be drawn twice, specifically, the tick marks at 0 through 10. Unlike the first method, this technique does not require regenerating the tick mark labels array, which would require considerably more logic to ensure the labeling of the correct tick mark. By using this approach, you can easily change the number of tick marks drawn between each labeled tick mark. For instance, if you wanted to draw three tick marks between each integer coordinate, dividing each interval into one-fourth length segments, you simply replace the *21* in the first call to *gCoordinateAxesDraw()* with *41*. This method of redrawing a graphic element multiple times using different parameters each time is quite useful in creating many types of graphic drawings, such as bar charts and pie charts. In this example, the same technique may be used to change the text font and/or character size for the tick mark labels. As each set of tick marks is plotted, the character size could be changed so that the differently spaced tick marks can be easily distinguished. For example, the midpoint labels could be drawn with smaller characters to make them less intrusive on the final plot, but at least still readable. Many different types of plot styles can be accommodated by various combinations of *gCoordinateAxesDraw()*. As shown in the next section on setting the plot scale, you can even accommodate individually positioned tick marks for special-purpose labeling, such as marking a critical data point on the plot.

Drawing the coordinate axes for a plot only addresses part of the problem. You still need to plot the actual function. The main issue here is how to determine the scale of the plot and, subsequently, how to convert the input, (x,y) plot coordinates, to screen pixel coordinates suitable for passing to the point- and line-drawing functions developed in the previous chapters.

Setting the Plot Scale

The problem of how to create a properly scaled and labeled plot of a function has been around ever since the development of the Cartesian coordinate system. Even for well-behaved functions (those whose appearance you already know), there is no single "correct" way to plot the function. The type of plot depends on what you wish to show about the function. For less well-behaved functions, it often takes several iterations to get the plot to look as intended. The previous section described how to define and draw a set of coordinate axes with tick marks and labels. Now you must determine how to set the scale of the plot. This requires addressing several aspects of the function being drawn:

What is the range of values of the independent variable, x, that the function should be plotted for? For instance, if $y = sin(x)$, then you might want to create the plot with *x* ranging from 0 to 2*π, or from -2*π to +2*π or some other suitable range.

Given the range of *x*-values, what is the corresponding range for the dependent variable *y*? For *y=sin(x)*, the answer is easy because you know the *sin()* ranges between -1 to +1. For most functions, however, the range of output values can vary widely depending on the range of *x* being plotted.

If the range of *x* and *y* are different, then how should they be scaled to fit on the screen. For instance, in creating the plot of *y = 100*sin(x)*, with *x* ranging from 0 to 2*π, *y* ranges from -100 to +100. If the *x* and *y* axes are drawn at the same scale on the screen, then the resulting plot would appear much taller than it is wide, a very undesirable result! Conversely, arbitrarily adjusting the scale of *x* and *y* without clearly labeling the two axes can result in a very deceptive looking graph.

Linear Scaling

The range of both the *x* and *y* values sets the scale of the plot. For example, in the plot of *y=sin(x)* of Figure 11-1, *x* ranges from 0 to 2*π. If the plot occupies the entire screen, then there are *gGetMaxX()* columns in the graph region, which must be mapped to the range of *x* from 0 to 2*π.

The problem is to convert between the plot coordinates, ranging from 0 to 2*π, to pixel coordinates of the screen in the graph region. The most straightforward way to do this is to use *linear scaling*. Linear scaling simply means that the plot coordinates are scaled to the screen coordinates using two fixed scale conversion factors, one for the *x*-coordinate and one for the *y*-coordinate. Thus, a point that is halfway across the plot, should appear halfway across the screen. For this example, *x* values that range from 0 to 2*π can be converted to pixels on the screen by scaling the coordinates using Equation 11-1:

*xpixel = x * ((float)(gGetMaxX() - 1) / (2.0*PI))* (Equation 11-1)

More generally, if the range of *x*-values for the function is *xmin* to *xmax* and the graph region lies between *xmin_pixel* and *xmax_pixel* on the screen, then the corresponding pixel coordinate on the screen for *x* can be found using Equation 11-2:

$$xpixel = ((x - xmin) * ((float)(xmax\_pixel - xmin\_pixel) / (xmax - xmin))) + xmin\_pixel$$

(Equation 11-2)

In the *y = sin(x)* example, *xmin_pixel* is 0, *xmax_pixel* is *gGetMaxX()-1*, *xmin* is 0.0, and *xmax* is 2*π. The same formula shown in Equation 11-2 is used to convert between a given range of *y* to a given range on the screen, with the appropriate substitutions of *y* for *x*. The form of Equation 11-2 is very similar to that of the rescaling of a drawing, a problem presented in Chapter 6. In fact, it is exactly the same problem. As shown in Chapter 6, the entire coordinate transformation can be reduced to generating an affine transformation which defines the conversion between the *(x,y)* coordinates of the plot, and the *(x,y)* coordinates of the graph region. The desired boundaries for the input plot coordinates and output screen coordinates are specified by two *gRectangle* structures. The first rectangle specifies the boundaries of the plot in the units used by the function being plotted. For instance, the *y=sin(x)* plot has *x* ranging from 0 to 2*π and *y* ranging from -1.0 to +1.0. This rectangle is referred to as the *source graph region* because it represents the bounding box of the graph region on the screen, specified in coordinates suitable to the function being plotted. The second rectangle defines the graph region, specified as pixel locations on the screen.

The graph region may be created from the plot region using the function *gCreateGraphRegion()* as shown previously. The function *gCreateCoordinateTransform()*, shown in Listing 11-2, creates the transformation matrix required to transform coordinates from the plot units to screen pixel coordinates. Since most plots have the *y*-coordinate increasing from the bottom of the plot to the top (the opposite of screen coordinates), *gCreateCoordinateTransform()* includes a reflection operation to create suitable screen coordinates. Note that the final offset uses *dest_rect->ymax* instead of *dest_rect->ymin* because the *y* coordinates have been reflected.

```
/* Function to create transformation matrix from
  between two rectangles using linear scaling */

gMatrix *gCreateCoordinateTransform(gRectangle *source_rect,
                                    gRectangle *dest_rect)
{
gMatrix *matrix = NULL;
float xscale, yscale;
gVector *temp_vec;

if(!source_rect || !dest_rect)
 return NULL;

xscale = (dest_rect->xmax - dest_rect->xmin) /
         (source_rect->xmax - source_rect->xmin);
yscale = (dest_rect->ymax - dest_rect->ymin) /
         (source_rect->ymax - source_rect->ymin);

temp_vec = gVectorCreate(-source_rect->xmin,
                         -source_rect->ymin);
/* Generate transformation */
/* First, source coordinates are offset relative to
   rectangle */
gMatrixTranslate(matrix, matrix, temp_vec);
/* Now scale the coordinates */
gVectorSet(temp_vec, xscale, yscale);
gMatrixScale(matrix, matrix, temp_vec);
/* Now, invert the coordinates about the x-axis (-y) */
gMatrixReflect(matrix, matrix, 0, 1);
/* Finally, offset them to put them into the rectangle */
gVectorSet(temp_vec, dest_rect->xmin, dest_rect->ymax);
gMatrixTranslate(matrix, matrix, temp_vec);

gVectorDelete(temp_vec);
return matrix;
}
```

Listing 11-2. The function gCreateCoordinateTransform( ) creates the transformation to convert from one coordinate system to another.

With the transformation matrix, you can now plot the function directly to the graph region. The function *gTransformPoints()* transforms each *(x,y)* coordinate to the appropriate location in the graph region. The plot of *y=sin(x)* using 40 points is created with the following code:

```
gMatrix *plotToScreen;
gRectangle source_region, *graph_region;
float x, y, step;
gPoint lastpoint, point;

step = 2*PI / 40.0;    /* 40 steps */
source_region.xmin = 0.0;
source_region.xmax = 2*PI;
source_region.ymin = -1.0;
source_region.ymax = 1.0;
plotToScreen = gCreateCoordinateTransform(&source_region,
                                          graph_region);

for(x=0.0; x <= 2*PI; x += step) {
 y = sin(x);
 point.x = x;
 point.y = y;
 /* Now transform to graph region coordinates */
 gTransformPoints(plotToScreen, &point, 1);
 if(x > 0.0) {
  gLineDraw(ROUND(lastpoint.x), ROUND(lastpoint.y),
            ROUND(point.x), ROUND(point.y), gWHITE);
 }
 lastpoint = point;
}

/* Clean up any temporary objects */
gMatrixDelete(plotToScreen);
```

Listing 11-3. Procedure to create the plot of y=sin(x) using 40 points

Note that the number of steps used can be changed to any desired value, with no other changes to the code other than changing 40.0 to the desired number of steps. A reasonable number of steps to choose would be the number of columns in the graph region. Instead of using 40, use (*graph_region->xmax - graph_region->xmin + 1*). This will ensure that new data points will be computed for each column of the screen, creating the highest resolution and most accurate plot for the specified size of the graph region. By using the transformation approach shown in this code segment, the plot may be resized or moved to any part of the screen without requiring any coding changes. This makes much more modular and reusable code than if it were, say, hard-coded to plot to the entire screen.

Finding the Minimum and Maximum

In most plots, the range of the *x* and *y* variables is not known ahead of time and must be determined. If the data is being read from a file, then the file can be scanned to find the minimum and maximum *x*- and *y*-values. If a mathematical function is being plotted, then a range for *x* must be specified and the range for *y* determined by using the function. In the previous example of *y=sin(x)*, the minimum and maximum *y*-coordinates could be found using a *for* loop such as this:

```
float ymin, ymax;

ymin = ymax = sin(0.0);
for(x=0.0; x <= 2*PI; x += step) {
 y = sin(x);
 ymin = MIN(ymin, y);
 ymax = MAX(ymax, y);
}

source_region.ymin = ymin;
source_region.ymax = ymax;
```

This approach works fine for setting the *x* and *y* ranges in most cases, but it can cause some problems depending on the step size used to step through *x*. In this example, *ymin* is likely to be a value such as -0.995 rather than exactly -1.0, because you do not evaluate the exact point at which *sin()* achieves its minimum value. The simple solution to this problem is to round up to the nearest integer for the maximum and round down for the minimum. This, however, will not produce correct results if the range of the data is 0.10 to 0.11. In general, not having the scale set to the exact limits of the function can simply be more annoying than truly problematic.

You must be careful in creating the tick-mark labels to make sure you get the label values you intended. For example, if the bottom-most tick mark is acually at -0.995 rather than at -1.0, the label might read -0.99 instead of -1.0 as desired. Your program can force the tick-mark labels to the desired display value if necessary, even when it does not exactly match the plot limits. You can force the labels to the correct values by rounding to the proper number of digits. In the previous example, first multiply the values by 100.0, round the result, and then divide by 100.0 to get two significant digits. These rounded values are then used to create the tick-mark labels.

While you typically set the scale of the plot with the minimum and maximum plot values, you may not always want to do it that way. For instance, you may want to increase the scale of, or magnify, a certain portion of the plot to examine it in detail. The only operation you must perform is setting the source-graph region *ymin* and *ymax* values to represent the range you want to see, and then generate a new transformation matrix with *gCreateCoordinateTransform()*. To make sure that the plot function does not draw outside the graph region, add the graph region as a clip region using a call such as the following:

```
gAddClipFunction(&gRectangleClipTest, graph_region);
```

When the plot is complete, be sure to remove the clipping region with the following call:

```
gRemoveClipFunction(&gRectangleClipTest, graph_region);
```

By using the clipping functions, you may freely change the scale of the plot as well as reposition the plot without having to worry about the plot overwriting other portions of the screen.

Another Aspect of Plotting

One problem frequently encountered in creating a plot is that the rectangle defining the source graph region is not square. If the graph region does not have the same proportions as the source graph region, then the resulting plot can look distorted. For instance, in the plot of *y=sin(x)*, the source graph region has a width of 2*π and a height of 2.0. If the graph region is square, the resulting plot looks compressed because the plot width is made to fit into the same length as the plot height. It is therefore desirable to have both the source graph region and the graph region have the same aspect ratio, that is, the ratio of the width and height for each rectangle is the same. In some cases you will want to adjust the source graph region to match the graph region, and in others, you will want to adjust the graph region to match the source graph region. The function *gRectangleMatchAspect()*, shown in Listing 11-4, takes two *gRectangle* structures and adjusts the second one to have the same aspect ratio as the first. The adjusted rectangle remains centered about the original (unadjusted) rectangle center and will always be contained within the original rectangle. This ensures that the plot is always contained on the screen.

```
gRectangle *gRectangleMatchAspect(gRectangle *source,
                                  gRectangle *dest)
{
gRectangle *newrect;
float s_aspect, d_aspect, xcent, ycent, xlength, ylength;

if(!source || !dest)
 return NULL;

newrect = gRectangleCopy(NULL, source);
s_aspect = (source->ymax - source->ymin) /
           (source->xmax - source->xmin);
xcent = (dest->xmin + dest->xmax) / 2.0;
ycent = (dest->ymin + dest->ymax) / 2.0;
xlength = (dest->xmax - dest->xmin);
ylength = (dest->ymax - dest->ymin);
d_aspect = ylength / xlength;
```

```
/* You want ylength / xlength == s_aspect */
/* So, either multiply xlength by d_aspect / s_aspect */
/* Or, multiply ylength by s_aspect / d_aspect */
/* Use the one which shrinks the rectangle */

if(s_aspect < d_aspect)
 /* Shrink y */
 ylength *= s_aspect / d_aspect;
else
 /* Shrink x */
 xlength *= d_aspect / s_aspect;
}

new_rect->xmin = xcent - xlength/2.0;
new_rect->xmax = xcent + xlength/2.0;
new_rect->ymin = ycent - ylength/2.0;
new_rect->ymax = ycent + ylength/2.0;

return new_rect;
} /* End of gRectangleMatchAspect */
```

Listing 11-4. The function gRectangleMatchAspect() creates a new rectangle that has the same aspect ratio as a given source rectangle and has the same center as, and is contained within, the second rectangle.

The basic procedure for creating an appropriate graph region is to use *gCreateGraphRegion()* to create an initial graph region from the overall plot region. A source graph region rectangle is then created for the function or data being plotted, just as it was created for the *y=sin(x)* plot. The function *gRectangleMatchAspect()* is then called to adjust the graph region to have the same aspect ratio as the source graph region. The graph region is now ready to be used in drawing coordinate axes and in creating the appropriate transformation function.

However, using *gRectangleMatchAspect()* is not a good idea if the ranges of the *x*- and *y*-coordinates are very different. For instance, a plot of *y = 100*x* where *x* ranges from 0 to 1 produces a range for *y* of 0 to 100. Passing a rectangle of this source graph region to *gRectangleMatchAspect()* would produce a very thin graph region! In general, if the ratio of the *x* and *y* sides of the plot region is greater than 2 or less than 1/2, then you should probably not use *gRec-*

tangleMatchAspect(). With the linear scaling methods discussed so far, you must either live with the different *x* and *y* scales on the axes or change the range of *x* or *y* (or both) to be approximately equal. However, another way to plot the data is to apply a function to the coordinate values that brings them into a more reasonable range. The most common such function is the logarithm.

Logarithmic Scaling

In many scientific disciplines, the range of data for plotting can either be very large or very small. For instance, in measuring the distance of stars from earth, an astronomer might deal with stars ranging from 10 light years to 100,000 light years, or more, away. In any linear plot of this data, the data points for 10 light years would not even be visible on the plot. One solution is to plot some other function of the measurements that produces more reasonable scaling. A common function to use is the base 10 logarithm. The ***base 10 logarithm*** of *a* positive number is the power 10 must be raised to equal the number, that is, if *b* is the base 10 logarithm of *a*, then $a = 10^b$. The logarithm of 1 is 0, and any number between 0 and 1 has a negative logarithm. Thus, the 10 light-year measurement has a logarithm of 1, and 100,000 has a logarithm of 6. A plot range of 1 to 6 is much more reasonable than 10 to 100,000 and all of the data is visible on the plot.

For logarithmic plots in which the range of the data is from *ymin* to *ymax*, it is standard practice to compute the *y* limits of the source graph region as follows:

```
gRectangle source_region;

if(ymin > 0.0)
 source_region.ymin = floor(log10(ymin));
else
 source_region.ymin = 0.0;

if(ymax > 0.0)
 source_region.ymax = ceil(log10(ymax));
else
 source_region.ymax = 1.0;
```

For the minimum value *ymin*, the *floor()* function finds the nearest integer less than or equal to the base 10 logarithm of *ymin*. This ensures that the entire plot is above the minimum and that the source region is bounded by integer powers of 10. If *ymin* is less than 0, the source region minimum is simply set equal to 0.0. Similarly, for the maximum value *ymax*, the *ceil()* function finds the nearest integer greater than or equal to the base 10 logarithm of *ymax*. Again, this ensures that the source graph region is at least large enough to contain the entire plot when logarithmically scaled.

The basic plotting routine now becomes:

```
for(x=xmin; x <= xmax; x += step) {
 y = (*f)(x);
 point.x = x;
 if(y > 0.0)
  y = log10(y);
 else
  y = 0.0;
 point.y = y;
 /* Now transform to graph region coordinates */
 gTransformPoints(plotToScreen, &point, 1);
 if(x > xmin) {
  gLineDraw(ROUND(lastpoint.x), ROUND(lastpoint.y),
            ROUND(point.x), ROUND(point.y), gWHITE);
 }
 lastpoint = point;
}
```

When creating tick marks and labels for a logarithmic plot, you must be careful to compute the inverse logarithm (using *exp10()*) to get the actual variable value corresponding to the tick mark. Another simple way to do this is to use a simple exponential notation where each label is created by the code:

```
for(i=0; i < numticks; i++) {
 sprintf(string, "10e%1d", i);
  ...
}
```

Here, the index *i* corresponds to the logarithm of the *y*-value for each tick mark. The example shown assumes that the range of values for *y* is from 1 to $10^{(numticks-1)}$. For other ranges, an appropriate offset can be added to *i* to account for the different ranges.

Logarithmic plots require some careful interpretation and can sometimes be quite confusing. A straight line in a logarithmic plot no longer corresponds to a linear relationship. Instead, it shows an exponential relationship between *x* and *y*, that is, $y = b^x$, where *b* is proportional to the logarithm of the slope of the line. Furthermore, if *y* is less than one, then the logarithm becomes negative. The closer *y* gets to zero, the larger the magnitude of the logarithm, although the logarithm is still negative. Thus, the parts of the graph in a logarithmic plot that have negative *y* coordinates correspond to very small values of the measured variable *y*.

With many different kinds of data sets, both the *x* and *y* axes must be scaled logarithmically. This can be done using exactly the same approach for the *x*-axis as you used for the *y*-axis. As was done for the *y*-values, the *x* limits of the source graph region must be chosen to ensure that the plot remains entirely on the screen.

Labeling a Plot

The plot is almost complete. The coordinate axes are drawn, and the data has been plotted. All that is left is the labelling of the plot. The function *gPlotLabels()* makes this an easy task. The function takes three arguments, a graph region rectangle for defining the area to plot, a character string for the top label, and a character string for the bottom label. Either character string may be *NULL* to indicate that no label should be drawn on either the top or bottom. You may, of course, set the character font and size prior to calling *gPlotLabels()* to create differently sized characters than used for the tick mark labels. The labels are drawn centered horizontally with respect to the graph region.

Creating a Complete Plot

Now that I have described all of the functions, you can now create a complete plot. As a demonstration, I have provided the function, *gPlotFunction()*, shown in Listing 11-5, in the enclosed software This function plots any C function that takes a single floating point argument and returns a single floating point result. Your may use one of the standard C functions like *sin()* or create a function of your own. Pass the address of the function to plot, the range of input values to create the plot for, the color for the plot, and an optional set of top and bottom label strings to *gPlotFunction()*. The plot will have 10 tick marks on both axes and appropriate labels. The labels will contain at most 5 characters, so the output range of the function should not require more than 4 significant digits for the labels. *gPlotFunction()* takes advantage of the facility in C for passing pointers to functions, just as was done when setting clipping functions. This function uses the entire screen, but can be easily modified by passing the plot region as an argument rather than having *gPlotFunction()* define it as shown in the following listing:

```
void gPlotFunction(float (*f)(float x),
          float xmin, float xmax, gColor color,
          gStyle *text_style,
          char *top_label, char *bottom_label)
{
float ymin, ymax;
gRectangle plot_region, source_region, *graph_region;
gMatrix *plotToScreen;
gPoint point, lastpoint;
float x, y, xstep, ystep, step;
int i;
char **xlabels, **ylabels, string[10];

plot_region.xmin = 0.0;
plot_region.ymin = 0.0;
plot_region.xmax = gGetMaxX() - 1;
plot_region.ymax = gGetMaxY() - 1;
graph_region = gCreateGraphRegion(plot_region,
                                  gAXES_LOWERLEFT, text_style);

/* Now find the minimum and maximum values */
step = (xmax - xmin) /
      (float)(graph_region->xmax - graph_region->xmin + 1);
ymin = ymax = (*f)(xmin);
for(x=xmin; x <= xmax; x += step) {
 y = (*f)(x);
```

```
    ymin = MIN(ymin, y);
    ymax = MAX(ymax, y);
   }

   source_region.xmin = xmin;
   source_region.xmax = xmax;
   source_region.ymin = ymin;
   source_region.ymax = ymax;

   /* Create tick mark labels */
   xlabels = (char **)gcalloc(11, sizeof(char *));
   ylabels = (char **)gcalloc(11, sizeof(char *));
   x = xmin;
   y = ymin;
   xstep = (xmax - xmin) / 10.0;
   ystep = (ymax - ymin) / 10.0;
   x = xmin;
   y = ymin;
   for(i=0; i < 11; i++) {
    string[0] = 0;
    /* Write appropriate label */
    sprintf(string, "%5g", x);
    xlabels[i] = (char *)gcalloc(strlen(string) + 1, sizeof(char));
    x += xstep;
    sprintf(string, "%5g", y);
    strcpy(xlabels[i], string);
    ylabels[i] = (char *)gcalloc(strlen(string) + 1, sizeof(char));
    strcpy(ylabels[i], string);
    y += ystep;
   }

   /* Draw the axes */
   gCoordinateAxesDraw(gAXES_LOWERLEFT, graph_region,
                       11, 11, text_style, xlabels, ylabels);

   /* Label it */
   gPlotLabels(graph_region, text_style, top_label, bottom_label);

   /* Now plot the function */
```

```
/* Create the transformation */
plotToScreen = gCreateCoordinateTransform(&source_region,
                                          graph_region);
/* Set the clipping region */
gSetClipFunction(&gRectangleClipTest, graph_region);

for(x=xmin; x <= xmax; x += step) {
 y = (*f)(x);
 point.x = x;
 point.y = y;
 /* Now transform to graph region coordinates */
 gTransformPoints(plotToScreen, &point, 1);
 if(x > xmin) {
  gLineDraw(ROUND(lastpoint.x), ROUND(lastpoint.y),
            ROUND(point.x), ROUND(point.y), color);
 }
 lastpoint = point;
}

/* Clean up any temporary objects */
gRemoveClipFunction(&gRectangleClipTest, graph_region);
gMatrixDelete(plotToScreen);
gRectangleDelete(graph_region);
for(i=0; i < 11; i++) {
 free(xlabels[i]);
 free(ylabels[i]);
}
free(xlabels);
free(ylabels);


return;
}
```

Listing 11-5. Procedure to modify gPlotFunction

Before actually plotting the function, the clipping region is set equal to the graph region using *gSetClipFunction()* and the rectangular clipping function discussed in Chapter 7. This ensures that the plot will not overwrite the axes or the labels. This is quite useful since you can now scale the plot any way you wish without having to worry about clipping the plot to the graph region; it is done automatically by the clipping function. For an example of how to use *gPlotFunction()*, look at the demonstration program *dplot.c* provided on the disk accompanying this book.

Parametric Functions

So far you have only dealt with plotting functions of the form *y=f(x)*. As mentioned in the beginning of the chapter, there are many other types of data that you may wish to plot. For example, there are the parametric curves such as the circle and the ellipse presented in Chapter 5. The line-plotting technique can be easily adapted to this type of curve. In fact, only two changes need to be made, one in the portion of the code that finds the minimum and maximum *x* and *y* values and another in the basic plotting routine, as shown in the following code:

```
xmin = xmax = xcurve(tmin);
ymin = ymax = ycurve(tmin);
for(t = tmin; t <= tmax; t += step) {
 x = xcurve(t);
 y = ycurve(t);
 xmin = MIN(xmin, x);
 xmax = MAX(xmax, x);
 ymin = MIN(ymin, y);
 ymax = MAX(ymax, y);
}

...

 for(t = tmin; t <= tmax; t += step) {
 point.x = xcurve(t);
 point.y = ycurve(t);
 /* Now transform to graph region coordinates */
 gTransformPoints(plotToScreen, &point, 1);
 if(x > xmin) {
  gLineDraw(ROUND(lastpoint.x), ROUND(lastpoint.y),
           ROUND(point.x), ROUND(point.y), color);
 }
```

```
lastpoint = point;
      }
```

The functions *xcurve()* and *ycurve()* are the parametric functions defining the specific curve. The variable *t* is now used to step through the functions, generating the appropriate *x*- and *y*-values at each step. This is almost exactly the same procedure that was used to draw the circle and the ellipse in Chapter 5. You did not need to find the minimum and maximum *x* -and *y*-coordinates of the *gCircle* and *gEllipse* objects since they are already specified in screen coordinates. The enclosed software provides the function *gPlotParametricFunction()* for plotting parametrically-defined curves. The only differences between *gPlotFunction()* and *gPlotParametricFunction()* are those shown in the previous block of code and a change in the argument list to pass the two functions *xcurve()* and *ycurve()* instead of the single function *f()*. As a side note, this drawing procedure may be used to draw arcs of a circle or an ellipse by allowing *t* to range over a smaller interval than 0 degrees to 360 degrees.

Scattergrams

While line plots are quite useful, they are by no means the only types of plots that you may encounter. The two other types I will discuss are scattergrams and bar charts. A scattergram is simply a collection of (*x*,*y*) data points in random order. Typically, both *x* and *y* represent simultaneous measurements of two distinct variables, for example, star mass and star brightness for a large number of stars . A scattergram plot is created in almost exactly the same way as a line plot, except that the points are not connected together by lines as they are drawn. Instead, the points are stored in an array of *gPoint* structures. They do not have to be stored that way. If there are very many points, then they can be computed as needed or read from the file they are stored in. The main drawing loop becomes the following:

```
gPoint temp_point, *points;
gMatrix plotToScreen;
int i, numpoints;
```

```
for(i=0; i < numpoints; i++) {
 /* If the points are not stored in an array
    then read it into temp_point here */
 temp_point = points[i];
 gTransformPoint(plotToScreen, &temp_point, 1);
 /* At this point, you may want to use gSetBrush() to
    draw a desired shape rather than a 1 pixel dot */
 gPlotPixel(ROUND(temp_point.x), ROUND(temp_point.y), color);
}
```

It is common practice to plot a brush instead of just a single pixel for each data point. For instance, using *gSetBrush()*, you can plot small circles or some other significant symbol at each data point. The symbols can be made even more useful, if, for example, you have other data associated with each point, such as a third measurement. By making the color and/or brush depend on the value of this other associated data, you can create a much more informative graph. Suppose, for example, that you had five distinct data sets that were taken on five different days. Create five different brushes to represent each data set and then plot each data set with it's corresponding brush type. Similarly, you could choose the color of the brush to correspond to another measurement, such as time of day, (blue for morning, green for afternoon, red for night, for instance), to provide even more information in the plot. With these types of combinations, it becomes much easier to visually see the relationships between the various data sets.

Symbol plotting (that is, using a brush) is also quite common in line plots. When the data is relatively sparse or spaced out, it is important to see where the actual data points are, as well as connecting them with lines. You can easily add this feature to your plots simply by setting a desired brush to use as a symbol, such as a small triangle or square, and plotting each data point with a call to *gPlotPixel()*, just as was done in the previous scattergram example. The connecting lines should be drawn first, followed by the symbols to ensure that the symbols are always visible. Again, by using color and shapes creatively, you can create plots that are more readable and interesting. However, a plot can also become quite cluttered and unreadable if too many different graphs are drawn on a single plot. Sometimes two or three separate plots drawn side by side are more understandable than a single plot with too many symbols and graphs. Deciding which is best for your needs is where the art of plotting begins.

Bar Charts

A bar chart is a useful way to present a small number of data sets. It often gives a clearer indication of the relative sizes of variables than is gained by looking at a line plot. The setup for creating a bar chart is nearly identical to that of the line plot. The only difference is that a bar chart requires drawing rectangular bars rather than connecting points with line segments. At each step along the *x*-axis, a rectangle is drawn whose height corresponds to the value of *y* and whose width is either explicitly set or is automatically computed. In the following example, the width is chosen to be 1/2 the spacing between adjacent data points. This example assumes that the data for the bar chart is stored in *float*, an array of *float* values. Here is an example plotting routine for a bar chart:

```
gPoint temp_point, *points;
gMatrix plotToScreen;
gRectangle temp_rect;
float x, width, step, *yvalues;
int i, numpoints;

step = (graph_region->xmax - graph_region->xmin) /
       (float)(numpoints+1);
width = step / 2.0;
/* Setup initial rectangle */
x = step;
temp_rect.ymax = graph_region->ymax;
temp_rect.xmin = graph_region->xmin + x - width/2.0;
temp_rect.xmax = graph_region->xmin + x + width/2.0;
for(i=0; i<numpoints; i++) {
 /* If the points are not stored in an array
    then read it into temp_point here */
 temp_point.x = x;
 temp_point.y = yvalues[i];
 gTransformPoint(plotToScreen, &temp_point, 1);
 /* Set the height of the rectangle */
 temp_rect.ymin = temp_point.y;
```

```
    gRectangleFill(&temp_rect, color);
    /* Now move the rectangle over */
    temp_rect.xmin += step;
    temp_rect.xmax += step;
}
```

In this example, the scaling of the *x*-coordinates is not used. The graph region is automatically subdivided into *numpoints* intervals, with a bar plotted in each interval. The scaling in *y* sets the height of the bar. An example bar chart created by using this example is shown in Figure 11-8.

There are many other options which can be used to create much more complete bar charts. For instance, the bars can be filled with a bitmap pattern, or each with a different color. The bars can be made more elaborate by creating a 3-dimensional effect, and labels can be placed on top of the bars to show a readable value. With a little effort, the tools provided in the enclosed software will enable you to create virtually any type of bar chart.

Multiple Plots

It is often useful not only to use different plotting methods for separate data sets, but to overlay different data sets onto the same plot. Similar to what was done with *gCoordinateAxesDraw()*, you can overlay multiple plots onto the same graph region simply by plotting multiple times. This can be quite useful in visualizing possible relationships between multiple data sets. For instance, you can overlay *sin()* with *cos()* by multiple calls to *gPlotFunction()*:

```
gPlotFunction(&sin, 0.0, 2*PI, gWHITE, NULL,
            "SIN(X), COS(X)", NULL);
gPlotFunction(&cos, 0.0, 2*PI, gGREEN, NULL, NULL, NULL);
```

You can present many different data sets in one plot by using various combinations of colors and brushes. To present even more data on a single screen, you can divide it into multiple plot regions. Be careful, however, not to carry this to an extreme where there is so too much data on the screen will make it difficult to see anything useful.

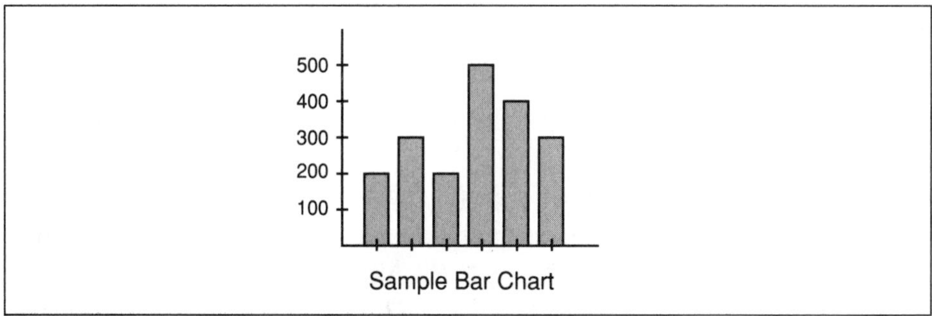

Figure 11-8. Sample bar chart

The Finished Plot

The demonstration program *dplot.c* provides a simple demonstration of the various types of plots that can be created using the tools presented in this chapter. This chapter provides a beginning set of graphing tools. By using all of the tools from the previous chapter, you can create fairly elaborate and useful graphs of many different types of data without a great deal of code. The affine transformation, once again, provides a straightforward means of scaling the plot data and placing it anywhere on the screen. I'm sure that you will find many ways to extend these tools to cover an even wider variety of plot types.

In the next chapter, I delve into the most unique aspect of computer graphics: its ability to provide interactive animation and dynamic simulation. When used in combination with the plotting capability, you can create interactive graphs that respond to your input or real-time measurements or can play back sequences of measurements. There is no other medium other than computer graphics which can provide this level of interaction and feedback. So, read on for an even more exciting plot!

Functions Found in This Chapter

Demonstration program

`dplot.exe`

This program demonstrates all of the different types of plots that can be created using the tools in this package. The program simply cycles through a series of plots showing the various plotting options.

Plotting functions

```
gRectangle *gCreateGraphRegion(gRectangle *plot_region,
                               gAXES_TYPE ctype,
                               gStyle *text_style);
```

Creates a suitable graph region with enough room for plot labels, tick marks, and tick mark labels. The variable *ctype* may be any of the values *gAXES_NONE*, *gAXES_LOWERLEFT*, or *gAXES_CENTER*. If *text_style* is *NULL*, then the default font is used for sizing characters, otherwise the passed style is used.

```
void gCoordinateAxesDraw(gAXES_TYPE ctype,
                         gRectangle *graph_region,
                         int nxticks, int nyticks,
                         gStyle *text_style,
                         char **xlabels, char **ylabels);
```

This function draws a suitable set of coordinate axes of the given type for the passed graph region. The number of tick marks along the *x* and *y* axes are specified by *nxticks* and *nyticks* respectively. An optional set of labels may be passed for the tick marks in *xlabels* and *ylabels*.

```
gMatrix *gCreateCoordinateTransform(gRectangle *source_rect,
                                    gRectangle *dest_rect);
```

This function creates a matrix to transform coordinates from the source units within the rectangle specified by *source_rect* to a rectangle on the screen, usually corresponding to a graph region, specified by *dest_rect*. The *y*-coordinate of the *source_rect* rectangle increases from bottom to top, so the transformation automatically inverts the coordinates, correctly orienting the plot on the screen.

```
void gPlotLabel(gRectangle *graph_region, gStyle *text_style,
        char *top_label, char *bottom_label);
```

Puts top and bottom labels above and below the graph region. If either pointer is *NULL*, then no label is drawn in that position.

```
void gPlotFunction(float (*f)(float x),
          float xmin, float xmax, gColor color,
          gStyle *text_style,
          char *top_label, char *bottom_label);
```

This function plots a C function that takes a single *float* argument and returns a *float* result. The *x*-axis is corresponds to the range *xmin* to *xmax*. The plot will contain lower-left style coordinate axes with 10 tick marks along each side and appropriate labels. The plot may be labeled by passing a non-*NULL* string pointer for the top and/or bottom label.

```
void gPlotParametricFunction(float (*xcurve)(float t),
                  float (*ycurve) (float t),
                  float tmin, float tmax, gColor color,
                  gStyle *text_style,
                  char *top_label, char *bottom_label);
```

This function is very similar to *gPlotFunction()*, except that it takes plots parametric functions. You must supply two functions, one that computes the *x*-coordinate as a function of the parameter *t*, and one that computes the *y*-coordinate. In all other respects, it functions the same as *gPlotFunction()*.

CHAPTER 12

Computer Animation Made Easy

The most unique aspect of computer graphics is its ability to provide interactive, dynamic, animated sequences. No other artistic medium can provide the type of user interaction and participation that a computer graphics system can. Most artistic media are static; the artist creates the image on a canvas or other surface and the image cannot be altered. In the cinematic arts, such as motion pictures and television, you can record and playback images complete with Dolby stereo sound, but the viewer cannot interact with the images to change their content, change the rate at which the images are played back, or examine portions of an image in detail by zooming in on or manipulating a particular region. Using your computer and its graphics display, you can make fully interactive drawings that respond either to direct user input, such as pressing a key on the keyboard or picking up an object with the mouse, or to a computer driven model that determines how to move objects around the screen. The interactivity, flexibility, and unprecedented artistic control provided by computer graphics are the main reasons it is currently such a popular medium, both artistically and commercially. This chapter will define and demonstrate the tools needed to create fully interactive drawings that you, (or the intended user), can manually control, dynamically alter, or just sit back and simply watch happen.

Principles of Animation

Creating the illusion of objects in motion on a screen is essentially an exercise in fooling the human eye. CRTs and movie screens can only show one image at a time. They fool your brain into believing that it is seeing continuous motion by displaying a series of images in rapid succession on the screen. Your eye and brain have the remarkable ability to take this series of static pictures and put them together so that you see it as a single moving picture. Animation is the process of recording or creating the individual frames depicting moving objects and then playing them back rapidly enough to create the illu-

One of the most powerful aspects of computer graphics is its ability to create dynamic, animated graphics. An animated drawing can convey a tremendous amount of information and, more importantly, it can change based on user input or new calculations. In this chapter, you'll teach your computer a few tricks of your own, and soon it will be doing the most amazing tricks!

sion of motion. Originally, animated sequences were created using a series of cards, called *flipcards*, with a single image on each one. Each individual image, or *frame*, shows one step in a motion sequence. By rapidly flipping through the cards, you would see a complete motion sequence. Even though this type of animation technique is rather crude, all animation uses exactly the same principle. The flipcards as a display medium have been vastly improved upon by CRTs and movie projectors, but the technique of rapidly flashing individual pictures to simulate motion is still the same.

One normally associates the term *animation* with cartoons. An animated cartoon sequence is one in which each individual frame of animation has been drawn by a cartoonist, or more likely, by an entire team of cartoonists. However, a television or movie camera also creates animation by recording live action rather than having someone draw each frame. In a movie camera, the film runs through the camera at a fixed rate of 24 frames per second. As each frame is drawn into position behind the camera shutter, the shutter opens and a picture of the current scene is captured on the frame as a still image. 1/24th of a second later, the next frame is loaded and another picture is taken. This process continues throughout the filming of the scene. When played back on the big screen, the film is still just a sequence of still images. Your brain, however, puts the images together to create the impression of smooth, continuous motion. Cartoon animation is exactly the same process, except that each frame is drawn, rather than recorded by filming live action.

Animation is not limited to depicting simple motion. For instance, a laser show is a type of computer animation in which objects appear to be constantly changing shape, size, and position. Any type of change in an object can be animated, including translation, rotation, scaling, changes in color, changes in the structure of the object (such as individual parts moving around), or change in any attribute you can think of that affects how the object appears on the screen. Cartoonists have been exploring the possibilities for decades. The computer, however, provides unprecedented flexibility, interaction, and absolute control of how objects look, behave, and respond to the viewer's actions. A great deal of information can be communicated with computer controlled animated displays.

Two important concepts required for any discussion of animation are the update rate and the refresh rate. The rate at which new images in a motion sequence are displayed is called the *update rate*. For motion pictures, the update rate is 24 frames per second, more commonly referred to simply as 24 Hz (abbreviation for Hertz, meaning cycles per second). The rate at which images are flashed on the screen is called the *refresh rate*. A movie projector actually flashes each frame of the movie on the screen twice to keep the screen from flickering. A movie is therefore displayed with a refresh rate of 48 Hz. The refresh rate and the update rate are not necessarily directly related. Even if a still image is shown (an update rate of 0 Hz), the image is still refreshed on the screen at the refresh rate, otherwise the screen would flicker quite noticeably. The same is true for your computer CRT. The refresh rate of a CRT is typically 60 Hz, although newer CRTs have refresh rates of 72 Hz and higher. The higher the refresh rate, the less perceptible the flicker as the CRT redraws the screen. The update rate, however, can be anything from 0 Hz (no motion at all) up to the refresh rate of the CRT.

Computer Animation

When a movie or television sequence is played back to the screen, the entire display is redrawn, even if nothing in the image has moved or been changed in any way. This is fine for film and television because the image is constantly recorded, even if no motion occurs. An animated cartoon, on the other hand, is not redrawn in this way. It shows the same frame repeatedly if nothing is moving. Animators want to minimize the number of new frames they must draw. Additionally, many cartoonists use fixed backgrounds and draw the animated characters over the top. The background does not change, the characters simply move against it. Thus, an animator has the much simpler task of animating just the characters, rather than the entire scene, for each frame. The characters are drawn on separate pieces of clear plastic that are then overlaid on top of the background in the desired position, as shown in Figure 12-1. The entire combination is then photographed to produce the completed image for the cartoon.

Computer animation uses the same basic technique to draw animated objects on the screen. Instead of redrawing the entire image every time something changes, the computer only updates the objects that have changed. For instance, to move a single object across the screen, such as a mouse cursor, the

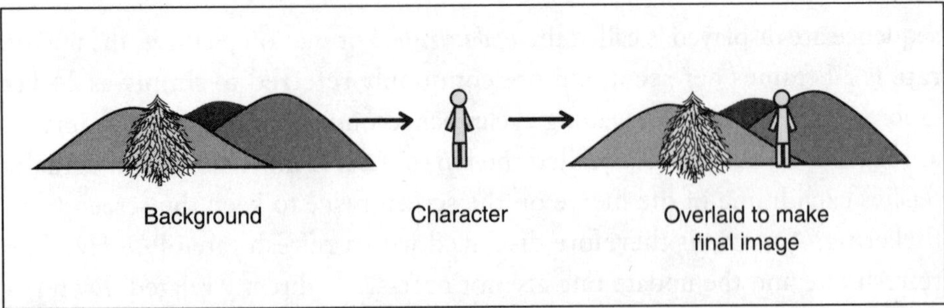

Figure 12-1. A background image and an animated character are overlaid to create a final frame in an animated sequence

cursor is erased from its current position on the screen and redrawn in the new position. The rate at which the computer can draw new objects is proportional to the total number of pixels comprising the objects that must be redrawn. The fewer the pixels that must be processed, the faster the computer can update the image, and the smoother the object motion will appear. The rest of the screen is left alone.

The basic procedure for animating an object on the screen can be summarized by a sequence of four steps:

1. Erase the object from its current position on the screen.
2. Compute the new position of the object on the screen.
3. Draw the object in the new position.
4. Go back to step 1.

This procedure is called an *animation loop*. The procedure may seem a little odd at first because it appears that the object is erased as soon as it is drawn. In fact, almost always, additional processing is needed between steps 3 and 4 to keep the object on the screen long enough for you to see it before it is erased and redrawn in the next position. Additionally, the process of drawing the object usually takes enough time for you to see the object as it is being drawn. If, however, the rate at which the animation loop is processed is close to the refresh rate of the CRT, then you may see objects flicker on the screen as they are continually drawn and erased.

Animating Bitmaps

The first type of object you will animate on the screen is a bitmap. Most computer animation in computer games and in windowing environments uses animated bitmaps to show dynamic events. Let's see how to create an animation loop that moves a 12 x 12 = 144-pixel bitmap of a plus sign horizontally across the screen. The following code segment shows the basic animation loop. Since animation can't be very dynamically demonstrated using book illustrations, all of the sample code described in this section is incorporated into a single program in the module *dbittest.c* that you can run on your computer. In this example, the plus sign is moved across the screen horizontally in 2 pixel steps for each iteration of the loop:

```
gBitmap *plus_sign;
gRectangle bitrect;
int finished = 0, x0, y0, xstep;

/* Create a rectangle the same size as the bitmap */
/* The rectangle is used to erase the bitmap before
   redrawing */
bitrect->xmin = 0.0;
bitrect->ymin = 0.0;
bitrect->xmax = plus_sign->wide - 1.0;
bitrect->ymax = plus_sign->tall - 1.0;

/* Initial position */
x0 = 20;
y0 = 20;
/* Put the rectangle in the right position */
bitrect->xmin += x0;
bitrect->xmax += x0;
/* Step by 2 pixels for each iteration
xstep = 2;

/* Main animation loop */
while(!finished) {
 /* Erase the old bitmap */
 gRectangleFill(&bitrect, gBLACK);
```

```
    /* Update the position of bitmap and rectangle */
    bitrect->xmin += xstep;
    bitrect->xmax += xstep;
    x0 += step;
    /* Now draw the bitmap in the new position */
    if(x0 < gGetMaxX() - 50)
     gBitmapDraw(x0, y0, plus_sign, plus_sign);
    else
     finished = 1;
}
```

Procedure 12-1. Moving a character across the screen

Let's analyze the various steps in this procedure. First, the code creates a rectangle the same size as the bitmap. This rectangle is used to erase the bitmap from its old position. The initial position of the bitmap places the upper left corner at (20, 20). (This code assumes that the hot spot for the bitmap is (0, 0).) The rectangle is then set to position it at the same location, covering exactly the same area as the bitmap. The main animation loop consists of the three major steps:

1. The bitmap is erased by drawing a filled, black rectangle
2. The position of both the rectangle and the bitmap is updated to move it 2 pixels to the right
3. The bitmap is drawn unless it is within 50 pixels of the right edge, in which case, the loop is terminated by setting *finished* to 1. The loop continues until *finished* becomes nonzero.

While the bitmap animation procedure does move the symbol across the screen, it is worth noting two limitations of this code. First, this procedure assumes that the screen has been blanked to a black background. The symbol is erased by drawing a filled black rectangle. If there were any sort of image in the background, it would be erased as well. This is often not the desired effect. The second point is that it erases all of the pixels in the bitmap rectangle instead of just the ones set by the clip mask. There is a minor performance penalty for a small bitmap such as the plus sign, but this could take a lot of extra processing time if the bitmap were large and only a few pixels actually needed to be written.

Saving The Background

The first problem can be dealt with by saving the portion of the screen underneath the bitmap prior to writing it to the screen. Instead of erasing the bitmap by drawing a rectangle, you can erase it by drawing the saved bitmap. This restores the image to its previous state before the bitmap was ever drawn. This is how the cursor bitmap is moved across the screen in a windowing environment. Every time the cursor is moved, the saved portion of the image underneath the cursor is written back to the screen. Next, the screen image at the new location for the cursor is copied to a temporary bitmap and the cursor is drawn in the new location. Using this approach, the cursor can be moved over any type of background image without disturbing it. The following listing shows the revised code to support this type of animation.

```
gBitmap *plus_sign;
gBitmap *save_region;
int finished = 0, x0, y0, xstep;

/* Create a background storage bitmap the same size as the
   bitmap being animated */
save_region = gBitmapCopy(NULL, plus_sign);
/* Initial position */
x0 = 20;
y0 = 20;
/* Step by 2 pixels for each iteration */
xstep = 2;
/* Get the initial region */
gBitmapRead(save_region, x0, y0);

/* Main animation loop */
while(!finished) {
 /* Erase the old bitmap, only the pixels in the mask
    need to be rewritten */
```

```
    gBitmapDraw(x0, y0, save_region, plus_sign);
    /* Update the position of the bitmap */
    x0 += step;
    /* Read the image where you want to plot */
    gBitmapRead(save_region, x0, y0);
    /* Now draw the bitmap in the new position */
    if(x0 < gGetMaxX() - 50)
     gBitmapDraw(x0, y0, plus_sign, plus_sign);
    else
     finished = 1;
   }
```

Using this method, you can now draw any type of image on the screen as a background image and move the bitmap across the screen without overwriting the background. The price of using this method is that there are now three separate bitmap operations that must be performed. The old bitmap position is rewritten; the new location is read into the temporary buffer; and the bitmap is drawn in the new position. If reading and drawing the bitmap is inefficient, then the animation will appear to be slow and might noticeably flicker. Most graphics packages provide highly optimized versions of the bitmap reading and writing routines so that there is no detectable flicker when the bitmaps are redrawn. These optimized versions are able (on most PCs) to perform all three bitmap operations for small bitmaps, at speeds that are faster than the refresh rate (typically 60 Hz) of the CRT. This means that the operation is completed before the screen is refreshed (redrawn from the frame buffer) again, and, thus, the motion looks smooth.

Note that, in this animation procedure, the bitmap is moving at a constant speed across the screen. For every iteration of the loop, the bitmap is in a new position and must be redrawn. If this procedure is used to move a cursor around the screen, then it would be important to add a test to see if the user has actually moved the cursor. If the cursor has not moved, then there is no need to redraw it. If the animation loop is executed continously, even when the cursor has not moved, then the cursor might appear to flicker on the screen as it is constantly erased and redrawn.

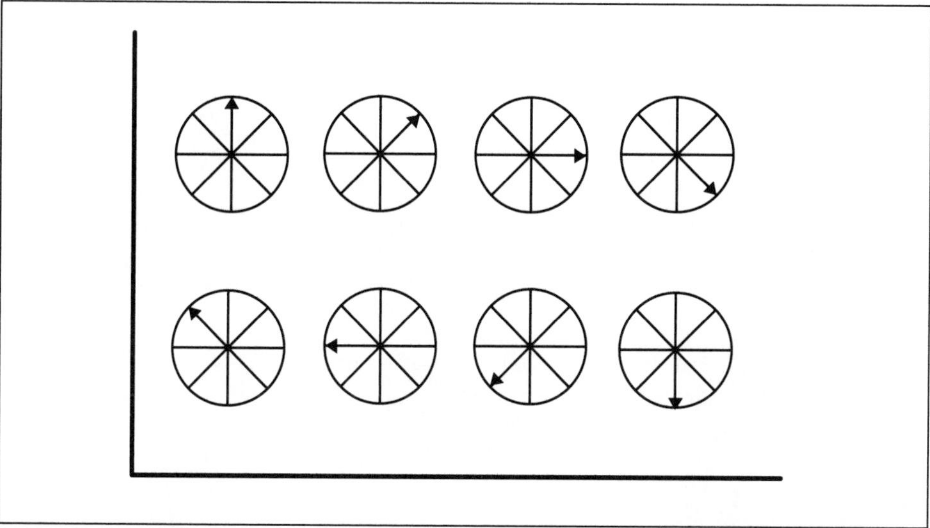

Figure 12-2. The eight states for depicting a simple spinning wheel. Each image is stored as a separate bitmap that can then be cyclically played back.

Flipping Bitmaps

As mentioned earlier in the chapter, animation does not have to be restricted to simple motion. Objects may be dynamically rescaled, resized, or drawn with different colors, to create interesting effects. Resizing or altering a bitmap during an animation sequence usually requires too much computation to keep the animation running at a reasonable update rate. Instead, employ the basic technique of cartoon animation by making several bitmaps that represent various states of motion. Within the animation loop, the program switches between bitmaps to create the illusion of animated characters, just as is done in a cartoon. Figure 12-2 shows a sequence of 8 bitmaps depicting various states of a simple spinning wheel.

The animation loop for displaying this rotating wheel is shown in the following code:

```
int nloops, mapnum;
gBitmap *wheel[8], *wheel_mask[8];

mapnum = 0;
```

```
/* Note that since the wheel does not move in x or y,
   you only have to save the background once */
gBitmapRead(save_region, x0, y0);
/* Main animation loop */
while(!finished) {
 /* Erase the old bitmap */
 gBitmapDraw(x0, y0, save_region, NULL);
 /* Switch to next bitmap */
 mapnum = (mapnum + 1) % 8;
 /* Now draw the bitmap in the new position */
 gBitmapDraw(x0, y0, wheel[mapnum], wheel_mask[mapnum]);
 /* Test to see if finished */
 if(++nloops > 100)
  finished = 1;
}
```

The background image is only saved once, prior to entering the animation loop, because the wheel is not moving across the screen. If it were moving, you would have to save the background inside the animation loop as was done previously. This animation loop can be made more efficient if you do not care about saving the underlying background image, that is, by allowing the bitmap to completely overwrite the screen in the region being drawn. A good example of this kind of animation might be a small clock or meter display that stays at a fixed location on the screen. If the bitmap can entirely overwrite the screen region, then you can simply remove the call that restores the old background image, *gBitmapDraw(x0, y0, save_region, NULL)*, from inside the animation loop. The succeeding bitmaps of the wheel animation will overwrite the previous ones. In this way, the wheel animation behaves exactly like flipcard animation—each new image of the wheel replaces the previous image. In general, if the bitmap does not change position on the screen and the next bitmap being drawn is the same size or larger, there is no need to erase the old bitmap. Drawing the new one gets rid of the old one for you.

Animation speed

There are two factors that control the apparent speed at which animated objects move or change. If the object is moving across the screen, the principal factor affecting the apparent speed is the step size. The *step size* sets how many pixels an object moves for each iteration of the animation loop. The step size does not have to be the same for each iteration nor does it have to be the same for *x* or *y*. An object can be moved at variable speeds by adjusting the step size during the animation loop. When you move the mouse, the computer determines the amount of displacement caused by your motion and redraws the cursor in a new position based on that motion. If the mouse is moved quickly, the cursor will appear to jump to the new position. If the mouse is moved slowly, the cursor will appear move to the new location with a much smoother, continuous motion.

The second factor affecting the apparent object speed on the screen is how quickly the animation loop executes. The number of things to do in the animation loop execution determines the update rate of the animated sequence. The more objects that must be drawn, or the more calculations that must be made to move the objects, the slower the update rate. The entire animation will slow down accordingly. You must balance the step size with the update rate to achieve a desired rate of motion. For instance, in the bitmap animation example of the plus sign used a step size of 2 pixels. If the animation loop executes 10 times a second (an update rate of 10 Hz), then the bitmap moves 20 pixels in one second. With a VGA screen resolution of 640 pixels across, it will take 640/20 = 32 seconds for the bitmap to cross the screen. If you change the program to move 2 bitmaps simultaneously, the update rate slows to 5 times a second, and the bitmaps will take 64 seconds to cross the screen. By adjusting the step size to 4 pixels this slowness can be compensated for, but the motion will appear less smooth. Another approach would be to change the screen resolution by using a different VGA mode. This way the step size may not have to be altered because the bitmaps take half as many iterations to get across the screen as before. However, they will now appear twice as large on the screen due to the reduced frame buffer resolution.

Just as the step size affects motion on the screen, the speed at which multiple bitmaps are switched determines how fast the object appears to move. In the rotating wheel example, the speed of rotation depends on how fast the animation loop executes. Since there are no other operations in that example, the wheel will rotate very quickly. You can change the update rate by introducing a delay to slow down the animation loop. One simple way to introduce a delay is to redraw the same bitmap a number of times in a row. By changing the number of times the bitmap is redrawn, you effectively speed up or slow down the animation. Another way to set the timing in an animation sequence is to use the function, *delay()*. *delay()* pauses your program an integral number of milliseconds before continuing. Thus, if you want the animation to have an update rate of 5 Hz, insert a call of *delay(200)*, (wait 200 milliseconds), after the last call to *gDrawBitmap()*, before the end of the animation loop. The problem with this method is that the amount of delay may have to be adjusted depending on the number of objects being drawn, the size of the objects, the complexity of the calculations to move the objects, and the speed of the computer on which the animation is being run.

By combining the two example animation procedures, the wheel can be rolled across the screen, rotating and translating simultaneously. To make the wheel appear as if it is rolling along an invisible horizontal line on the screen, the step size is set equal to length of the wheel hub between each rotation angle. In this example, the wheel rotates 45 degrees for each new bitmap, so the step size should be approximately equal to 1/8th of the circumference of the circle. The wheel bitmaps were defined using 10 x 10 bitmaps, so a 45-degree arc of the circle has a length of $2 * \pi * 5/8 = 3.9$, or approximately 4 pixels. A step size of 4 pixels produces a reasonable approximation of the wheel rolling across the screen. All of the examples described in this section on bitmap animation are incorporated into the demonstration program *dbittest.exe* provided on the disk that accompanies this book.

The various methods of bitmap animation shown in this section are effective if the size of the bitmap being moved is relatively small. A 16 x 16 bitmap, for instance, only requires 256 pixels of storage. Reading and writing this amount of data to the screen is generally very fast. However, if the bitmap is 100 x 100, or 10,000 pixels, then the animation will be slowed down considerably (reading and writing the bitmap will take approximately 10,000 / 256, or 40 times longer) without the assistance of special-purpose graphics hardware. It is important when designing an animation program to be aware of the total number of pixels that will be moved around the screen. The more pixels being processed, the slower the animation will be (or the faster the computer you will need!).

You will find that in most animation programs, you need all of the processing horsepower you can obtain.

Animated Line Drawings

Bitmaps are only one type of object that you might need to animate. Several of the demonstration programs from the previous chapters used animated polygons to illustrate various features in a dynamic fashion. The *dxform.exe* program from Chapter 6 animated a polygon by incrementally changing an affine transformation for each iteration of an animation loop. For each pass of the animation loop, the polygon is erased from the old position, the transformation is updated for the new position, and the polygon is redrawn using the updated transformation. This is basically the same approach used in bitmap animation, and it has the same problem as the first bitmap animation example had. If the polygons are animated on top of a background image, then portions of the background image will be lost each time a polygon is erased. There are several solutions to this problem.

The most obvious solution is to save the background region in a temporary bitmap, just as was done in bitmap animation. This is a reasonable solution if the polygon occupies a small screen area, comparable to that of a small bitmap of 10 x 10 pixels. But suppose you wish to move something like a 200 x 200-pixel rectangle around a screen. To save the area contained within the rectangle requires reading in a bitmap of 40,000 pixels and then rewriting it whenever the rectangle is moved. This type of redrawing would be slow and, thus, produce a poor animation. Furthermore, it wastes memory because the only part of the background image that really needs to be saved is the part under the edges of the rectangle, not the interior. Animating the rectangle only requires erasing and redrawing the rectangle boundary, not everything in the interior. For a non-rotated rectangle, you can save just the portion of the background underneath each edge using code like the following:

```
gBitmap *left_side, *right_side, *top_side, *bottom_side;
gRectangle rect;

width = ceil(rect.xmax - rect.xmin + 1.0);
```

```
height = ceil(rect.ymax - rect.ymin + 1.0);

/* Create bitmaps for the left & right sides */
left_side = gBitmapCreate(1, height, 0, 0);
right_side = gBitmapCreate(1, height, 0, 0);

/* Create bitmaps for the top & bottom */
top_side = gBitmapCreate(width, 1, 0, 0);
right_side = gBitmapCreate(height, 1, 0, 0);
```

Whenever the rectangle is drawn, the background image underneath all four sides is saved into the four separate bitmaps and the rectangle is drawn on the screen. When the rectangle is moved sometime later, the data underneath the rectangle is restored from the bitmaps. This works fine as long as the rectangle is not resized or rotated. Each time the rectangle is resized, you must either create new bitmaps to reflect the lengths of the edges or simply allocate bitmaps that are the maximum sizes (*gGetMaxX()* horizontally and *gGetMaxY()* vertically) at the beginning. A rotated rectangle causes even more of a problem since now the edges are not lined up with the *x*- and *y*-axes, which is a requirement for the bitmaps. Furthermore, even for a nonrotated rectangle, you must make sure to delete the bitmaps whenever the rectangle is deleted. This method of trying to save the pixels underneath the object edges is not very adaptable to more complex shapes such as circles, ellipses, and other nonrectangular polygons. I will now, however, explain other approaches, that are much easier to use with these shapes.

Graphics—Bit by Bit

To animate objects on top of a background, a graphics programmer would ideally like to use the animation techniques of cartoon animation: separate background and animation layers. In a sense, you would like to have several separate frame buffers that can each be treated independently and then have their separate video overlaid on top of one another, like layers of cartoon animation cels. This section will explore two basic techniques, *XOR* animation and plane masks, for taking the single frame buffer and splitting it into a number of separate, independent frame buffers that can be manipulated so the animated characters can be erased and redrawn without having to worry about disturbing the background image, or other parts of the animation.

To see how to separate your single frame buffer into independent layers, you must learn some more about the kinds of processing you can do with the pixels of the frame buffer. Most graphics-display hardware packages have the capability to perform some simple manipulations of pixels before they are written to the screen. The types of operations that can be performed by the on-board hardware are generally limited to combining the pixel currently on the screen with the new pixel being written to the screen. The only function presented so far is simple replacement: the new pixel overwrites the current pixel on the screen. The other functions are the simple *bit-wise* functions, such as *AND*, *OR*, *NOT*, *NAND*, and others where the result is based on a bit-by-bit combination of two numbers. The four operations most useful for graphics are AND (the C operator, &), *OR* (the C operator, |), *XOR* (exclusive *OR*, the C operator, ^), and *NOT* (the C operator, !).

The *AND* function performs the following operation for each bit: if both bits are one, then the result is one, otherwise the result is zero. Here are some simple examples of applying *AND* to two 8-bit values (each 8-bit value is shown using binary notation so you can see which bits are changed and which are unaffected by this operation):

```
10101010 & 00001111 = 00001010
11110000 & 00001111 = 00000000
00110011 & 11110000 = 00110000
```

The *OR* operator uses the rule that if either bit is one, then the result is one. Otherwise, the result is zero. Here I have given some examples of the *OR* operator:

```
10101010 | 00001111 = 10101111
11110000 | 00001111 = 11111111
00110011 | 11110000 = 11110011
```

The *NOT* operator takes only a single argument and simply inverts the bits. If a bit in the argument is one, it is set to zero in the result. If a bit in the argument is zero, then the corresponding bit is set to one. These are some examples of *NOT*:

```
!(00001111) = 11110000
!(01010101) = 10101010
!(00110011) = 11001100
```

The *XOR* operator uses the following logic for each bit: if either bit is one, but not both, then the result is one, otherwise the result is zero. Following are some examples of the *XOR* (the C operator ^):

```
10101010 ^ 00001111 = 10100101
11110000 ^ 00001111 = 11111111
00110011 ^ 11110000 = 11000011
```

XOR is the most useful operator for animation because it possesses two basic properties for animation:

1. Any value XORed with itself yields zero
2. Zero *XOR*ed with any value, yields that value. Using these two properties yields the result:

$$b \wedge (b \wedge a) = (b \wedge b) \wedge a = 0 \wedge a = a \qquad \text{Equation 12-1}$$

Now, how are these pixel functions used to solve the animation problem? Instead of drawing the object using simple pixel replacement, you instead *XOR* the color of the object with the pixels of the background. For each pixel, the current background image is the value *a* in Equation 12-1, and the new object color is *b*. Thus, the pixel on the screen now contains the value $(b \wedge a)$. When the object is moved, you can erase it by redrawing it again using *XOR*. Each pixel value now becomes $b \wedge (b \wedge a) = a$. The background pixels magically reappear, just as they were before the object was drawn, due to the property shown in Equation 12-1.

This provides one solution to our animation problem. By using *XOR* mode to both draw and then erase the object, you can move the object over the background image without erasing any of the background pixels and thus, save a step. In most windowing systems, this is how the picking up and the moving of a window is depicted. When the window is selected with the mouse, the operating system creates and draws an *XOR* rectangle the size of the window. You may then move this rectangular outline anywhere around the screen, without overwriting any other parts of the screen. After you position the outline to where you want the window to move, the rectangle is erased and the window is redrawn in the new position you selected. This mode, by definition, works with any type of object including circles, ellipses, and polygons.

Writing pixels using the *XOR* function is implemented in our graphics package as yet another mode of *gPlotPixel( )*. The function *gSetPlotPixelMode( )* determines the bit-wise function *gPlotPixel( )* uses when writing pixels. There are currently two operations that may be set with this function, defined using the following *enum* type:

```
typedef enum {
gPIXELMODE_COPY = 0,
gPIXELMODE_XOR
} gPixel_Mode;
```

Once the pixel-writing mode is set with *gSetPlotPixelMode( )*, all subsequent calls to *gPlotPixel( )* (and consequently, any drawing functions in the software) will write pixels using that mode. The default mode is *gPIXELMODE_COPY*, which writes the new pixels over the old pixels, as you have done all along. The other mode, *gPIXELMODE_XOR*, activates the *XOR* function. The *XOR* function is implemented without assuming any special graphics hardware is available. Thus, the *XOR* function is implemented by reading the current pixel from the frame buffer, performing the appropriate function, and then writing the result back to the frame buffer. So every call to *gPlotPixel()* must both read and write a pixel. If you have a specialized graphics card that can perform these functions directly, then you can substantially improve the performance of *gPlot-*

Pixel() by using the graphics hardware to implement these functions, avoiding the problem of reading pixels from the frame buffer.

The only problem with this animation method is that the displayed colors for the object will usually not be the same as the color specified in the call to draw the object. Therefore, the background is entirely zero, the edges of the object will appear multi-colored because the frame buffer contains the *XOR* values, not the color of the object. You can see this effect whenever you move a window in a windowing system. The rectangle edges will change color depending on the color the background image it moves across. This is not a serious problem when you have a task like positioning a window on the screen. The rectangle acts only as a guide; its color is not important to the task being performed. Though, in the case of animated objects, It is always better, and in many cases necessary, to draw them using the intended colors, rather than colors resulting from the *XOR* mode.

Plane Masks

Recall that the ideal solution to the animation problem was to try to break the frame buffer up into a number of separate layers that could be manipulated independently. You can do this by observing that if the background image does not use the full 256 colors of the palette, then there are unused bits for every pixel in the frame buffer. Suppose, for instance, that the background image only uses the first 16 colors, entries 0 through 15. Only 4 binary bits are needed to represent 16 colors. In 256-color VGA mode, a pixel is stored as an 8-bit quantity. With a 16-color image, only the least significant (or lower) 4 bits of each pixel are used to store the background image, the most significant (or upper) 4 bits are all 0. The upper 4 bits are therefore available to store other graphic data. To make use of these unused bits to color the animated parts of the image, you should write pixels using color values greater than 15, values that use the upper 4 bits. Furthermore, when these values are written, you don't want to overwrite the lower 4 bits already used by the background image. For instance, suppose a pixel contains the value 10, which has the 8-bit binary representation 00001010. You can write any value you like into the upper 4 bits, as long as the lower 4 bits remain unchanged. Later, if the upper 4 bits are set back to 0, the original value of the pixel (10) is restored. Thus, an animated object may be drawn by setting the upper 4 bits to an appropriate color value and later erased by setting the upper 4 bits back to 0. This is the fundamental means of separating a single frame buffer into multiple independent frame buffers, by using different groups of bits for each pixel.

In computer graphics, the term *graphics plane* is used to refer to a single bit in a pixel. For instance, if there are 8 bits per pixel in the frame buffer, the frame buffer is said to consist of 8 graphics planes. You can think of a graphics plane as a frame buffer with pixels only 1 bit deep. Thus a frame buffer can be treated as a single array of pixels 8-bits deep, or as 8 arrays of pixels 1 bit deep each, or as 4 arrays of pixels 2 bits deep, or any combination of bits you like. By treating the frame buffer as being composed of separate graphics planes, you have achieved your goal of creating separate, independent layers. Now let's learn how to specify which bits to use for each graphics layer.

A special control quantity, called a *plane mask*, is used to select which bits in the frame buffer can be written to. The plane mask is a variable of type *gColor*. If a bit in the plane mask is one, the corresponding bit of each pixel in the frame buffer is *enabled*, meaning it can be written to. If a bit in the plane mask is zero, then the corresponding bit of each frame buffer pixel is *disabled*, and cannot be changed when new pixels are written. *gPlotPixel( )* uses the plane mask to determine which bits of new pixel data are actually written to the frame buffer. Only the bits which have been enabled by the plane mask are written, the other bits of the pixel are ignored. The significance of this is that the unaffected bits can be used to store background image data. Only the enabled bits can be changed, allowing us to draw an image on top of a background image. For this discussion, the plane mask is assumed to be an 8-bit quantity, but it could be any size depending on the number of bits per pixel in the frame buffer. Furthermore, I will use hexadecimal and binary notation to describe a plane mask, so that it is obvious which bits are actually being set. A plane mask made up of all zeros disables all writing to the frame buffer. A plane mask of *0 x FF* in hexadecimal (11111111 binary) allows all bits to be changed. This is the default setting. A plane mask of *0 x 0F*, (00001111 binary), allows only the lower 4 bits to be changed. A plane mask of *0 x F0*, (11110000) binary, allows only the upper 4 bits to be changed. To set the plane mask, use the function, *gSetPlaneMask( )*. It will remain in effect until it is called again. The plane mask is implemented in *gPlotPixel()* using the following algorithm:

```
gColor plane_mask, pixel, new_pixel, old_pixel;

/* Get the current value in the frame buffer */
old_pixel = gReadPixel(x, y);
pixel = (new_pixel & plane_mask) |
    (old_pixel & !plane_mask);
/* Now write the value in pixel to the frame buffer */
```

Let's examine this algorithm in detail. The expression *(new_pixel & plane_mask)* uses the bit-wise function *AND* to create a value where all of the bits disabled by the plane mask (a plane mask consisting of all 0 bits) are set to 0 in *new_pixel*. For instance, if the plane mask is 11110000 and *new_pixel* is 00010001, then the result of the expression is 00010000; the lower 4 bits are all set to 0. The second expression *(old_pixel & !plane_mask)* does the opposite. It sets to 0 the bits in *old_pixel* that correspond to the 1s in *plane_mask*. If the plane mask is 11110000, then *!plane_mask* is 00001111. For instance, if *old_pixel* is 00010000, and the plane mask is 11110000, then the result is 00000000. Finally, the results of these two expressions are *OR*ed together. This last step replaces the upper 4 bits of *old_pixel* with the upper 4 bits of *new_pixel*, assuming a plane mask of 11110000. Table 12-1 shows several examples of how this method works using a plane mask of 11110000 (upper 4 bits are enabled):

Table 12-1. Examples of plane mask

new_pixel	*(new_pixel & plane_mask)*	*old_pixel*	*(old_pixel & !plane_mask)*	*Result*
11111111	11110000	00000000	00000000	11110000
00110011	00110000	00001111	00001111	00111111
01010101	01010000	01010101	00000101	01010101
01110111	01110000	00001111	00001111	

While the explanation of this algorithm is fairly complex, using it to animate an object is not. For example, suppose you want to animate a white circle on top of some elaborate background image you have created. First, call *gSetPlaneMask(O x FØ)* to enable writing to the upper 4 bits only. Next, call *gCircleDraw( )* to draw the circle, but instead of using *gWHITE* as the color, you must shift it up into the upper 4 bits. This can be done in one of two ways, by multiplying by 16, or using the C left bit-shift operator <<:

```
gCircleDraw(circle, gWHITE << 4);
```

The bit shift operator << takes its first argument and shifts it to the left by the number of bits specified as the second argument to occupy the desired bits. This takes the value for *gWHITE* (15) and puts in the upper 4 bits. Multiplication by 16 produces the same result, but using the << operator is clearer because it explicitly indicates that the value is being shifted up by 4 bits. If you use a different number of bits, then simply specify how many bits the value needs to be shifted.

Getting The Color Right

By setting the plane mask and using this color for the call to *gCircleDraw( )*, a circle will now be drawn into the upper (unused) 4 bits of the image. For each pixel drawn for the circle, the upper 4 bits will now have the value *gWHITE*. So now you have followed this procedure, but the circle does not show up as white! The problem now is that the palette must be set such that every pixel value with the value *gWHITE* in the upper 4 bits displays the color white. Since *gWHITE* equals 15, 1111 in binary, this corresponds to the 16 values from 11110000 (= 240) to 11111111 (= 255). The palette can be set using the following code segment:

```
gPalette *pal;
int i, index;

/* Make a palette with 1 entry, white */
pal = gPaletteCreate(1);
gSetPaletteEntry(pal, 0, 255, 255, 255);
```

```
/* Now set all entries for WHITE */
index = gWHITE << 4;
for(i=0; i < 16; i++)
 gPalettePut(index + i, pal);

gPaletteDelete(pal);
```

Now a pixel written with the value (*gWHITE* << 4) will show up as white, regardless of what the background pixel it is on top of. The circle may be erased by drawing the circle with a value of 0. This sets all 4 upper bits to 0, leaving the background bits unchanged since the plane mask does not allow modification of the lower 4 bits.

In this example, you only needed one color to draw the circle, namely white. You only need a single bit to represent one value if you set the color palette appropriately. Instead of using 4 bits to do this, you could have used only 1 bit by using a plane mask of 10000000, equal to 0x80 hexadecimal. Just as with the 4-bit graphics plane, you must set the palette so that all pixel values with the most signicant bit set are displayed as white. This requires setting the values 128 through 255, using the following code segment:

```
/* Make a palette with 1 entry, white */
pal = gPaletteCreate(1);
gSetPaletteEntry(pal, 0, 255, 255, 255);

/* Now set all entries for WHITE */
for(index=128; index <= 255; index++)
 gPalettePut(index, pal);
```

The color used for drawing into this graphics plane can, of course, be set to any desired color. By using only 1 bit for the animated objects, there are now 7 bits available for the background image, providing 128 separate colors.

Multiple Graphics Planes

The plane mask can be used to support more than a single graphics overlay over a background image. For instance, consider Figure 12-3 in which three

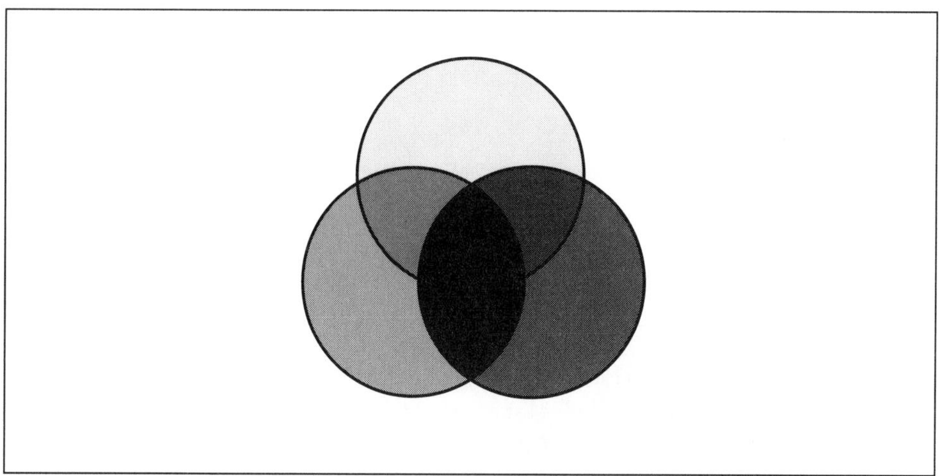

Figure 12-3. Three overlapping rings. The rings can be easily moved if they are drawn into three separate graphics planes.

overlapping rings of different colors are shown. If each ring is drawn using a separate graphics plane, then any one of them may be moved without having to redraw the others or the background. If all three circles were drawn as part of a single 4-bit graphics overlay, as in the previous section, then when a circle is moved (erased and redrawn), the other circles must be redrawn as well because they overlap. Drawing the circles in separate graphics planes avoids that problem all together. For instance, the three plane masks of 10000000 (0 x 80), 01000000 (0 x 40), and 00100000 (0 x 20) can be used for each circle. This uses the most significant 3 bits to draw the circles, leaving 5 remaining bits (= 32 colors) for the background image. You may have as many graphics planes as there are bits per pixel. However, the more graphics planes you use, the fewer the number of colors that are available for the background image.

Using a single bit plane for a graphics image requires that the palette be set properly to show the desired color for the bit plane. All graphics drawn into that bit plane are drawn in a single color. To have a multicolor graphics overlay, you must use more than a single bit, as you did with the 4-bit graphics overlay of the previous section. The function *gSetPlaneMaskColor()*, shown in Listing 12-1, will set the palette so that all graphics written using the passed plane mask are shown in the specified color.

```
void gSetPlaneMaskColor(gColor plane_mask,
            int red, int green, int blue)
{
gPalette *pal;
gColor i;

/* Make a palette with 1 entry, white */
pal = gPaletteCreate(1);
gSetPaletteEntry(pal, 0, red, green, blue);

/* Now scan the palette for colors that have the
   same entries as the plane mask */
for(i=0; i < gPaletteGetSize(); i++) {
 if(i & plane_mask)
  gPalettePut(i, pal);
}

gPaletteDelete(pal);

return;
}
```

Listing 12-1. The function gSetPlaneMaskColor( ) sets the palette so that any graphics drawn using that plane mask appears in the correct color.

gSetPlaneMaskColor() should be used for plane masks in which only a single bit is set, such as 0x80, 0x40, 0x20, and so forth. To determine if a palette entry must be set, *gSetPlaneMaskColor()* loops through all of the possible palette entries and for each entry *i*, evaluates the expression: *i & plane_mask* (the *AND* of *i* and *plane_mask*). If palette entry *i* has any of the same bits' sets as the plane mask, then the result of the *AND* operator will be nonzero. For instance, suppose *plane_mask* equals 0 x 80. Then any palette entry number with its most significant (or highest numbered) bit equal to 1, when *AND*ed with 0 x 80, will produce 0x80 again, which is nonzero. If the most significant bit is not set, then the result is 0. This function is a convienient way to set the colors for any number of single-bit graphics planes. For instance, the following example draws the three circles shown in Figure 12-3:

```
gCircle *red_circle, *green_circle, *blue_circle;
gColor *plane_mask;

red_circle = gCircleCreate(100.0, 100.0, 50.0);
green_circle = gCircleCreate(150.0, 100.0, 50.0);
blue_circle = gCircleCreate(200.0, 100.0, 50.0);

/* Set the colors of the graphics planes */
gSetPlaneMaskColor(0 x 80, 255, 0, 0);
gSetPlaneMaskColor(0 x 40, 0, 255, 0);
gSetPlaneMaskColor(0 x 20, 0, 0, 255);

/* Now draw the objects */
gSetPlaneMask(0 x 80);
gCircleDraw(red_circle, 0 x FF);
gSetPlaneMask(0 x 40);
gCircleDraw(green_circle, 0 x FF);
gSetPlaneMask(0 x 20);
gCircleDraw(blue_circle, 0 x FF);
```

Notice in this example, that each circle is drawn using the color *0 x FF*, and all bits in the color are set to one, rather than to one of the standard colors. Remember that only the bits enabled by the plane mask are actually written. Graphics written using a 1-bit plane mask are displayed only in the one color set by *gSetPlaneMaskColor( )*. By using 0 x FF, you ensure that the object is drawn, no matter which plane mask bit is set. Whenever you use a single-bit plane mask, think of the color for an object as being set by *gSetPlaneMaskColor( )*, rather than by the color argument passed to *gCircleDraw( )*.

While you have accomplished your basic goal of separating the image into separate layers, there is, of course, a trade-off. The background image must use fewer than the maximum number of colors in order to make bits available for the animated objects. Furthermore, a 1-bit graphics plane can only display objects of one color. You could, for instance, use the upper 4 bits to have separate red, green, blue, and white graphics overlays. Or the upper 4 bits can be used for a single graphics overlay, but now objects using 16 colors can be represented. The problem is that if you have multiple animated objects drawn in a single layer, and any one of them is moved, then they all must be redrawn. If they are drawn in separate graphics planes, then each object can be treated independently.

The choice of deciding how many graphics planes to use depends on how many objects you will be animating at one time and how long it takes to redraw them. For instance, suppose you create a complex plot using the tools in Chapter 11. You can overlay multiple additional plots on top of the base plot (the background image) and change them dynamically by assigning each new plot to separate graphics planes. If your base plot only used eight colors (3 bits), then up to five other indepedent plots may be overlaid on top of the base plot and freely changed without having to redraw any of the other plots. This provides enormous flexibility to combine multiple graphics images and to animate objects on top of other objects in a non-destructive manner. The demonstration programs described in Chapter 14 and listed in Appendix B show many examples of how to use plane masks to easily animate multiple objects over a background image.

Getting User Input

In most animation programs, you need to allow the user to provide input, either to direct the flow of the program, provide data, change the program state, or even just to exit the program. So far, there is no graceful way to do this in the animation loop. The animation simply keeps running until some preset condition is met; the user cannot interrupt the program. To add this capability to your programs, the graphics package provides two keyboard functions, *gKeyPressed()* and *gGetch()*. The function *gKeyPressed()* returns 1 if the user has struck a key on the keyboard, 0 otherwise. The function *gGetch()* returns the last character typed by the user on the keyboard. You use the two functions within an animation loop as follows:

```
char ch;

/* Main animation loop */
while(!finished) {
 /* Erase, update, and redraw the objects */
 ...
```

```
    if(gKeyPressed()) {
     /* User struck a key, find out which one */
     ch = gGetch();
     switch(ch) {
     /* Take actions based on key that was struck */
     }
    }
  }
```

Until the user strikes a key, the animation loop will proceed normally. You may take whatever action you like when a key is pressed, based on which key is struck. For instance, you might use *x* to exit the program, or '+' and '-' to speed up or slow down the animation. A useful convention to adopt is if the user enters a *?* character, then display a short help screen showing what other keys the user may enter. Some of the demonstration programs in the previous chapters exemplify this function. They let you switch various parameters based on which keys were entered.

Another good use for *gGetch()* is to pause the program and wait for another key to be entered before continuing. This is useful inside the animation loop. The user can pause the animation to examine the screen and then restart the animation by pressing another key. Our convention is to use the space key as the pause key.

Your Future in Animation

The functions described in this chapter provide the means for animating any drawable object on the screen. By using the various affine transformations, objects may be moved, rotated, or scaled dynamically, right before your very eyes. In addition, other attributes of an object may be animated such as color, brush styles, and fill patterns. With bitmap animation, you can create animated character sequences that are as detailed and elaborate as any cartoonist could create. Unlike a cartoon, you can create the program that decides what the characters should do and when in a fully interactive manner. Using your artistic creativity and patience, you can create animated graphs, games, and simulations with a level of flexibility and interactivity that cannot be performed by any other means except computer graphics. Chapter 14 provides several more example programs of how to use the animation techniques presented in this chapter. You should examine those programs carefully and then begin expanding them and experimenting for yourself. The tools are now in your hands, have fun with it!

Animated sequences tend to emphasize another problem with computer-generated raster images, jagged edges. As objects are rotated or scaled, the fact that lines are not perfectly straight but are composed of individual pixels becomes even more apparent, and often distracting. In the next chapter, I will discuss various means of removing, or at least making less distracting, the jagged edge artifacts inherent in using a raster frame buffer for drawing. When these smoothing techniques are applied to animated objects, the animation becomes more pleasing and natural looking. So, on to the next chapter where you will learn some of the secrets of anti-aliasing.

Functions Found in This Chapter

Demonstration programs

`dbittest.exe`

This program and its source module, *dbittest.c*, contain all of the example code presented in this chapter, with the additional code to make a complete program.

Frame buffer functions

`void gSetPlotPixelMode(gPixel_Mode mode);`

Sets the mode for writing to the frame buffer. Currently, there are only two valid modes, *gPIXELMODE_COPY* which performs pixel replacement, and *gPIXEL-MODE_XOR*, which *XOR*s new pixels into the frame buffer.

```
void gSetPlaneMask(gColor *plane_mask);
```

Determines which bits are enabled for all subsequent pixel writes to the frame buffer with *gPlotPixel()*. By disabling selected sets of bits, the frame buffer can be divided into a background image and a number of graphics overlays.

```
void gSetPlaneMaskColor(gColor *plane_mask,
        int red, int green, int blue);
```

Sets the color palette such that all graphics to the bit planes enabled by *plane_mask* will appear as the specified color. Graphic objects drawn using a single bit plane mask should use this call to set the color. All objects drawn to that bit plane will appear in this color.

Keyboard input functions

```
int gKeyPressed(void);
```

Returns 1 if a key has been pressed on the keyboard, 0 otherwise. Use this function in an animation loop to see if the user wants to enter some new data or change something about the animation.

```
char gGetch(void);
```

Returns the last character entered by a user. If no character has been entered, waits until a key is pressed before returning. *gGetch()* is used after a successful call to *gKeyPressed()* to determine which key was pressed.

CHAPTER 13

Making a Better Picture

The final, major drawing technique to cover concerns the problem that, despite previous claims to the contrary, raster graphics is not a perfect graphics medium. The finest resolution you can achieve on a raster display is limited by the pixel size on the screen. Whenever any type of curve is drawn on the screen, the pixels nearest to the curve are plotted, but these pixels are almost never exactly on the curve. For instance, the line-drawing routines plot the pixels that are closest to the line, but they are never exactly on the line except when the line is vertical, horizontal, or aligned at a 45-degree angle. When viewed up close, as in Figure 13-1, the pixels form a stair-step pattern. It is this stair-step effect that gives lines, circles, and other curves their jagged appearance on the screen. You can clearly see this effect when you run the *dline.exe* demonstration program from Chapter 4. All of the lines, except for the horizontal, vertical, and 45-degree ones, appear slightly jagged. This effect is also clearly evident in the circle- and ellipse-drawing programs. Clearly, straight lines that appear straight, without the jagged edges, are preferable. The question is, can you do anything about it?

And the answer is: you certainly can. Solving the problem of drawing smooth curves on raster displays is one of the most researched topics in computer graphics. The solution to this and other related problems is called *anti-aliasing*. When any type of curve is drawn on a raster display, you must decide which pixels to turn on to best represent the curve. The simplest and fastest method is to turn on the nearest pixels to the curve, which is what all of your drawing routines have done so far. However, because the pixels are only an approximation to the curve, the curve is said to *alias* or to possess aliasing artifacts. There are many other types of aliasing problems which are especially frustrating in three-dimensional computer graphics. This chapter will be limited to solving the problem of removing, or at least substantially reducing, the jagged edges and stair-stepping from computer drawings.

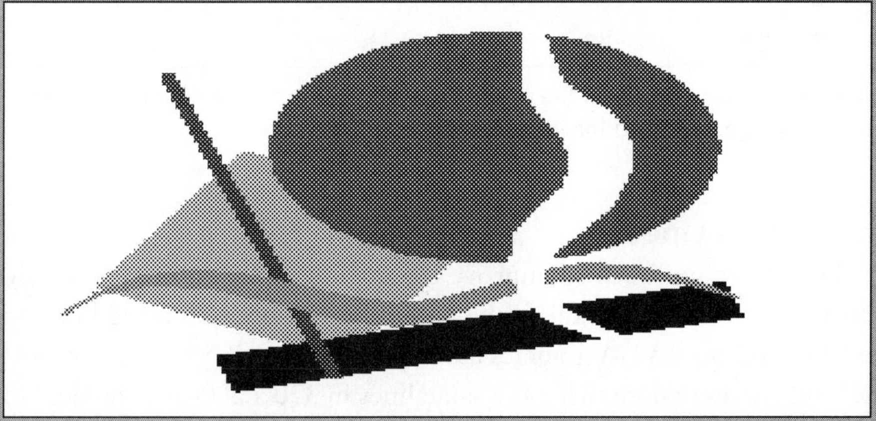

No matter what kind of graphics display you have, you'll want to get the most out of it. Even with a high resolution SVGA display, your images can still exhibit rough edges, often referred to as the jaggies. Anti-aliasing is the name for a number of techniques for smoothing out these jagged edges and making the image more pleasing to look at. By using various anti-aliasing methods, you can improve the look of your images without buying more expensive, higher resolution graphics hardware.

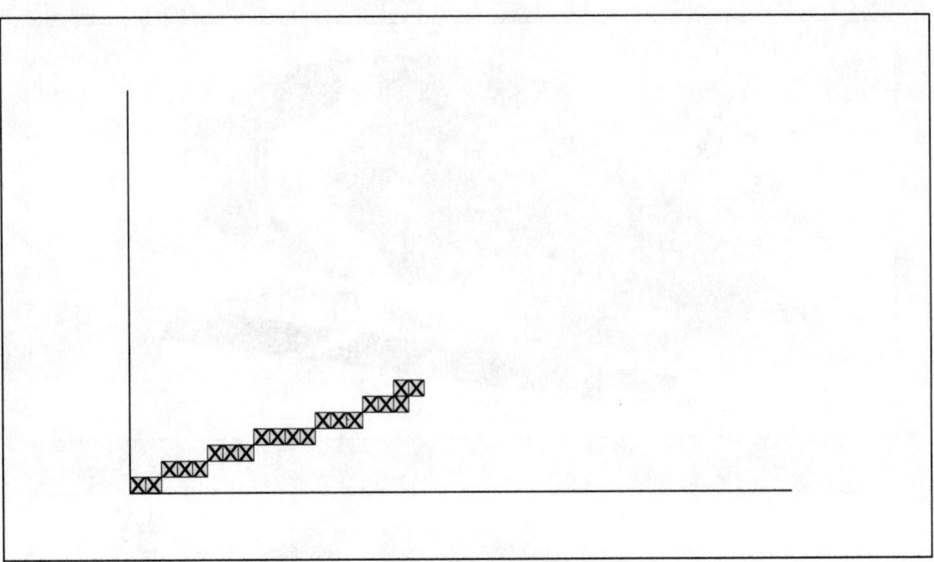

Figure 13-1. Close-up of how the pixels drawn for a line form a stair-step pattern, creating a jagged edge on the screen

Anti-Aliased Lines

The direct approach to improve the quality of drawn lines is simply to increase the resolution of the frame buffer. For instance, drawing lines using the 640 x 400-pixel VGA graphics mode produces significantly better looking lines and curves than drawing the same lines in 320 x 200-pixel mode. However, even with the maximum display resolution supported by your graphics card and monitor, lines will still appear jagged. So, you are still left with the problem of trying to eliminate the stair-step appearance as much as possible.

By using anti-aliased line drawing, you can create a drawing using a lower resolution display that will appear to be of equal or better quality than the same drawing on a higher resolution display without anti-aliasing. This can be of great significance in some applications such as flight simulation and mechanical CAD, where the size of the frame buffer used is a significant expense. Any means of reducing the frame buffer size without sacrificing overall image quality is, financially, very beneficial.

Over the last 20 years, many researchers have developed and implemented many types of anti-aliasing algorithms. Some methods are very simple minded and do not produce very good results in many cases. Others are quite computationally complex and while they produce very good results, are not practical in many applications because they take too long to draw. Others work very well on specific types of curves, but are not easily adaptable to drawing other types. There are three basic properties to strive for in an "ideal" anti-aliasing routine:

1. It is efficient, in that anti-aliased line drawing takes only slightly longer to draw than the normal line drawing.
2. It is effective. This means that it smooths out the stair-step appearance.
3. The algorithm can be easily generalized to drawing other types of curves.

Achieving all three criteria is, of course, impossible. The algorithm implemented in this software was chosen because it meets most of the conditions and is especially efficient. This algorithm is based on the work of Mr. Xiaolin Wu from the department of computer science at the University of Western Ontario. The basic algorithm was presented in a paper in the Siggraph 1991 proceedings. See the Bibliography for a complete reference.

Up to this point, all of the curves have been considered to be infinitely thin, mathematical curves, and all of the pixels to be mathematical points. This is not an accurate representation. A pixel is actually a small rectangular area of the screen, not a point. When I talk about drawing "curves," this actually means "curves with a finite width," namely one pixel. Figure 13-2 shows a magnified view of the drawing of a line. Line-drawing methods up to this point in the book have simply filled in the nearest pixels to the curve. A more accurate method would color the pixel using an intensity based on the amount of overlap between the pixel and the one-pixel wide line. The larger the amount of overlap, the brighter the pixel; the smaller the amount of overlap, the dimmer the pixel. At normal screen resolutions, your eye does a remarkable job of integration of the pixels. You will perceive a smoother straight line. The stair-step of the non anti-aliased lines is substantially reduced. Computing the actual area of overlap between the line and each pixel is a computationally expensive task. Instead, the anti-aliasing method used here makes a reasonable approximation for the amount of overlap.

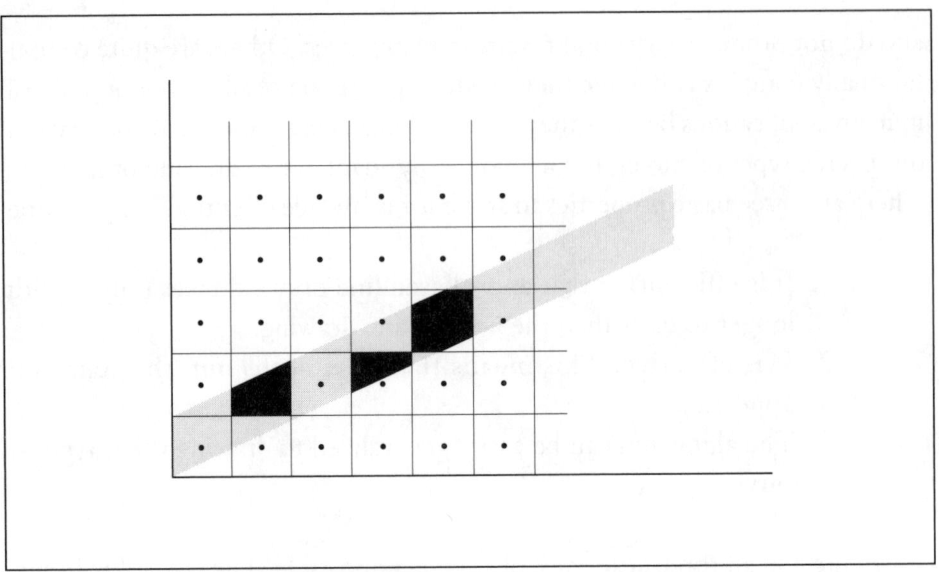

Figure 13-2. A line is drawn as a one-pixel wide curve. Pixels represent small areas on the screen, not single points. The intensity of a pixel should be proportional to the amount of overlap between the line and the pixel.

Figure 13-3 illustrates the basic anti-aliasing method. Assume that the line is being drawn with a color, (red, green, blue), where each of the color components is in the range from zero to 255. The line-drawing algorithms of Chapter 4 choose the pixels nearest the line. Consider the point at which the line intersects the vertical line for $x = xi$. The line precisely intersects this edge at the point $y = yideal$. You need to figure out the amount of overlap between the line and the two pixels above and below the intersection point at (xi,yi) and $(xi,yi+1)$, respectively. As you can see from figures 13-2 and 13-3, a very reasonable approximation to the amount of overlap is the vertical distance of the point $(x0,yideal)$ from the center of both of the pixels. The closer the line is to passing through the center of the pixel, the greater the overlap of the line with the pixel. In Figure 13-3, the smaller the value of dy, the more the line overlaps the pixel. Equation 13-1 shows how the intensity at each pixel is computed based on this distance.

Let $dy = (yideal - yi)$, then the color to plot at each pixel is:

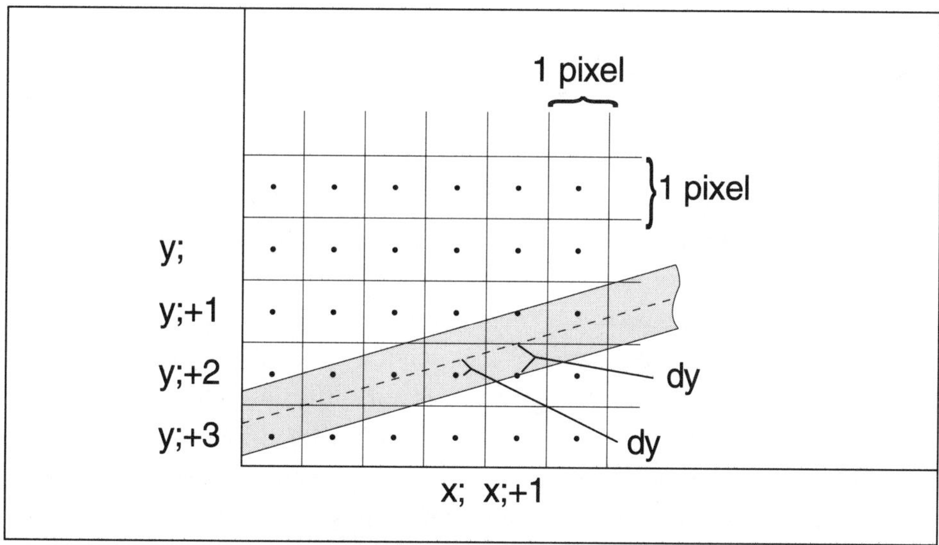

Figure 13-3. Area overlap between a line and a pixel is approximated by calculating the value dy, the vertical distance between the intersection point of the line and the center of the pixels above and below. The smaller the value of dy, the greater the overlap. If dy equals zero, then the line passes directly through the pixel center and is considered to completely cover the pixel.

$$(x_i,y_i) = (\text{red}*dy, \quad \text{green}*dy, \quad \text{blue}*dy)$$
$$(x_i,y_{i+1}) = (\text{red}*(1.0 - dy),\text{green}*(1.0 - dy),\text{blue}*(1.0 - dy)) \quad \text{Equation 13-1.}$$

The value *dy* modifies the intensity of the color. Using these equations, each of the pixels is drawn with an intensity inversely proportional to how close it is to the actual line. The closer the line is to a pixel, the more overlap there will be, and the brighter the pixel will be. Conversely, the further away the line is, the darker (less intense) the pixel will be. While this approximation is not an exact calculation of overlapping areas, it is reasonably close and is easy to compute.

An Anti-Aliasing Color Palette

Before diving into how to actually implement this anti-aliasing method, you must consider how to get all of the colors you need to draw the line. The main problem with this, or any other, anti-aliasing technique is that it requires more than one color to draw any curve. In this case, you could potentially need 256 intensity levels of white to draw one line, since the value *cw* can be any value between zero and one. Fortunately, this many intensity levels is not really required. Several studies have empirically determined that using 32 intensity levels is almost always sufficient to represent the anti-aliased line. Finer gradations in intensity levels simply do not significantly improve the perceived image quality of the line.

However, even with 32 levels, there is still a considerable limitation for non 24-bit displays. The first limitation is that you must use a 256-color VGA mode for these routines to work; EGA graphics is not sufficient. The second limititation is that you are limited to usng only 8 different colors simultaneously. Since 32 intensity levels are required to represent an anti-aliased line of a certain color, a color palette of 256 colors can only support 256/32 = 8 indepedent colors. Thus, the color palette must be divided into 8 (or fewer) separate 32-color partitions. Each partition contains all of the intensities for a given color, divided into 32 levels from darkest (black) to brightest (maximum intensity). For instance, the following code sets the palette entries from 32 to 63 for 32 intensity levels of white:

```
gPalette *palette;
int i, red, green, blue;

palette = gPaletteCreate(32);
                        /* Create a palette of 32 elements */
red = 0; green = 0; blue = 0;
for(i=0; i<32; i++) {
  gSetPaletteEntry(palette, i, red, green, blue);
  red += 8;
  green += 8;
  blue += 8;
  red = MIN(red, 255);
  green = MIN(green, 255);
  blue = MIN(blue, 255);
}
gPalettePut(gAA_WHITE, palette, 32);
```

The routine *gSetAntiAliasPalette()* may be used to automatically set up the palette with the 32 intensity levels for all six primary and secondary colors and for white. The first 16 entries of the palette are left with their default entries so you can still use the standard color set to draw any of the other object types along with the anti-aliased lines. Since an anti-aliased line requires more than a single color, you cannot use the normal color macros, such as *gWHITE* and *gBLACK*, with the anti-aliased drawing routines. Instead, I have provided another set of macros to specify the color of the line once the palette has been set by *gSetAntiAliasPalette()*. The macro names are as follows:

```
#define gAA_WHITE      32
#define gAA_RED                 64
#define gAA_GREEN      96
#define gAA_BLUE                128
#define gAA_YELLOW     160
#define gAA_CYAN                192
#define gAA_MAGENTA    224
```

Whenever a color value is expected for an anti-aliased drawing routine, one of the above macro values should be passed. In all other respects, the anti-aliased drawing routines use the same arguments as the non anti-aliased drawing routines do.

Drawing the Anti-Aliased Line

For your first implementation, let's adapt the DDA line-drawing algorithm to use this anti-aliasing method. As in Chapter 4, you will first consider the case of a line with slope between -45 degrees and +45 degrees. Recall that the DDA algorithm looped for all values of x and updated y by adding the slope of the line for each increment in x. The pixel to plot was determined by computing *ROUND*(y) and then plotting the pixel at (x, *ROUND*(y)). Instead, you want to fill in the pixels both above and below the actual intersection point. Instead of implementing *ROUND()*, use the function *floor()* to find the largest integer that is less than or equal to y. By definition, y is between *floor*(y) and *floor*(y) + 1. The distance from the intersection point to the pixel at (x, *floor*(y)) is then simply (y - *floor*(y)), as shown in Figure 13-3. This is always a number between zero and one. You must then use this value to find which color index to write with. Since the palette has been set up with the 32 intensity levels, you take (*y* - *floor(y)*) and multiply it by 32, to get an intensity level between zero and 31. This value is then cast to an integer to get the appropriate color index. Once the color index is computed, you can select the appropriate color value to use for both pixels. The following code shows how this is implemented for the DDA line-drawing algorithm:

```
float y, m;
int x, iy;
gColor aa_color, maxcolor;

m = (float)(y2 - y1) / (float)(x2 - x1);
/* aa_color is the color index passed in, it
   represents an intensity of zero. maxcolor is the
   index for the maximum intensity */
maxcolor = aa_color + 31;
y = y1;
for(x=x1; x<=x2; x++) {
  iy = floor(y);
  /* Plot pixel at iy and iy + 1 */
  index = MIN(ROUND((y - iy)*32), 31);
  /* Okay, now plot iy with maxcolor - index */
  /* The closer (y - iy) is to zero, the more intense the
     color, which means use maxcolor - index */
  gPlotPixel(x, iy, maxcolor - index);
  /* And plot iy with aa_color + index */
  gPlotPixel(x, iy + 1, aa_color + index);
  /* Update y */
  y += m;
}
```

Compared with the original DDA code, the amount of extra calculation needed for the anti-aliasing is quite small. You can, in fact, make this routine more efficient by prescaling all of the *y*-values by 32. Then the floating point value, *y*, can be directly cast to an integer. To get the pixel *y*-coordinates, you must divide *ROUND(y)* by 32 using the C right-shift operator. The low order 5 bits are equal to [(*y* - *floor*(*y*)) * 32], which is the desired color index value. The revised algorithm is shown in the following code:

```
float y, m;
int x, iy, iyscreen, index;
gColor aa_color, maxcolor;

m = (float)(y2 - y1) / (float)(x2 - x1);
m *= 32.0;
/* aa_color is the color index passed in, it
   represents an intensity of zero. maxcolor is the
   index for the maximum intensity */
maxcolor = aa_color + 31;
y = y1 * 32;
for(x=x1; x<=x2; x++) {
  iy = ROUND(y);
  /* Plot pixel at iy and iy+1 */
  index = iy & 0x4F;
  /* Get low order 5 bits */
  /* Okay, now plot iy with maxcolor - index */
  /* The closer (y - iy) is to zero, the more intense the
     color, which means use maxcolor - index */
  iyscreen = iy >> 5; /* Remove low order 5 bits */
  gPlotPixel(x, iyscreen, maxcolor - index);
  /* And plot iy with aa_color + index */
  gPlotPixel(x, iyscreen+1, aa_color + index);
  /* Update y */
  y += m;
}
```

Now all additional floating-point operations have been removed from inside the inner loop. The algorithm is easily extensible to handle the other case for lines with slope greater than 45 degrees. For those cases, reverse the role of *x* and *y* and plot the two pixels at (*floor*(*x*), *y*) and (*floor*(*x*) + 1,*y*), as you increment in *y*. The complete DDA line-drawing code with this anti-aliasing method can be found in the routine *gAA_LineDraw()* in the module *gAlias.c*.

Many drawings are based on drawing polylines and polygons, which are themselves drawn as a connected series of line segments. Anti-aliased polylines and polygons can be drawn by using *gAA_LineDraw( )* instead of *gLineDraw( )* in the functions *gPolygonDraw( )* and *gPolylineDraw( )*. Instead of creating a separate, anti-aliased version of *gPolygonDraw( )* and *gPolylineDraw( )* that uses *gAA_LineDraw( )*, use the function *gSetAntiAliasEnable( )* to enable or disable anti-aliasing. The function *gLineDraw( )* checks to see if anti-aliasing has been enabled, and if so, calls *gAA_LineDraw( )* instead of using the normal midpoint line-drawing algorithm. This approach lets any of the drawing routines that use *gLineDraw( )* draw anti-aliased lines instead. There are, however, several restrictions with this mode. First, anti-aliasing cannot be used if the palette size is less than 256 entries. Second, *gSetAntiAliasEnable( )* automatically calls *gSetAntiAliasPalette( )* to set the appropriate color palette when anti-aliasing is enabled. Any palette entries in the range 32 - 255 are lost. The values in indices 0 through 31 are not changed. If you wish to restore the palette to its original setting, you must explicitly save it in your own palette structure. Finally, only the colors white, red, green, blue, yellow, cyan (green and blue), and magenta (red and blue) may be used in this mode. Any other colors will be plotted as white.

For example, suppose you wanted to draw an anti-aliased, rotated rectangle. The following code shows how to do this:

```
gRectangle rect;
gMatrix *matrix;

matrix = gMatrixRotate(NULL, NULL, 20.0);
gMatrixTranslate(matrix, matrix, 200.0, 200.0);
rect.xmin = -100.0;
rect.xmax = 100.0;
rect.ymin = -100.0;
rect.ymax = 100.0;
rect.matrix = matrix;

gSetAntiAliasEnable(1); /* Turn anti-aliasing on */
gRectangleDraw(&rect, gWHITE);
```

The color passed to the drawing function must be one of the following: *gWHITE, gRED, gGREEN, gBLUE, gCYAN, gMAGENTA, gYELLOW,* or *gBLACK.* Any other color or palette index value will be treated as if *gWHITE* were passed. *gLineDraw()* uses a static lookup table to convert each of these color values into one of the anti-alias color values needed by *gAA_LineDraw()*.

One of the main uses for the anti-aliasing operations is for drawing anti-aliased polyline characters. The demonstration program *galias.exe* shows a number of examples of anti-aliased shapes, including text. You can see for yourself that anti-aliasing enhances the appearance of the text by smoothing out some of the rough edges.

Anti-Aliased Circles

One of the main reasons I chose this anti-aliasing method was its extensibility to other types of curves. Now that you have anti-aliased lines, you can see how to adapt the algorithm to drawing circles and ellipses. As was done for the line, you begin by using the DDA method for drawing a circle. To improve its overall efficiency, I have modified the DDA algorithm to take advantage of the eight-fold symmetry of the circle. This modified version uses the same method as the midpoint algorithm except that it does not use a decision variable. Instead, this version simply computes the *y*-coordinate directly, using the equation of the circle. The basic DDA circle-drawing algorithm becomes the following:

```
int x, y;
float r2;

r2 = (circle.radius * circle.radius);
y = circle.radius;
while(y > x) {
  y = ROUND(sqrt(r2 - (x*x)));
  gCircleDrawEight(&circle, x, y, color);
  x++;
}
```

To apply this anti-aliasing method requires that you do two things. First, performing the same trick used for the line, you multiply the *y*-coordinate values by 32. The low-order 5 bits can be used to determine the distance of the pixels above and below the curve from the actual curve. Second, a new version of *gCircleDrawEight()* is needed to plot the corresponding pairs of pixels for each of the eight symmetric points. The function *gAA_CircleDrawEight()* shown in Listing 13-1 performs that function.

```
void gAA_CircleDrawEight(gCircle *circle, int x, int y,
                         gColor aa_color);
{
int x, iy, ixscreen, iyscreen, index;
int ixc, iyc;
gColor colorA, colorB;

/* aa_color is the color index passed in, it
   represents an intensity of zero. maxcolor is the
   index for the maximum intensity */
ixscreen = ix >> 5;
iyscreen = iy >> 5;
ixc = circle->x;
iyc = circle->y;
index = iy && 0x4F;
colorA = aa_color + 31 - index;
colorB = aa_color + index;

/* Point #1 (x, y) */
gPlotPixel(ixc + ixscreen, iyc + iyscreen, colorA);
gPlotPixel(ixc + ixscreen, iyc + iyscreen + 1, colorB);

/* Point #2 (-x, y) */
gPlotPixel(ixc - ixscreen, iyc + iyscreen, colorA);
gPlotPixel(ixc - ixscreen, iyc + iyscreen + 1, colorB);

/* Point #3 (x, -y) */
gPlotPixel(ixc + ixscreen, iyc - iyscreen, colorA);
gPlotPixel(ixc + ixscreen, iyc - (iyscreen + 1), colorB);

/* Point #4 (-x, -y) */
gPlotPixel(ixc - ixscreen, iyc - iyscreen, colorA);
```

```
gPlotPixel(ixc - ixscreen, iyc - (iyscreen + 1), colorB);

/* Now reverse x and y, anti-aliasing is now applied
   along horizontal pieces */

/* Point #5 (y, x) */
gPlotPixel(iyc + iyscreen, ixc + ixscreen, colorA);
gPlotPixel(iyc + iyscreen + 1, ixc + ixscreen, colorB);

/* Point #6 (-y, x) */
gPlotPixel(iyc - iyscreen, ixc + ixscreen, colorA);
gPlotPixel(iyc - (iyscreen + 1), ixc + ixscreen, colorB);

/* Point #7 (y, -x) */
gPlotPixel(iyc + iyscreen, ixc - ixscreen, colorA);
gPlotPixel(iyc + (iyscreen + 1), ixc - ixscreen, colorB);

/* Point #8 (-y, -x) */
gPlotPixel(iyc - iyscreen, ixc - ixscreen, colorA);
gPlotPixel(iyc - (iyscreen + 1), ixc - ixscreen, colorB);

return;
}
```

Listing 13-1. The function gAA_CircleDrawEight() draws the eight symmetric points of the circle using the basic anti-aliasing algorithm

Using *gAA_CircleDrawEight()*, the complete anti-aliased circle-drawing function becomes the following:

```
void gAA_CircleDraw(gCircle *circle, gColor aa_color)
{
int x, y;
float r2;

/* Scale both x and y by 32 */
r2 = (circle.radius * circle.radius * 1024.0);
y = circle.radius * 32;
x = 0;
```

```
    while(y > x) {
      y = ROUND(sqrt(r2 - (x*x)));
      gAA_CircleDrawEight(&circle, x, y, color);
      x += 32;
    }

    return;
    }
```

The anti-aliased ellipse-drawing functions work in exactly the same manner. The only real difference in the ellipse-drawing functions is that they use the equation of an ellipse rather than a circle. The functions *gAA_EllipseDraw()* and *gAA_EllipseDrawFour()* can be found in the *galias.c* module on the enclosed software diskette along with the anti-aliased circle- and line-drawing routines.

The anti-aliased circle- and ellipse-drawing routines are integrated into the functions *gCircleDraw()* and *gEllipseDraw()*, respectively. Whenever anti-aliased drawing mode is enabled with a call to *gSetAntiAliasMode()*, *gCircleDraw()* calls *gAA_CircleDraw()* and *gEllipseDraw()* calls *gAA_EllipseDraw()* instead of using their usual midpoint-drawing routines. Thus, you can create anti-aliased drawings without having to change any of your code except for calling *gSetAntiAliasMode()*.

Drawing Anti-Aliased Transformed Ellipses

While the previous drawing routines handled non-transformed circles and ellipses well, they are not quite what you need for transformed ellipses. Recall that drawing transformed ellipses involved making a polyline approximation to the curve and drawing it parametrically. Parametric curve drawing works by evaluating the parametric equations for x and y at two different values of a parameter, t. A line is then drawn between these two computed points. In most cases, these are not integer screen-coordinates, and so, are rounded to the nearest integer to get valid screen-coordinates for *gLineDraw()*. Your line-drawing routine draws anti-aliased lines, but it makes the assumption that the line always begins and ends at integer coordinates. You can remove this assumption by createing another version of *gAA_LineDraw()* that takes floating-point coordinates as arguments. If the line segment has a slope between -45 degrees and +45 degrees, then you explicitly find the intersection with the first column of pixels to the right of the starting point. This situation is shown in Figure 13-4. Once this first point is found, you proceed incrementally as in the normal line-drawing procedure. The algorithm is shown in the following code segment:

```
/* Now (x1, y1) and (x2, y2) are floats */
/* It is assumed here that x2 >= x1 */

float y, m;
int x, iy, iyscreen, index;
gColor aa_color, maxcolor;

m = (float)(y2 - y1) / (float)(x2 - x1);
m *= 32.0;
/* aa_color is the color index passed in, it
   represents an intensity of zero. maxcolor is the
   index for the maximum intensity */
maxcolor = aa_color + 31;
/* Find first point */
y = y1*32.0 + m*(ceil(x1) - x1);
for(x=ceil(x1); x<=floor(x2); x++) {
  iy = ROUND(y);
  /* Plot pixel at (iy) and (iy + 1) */
  index = iy & 0x4F;
  /* Get low order 5 bits */
  /* Okay, now plot iy with maxcolor - index */
  /* The closer (y - iy) is to zero, the more intense the
     color, which means use maxcolor - index */
  iyscreen = iy >> 5;/* Remove low order 5 bits */
  gPlotPixel(x, iyscreen, maxcolor - index);
  /* And plot iy with aa_color + index */
  gPlotPixel(x, iyscreen+1, aa_color + index);
  /* Update y */
  y += m;
}
```

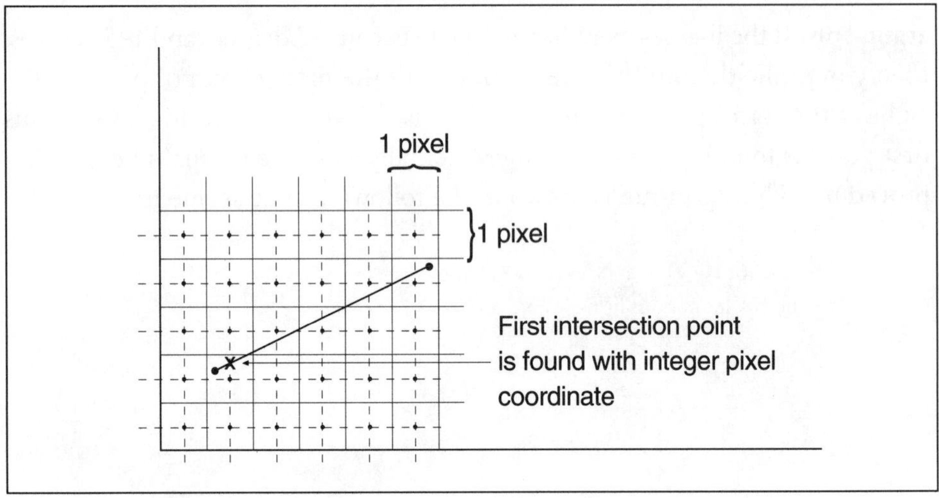

Figure 13-4. Drawing a line segment with floating-point screen coordinates. The intersection with the first vertical edge is found. From that point on, the normal incremental algorithm may be used.

The function *gAA_LineDrawFloat()* implements the line-drawing method using floating point rather than integer coordinates. Listing 13-2 shows the modified version of the parametric circle-drawing function from Chapter 5. By using *gAA_LineDrawFloat()*, the transformed curve will now be correctly anti-aliased. As you will recall from Chapter 5, the transformed ellipse-drawing routine *gEllipseDrawTransformed()* simply calls *gCircleDrawTransformed()*. Therefore, you do not need a separate anti-aliased ellipse-drawing function.

As was done with *gCircleDraw()*, *gCircleDrawTransformed()* checks to see if anti-aliasing mode has been enabled, and if it has been, calls *gAA_CircleDrawTransformed()* to draw the anti-aliased circle.

```
void gAA_CircleDrawTransformed(gCircle *circle
                               gColor aa_color)
{
gMatrix *matrix;/* Transform matrix */
float x, y;
float newx, newy, lastx, lasty;
float t, tinc;
```

```
ratio = FindScalingRatio(circle->matrix);
/* Get first point */
tinc = (1.0 / circle->radius) * ratio;
matrix = circle->matrix;
vertex = gVectorSet(NULL, circle->radius, 0.0);
gTransformVector(matrix, vertex, vertex);
gVectorGet(vertex, &x, &y);
lastx = x + circle->x;
lasty = y + circle->y;
/* t represents an angle that measures between
   0 and 2 * PI in radians */
for(t=0.0; t <= 2.0*PI; t += tinc) {
  xp = circle->radius * cos(MIN(t, 2*PI));
  yp = circle->radius * sin(MIN(t, 2*PI));
  vertex = gVectorSet(vertex, xp, yp);
  /* Transform it */
  gTransformVector(matrix, vertex, vertex);
  gVectorGet(vertex, &x, &y);
  newx = x + circle->x; newy = y + circle->y;
  /* Only draw it if this point is different */
  /* Check to see if you have moved out of a pixel */
  if( floor(newx) != floor(lastx) ||
      floor(newy) != floor(lasty)) {
    gAA_LineDrawFloat(lastx, lasty, newx, newy, aa_color);
    lastx = newx;
    lasty = newy;
  }
}
/* Make sure the last point is drawn */
vertex = gVectorSet(vertex, circle->radius, 0.0);
gTransformVector(circle->matrix, vertex, vertex);
newx = x + circle->x;
newy = y + circle->y;
```

```
    if( floor(newx) != floor(lastx) ||
        floor(newy) != floor(lasty)) {
      gAA_LineDrawFloat(lastx, lasty, newx, newy, aa_color);
    }

    return;
    }
```

Listing 13-2. A modified version of gCircleDrawTransformed() that correctly anti-aliases a transformed circle or ellipse

Just as you needed to use *gAA_LineDrawFloat()* for the transformed circles and ellipses, you also need it to be able to draw other transformed objects, including polylines and polygons. In a transformed polyline or polygon, each vertex is transformed and then line segments are drawn between the vertices. To correctly anti-alias the object, the new vertex coordinates must not be rounded to the nearest pixel. Instead, the transformed floating-point coordinates must be directly used to draw the object. Thus, I have provided anti-aliasing versions of each object-drawing routine, such as *gAA_PolylineDraw()* and *gAA_PolygonDraw()*, in the *galias.c* module found on the enclosed diskette.

The addition of *gAA_CircleDrawTransformed()*, completes the list of anti-aliasing functions for all of the line-drawing functions. By integrating these functions into the normal drawing functions, you need only implement *gSetAntiAliasEnable()* to use them for your drawings. Drawing with the anti-aliasing functions is slower than the normal drawing functions primarily because twice as many pixels need to be set. However, these functions produce better looking lines and figures. Whether you need to use them or not in a particular drawing depends on the application.

Prove It!

The demonstration program *dalias.exe* illustrates how the anti-alias functions improve the image quality for the various shapes. The program divides the screen into two vertical halves, as is done by the *dline.exe* demonstration program. In the left half of the screen, various lines, circles, ellipses, polylines, and text are drawn using the standard drawing routines. In the right half, the anti-aliased versions are drawn. I think you'll agree there is a noticeable difference between the two images. The program cycles through a number of different screens to illustrate the effects on each type of object.

Other Anti-Aliasing Features

While the anti-aliasing algorithms in this package are effective for single-pixel wide curves, they do not constitute a complete anti-aliasing package. For instance, the methods presented here assume that all of the objects are drawn against a black background. Recall that the intensity of a pixel is determined by the amount of overlap between the curve and the pixel. If the pixel already has a color in it from a background image, then the new pixel color should actually be a mix of the color of the line and the background color. Think of the curve as covering up a portion of the pixel. The new color of the pixel is a combination of the part of the curve covering the pixel, and the part that "shows through" where the curve has not covered the pixel. The new pixel color should be a weighted average of the color of the curve and the color of the background based on the amount of overlap between the curve and the pixel. For example, if the color of the curve being anti-aliased is (red1, green1, blue1) and the background color is (red2, green2, blue2), then combine the colors by computing a weighted average of the two colors for each color component. Using the distance factor *cw* from Equation 13-1, the new color for the pixel becomes the following:

(*cw**red1 + (1.0 - *cw*) * red2, *cw* * green1 + (1.0-*cw*) * green2, *cw* * blue1 + (1.0-*cw*) * blue2)

The problem is that 256 colors are just not enough colors to represent every possible combination of background colors with anti-aliased colors. To perform this calculation accurately requires a 24-bit buffer, in which red, green, and blue can be separately manipulated. In the absence of a 24-bit buffer, you must limit the anti-alias curve drawing to a black background.

This software package does not deal with drawing-filled, anti-aliased shapes either. The extension to anti-alias, solid-filled polygons is straightforward, but the extension for pattern-filled polygons requires more effort. The real problem is not so much in implementing the anti-aliasing, but what to do when filled objects overlap. Without being able to compute the weighted average between pixels, any overlapping portions will have an outline drawn around them due to the anti-aliasing. Anti-aliasing overlapping solid objects requires much more effort and a 24-bit frame buffer to correctly implement.

Finally, the anti-aliasing algorithms will not work correctly when using brushes with the objects. Once again, anti-aliasing a brush requires more effort to implement and you still have the problem of having two overlapping objects, both drawn with brushes leaving incorrect edges from the anti-aliasing operation. There are actually very few graphics packages that provide general purpose routines for solving this problem, primarily because it is a computationally expensive and complex problem to anti-alias an arbitrary bitmap brush against a background image.

Major Programs Ahead

In this chapter, you have seen how anti-aliasing can substantially improve the appearance of many line drawings. As was done with other types of operations such as clipping and transforming, the anti-aliasing functions have been integrated into the basic drawing operations so that only a single function call is required to enable or disable drawing anti-aliased figures. As with all of the other features in the package, you should experiment with anti-aliasing each of the different object types and see the effects for yourself.

This chapter contains the final set of drawing routines for the book. In the next chapter, you will put them all together to create some interesting and fun applications. As you will see, the real power in this, or any other, graphics package is the ability to combine many different features quickly and easily to create dramatic and dynamic applications. Because all of the features such as anti-aliasing, clipping, and transforming can be applied in any combination to any of the objects, you can create a huge variety of different types of drawings. So, carry on to the next chapter—you have made it to the fun part!

Functions Found in This Chapter

Demonstration programs

`dalias.exe`

Demonstrates the differences between anti-aliased and non-anti-aliased images. The screen is divided into two halves, with the left half being non anti-aliased and the right half being anti-aliased. The program then cycles through a number of different drawings to illustrate the basic differences in image quality. This program, as do all of the anti-aliasing options, requires a VGA or SVGA graphics card.

Drawing functions

`void gSetAntiAliasPalette(void);`

Sets up the color palette for the anti-alias drawing routines. Palette entries zero through 31 are not affected by this call, but values 32 through 255 are all changed.

`void gSetAntiAliasMode(int enable);`

Enables (*enable* = 1) or disables (*enable* = *0*) anti-aliasing mode. When anti-aliasing is enabled, the various drawing routines automatically call the appropriate anti-alias drawing routine. This function also calls *gSetAntiAliasPalette()* to set the palette up properly.

Internal drawing functions

The following routines may be used explicitly, but for the most part you do not need them. By enabling anti-aliasing with *gSetAntiAliasMode(1)*, these routines are automatically called by the normal drawing functions.

```
void gAA_LineDraw(int x1, int y1, int x2, int y2,
                  gColor aa_color);
```

Draws an anti-aliased line between the two points. The passed color must be one of the anti-alias color values such as *gAA_WHITE*.

```
void gAA_LineDrawFloat(float x1, float y1, float x2, float y2,
                       gColor aa_color);
```

Same as *gAA_LineDraw()* except that this accepts and accounts for floating-point screen coordinates. Used by all of the anti-alias drawing routines to handle transformed polylines.

```
void gAA_CircleDraw(gCircle *circle, gColor aa_color);
```

Draws an anti-aliased circle.

```
void gAA_CircleDrawEight(gCircle *circle, int x, int y,
                         gColor aa_color);
```

Draws the 8 symmetric points on a circle for the passed *x*- and *y*-values. These values first need to be scaled by a factor of 32 for this routine.

```
void gAA_EllipseDraw(gEllipse *ellipse, gColor aa_color);
```

Draws an anti-aliased ellipse.

```
void gAA_EllipseDrawFour(gEllipse *circle, int x, int y,
                         gColor aa_color);
```

Draws the 4 symmetric points on an ellipse for the passed *x*- and *y*-values. For this routine, these values first need to be scaled by a factor of 32 for this routine.

```
void gAA_CircleDrawTransformed(gCircle *circle, gColor aa_color);
```

Draws an anti-aliased circle that has been arbitarily transformed.

```
void gAA_EllipseDrawTransformed(gEllipse *ellipse,
                                gColor aa_color);
```

Draws an anti-aliased ellipse that has been arbitarily transformed.

```
void gAA_PolylineDraw(gPolyline *poly, gColor aa_color);
```

Draws an anti-aliased polyline.

```
void gAA_PolygonDraw(gPolygon *poly, gColor aa_color);
```

Draws an anti-aliased polygon.

```
void gAA_RectangleDraw(gRectangle *rect, gColor aa_color);
```

Draws an anti-aliased rectangle. Note that this call is only necessary if the rectangle has been transformed and is no longer aligned with horizontal and vertical axes.

CHAPTER 14

Putting It All Together

You made it! Now that you're armed with all the amazing graphics tools from this book, it's time to put them to use and create some interesting and, more importantly, fun applications. There are many programs available that let you draw, paint, and create interesting plots and graphs. For this chapter, I have selected interactive applications that demonstrate other unique uses of computer graphics techniques.

There are three complete demonstration programs included on the disk that accompanies this book, an analog clock display with multiple personalities, a variation of the game of life in which fish and sharks battle one another for supremacy, and finally, a noisy simulation of gas molecules bouncing and reacting in a closed chamber. Each program shows various creative and, dare I say it, clever ways to use the graphics tools in this book to create dynamic and interactive programs. I strongly encourage you to run the programs, examine the source code to see how the graphics calls are used, and then expand, improve, and adapt them for your own fun and games.

The common thread of these programs is the dynamic and interactive behavior that each displays. Every program lets you change the conditions while it is executing, and then immediately see the result of the change. If you take away the interactivity, these programs are not very interesting. There are many ways to put nice looking static images on your graphics display. You can use the tools in this package, or you can use any of the unending variations of programs for painting and drawing, or you can scan in photographs using anything from a $200 hand-held scanner to a $20,000 high resolution optical scanner. Of course, you can create better looking static imagery using cameras, photographs, paint canvases, or a variety of other artistic media. The unique advantage of using computer graphics is that you gain the innate ability to interactively animate objects any way you wish. Since you make the rules in computer graphics, you can change them whenever you want.

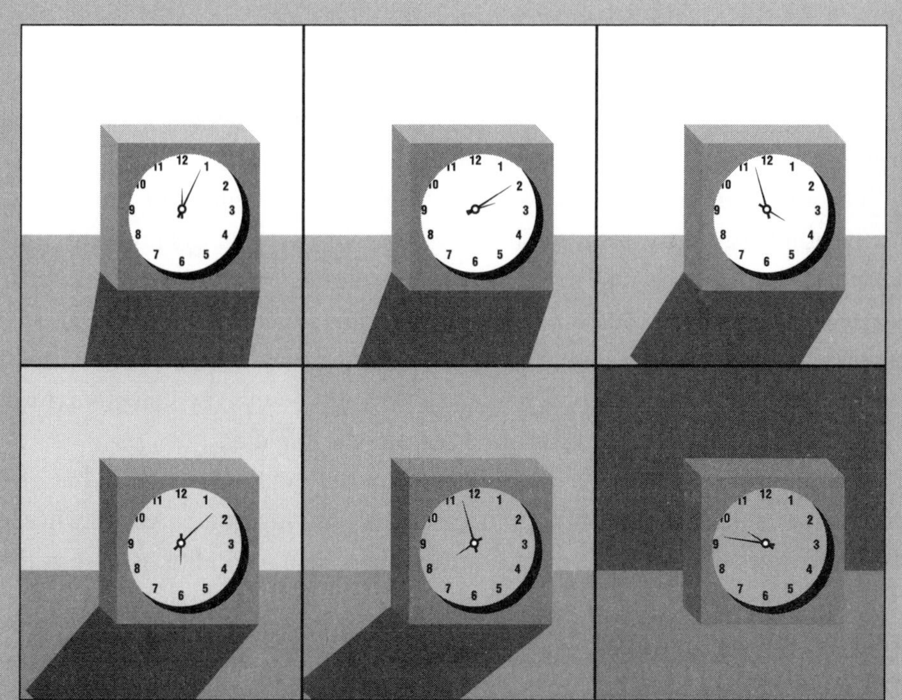

Given the extensive graphics calls library in this book, you will need to learn how to put them together in order to create complete applications. Animation programs provide the most fun and often the most useful means of presenting information.

The programs in this chapter demonstrate how all the graphics tools can be used to create elaborate applications, such as a schizophrenic clock, a life-and-death simulation, and a look at the behavior of two-dimensional gas molecules. These applications, as well as the demonstration programs that you'll find throughout this book, provide extensive working examples of the kinds of programs that you can build using the tools in this book. These programs are meant to entice you with the possibilities of computer graphics; the rest is up to you.

Interacting with an environment that you can create, control, redefine, or destroy should be very appealing and, incidentally, quite useful. The life simulation of the fish and sharks, besides being fun to watch, provides a simplified model of predator/prey relationships in nature.

The ability to run an interactive simulation requiring millions of calculations, and the ability to see the results is a powerful means of studying a problem. Furthermore, you don't have to settle for a simple plot or reams of numbers as the output of your program. Instead, you see the results in a visually intuitive and far more meaningful way. For instance, the fish and sharks simulation would be quite boring if all it told you were how many fish died and how many sharks survived. It is far better to view the simulation to see *why* the fish died.

A computer simulation is the ultimate experimental environment because you can model virtually any process without ever leaving home! As you will see in the examples, you can change any of the experimental conditions, restart the simulation, or change the mathematical model to whatever you want, from trying to accurately model reality to creating a new or virtual reality that can only exist inside the computer.

A Clock In Time

The first of the applications is the program *dclock.exe*. This program provides an analog clock display for your screen, complete with hour, minute, and second hands. This display uses the circle-pattern filling algorithms to draw the clock face and a circle around each of the numerals on the clock. The hour and minute hands are drawn as pattern-filled polygons, and the second hand is drawn as an unfilled polygon. Each of the hands is rotated using the *gMatrixRotate()* function to set the angle of the hand. This makes for very succinct code for drawing and moving the hands around the screen.

The clock uses the plane-mask functions described in Chapter 12. The hour, minute, and second hands are each drawn in separate graphics planes from the background. So, whenever one of the hands is updated, only the hand being moved is redrawn. By using separate graphics planes, redrawing any one hand does not affect any others. If the second hand were not drawn this way, then any part of the clock's face that the second hand overwrites, such as the numbers or the hour and minute hands, would have to be updated every second.

The clock requires a fixed-time animation loop; that is, the clock must be updated at a fixed-time interval, namely, once a second. To accomplish this, you use the ANSI C functions *time()*, *ctime()*, and *difftime()*. The function *time()* returns the elapsed time in seconds since Jan. 1, 1970. The value is stored in the data type *time_t*. *ctime()* takes a *time()* value and generates a character string representing the current date and time in the form:

Day Mon Date hh:mm:ss year
for example: Mon 04 Jan 15:01:00 1994

From this string, you can extract the needed fields, such as the hours, minutes, seconds, and date, using the *sscanf()*. The function *difftime()* returns the difference in seconds between two different times. The returned value is of type *double*. The basic animation loop for the clock is as follows:

```
#include <time.h>

time_t time1, time2;
char *time_string;
char day[4], month[4], prev_day[4], prev_month[4];
int date, year, hour, min, sec;
int prev_date, prev_year, prev_hour, prev_min, prev_sec;

/* Make valid strings by putting NULL at the end */
day[3] = month[3] = prev_day[3] = prev_mont[3] = 0;

/* Other initialization */
...

/* Main animation loop */
while(!finished) {
 time1 = time();
 time_string = ctime(time1);
 /* Extract the data from the string */
 sscanf(time_string,"%3c %2d %3c %2d:%2d:%2d %4d",
        day, date, month, hour, min, sec, year);
```

```
/* Redraw the portions that needs redrawing by checking new values
   against previous values to see what has changed */
...
/* Now save these current values */
prev_date = date;
prev_year = year;
prev_hour = hour;
prev_min = min;
prev_sec = sec;
strcpy(prev_day, day);
strcpy(prev_month, month);
/* Check for any keyboard activity */
if(gKeyPressed()) {
 /* Take appropriate action */
}

/* Wait for at least 1 second to pass */
do {
 time2 = time();
} while(difftime(time2, time1) < 1.0)

} /* End of animation loop */
```

At the end of the animation loop, *difftime()* is used to wait until at least one second has past. Notice that the clock does not get out of sync, because it always reads the time at the start of the animation loop. So, if more than one second passes because all the hands were moved, it will still report the correct time.

A number of features have been added to this clock that you are not likely to find in the clocks around your house. First, the numbers on the clock's face can be displayed either as Arabic or Roman numerals. Second, the date and time are displayed digitally on the clock's face and the digital time may be shown in Roman numerals as well. Since any decent analog clock should have a ticking sound for the second hand and the ability to chime the hour, the following functions are provided: *gSound()*, which turns the PC speaker on, *gNoSound()*, which turns the PC speaker off, and *gDelay()*, which waits a specified number of milliseconds before turning a tone on and then off. These functions directly call the BORLAND C++ *sound()*, *nosound()*, and *delay()* functions. *gSound()* turns the PC speaker on with a fixed frequency specified in hertz (cycles per second). The tone will continue to be played until *gNoSound()* is called. The function *gDelay()* causes your program to wait a specified number of milliseconds. Again, this is used to turn a tone on for a specified time period and then turn it off, for example:

```
gSound(400); /* Make 400-Hz tone */
gDelay(200); /* Wait 200 msec = 1/5 second */
gNoSound(); /* Shut it off */
```

By using various combinations of frequencies and delays, you can create a number of sound effects, though the audio quality is greatly limited by the PC speaker. *dclock.c* creates a second-hand ticking noise when the clock is running and sounds the start of every hour.

There are two other dynamic features in the clock. First, the patterns used in filling each part of the clock are switched every five minutes. The entire clock is redrawn with each element drawn with a new pattern. You can easily modify the program and add your own patterns. So, try adding your own patterns, and see the effects for yourself!

Second, the palette is cycled at five-minute intervals to display the patterns with different color combinations. Changing the palette does not require any redrawing of the screen; so it can be done quickly. Altering the palette provides a fast and easy way of changing a displayed image without requiring a lot of computer drawing time. The palette in the clock is shifted every 2.5 minutes after the patterns are switched. Even with the relatively few fill patterns provided, there are several different color and bitmap combinations that are displayed before the clock repeats the exact same display. By combining dynamic color changes with different fill patterns, you can make even a relatively simple drawing appear quite complex.

While the clock is running, there are a number of keys that you can press to change the display. Each key, and its effect, is shown in Table 14-1.

Table 14-1. Keyboard options for altering the clock program

Keyboard Key	Description
Escape	Exits the clock program
X	Exits the clock program
?	Prints a list of valid keys
R	Toggles between Roman and Arabic numbers
D	Toggles the digital clock display on or off
P	Switches the bitmap patterns used for filling, otherwise the switch occurs every five minutes
S	Toggles the sound on and off

An Ecosystem Simulation

Next, you'll find the fish and sharks simulation program, *dfish.exe*. This program is a variation of the many different life simulations that can be done on a computer. Originally, these types of simulations were developed to study how predator/prey populations coexist in a closed ecosystem. In this particular environment, there are prey creatures, which could be microscopic bacteria, herds of sheep, alien creatures, or whatever else you'd like to study.

The prey population is assumed to be composed of herbivorous creatures that, in the absence of predators, will continue to increase their population until either all the food is gone or there is no space for them. The predator population survives by eating members of the prey population. If there is no prey, then the predators will die out. If there are too many predators, the prey population will be wiped out first, soon followed by the predator population.

The main question that you need to answer is: Under what conditions is the population stable? By stable, I mean that the populations vary up and down, but never reach the point where one or the other dies out. The fish and sharks program provides an interactive means of exploring the problem by adjusting various parameters of the simulation.

In a life simulation program, the world is two-dimensional, and it's defined by the screen. The world can either be confined to the boundaries of the screen, or it can "wrap around" the screen, meaning that when the world breaks the screen's boundaries from any side, it appears, or continues, on the opposite side of the screen. Both types of worlds can be interesting to study. The fish and sharks program uses a wrap-around world, but you, of course, can change it to a confined world with only a few slight coding changes.

The creatures may move anywhere within the world, subject to various restrictions placed on their motion. All creatures move in discrete steps that are based on dividing the screen into a rectangular grid of cells. The fish and sharks program lets you select the number of cells that the screen will be divided into, both vertically and horizontally, up to a maximum of 32,000 cells. All movement is restricted to one of eight directions, either horizontally, vertically, or diagonally. In more sophisticated simulations, movement at other angles is allowed as well.

The behavior of the fish and sharks are governed by a set of rules, many of which have adjustable parameters. Prey creatures follow rules for moving, reproducing, and avoiding predators. Predator creatures also follow rules for moving and reproducing along with rules for hunting prey and dying if they have not eaten enough food in a certain amount of time. For each cycle of the main animation loop, all the creatures are updated, and then redrawn in their new positions (unless, of course, they died or were eaten that cycle). After each cycle, the program checks every creature's status against the rules to see what happened during that cycle. The program then updates the screen accordingly. The program continues the simulation until a termination condition is reached. For the fish and sharks, this condition occurs whenever all the predators die off either by eating all the fish or by not reproducing rapidly enough.

The rules for the fish, or prey creatures, are:

Fish reproduction

- Each fish produces new fish after a certain number of cycles have passed. The number of cycles for reproduction is a random amount for each fish, based on an average birthrate and a random variation from fish to fish. In effect, each fish has its own biological clock, implemented as a simple counter, to determine when it can reproduce. The number of offspring produced at a time is a parameter of the simulation.

- A fish cannot reproduce if all eight adjacent cells are occupied. If this occurs, the fish's biological clock is reset.
- If a fish reproduces, the offspring randomly occupies one of the empty cells adjacent to the parent and initially moves in the same direction as the parent.

Fish movement

- There can be no more than one fish or shark per cell.
- Unless a fish sees a shark, it continues to move in the same direction it is going. (Sight distances are measured in the number of cells, or "distance," between a shark and a fish.)
- All fish move at the same rate of 1 cell per cycle.
- If the fish runs into another fish by attempting to move into a cell occupied by another fish, then the fish starts moving in the same direction as the other fish. This promotes schooling of fish. Once fish are adjacent to one another, they all start moving the same way.
- If the fish sees a shark, it moves in the direction opposite the direction that the shark is moving. So, if one fish in a school sees a shark, the entire school starts moving away.
- When a fish is born, it initially moves in the direction of its parent.

Sharks, or predators, use the following rules:

Shark reproduction

- Sharks must eat fish to survive.
- Each fish is worth a certain number of food points.
- Moving and reproducing use food points. Unlike fish, a shark must continue to eat in order to reproduce and live.
- When a certain food-point threshold is reached or exceeded by eating enough fish, the shark may reproduce. If a shark attains, and then drops below the threshold because it has burned up food points by moving, it won't reproduce. If, however, the fish is happily munching away, it will almost certainly reproduce.

- A newborn shark appears in one of eight adjacent cells to the mother shark, but it does not necessarily move in the same direction as the mother. The energy that a newborn shark receives from its parent is a parameter that you set.

Shark movement

- A shark burns up a certain number of food points for every cycle of movement.
- A shark generally moves faster than a fish. The speed of the sharks is a parameter of the simulation and may be set anywhere from one to two times as fast as the fish. The faster a shark is, the more likely it is to catch fish and survive.
- A shark continues to swim in a particular direction until it sees a fish. The fish must be within the shark's sight distance to be seen.
- When a fish is spotted, the shark moves toward the fish. If it occupies the same cell as the fish, the shark eats the fish. The shark will continue to follow a fish until it cannot see that fish any more, even if there are other fish closer.
- Sharks do not eat each other.
- If a shark's food points drop below zero, the shark dies.

The program uses graphics tools developed in the previous chapters. The fish and sharks are drawn as bitmaps with clip masks to make them appear as fish on the screen. Several bitmaps are used for the shark to provide an indication of how many food points the shark has left and when it is about to reproduce. The background is set to all zeroes with the palette set to display the value zero as blue. As such, the bitmaps may be drawn using *XOR* mode. This creates some interesting visual effects when the fish start to school and the size of a cell is less than the size of the bitmap, because the bitmaps overlap. The current status of the simulation, including the number of fish, sharks, and cycles, is updated for each cycle of the simulation.

Each fish and shark is defined by a structure that contains all the attributes. These structures are stored in a linked list that contains the entire population of each. For each cycle, all the fish are checked to see where they are to move next and whether or not they should reproduce. If a fish is born, it is added to the end of the list of fish. Similarly, all the sharks are processed to see if they can eat a fish, move toward a fish, reproduce, or just keep on swimming. If a fish is eaten, it is removed from the list of fish. The world is stored as a two-dimensional array of cells. The array simply keeps track of what, if anything, occupies the cell. The world array is primarily used to determine if a fish can see a shark and vice versa.

To produce fish with various random characteristics, such as reproductive time, *dfish.exe* uses the ANSI random-number generator *rand()* and the random-number initializer *srand()*. *rand()* generates a positive random integer from 0 to *RAND_MAX*, defined as $2^{15} - 1$. *rand()* uses a repetitive method to generate successive random numbers. A random number in sequence is initialized by calling *srand()* with an integer value known as a *seed*. Whenever the same seed is set with *srand()*, the same sequence of random numbers will be generated by *rand()*. This is useful since sometimes you must rerun a simulation with the exact same values. Using *srand()* ensures that this can be done. To help simplify some of the calculations involving random numbers, I have provided another function, *gfrand()*, that uses *rand()* to generate random values of type *float* between -1.0 and +1.0. For instance, whenever a new fish is born, it is assigned a length of time before it can reproduce using the following equation:

fish->birthrate = fish_mean_birthrate + (Equation 14-1)
*gfrand()*fish_var_birthrate;*

The variable *fish_mean_birthrate* represents the average number of cycles that pass before a fish gives birth and *fish_var_birthrate* is the deviation from that average.

The basic parameters of the simulation may be set both at startup and during the simulation. As you'll recall, all sight distances are measured in the number of cells between the prey and predator. All rates, such as birthrate, are measured in number of cycles. The keys that may be used to alter the simulation are listed in Table 14-2.

Table 14-2. Keyboard options for altering the fish and shark program

Keyboard Key	Description
Escape	Exits the program
X	Exits the program
?	Prints a list of valid keys
R	Enters new fish reproduction rate statistics, both the mean and variance
B	Enters the number of offspring a fish produces when it spawns
L	Enters the minimum number of food points a shark must have before it may reproduce
P	Enters the probability that a shark reproduces if it reaches the minimum food-point level. (This is a number between 0.0 and 1.0.)
E	Enters new sight distances for both fish and sharks. These determine how far away each one can see the other.
V	Enters new food-point value for a fish. This determines how many fish a shark must eat before it can reproduce.
M	Enters the cost in food points and the distance for 1 cycle of movement for a shark. This must be significantly lower than the food value of a fish, or else the sharks will quickly starve.
C	Enters the food-point cost for a shark reproducing. Generally, this should be at least half the minimum food-point level for reproduction.
I	Enters a new initial number of fish and sharks and restarts the simulation

In addition to controlling the parameters during the simulation, you can set them along with additional ones as options on the command line when the program is started. Each command-line option has the same name as its keyboard key. If an option is used for both the fish and sharks, you use an *F* or *S* as a prefix to the name. You enter reproduction rates for fish with option *-RM* (reproductive mean), which sets the mean, and with option *-RV* (reproductive variance), which sets the variance. To enter the movement rate for sharks, you enter *-M* (movement cost) to specify the food-point cost for movement and as *-MS* (movement speed) to enter the number of cells per cycle that the shark can move. Upper- or lowercase characters may be used. For example, a typical command line might be:

dfishy -m1 -v20 -fi30 -si5 -l100

The previous command line sets the initial number of fish at 30, the initial number of sharks at 5, the food value of a fish at 20, the cost of shark movement at 1 food point, and the food points required for shark reproduction at 100.

There are some additional parameters, which you may specify on the command line, that have no corresponding keyboard keys. The *-SB* option specifies how much energy the offspring of a shark should have. This parameter must be less than the reproduction cost specified by *-C*. Whatever energy is transferred to the baby shark is subtracted from the energy level of the mother shark. The speed of a shark is set using the *—N* option. This parameter specifies how often a shark can move two cells in a single turn. For instance, *-N1* lets the sharks move two cells every turn, making them twice as fast as the fish. A setting of *-N5* lets the sharks move two cells every fifth turn, making their effective speed 1.2 times the speed of the fish.

Three parameters that affect the overall simulation are *-W*, *-T*, and *-A*. The *-W* and *-T* options specify the width and height in pixels respectively, of the cells comprising the world. The *-A* option lets you specify a different initial random seed to be passed to *srand()* before the simulation begins. If you do not specify a random seed, the program selects one based on the current time. So you will not get the same simulation unless each time you run the program an explicit initial seed is set with the *-A* option.

The fish and sharks simulation can be expanded a number of different ways. Predicting and then verifying how the various rules and parameters affect the final outcome can be quite challenging. Once you start changing the rules or adding new rules, it's hard to know where to stop because the possibilitiers are literally endless. An alternative to this is adding a third population, such as plants, that the fish must feed on to survive. More complex models of behavior, such as having sharks attack each other if they are hungry enough or having sharks reproducing more than a single creature when they give birth, may be applied to see what, if any affect, this has on population stability. Give it a try; you'll find it an interesting game finding the parameters that create a consistently stable population.

A More Physical Simulation

The final program, *dgas.exe*, started as a model of pool balls bouncing around a frictionless pool table. Then, as a result of my predilection for tinkering, it evolved into a more elaborate model of interacting molecular gases in a two-dimensional container. Still, it contains many of the same elements as the simpler pool-table model; so let's begin with that.

A game of pool

To model two-dimensional pool balls, you create a collection of balls, each assigned a finite mass. (Originally, I drew the balls as circles but despite the efficiency of the circle-drawing algorithm, it was faster to draw them as simple polygons. The polygons were changed to bitmaps for this book.) The data for each ball is stored in a structure called *circle_data*. The balls are stored as a simple array of pointers to each individual ball. For the following discussion, the variable *ball* is a pointer to an individual ball.

Each ball moves about the screen in a straight line until it either collides with an edge or with another ball. Unlike the fish and sharks simulation, pool balls are allowed to move at any angle on the screen, not just one of the eight directions governed by cells. The velocity of a ball is specified by two values, *vx* and *vy*, which determine the number of pixels to move the ball in the *x*- and *y*-directions for each animation cycle. The first problem to solve is to make the balls bounce off the edges of the screen. Since the edges are assumed to be infinitely hard and massive, a ball bounces by reversing the velocity component perpendicular to the edge. If a ball hits the left or right edge of the screen, then *vx* is negated. If a ball strikes the top or bottom edge, then *vy* is negated. A ball strikes an edge if the *(x,y)* center coordinate of the ball is within the radius of the ball from the edge. For instance, the ball strikes the top edge if *ball->y < ball->radius*. Similarly, the ball strikes the bottom edge if *ball->y > gGetMaxY() - ball->radius*. If this condition occurs for any edge, the corresponding velocity component is negated.

So, now the balls are bouncing around the screen. The next feature I added was the ability for the balls to collide with one another realistically. Two balls collide if the distance between their centers is less than the sums of their respective radii. If the balls collide, then you must change their respective velocities based on the laws of physics. This is an elementary physics problem, which can be solved using the law of energy and momentum conservation. In the collision between the two balls, let *vx1* and *vy1* be the *x*- and *y*- velocity components of ball 1 before the collision, and *vx2* and *vy2* be the velocity components of ball 2. The velocities after the collision are called *vx1'*, *vy1'* and *vx2'*, *vy2'*. The general solution for the velocities after the collision for ball 1 is:

vx1' = ***alpha1*** * *vx1* + ***beta1*** * *vx2* (Equation 14-2)
vy1' = ***alpha1*** * *vy1* + ***beta1*** * *vy2*

where ***alpha1*** = *(Mass1 - Mass2) / (Mass1 + Mass2)*
beta1 = 2 * *Mass2 / (Mass1 + Mass2)*

The solution for ball 2 is:

$$vx2' = alpha2 * vx2 + beta2 * vx1 \qquad \text{(Equation 14-3)}$$
$$vy2' = alpha2 * vy2 + beta2 * vy1$$

where $alpha1 = (Mass2 - Mass1) / (Mass1 + Mass2)$
$beta1 = 2 * Mass1 / (Mass1 + Mass2)$

The program must check each pair of balls to see if they collide. If the balls do collide, then the velocities of both balls are changed according to Equation 14-1 and Equation 14-2. Now the balls not only collide with the edges of the screen but with each other. The basic animation loop cycle in *dgas.exe* is:

```
Circle_Data *balli, *ballj, ball[MAX_BALLS];

while(!finished()) {
 for(i=0; i < numballs; i++) {
  balli = ball[i];
  /* Erase balli */
  draw_ball(balli);          /* Using XOR mode */
  /* Now update the position of the ball.
    Check to see if this ball hits an edge */
  ...
  /* Now check for collisions */
  /* You only have to check this ball against balls
    further down the array, since collision
    detection updates both balls at the same time */
  for(j=i+1; j < numballs; j++) {
   ballj = ball[j];
   /* Check to see if balli and ballj collided */
```

```
      if(collide(balli, ballj)) {
        /* Take appropriate action for collision */
      }
    }
    /* Done; now redraw it */
    draw_ball(balli);
  }
  /* Perform other animation tasks, such as checking for keys */
  ...
}
```

This program was originally developed on a machine without a floating-point coprocessor. The problem with using the general equations for the collision between masses of different sizes is the extensive amount of floating-point operations required. To gain sufficient resolution to accurately model the collisions, I stored the velocity components *vx* and *vy* and the positions *x* and *y* as floating-point numbers. This, however, proved to be too much floating-point arithmetic for running the simulation at reasonable update rates. To avoid this problem, I used a fairly standard computational trick. The velocity and position of each ball are stored as integers, but scaled by a factor of 32. The motion arithmetic is done using integer calculations. The screen coordinate of the ball center is computed by dividing the *x*- and *y*-components of the ball's center position by 32, or equivalently, using the *C* >> right-shift operator to lower the values by 5 bits. Using scaled integers to represent floating-point numbers in this fashion is called a *fixed-point representation*. In effect, you have positional resolution of 1/32 a pixel. This provides ample resolution for any of the calculations.

The collision calculations using *alpha* and *beta* are still done in floating point. However, the frequency of collisions is usually quite low, so the extra overhead is not very noticeable. This is a common issue in simulation programs. Calculations that must occur every cycle of the animation loop should be made as efficient as possible. With the pool table simulation, the balls are moved every cycle; so the motion computations must be done efficiently. Calculations that only occur when a special condition is met, such as two balls colliding, do not have to be as efficient because they occur less frequently, and they have a lesser effect on overall animation speed.

Molecular modeling

So, how did the bouncing pool balls become the molecular gas simulation? By fiddling with the program, of course! Once the basic simulation was in place, I found it irresistible to add more features. Each ball is assumed to be of constant density; so the mass of the ball is made proportional to its area on the screen. When the simulation is started, you specify the number of molecules to create and then the program creates that number with a random distribution of size and color. Second, so-called chemical reactions occur when the balls collide. The color of a ball determines which type of molecule it is. If two different molecules collide, then they react by either absorbing one another (becoming one molecule) or by creating a new molecule as a by-product of the reaction. Sound was added to let you know when the balls collide. The *gSound()* and *gNoSound()* functions are used to create different sounds for the different reactions. The frequency of the sound depends on the type of reaction that occurs. Another feature provides you with the ability to raise or lower the temperature, by increasing or decreasing the velocity of the molecules.

The most recent addition that I made was to include a single rogue polar molecule that attracts certain kinds of molecules and repels others. A simple force model causes the rogue molecule to attract some types of molecules and to repel others. The rogue molecule is highlighted by constantly cycling through the color used to display it; this gives it a pulsating appearance. In addition, the extent of the force boundary is drawn as a diamond-shaped boundary around the rogue to show its region of influence. The amount of force exerted by the rogue on other molecules is based on the distance that the two molecules are apart. The force model, however, does not use normal Euclidean distance, $sqrt(x^2 + y^2)$, but a simpler distance function that does not require floating-point calculations, namely *(ABS(x) + ABS(y))*. In this model, the applied force is inversely proportional to the distance separating the molecules. The strength of the force applied by the rogue molecule can also be adjusted during the simulation to create some interesting effects.

dgas.exe uses the *XOR* mode to draw all the objects. Using *XOR* mode lets the simulation have a more interesting background than merely a black background that you initially provided. I invite you to use your favorite picture as a background image. Multiple bitmaps are used to animate gas molecules as they move about in the container. This simulation makes use of sound not only to provide random beeps and other noise, but also to give you an idea of what is happening. For instance, as the temperature is raised, the frequency of collisions goes up and, correspondingly, the frequency of the collision beeps increases. As the temperature is lowered, the frequency of beeps also decreases. This gives you audible feedback about what is occurring during the simulation.

The simulation may be altered dynamically while it is running. The following keys may be used to change the parameters of a simulation:

Table 14-3. Keyboard options for altering a simulation's parameters

Keyboard Key	Description
Escape	Exits the program
X	Exits the program
?	Prints a list of valid keys
Space	Pauses the simulation. Press the spacebar again to continue the simulation.
R	Restarts the simulation with a new number of initial molecules
S	Toggles the sound on or off
F	Toggles the up and down arrows to modify the force of the rogue molecule, or the temperature. When the temperature is being modified, the background is black. When the force is being modified, the background is red.
up/down arrow	Raises/lowers the temperature, or the strength of the rogue molecule's attraction/repulsion

As with the fish and sharks simulation, there are many ways to enhance *dgas.exe* to provide a more realistic simulation. For instance, all the molecules could be modeled as exerting forces on one another. The force model could be altered to use true Euclidean distance on machines with floating-point coprocessors, and it could use different distance functions, such as $1/(distance)^2$. The collision reactions that create and destroy molecules are entirely contrived for demonstration purposes. Changing the collision processing to create a more realistic reaction model, such as hydrogen and oxygen forming water, would produce a more realistic tool for testing models of chemical reactions. Another interesting possibility is to model it with a wrap-around screen and see what, if any, difference this makes.

An Interactive Conclusion

The demonstration programs presented in this chapter provide examples of how the graphics routines developed in this book can be combined to create dynamic simulations of real-life phenomena. As you know, computer graphics is a powerful means of exploring your understanding of the world and communicating ideas to others. You now have the tools to express yourself graphically in many different ways, from business graphics with bar charts, graphs, and pie charts to elaborate simulations of physics, chemistry, and nature. The computer can bring your graphics to life with animation and color. But above all, computer graphics is a lot of fun. It provides the gratification of instant feedback: you see the results as soon as the program runs. You can quickly make changes, improve the model, change the scale and color, and create whole new environments that can exist only in your mind and, with your effort and the right tools, on your screen for all to see. And unlike most artistic media, there's nothing to clean up when the work is complete (except, perhaps, a few scattered listings)!

Take a little time to play with all the programs throughout this book. Most of them are fun and will guide you in making new programs in which to create your drawings and your worlds. The fun with computer graphics, like the movies, is seeing the screen come alive with a story or world you created. The actors in computer graphics are objects, such as the line, circle, polygon, and bitmap. They are there for your direction, and they're a whole lot cheaper than live ones. Have fun with them; after all, their union is far less strict.

In the next chapter, you'll learn how to explore other aspects of computer graphics. So, for further adventures, on to the final chapter.

Functions Found in This Chapter

Demonstration program

`dclock.exe`

Puts a working analog clock on the screen. Reasonable screen-saver program.

`dfishy.exe`

Fish and sharks life simulation program. Watch the fish and sharks battle for supremacy in a real-life world.

`dgas.exe`

Simulation of two-dimensional gas molecules in a closed container. Molecules bounce off one another and react to create and destroy themselves.

Utility functions

`void gSound(int frequency)`

Turns on the PC speaker at a specified frequency in hertz (cycles per second). The tone will continue to play until *gNoSound()* is used.

`void gNoSound(void)`

Turns the PC speaker off.

`void gDelay(int msec)`

Delays the program by a fixed number of milliseconds. This is often used with the sound functions to sound a tone for a fixed length of time.

`double gfrand(void)`

Returns a random number between -1.0 and +1.0 using the ANSI C *rand()* function.

CHAPTER 15

Where to Now?

There has been an explosion in the use of computer graphics. Computer-generated images now appear wherever something is presented visually. From major motion pictures to television shows and commercials to books, magazines, paintings, and sculptures, computer graphics is being used everywhere. People are fascinated not only with the breadth of imagery that can be produced on a computer, but they are also impressed with the computer's ability to provide more control and flexibility than ever before. Any type of motion, action, or reaction that you can program can be realized on the CRT of your computer. Computer graphics is not a substitute for any existing artistic media; it is a new medium in and of itself. There is no other medium that lets you create beautiful images of both the real and surreal, while still letting you animate and, most importantly, interact with your creation. The software presented in this book provides a beginning for your exploration of computer graphics, but by no means encompasses all or even most of computer graphics today.

Why is computer graphics so popular today when 30 years ago it was unheard of? The answer is simple; the computers are now fast enough and the displays inexpensive enough to make interactive graphics affordable. The development of computer graphics precisely parallels the development of the computer. As computers have become more accessible, more people have been able to experiment with computer animation and drawing. Increasing computer power has meant more complex drawings and, more importantly, more interactive drawings. Once a system could draw images—even simple line drawings—at reasonable rates, animated graphics became possible. Interactive animation is a tremendous means of communicating with people since everyone is primarily a visual creature. The human brain is attuned to processing images, not numbers. This unique ability to present programmable and dynamic images has led to the current graphics revolution in which all people and computer interaction is essentially through a graphic display of some sort.

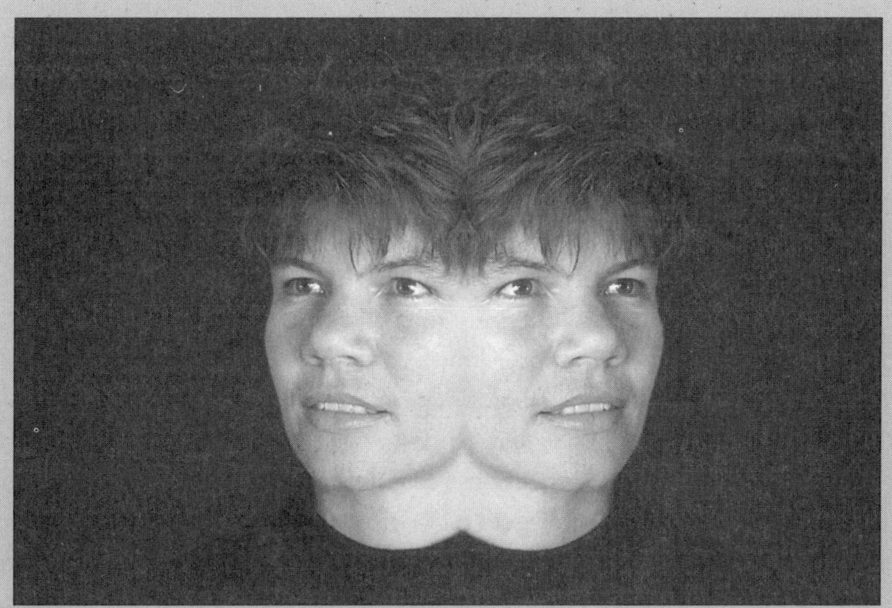

Computer graphics is such a broad field that it is difficult to know where to turn next. Three-dimensional graphics, advanced simulation, movie production, generating realistic animated figures, and advanced plotting techniques are only a few of the areas you can explore. The computer is a very powerful graphics medium. It gives you complete interactive control over a drawing, and it can be used in ways that are just not possible with other types of graphics.

Now that computers are relatively low cost, they are accessible to almost everyone. Using the tools presented in this book, you can create a number of useful applications, but more importantly, you can have fun using your computer. You not only get the satisfaction of creating attractive pictures on the screen, but you can make the pictures change according to rules you define.

The ability to interact with an application is a powerful feature of a computer-generated display. Computer games use the same tool types as those found in this book's software libraries. Take advantage of them, and use this book as a starting point in exploring the possibilities of computer graphics.

The software discussed in this book covers many aspects of two-dimensional computer graphics, but it does not directly provide many applications. The plotting software in Chapter 11 covers only the basics of plotting, and certainly does not support every type of plot that you might want to make. The tools developed here form the foundation on which to build other applications.

Revolutionary Graphics

The graphics revolution occurring today had humble beginnings, as most revolutions do. The first computer graphics applications were created by scientists and engineers wanting to automate the more mundane and repetitive drawing tasks required for their day-to-day work.

Plotting recorded data or equations accurately by hand gets old very quickly. The computer, however, never gets tired of doing this no matter how many times you redraw the plot, change the scale, or add new data. With the advent of low cost CRTs connected to a computer, people now realize that not only can they create plots more quickly, but they can also change the plot in response to new data. As mentioned in Chapter 11, the computer can be programmed to perform complex calculations on more data points and in more ways than any person could possibly hope to do.

So, the computer provides the means to study phenomena and perform analyses that are not possible by any other means. Not only does computer graphics significantly improve the presentation of data in traditional ways, such as line graphs and bar charts, but it also provides a medium for visualizing data and processes in totally new and different ways.

Another Dimension of Computer Graphics

A major topic in computer graphics that this book does not cover is three-dimensional graphics. The computer is well adapted to perform the necessary calculations to create a perspective view of a three-dimensional model. Although three-dimensional graphics is not covered in this book, there are many other books on the topic. It is a broad subject because not everyone needs the same level of sophistication. For instance, an architectural draftsperson may only need to see three-dimensional wire-frame (line-drawing) models of a building.

However, an architect might want to see a photorealistic drawing that accurately depicts how the finished building will look before the site is surveyed.

All three-dimensional graphics are based on similar software tools as those used in this book. A three-dimensional model is drawn using perspective calculations that convert three-dimensional surfaces into two-dimensional objects. The exact same types of affine transformations that you have developed for two-dimensional manipulation also work in three-dimensions. Once you have the two-dimensional projection of an object, it can be drawn on the screen using the tools found in this book.

One of the more fascinating aspects of three-dimensional modeling is its ability to realistically simulate the three-dimensional motion of objects. The development of both three-dimensional graphics and computer animation was, and continues to be, heavily influenced by flight-simulation applications. A *flight simulator* is a device designed to help train pilots to fly an airplane by recreating the cockpit environment. A key component of a flight simulator is the visual system that creates a realistic view of what the pilot would see outside a real aircraft window.

The demands on a computer graphics system for such an application are enormous. The visual system must generate a complete three-dimensional view of an airport with runways, runway lights, and taxiways at real-time rates (typically 30 times a second). Most initial high performance graphics algorithms were developed primarily to speed up the drawing process for flight simulator visual systems. Back in the early 1970s, flight simulator visuals were crude, usually just showing the runway lights and nothing more. Today, state-of-the-art flight simulators depict very realistic scenes that border on photorealism.

As you have undoubtedly seen in recent movies, computer animation can also depict the surreal and the physically impossible. Animated features, such as Walt Disney Productions' *Beauty and the Beast* and *Aladdin*, illustrate how you can create dynamically animated images of places that have never been. Special effects seen on television show an incredible depth of visual expression made possible by computer graphics. Computer graphics lets you explore places you can never physically visit, such as inside a molecule or atop a star's surface.

In Chapter 14, you saw how computer simulation and graphics can be combined to model events that you cannot directly observe, such as atoms bouncing in a container. Computer simulation lets you increase your understanding of the world by performing experiments under very controlled conditions, as with the fish and sharks. Computer graphics plays a key role in most simulation applications by presenting the results in an informative, interactive, and intuitive manner.

Standard Graphics

In this book, I've tried to make the software portable to as many computers and operating systems as possible. I've included several routines, such as *gGetMaxX()* and *gGetMaxY()*, to help make your programs device independent. The diversity of graphics hardware and computers makes creating device-independent software especially difficult. As more graphics applications are developed, device and operating-system independence have become major software issues.

Many programmers and engineers want standard graphics routines for no other reason than to keep from having to constantly retranslate their software for new operating systems and new graphics hardware. The software package in this book is not in any sense a standard, nor is it intended to be. This software does not cover all of today's possible graphics environments. In fact, despite the protests of hardware and software manufacturers, there is not now, nor will there ever be, a single set of standard routines for computer graphics software.

The primary reason for this lack of a universal graphics standard is simply one of efficiency versus generality. If your application has very specialized needs, such as real-time animation, you'll want to optimize the code to perform the functions you need as quickly as possible. You probably don't really care if the graphics package supports patterned italicized text, especially if providing the support slows the drawing operations. On the other hand, if you are designing a more general-purpose software package, such as a paint program, you'll want to incorporate as many features as possible and have it run on as many different hardware and operating system configurations as possible. Furthermore, you want the flexibility to combine operations in as many different ways as possible; often, these in ways are infeasible to incorporate into hardware.

The software in this book is designed to serve the following two basic purposes:

1. To be a general-purpose, portable package that supports many basic drawing features
2. To show how the various drawing functions actually work

The portability of the package's design has all the drawing routines use *gPlotPixel()* to write to the frame buffer. So, if you make *gPlotPixel()* work on your display, the rest of the routines will work as well. The software is not designed to be the fastest graphics package.

If speed is your goal, then you should put most of the basic routines in assembler code, but this would not be very easy to follow or port to another environment. For example, the function *gPlotPixel()* performs a lot of conditional tests that support features such as clipping functions and brush drawing. These tests introduce extra computational overhead because they occur each time you draw a pixel.

If you want optimal performance, and you do not need these features, you can remove them from the code. If you feel the need for even more speed, consider converting some of the lower level functions like *gLineDraw()* into fast assembly code. But there is always some trade-offs between having general-purpose features and optimum performance in specialized applications. You'll want to chose the former option since you can always take a subset of the code and adapt it for specialized applications.

The graphics package in this book is also designed to be very modular. Rather than having lots of separate routines for drawing rectangles, scaled rectangles, rotated rectangles, scaled circles, and so forth, I use affine transformations to specify any combination of transformations and I also use it in an object's single drawing routine. Similarly, other features, such as clipping and brush drawing, work with all object types rather than just a few types. This type of approach actually makes for more efficient software while retaining the desired generality.

If you are developing applications in an environment where speed is paramount, such as flight simulation or real-time data acquisition, you'll want to take advantage of the fastest code and hardware available. However, once you take advantage of the faster hardware or specialized code, you cannot easily go back to a system that does not support it. Many of the more sophisticated graphics packages, such as MS-Windows on the PC and X-Windows on UNIX workstations provide a higher level software interface to support more complete device independence. If your hardware supports a particular operation, such as rapidly filling polygons, then the software takes advantage of it. The problem is that you must constantly ensure that the libraries are updated to take advantage of this powerful hardware feature. Furthermore, hardware implementations of specialized algorithms have a knack for introducing more restrictions than their software counterparts. For instance, a hardware polygon fill may only work on convex polygons. This places the burden on your program to convert nonconvex polygons into convex polygonal pieces. Also, having the graphics libraries check to see if a particular option is supported in your hardware introduces extra computational overhead and, consequently, makes the program run slower than if the program were hard-coded for a particular hardware configuration.

Although there are no *universal* standards, there are graphics standards. In fact, there are several. On the PC, you basically choose between running under DOS or MS-Windows. In DOS, there is a limited set of graphic functions, but as you can see by examining the source code for functions like *gPlotPixel()*, the DOS calls provide only basic functions, such as plotting a pixel. In order to do anything useful, you need a more extensive graphics package, such as the one in this book. The set of DOS graphics calls do not provide any direct support for the newer SVGA graphics cards; so software makers are forced to provide support for a plethora of different hardware vendors cards.

MS-Windows provides a more extensive set of graphics functions than DOS or the software in this book. Although the graphics package in the book provides many drawing functions, it does not handle other graphics operations that you might need, such as support for window-based graphics. The Microsoft Windows API (application programmer interface) is a software library that provides a set of calls for drawing graphics under Windows. For instance, if you write text to an open window under MS-Windows, the operating system handles the details of where the window is physically located on the screen, whether the window changes size, and whether the text needs to be clipped because there is another window on top of the one to which you are drawing. As you can see, routines for drawing to a window handle many of the more mundane details of window-based graphics; so your program does not have to. Windows isolates the specifics of how the graphics card works. From your program's standpoint, you always draw to a window no matter what type of graphics card is being used.

In the workstation environment, the most prevalent graphics standard is X-Windows, though by no means is it the only one. In many respects, it is very similar to MS-Windows, however, the two do not use the same function names or even provide the same functions. For instance, the equivalent to *gLineDraw()* function in X-Windows is *XDrawLine()*, and in MS-Windows, it is a combination of calls to *MoveTo()* and *LineTo()*. On the Macintosh, it is different yet again. Several entrepreneurial software companies are making a lot of money by selling software toolkits that support all the different graphics standards. Basically, they are profiting from the lack of currently accepted standards.

Despite the problems, various graphics packages and standards are slowly merging. All these packages, for instance, possess equivalents to most basic drawing functions, such as drawing lines, rectangles, and circles. Some of the newer standards, such as OpenGL, Hoops, and Phigs, provide the same kind of affine transformation support that I have provided as well as standardized three-dimensional graphics drawing functions. However, not all of these packages provide all the features or functions that you may need, and future additions are sure to be needed as computer graphics software and hardware continue to rapidly evolve. The software library in this book is easily adapted to any of these other environments, so you may take advantage of what those graphics packages offer, as well as the additional features I have provided.

Hard Copy

Another area not addressed by this software is creating hard copy. Printing graphics is a whole discipline of its own, and the discipline has its own unique set of problems. Since I have taken a device-independent approach to graphics, you can adapt the graphics software in this book to display images on a printer rather than to a frame buffer. Many printers now support explicit pixel operations, making it possible for *gPlotPixel()* to set an individual dot on a page. As with any other graphics device, you must make the functions *gInitDisplay()*, *gPlotPixel()*, and *gCloseDisplay()* perform equivalent operations on the printer.

Since all other calls are based on these, once those calls are made functional, the rest will follow.

In fact, you can direct the drawing output to a printer in two ways. With the first approach, you simply make *gInitDisplay()* open the printer, *gPlotPixel()* write dots on a page, and *gCloseDisplay()* close the access to the printer. This approach, however, is not very efficient because it requires a lot of communication between the computer and the printer to set individual dots on a page. A more robust approach is for you to create a bitmap to store your image and to redirect your output to this bitmap with a call to *gSetOutputBitmap()*. Your drawing program then draws into the bitmap. Once your drawing is finished and stored in the bitmap, the bitmap may then be sent to the printer in one drawing operation. Generally, this will be more efficient than having every call to *gPlotPixel()* send the commands to plot a single dot on the printer. You must keep in mind, however, that in the current implementation of this software under DOS, a single bitmap cannot be larger than 64 KB. This places a limitation on the size of the output image that you can create, although this can be overcome by drawing the image in 64-KB sections and then sending each section to the printer until a complete page is printed.

The bitmap approach is easily generalized to write the finished image to any output device, including writing to a file. By sending the bitmap to a file, you create files in one of the most common file formats, such as GIF, TIF, or PCX. You may want to create separate initialization calls for the different devices, such as *gInitPrinter()* and *gInitFile()*. These calls would take the necessary steps to set up the output device to receive the bitmap data. You must create a call with a name like *gSendBitmapToOutput()* to take a bitmap and actually write it to the appropriate output device, which converts the bitmap pixels into the correct format for the particular printer or disk-file type. Using this technique, you can send your drawings to any number of output devices once you determine how to set pixels on that device. The book *Bitmapped Graphics* by Steve Rimmer (Tab, 1992) is a good reference on the most common graphics file formats. It provides the necessary information for coding the function *gSendBitmapToOutput()* to write the bitmap into the appropriate file format.

Drawing to a Close

Low cost computers and high performance color graphics cards now make computer graphics available to more people than even five years ago. The software package included in this book provides a powerful set of tools for creating and interacting with a wide range of graphic images. As I hope you've seen, incorporating features, such as the affine transformations, clipping, brush and pattern drawing, and animation, gives you considerable flexibility in the types of images you can make. By combining these features in creative ways, you can create an astonishing variety of drawings, graphs, and games while having fun, as the demonstration programs illustrate. The only limit on the images you can create is time and your imagination. Despite the seemingly overwhelming amount of research and development in computer graphics, we are still only beginning to exploit the possibilities. You are now on the frontier; it's time to go exploring.

As I mentioned at the beginning of this chapter, this software provides a foundation on which to build more advanced graphics packages and applications. There is so much more you can do with computer graphics software. And often it is difficult to know where to look for further information. Several engineering organizations have societies dedicated to pursuing and reporting about various aspects of computer graphics. Some of the largest are as follows:

Association for Computing Machinery (ACM)
11 W. 42nd St.
New York, NY 10036
ACM/SIGGRAPH (Special Interest Group on Computer Graphics)

The annual SIGGRAPH conference covers the state-of-the-art in computer graphics research and applications.

IEEE Computer Society
10662 Los Vaqueros Circle
Los Alamitos, CA 90720

IEEE Computer Graphics and Applications, a monthly publication, is a good source of information on the latest academic research regarding computer graphics.

Computer bookstores are filled with books on graphics. Some of the more useful books on advanced computer graphics topics are as follows:

Feiner, Steven K., James D. Foley, John F. Hughes, and Andries van Dam. *Computer Graphics: Principles and Practice*. 2nd ed. Addison-Wesley Publishing Company, Inc., 1990.

Sharp, Larry and Christopher D. Watkins. *Programming in 3 Dimensions*. M&T Books, 1992.

Coy, Stephen, Mark Finlay, and Christopher D. Watkins. *Photorealism and Ray Tracing in C*. M&T Books, 1992.

From C to C++

The code in this book has been written in ANSI C to make it accessible to the greatest number of users. C++, however, is becoming the language of choice for many applications and is well suited for computer graphics. C++ will continue to gain popularity as more people learn about the benefits of object-oriented programming. One goal for the software in this book was to take an object-oriented approach to the design and do the best I could using C. Converting the code over to C++ is actually not as difficult with this package as it is for many others. This appendix provides a recipe for converting the code into C++ which takes advantages of the features of C++. This appendix assumes you have a working knowledge of C++. If you are interested in learning more about C++, there are several references listed in the Bibliography which provide much more detailed information about the language and effective ways to use it for graphics and many other applications.

Matrix and Vector Classes

The *gMatrix* and *gVector* types are ideal candidates for classes and to use with overloaded operators such as +, *, -, and /. In particular, the *gVector* structure can be recast as a class with the following declaration:

```
        class gVector {
         private:
         float i,j,t;
         protected:
         public:
// Declare all public functions
//    First, the constructors
         gVector(void);
         gVector(float x1, float y1);
         gVector(gVector &vector);
```

```
// Destructor
     ~gVector();
// Set the values explicitly
     void set(float x1, float y1);
// Overload the = operator
     gVector& operator = (gVector &vector1,
                          gVector &vector2);
// Overload the binary operators
     friend gVector operator + (gVector &vector1,
                                gVector &vector2);
// Declare all of the other operators as well
  .
  .
  .
};
```

By overloading the binary operators, like +, -, *, and /, you can perform all of the functions like *gVectorCombine()* with arithmetic expressions as in the following example:

```
gVector vec1, vec2, vecout;

vec1.set(1.0, 1.0);
vec2.set(2.0, 2.0);
vecout = vec1 / (vec1 + vec2);
```

The *set()* member function performs the equivalent of the *gVectorSet()* function. In the above declaration, I have also overloaded the = operator. In C++, this good practice ensures that expressions like *a* = *b* always copy the correct data.

The *gMatrix* data type may be converted to a class in a similar manner to creating the vector class. In addition to the binary operators where two matrices or two vectors are supplied as arguments, you can also define the operators to perform the various transformation operations. For instance, you can define an overloaded version of the * operator to apply a transformation to a vector:

```
gVector operator * (gMatrix& matrix, gVector &vector)
{
 gVector vout;

 vout->i = mat.a00 * vector.i + mat.a01 * vector.j +
           mat.a02 * vector.t;
 vout->j = mat.a10 * vector.i + mat.a11 * vector.j +
           mat.a12 * vector.t;
 vout->t = mat.a20 * vector.i + mat.a21 * vector.j +
           mat.a22 * vector.t;
 return vout;
}
```

This function must be declared as a *friend* function in the *gVector* class declaration so that it can access the private members of the *gVector* class directly. With this overloaded operator, you can apply a matrix to a vector using this standard notation:

```
gMatrix matrix;
gVector vec1, vect;

/* Transform vec1 */
vect = matrix * vec1;
```

All of the matrix and vector functions can be easily recast as overloaded operators, allowing more readable and compact expressions.

For matrices, the translate, scale, rotate, and reflect operators must also be provided. The simplest approach is to provide *translate()*, *scale()*, *rotate()*, and *reflect()* member functions in the *gMatrix* class. These member functions should use the exact same syntax as the corresponding C functions: *gMatrixTranslate()*, *gMatrixScale()*, *gMatrixRotate()*, and *gMatrixReflect()*. Once the matrix classes have been defined, manipulating objects with matrices becomes easier if you derive a graphics objects class from the matrix class, thus inheriting all of the properties of the matrix class.

Graphics Objects

Whenever we introduced a new type of drawing object, such as the circle or ellipse, we provided functions to create, copy, delete, draw, fill, and manipulate the object as appropriate. For instance, the *gCircle* type has the functions *gCircleCreate( )*, *gCircleCopy( )*, *gCircleDelete( )*, *gCircleDraw( )*, and *gCircleFill( )* to perform the various operations on a circle. In C++, these functions would be member functions for the *gCircle* class. However, you can do more than just rewrite these functions as member functions. The above set of operations are necessary for all object types, not just circles. Therefore, you define a base class for all objects, and derive the specific objects like circle, ellipse, rectangle, and so forth, from this base class. The following is a sample definition for a base class called *gObject*::

```
class gObject: public gMatrix {
 private:
 protected:
 public:
 virtual ~gObject();
 virtual gObjectType IsA();    // What am I?
 virtual void draw(gColor color);
 virtual void fill(gColor color);
 gObject& operator = (gMatrix &matrix);
};
```

Notice that *gObject* is derived from *gMatrix*. The reason is to allow an object to inherit all of the matrix operators and functions. The affine transformations are now built into the object definition. Now you can scale, translate, and rotate any object using the overloaded binary operators, like + and *, defined for matrices. This feature of C++, called *inheritance*, is a very powerful way of building hierarchical structures. Since *gObject* is derived from the *gMatrix* class, any change in the *gMatrix* data type or any of its member functions will automatically appear in any *gObject* type.

Notice that there is no data in the *gObject* class and that almost all of the functions are *virtual*. You will not create any *gObject* types directly. *gObject* simply serves as a definition from which to derive any of the other types. For instance, the *gCircle* type can be derived as follows:

```
class gCircle : public gObject {
 private:
 protected:
 public:
 float x, y, r;
// Function definitions
 void IsA() {return gObject_Circle};
 void draw(gColor color);
 void fill(gColor color);
};
```

The functions *gCircleDraw()* and *gCircleFill()* would become the member functions *draw()* and *fill()* respectively. The member function *IsA()* provides a way for your functions to determine what kind of object they are processing. The symbol *gObject_Circle* would be part of an *enum* type listing all of the possible data types, such as *type enum* {, *gObject_Rectangle*, *gObject_Circle*, *gObject_Ellipse*, and } *OBJECT_TYPES*.

The one non-virtual function shown in the definition of *gObject* is the overloaded assignment operator, =. The reason for this is to let you use a *gObject* anywhere in an expression that a matrix can be used, including the left hand side of an assignment statement. The definition of this operator is simply to copy the matrix on the right-hand side of an expression into the matrix portion of the *gObject* object. Thus, you may set the transformation for an object with a simple expression such as: *object = matrix*.

One of the advantages in using the *gObject* type is that it enables you to create functions that draw object lists of different types, which simplifies storing and manipulating complex drawings. For instance, suppose you have a drawing composed of circles, ellipses, and rectangles. Pointers to any of these objects may be stored in an array of *gObject* pointers. To rescale all of the objects and then redraw all of the objects in the list, you can simply loop through the pointer array:

```
gObject *object, *objlist[100]; // Array of objects
gMatrix zoom_matrix;
int i;

for(i=0; i < numobjects; i++) {
 *(objlist[i]) = zoom_matrix * (*(objlist[i]));
 objlist[i]->draw();
}
```

With this approach, you do not have to check to see what type of object is being pointed to by each pointer in the array. The correct drawing function will automatically be called for the type of object. Since *gObject* is derived from *gMatrix*, the matrix operators may be applied to any object derived from *gObject*. Thus, the rescaling operation is the same for any object type.

There is no easy way to store an equivalent list of objects in a C program. You are stuck with keeping around separate lists of circles, ellipses, rectangles, and whatever other kinds of objects are supported. For example, you could define an object list structure as the following:

```
typedef struct gObjectList_struct {
 gRectangle **rects;
 gCircle  **circles;
 gEllipse  **ellipses;
 gPolyline **polylines;
 gPolygon  **polygon;
} gObjectList;
```

Whenever you want to add a new object type, like a spline curve type, you must modify the object list structure to include an array of pointers for that type. Furthermore, any function which uses a *gObjectList* would have to be updated to recognize and support the new data type. A separate set of functions would have to be developed to add each kind of pointer to the object list, such as *gObjectListAddCircle()*, *gObjectistAddRectangle()*, and so forth. The C++ approach provides a much more elegant way of storing collections of objects with common characteristics. C++ ensures that any new objects are fully supported throughout all of your functions. This is the essence of object-oriented programming. Each new object defines its own method of accomplishing some task, such as drawing or filling on the screen. Whenever an object of that type is used, the appropriate function for that object is used. The application program does not worry about how the task is accomplished or any specifics of the object implementation.

The *gObject* concept can be extended further by considering how to manipulate collections of objects. For instance, a typical architectural drawing consists of lines, rectangles, circles, ellipses, and perhaps many other types of objects. You often want to group objects together and apply an operation like scaling or rotation to the entire group. A group of objects can be maintained as a simple list of pointers, as demonstrated by the array of *gObject* pointers. Let's define a new class, *gObjectGroup*, as a list of objects. The member function *draw()* can be defined for the *gObjectGroup* class that simply draws all of the objects in the list. Similarly, all the matrix and vector operators may be defined for the *gObjectGroup* class, by applying the matrix (or adding a vector) to all of the objects in the list. You now have what you need. A *gObjectGroup* object may be treated just like any other object in that it can be drawn, scaled, rotated, moved, or use any operation which a *gObject* can use. Thus, you can create complex collections of figures and treat them as a single object. The ability to encapsulate common features between different types of objects is a prime benefit to using C++ in many applications, including computer graphics.

C++ Finale

The two major changes required to create an object-oriented version of the code are: 1) convert the *gVector* and *gMatrix* structures into classes with overloaded binary operators for each type; and 2) create a *gObject* base class and derive each of the graphics object types from this base class. Most of the other functions can remain the way they are. You will probably need to incrementally convert them into classes as you need them.

The *gStyle* structure may be converted to a class if desired. The various *gStyle* functions which set text attributes become member functions of the *gStyle* class. This is not really necessary unless you plan to use *gStyle* with other data types, for instance, to specify various styles of fill patterns for other objects. However, it is very useful to create a *gFont* base class and derive the *gBitmap-*

Font and *gPolyFont* classes from this base class. This eliminates the need for the *gStyle* structure to maintain separate pointers for each type of font. It also makes it much easier to implement other types of fonts, such as spline-based fonts, in the future. The *gTextDraw()* function would then use the member function of the font to transform and draw the characters.

Graphics applications are an excellent way to learn C++ because you already think in terms of graphical objects. Complex objects are built from simpler ones. For instance, you might build an animated figure as a combination of polygons for the body and a circle for the head. You want to be able to treat this object as a group. The *gObjectGroup* class provides a simple way to support this kind of structure in a natural and intuitive way. Accomplishing the same type of operation in C requires a lot of additional code and is difficult to understand and support.

Converting the software in this book to C++ is an good exercise in learning C++. Most of the conversions are straightforward and with C++, you can proceed at your own pace since C++ is fully compatible with C. Try creating the vector and matrix classes first, and then starting adding the *gObject* types. You will see that it isn't so tough after all and the benefits can be most rewarding.

APPENDIX B

Installing the Software

The enclosed diskette contains all of the source, Borland C++ project, and executable files stored in two compressed ZIP files: *source.zip* and *exec.zip*. These files are decompressed using the utility *pkunzip.exe*, also provided on the diskette. You should copy the entire contents of the diskette to a suitable subdirectory on your hard drive, such as *c:\ggraph*. Once you have copied the contents of the diskette, you decompress the files by typing:

```
c:
cd \ggraph
install
```

The *install.bat* file will decompress both of the *zip* files. You will need approximately 2 MB of free disk space to store all of the source and executables. Once the files are decompressed, you may delete both .ZIP files from your hard drive.

In addition to the C source files and executables, there are two other files: *makefile* and *links*. These two files are used by *make* to compile all of the modules and link each of the demonstration programs to produce executable programs. The executable files (*.exe* extension) for all of the demonstration programs described in each chapter are already provided on the diskette, so you do not have to make them. You may run any of these programs simply by typing the desired program name from the DOS command prompt. By default, the executables look for an EGA or VGA display mode. If you do not have either of these options, simply run the program with the following command line:

```
dprogram mode4
```

The *mode4* option forces the program to run in CGA graphics mode. You may specify any DOS graphics mode from 1 to 19 for the *mode* option if you wish to run the demonstration in a particular graphics mode.

The file *makefile* is provided as an example of how to compile and link your own programs. The makefile can also be used to rebuild all of the demonstration programs. The makefile is currently set up for the Borland C++, version 3.1, compiler and libraries. If you have Borland C++, you can create all of the demonstration programs simply by changing to the directory where the files were copied and typing *make*:

```
c:
cd \ggraph
make
```

The *makefile* currently assumes that you have installed Borland C++ onto your C: drive in the standard directories. You will need approximately 1 Megabyte of additional hard disk space for all of the object files (.OBJ extension) produced when the modules are compiled. The makefile is shown in listing B-1.

```
all: DBITMAP.exe DFILL.exe DDRAW.exe DLINE.exe DXFORM.exe \
     DPALET.exe DTEXT.exe DPLOT.exe DBITTEST.exe \
     DCLOCK.exe DFISH.exe DGAS.exe DALIAS.exe DCLIP.exe

# Set your library and include directories here
LIB_DIR = c:\borlandc\lib
INC_DIR = c:\borlandc\include

CFLAGS = -ml -I$(INC_DIR) -c
CC = bcc
LINK = tlink /L$(LIB_DIR)

#All of the modules listed here must be linked in for each
#of the demonstration programs

COMMON_OBJ = \
      GDEMO.obj    GGRAPH.obj   GSCAN.obj    GFCIRC.obj    \
      GELLIP.obj   GSPEC.obj    GBITMAP.obj  GLINALG.obj   \
      GBOUND.obj   GPOLY.obj    GCIRCLE.obj  GLINE.obj     \
      GFONT.obj    GSTYLE.obj   GPLOT.obj
```

```
dbitmap.exe  : $(COMMON_OBJ)
dfill.exe    : $(COMMON_OBJ)
ddraw.exe    : $(COMMON_OBJ)
dline.exe    : $(COMMON_OBJ)
dxform.exe   : $(COMMON_OBJ)
dpalet.exe   : $(COMMON_OBJ)
dtext.exe    : $(COMMON_OBJ)
dplot.exe    : $(COMMON_OBJ)
dbittest.exe : $(COMMON_OBJ)
dclock.exe   : $(COMMON_OBJ)
dfish.exe    : $(COMMON_OBJ)
dgas.exe     : $(COMMON_OBJ)
dclip.exe    : $(COMMON_OBJ)
dalias.exe   : $(COMMON_OBJ)

.obj.exe:
     $(LINK) c0L $*.obj @links $*.exe, , emu mathl cl

.c.obj:
     $(CC) $(CFLAGS) $*.c
```

Listing B-1. The makefile to create the demonstration programs

If your compiler include directories or libraries are installed in a different directory, then you must specify where *make* should look for them by changing the symbols *INC_DIR* (include directories) and *LIB_DIR* (library directories) to the appropriate locations. If you are using a different compiler, you will need to make the appropriate changes to *makefile* for your compiler's version of *make*. You must also provide the correct command line for the compiler by changing the definition of the *CC* symbol and the *LINK* symbol of *makefile*.

To link a program of your own creation, you must link with all of the modules specified by the symbol *COMMON_OBJ* shown in listing B-1. If you are using the Borland project files, then you must include all of the modules as part of the project. Project files for each of the demonstration programs are included on the diskette. However, these project files assumes that the include and library directories are the standard ones. You must also be sure to include *ggraph.h* in your source files.

A complete listing of the contents of the enclosed disk and the individual *zip* files is shown in the following series of tables.

Files on the Disk

File:		Description:
PKUNZIP	EXE	Decompresses the files
INSTALL	BAT	Runs pkunzip on the two compressed files
SOURCE	ZIP	All C source files and Borland project files
EXEC	ZIP	Executable copies of all demonstration programs

Files for make

LINKS	98	
MAKEFILE	830	
README		Last minute changes or enhancements

Demonstration program source files *(source.zip)*

Program source file:			Program is described in:
DALIAS	C	9458	Chapter 13
DBITMAP	C	10472	Chapter 9
DBITTEST	C	10928	Chapter 12
DCLIP	C	1421	Chapter 7
DCLOCK	C	10422	Chapter 14
DDRAW	C	6884	Chapter 5
DFILL	C	13117	Chapter 8
DFISH	C	14108	Chapter 14
DGAS	C	10495	Chapter 14
DLINE	C	5797	Chapter 4
DPALET	C	3025	Chapter 4
DPLOT	C	2380	Chapter 11
DTEXT	C	15886	Chapter 10

DXFORM	C	10772	Chapter 6
GDEMO	C	7475	Special routines for magnified pixels

Graphics module source files *(source.zip)*

Source File:			Module is described in:
BITFONT	C	3601	Chapter 10
GALIAS	C	7605	Chapter 13
GBITMAP	C	4464	Chapter 9
GBOUND	C	11957	Chapter 7
GCIRCLE	C	3097	Chapter 5
GELLIP	C	3153	Chapter 5
GFCIRC	C	2660	Chapter 5
GFONT	C	21107	Chapter 10
GGRAPH	C	18724	Chapter 4
GLINALG	C	8482	Chapter 6
GLINE	C	9611	Chapter 4
GPLOT	C	12105	Chapter 11
GPOLY	C	3363	Chapter 5
GSCAN	C	9396	Chapter 8
GSPEC	C	1143	Chapter 9
GSTYLE	C	2557	Chapter 10
POLYFONT	C	12702	Chapter 10

Header files *(source.zip)*

GDEMO	H	1266	Used only by the demo programs
GGRAPH	H	12594	
GSIMPLE	H	697	Used only for the DDA drawing routines
GTYPES	H	3955	

Project files *(source.zip)*

```
DALIAS   PRJ
DBITMAP  PRJ
DBITTEST PRJ
DCLIP    PRJ
DCLOCK   PRJ
DDRAW    PRJ
DFILL    PRJ
DFISH    PRJ
DGAS     PRJ
DLINE    PRJ
DPALET   PRJ
DPLOT    PRJ
DTEXT    PRJ
DXFORM   PRJ
```

Demonstration program executables *(exec.zip)*

```
DALIAS   EXE
DBITMAP  EXE
DBITTEST EXE
DCLIP    EXE
DCLOCK   EXE
DDRAW    EXE
DFILL    EXE
DFISH    EXE
DGAS     EXE
DLINE    EXE
DPALET   EXE
DPLOT    EXE
DTEXT    EXE
DXFORM   EXE
```

Bibliography

Bresenham, J. E. "Algorithm for Control of a Digital Plotter." *IBM Systems Journal* 4(1) (1965): 25–30.

Bresenham, J. E., D. G. Grice, and S. C. Pi. "A Linear Algorithm for Incremental Digital Display of Circular Arcs" *Communications of the ACM* 20(2) (1977): 100–106.

Coueignous, P. "Character Generation by Computer." *Computer Graphics and Image Processing*. 16 (1981): 240–269.

Coy, Stephen B., Mark Finlay, and Christopher D. Watkins. *Photorealism and Ray Tracing in C*. M&T Books, 1992.

Davis, Philip J. and Reuben Hersh. *The Mathematical Experience*. Houghton Mifflin Company, 1981.

Encyclopaedia Britannica. Vol. 11. *Macropedia*. "History of Mathematics." 630–696.

Feiner, Steven K., James D. Foley, John F. Hughes, and Andries van Dam. *Computer Graphics: Principles and Practice*. 2nd ed. Addison-Wesley Publishing Company, Inc., 1990.

Field, D. "Algorithms for Drawing Anti-Aliased Circles and Ellipses." *Computer Vision, Graphics, and Image Processing* 33 (1986): 1–15.

Kernighan, Brian W. and Dennis M. Ritchie. *The C Programming Language*. Prentice Hall Computer Publishing, 1978.

Lippman, Stanley B. *A C++ Primer*. Addison-Wesley Publishing Company, Inc., 1989.

Norton, Peter and Richard Wilton. *The New Peter Norton Programmer's Guide to the IBM PC and PS/2*. 2nd ed. Microsoft Press, 1988.

Nye, Adrian. *Xlib Programming Manual*. 3rd ed. Vol. 1. O'Reilly & Associates, Inc., 1988.

Resnick, Robert and David Halliday. *Physics, Part 1*. John Wiley & Sons, Inc., 1966.

Rubinstein, R., *Digital Typography: An Introduction to Type Composition for Computer System Design*. Addison-Wesley Publishing Company, Inc., 1988.

Sharp, Larry and Christopher D. Watkins. *Programming in 3 Dimensions*. M&T Books, 1992.

Sutherland, I.E., and G. W. Hodgman. "Reentrant Polygon Clipping." *CACM* 17(1) (1974): 32–42.

Thomas, George B. *Calculus and Analytic Geometry*. Addison-Wesley Publishing Company, Inc., 1972.

Watt, Alan. *Fundamentals of Three-Dimensional Computer Graphics*. Addison-Wesley Publishing Company, Inc., 1989.

Wilton. Richard. *Programmer's Guide to PC and PS/2 Video Systems*. Microsoft Press, 1987.

Wu, Xiaolin. "An Efficient Anti-aliasing Technique." *Computer Graphics*. SIGGRAPH 1991 proceedings 25(4) (July): 143–152. New York: ACM SIGGRAPH, 1991.

Index

C

D

E

F

G

H

I

N

O

P

S

Tell us what you think and we'll send you a free M&T Books catalog

It is our goal at M&T Books to produce the best technical books available. But you can help us make our books even better by letting us know what you think about this particular title.Please take a moment to fill out this card and mail it to us. Your opinion is appreciated.

Tell us about yourself

Name____________________

Company____________________

Address____________________

City____________________

State/Zip____________________

Title of this book?

Where did you purchase this book?

- ☐ Bookstore
- ☐ Catalog
- ☐ Direct Mail
- ☐ Magazine Ad
- ☐ Postcard Pack
- ☐ Other

Why did you choose this book?

- ☐ Recommended
- ☐ Read book review
- ☐ Read ad/catalog copy
- ☐ Responded to a special offer
- ☐ M&T Books' reputation
- ☐ Price
- ☐ Nice Cover

How would you rate the overall content of this book?

- ☐ Excellent
- ☐ Good
- ☐ Fair
- ☐ Poor

Why?

What chapters did you find valuable?

What did you find least useful?

What topic(s) would you add to future editions of this book?

What other titles would you like to see M&T Books publish?

Which format do you prefer for the optional disk?

☐ 5.25" ☐ 3.5"

Any other comments?

☐ Check here for M&T Books Catalog

M&T BOOKS

2829

NO POSTAGE
NECESSARY
IF MAILED
IN THE
UNITED STATES

BUSINESS REPLY MAIL

FIRST CLASS MAIL PERMIT 2660 SAN MATEO, CA

POSTAGE WILL BE PAID BY ADDRESSEE

M&T BOOKS

411 Borel Avenue, Suite 100
San Mateo, CA 94402-9885

PLEASE FOLD ALONG LINE AND STAPLE OR TAPE CLOSED